Publications of the Palestinian Institute of Archaeology
Excavations and Surveys

Tell Taannek 1963-1968

IV: Miscellaneous
2: The Iron Age Cultic Structure

BIRZEIT UNIVERSITY

Publications of the Palestinian Institute of Archaeology
Excavations and Surveys

The "Tell Taannek 1963-1968" publication program continues the "Taanach" series, the first volume of which was W. E. Rast, *Taanach I: Studies in the Iron Age Pottery*. Cambridge, MA: American Schools of Oriental Research, 1978.

Tell Taannek 1963-1968
IV/2
The Iron Age Cultic Structure

by
Frank S. Frick

Published with the Sponsorship
of the
American Schools of Oriental Research

Excavations and Surveys
Tell Taannek 1963-1968 IV/2
Palestinian Institute of Archaeology - Birzeit University
Project Directors: Khaled Nashef and Walter E. Rast

تنقيبات ومسوحات
تل تعنك ١٩٦٣-١٩٦٨ IV/٢
معهد الآثار الفلسطيني - جامعة بيرزيت
مديرا مشروع النشر: خالد الناشف ووالتر أ . راست

مشروع نشر تنقيبات تل تعنك ١٩٦٣-١٩٦٨ مرتبط بالمدارس الاميركية للابحاث الشرقية
The Publication Project of the Tell Taannek 1963-1968 Excavations
is affiliated with the American Schools of Oriental Research

© 2000, Palestinian Institute of Archaeology

جميع الحقوق محفوظة لمعهد الآثار الفلسطيني، ٢٠٠٠

Frank S. Frick
The Iron Age Cultic Structure

فرانك س. فريك
المبنى الطقوسي من العصر الحديدي

ISBN 0-89757-050-2

Inquiries:
Palestinian Institute of Archaeology - Birzeit University
P. O. Box 14
Birzeit - Palestine
Tel: (02) 2982974; Fax: (02) 2810656
Email: pia@birzeit.edu

للاستفسار:
معهد الآثار الفلسطيني - جامعة بيرزيت
ص. ب ١٤
بيرزيت - فلسطين
ت: ٢٩٨٢٩٧٤ (٠٢)؛ فاكس: ٢٨١٠٦٥٦ (٠٢)
البريد الالكتروني: pia@birzeit.edu

CONTENTS

Preface and Acknowledgments		vii
Part I	The Archaeology of Cult	1
Part II	The Cultic Structure at Taanach in its Geographical and Archaeological Context	17
Part III	The Architecture and History of the Cultic Structure at Taanach	29
	III.A Major Excavations at Taanach's Cultic Structure	29
	III.B The Stratigraphy of Area B at Taanach	33
Part IV	Objects and Artifacts Associated with the Taanach Cultic Structure	55
	IV.A Basin 75 in SW 2-7	55
	IV.B Astragali	65
	IV.C Stone Objects	80
	IV.D Ceramic Objects	94
	IV.E Calcite Items	136
	IV.F Shells	137
	IV.G Bone and Ivory Objects	142
	IV.H Metal Objects	148
Conclusions		168
Appendix A	Section Drawings of SW 1-7, SW 1-8, SW 2-7, and SW 2-8	172
Appendix B	Descriptions of Principal Loci in SW 1-7, SW 1-8, SW 2-7, and SW 2-8	190
Appendix C	Registered Objects found in SW 1-7, SW 2-7, SW 1-8, and SW 2-8	229
Appendix D	Registered Objects found in SW 1-7, SW 2-7, SW 1-8, and SW 2-8 from Period IIB (960-918 BCE)	272
Appendix E	Astragali from the Cultic Structure	304
Appendix F	Overall Taanach Astragali Data	322
Sources Consulted		344

Preface and Acknowledgments

For the first time since the publication of the Iron Age pottery from Tell Taannek by Walter Rast in 1978, the Palestinian Institute of Archaeology has launched, in affiliation with the American Schools of Oriental Research, a series of publications of one of the most important excavations of this century, the excavations at Tell Taannek that were carried out from 1963-1968. The co-directors of this project are Khaled Nashef of the Palestinian Institute of Archaeology and Walter Rast of the American Schools of Oriental Research. The series will consist of a number of volumes dealing with specific aspects of the excavations of Tell Taannek, including the site's stratigraphy, the Early Bronze Age pottery, glyptics, loom weights, stone objects, animal bones, and this study dealing with the Iron Age cultic structure. I am honored to be a part of what promises to be a significant series of publications, which will finally bring to light aspects of the results of the excavations at Tell Taannek that have only been available to the public until now in specialized studies of particular artifacts and in preliminary reports. These earlier specialized studies have been both scattered and incomplete, and the present series of publications, when completed, should provide a holistic picture of the results of the excavation.

There are many persons who have assisted me in the preparation of this study of the Iron Age cultic structure, some of whom I wish to acknowledge by name here. I thank Dr. Nancy Lapp, the widow Paul Lapp the principal excavator of Tell Taannek, who invited me to participate in this project and also assisted me in its later stages. I also thank Lois Glock, the widow of the late Al Glock, who was at the Palestinian Institute of Archaeology where the Taannek materials are kept until his untimely passing. Lois was of invaluable assistance to me during my first two trips to the West

Bank to work with the Taannek materials. Munir and Sumaya Farhat Naser were gracious hosts to me in the summer of 1995, when my visit to Birzeit was aborted early due to the unexpected death of my father. They also hosted my wife and I during a longer stay in Birzeit in the summer of 1996. I also wish to acknowledge the assistance of Dr. Khaled Nashef and other members of the staff of the Palestinian Institute of Archaeology, who helped me gain access to and understand the Taannek materials. A special thank you to my former student, Wendi Mrozinski, who helped me think through some of the theoretical issues in this project's early stages. Kimberly Frick Arndts offered an invaluable service by reading the manuscript in its final stages, suggesting stylistic changes. Finally, I owe a huge debt of gratitude to my wife, Bonnie, who not only worked as my research assistant in Birzeit during the summer of 1996, but has also been involved in significant ways in this project from its inception, including supporting me when I became more irascible than usual.

This work was supported by a grant from the Hewlett-Mellon Fund for Faculty Development at Albion College, Albion, Michigan, and by funds made available to me as the Stanley S. Kresge Professor of Religious Studies at Albion College.

Frank S. Frick
Stanley S. Kresge Professor of Religious Studies
Albion College
Albion, Michigan
Fall 1997

Part I. THE ARCHAEOLOGY OF CULT

The identification of cultic activity in the archaeological record is an area of archaeology that has been plagued by continuing contention. Many archaeological studies of conjectured cultic sites and cultic objects have suffered from a conspicuous circularity in which an artifact is identified as cultic because it was found in a cultic structure; a structure is labeled cultic because it incorporated cultic artifacts. Few archaeological studies have given serious consideration to the functional or spatial correlates of "cultic" assemblages excavated in so-called "temples" or "shrines." Instead, as Binford (1981: 293) observes, there has been a notable tendency on the part of archaeologists to make poorly-supported claims about the behavioral significance of the archaeological record. Unfounded pictures of past human behavior have accompanied such claims, especially in the archaeology of cult.

Correcting an earlier tendency, there has also been on the part of many archaeologists and archaeological interpreters a move away from "biblical archaeology" when dealing with cult—i.e., a dependency on the Bible to generate theses and interpretations of the archaeological record. While the biblical text can be used to some degree and with appropriate caution in formulating hypotheses about cultic behavior patterns in ancient Palestine, these hypotheses must then be tested systemically, processually, and scientifically. Certainly, the relationship between archaeology and the study of cultic behavior is not advanced simply by positing the identification of a structure as a cultic site, based on the similarities between the structure and biblical descriptions of cultic structures, as Zertal appears to do (1994: 63). While the biblical text can be used to some extent in formulating hypotheses about behavior patterns in the ancient Israelite cult, it must be remembered that for the most part the Hebrew Bible contains little information about "popular" religious practices, except for warnings about how they deviate from "official" religion. The study of ancient religious behavior as it was practiced by people, not as some kind of official norm, must, to a large degree, be based on the analysis of its material culture correlates, i.e., on the remains of cultic sites and their contents, as recognized by an archaeology that is systemic, processual, and scientific. While much has been written about cult in archaeological contexts, there are few systematic, theoretical approaches to identifying cultic remains. There has been instead a disturbing inclination over many years to label as cultic those objects for which no other apparent function can be conjectured. In an insightful essay, McCown, nearly fifty years ago, pointed out this misleading presupposition, together with two others that have misled Palestinian archaeologists and biblical scholars working with supposed cultic materials:

> Excavators in Palestine have been led into temptation by various presuppositions. The initial difficulty was a subconscious feeling that the Holy Land must be covered with Holy Places. . . . Another temptation to which the Old Testament scholar was especially liable was the assumption that all standing stones were *masseboth*. . . . A third misconception, naturally consequent upon the first, was the idea that all unusual, specially decorated, or unexplained articles must have served the purposes of cult (1950: 209).

As already noted, to focus on either architecture or artifacts can lead one into a vicious circle. A more fruitful approach, one that takes seriously the behavioral significance of the archaeological record, is one outlined by P. M. Michèle Daviau (1994). Daviau maintains that cultic behavior included a discrete number of activities, whose specificity can be discerned, at least partially, on the basis of artifact classification, and whose location can be identified by spatial distribution. In an analysis of cultic behavior based on the observation of its cultural material correlates, the focus is on the functional characteristics of the artifactual evidence, organized in locus groups and activity sets. The underlying assumption is that the distribution of finds in a given architectural space may reflect patterned activity, and that this activity can be identified once the function of individual artifacts and the possible uses of specific activity sets has been determined. Ideally, of course, a one-to-one correlation of material correlates to cultic activities could serve as a control for purposes of functional identification. Lacking such a precise correlation, this study of architectural space and artifact distribution in the Iron Age cultic structure at Taanach, as Daviau does for the Bronze Age orthostat temple at Hazor, can suggest how artifactual finds are associated with cultic activities. Daviau's strategy suggests the basis for an analytical evaluation of cultic artifacts and for what constitutes a cultic assemblage. The presence of numerous ordinary domestic pottery types such as cooking pots, bowls, and jars, together with more unusual artifacts in contexts that were most likely cultic ones, such as the orthostat temple at Hazor, certainly suggests that ordinary domestic vessels were sometimes used for cultic purposes. It also indicates that so-called "domestic" tasks such as the preparation and consumption of food could and did take place in cultic contexts, implying that an either/or interpretation of cultic artifacts and structures is inappropriate.

Many flawed explanatory attempts dealing with archaeology and cult derive from the failure to situate cultic or ritual activity firmly in a social matrix, as part of a social system, and to define carefully what is involved in categorizing acts as religious rituals or a site as a cultic site. As Levine has argued, cult does not exist outside the matrix of the society in which it operates, and cult is only one expression within this matrix. *Cult is often used for other than cultic purposes* [emphasis mine]. Formal material characteristics can be deceptive, to say the least, and without a corresponding handle on other aspects of the complex belief symbols and their formal expression, they can often mislead us. When talking about cult, one must look at context (Levine 1993: 267).

With respect to the behavioral significance of the archaeological record dealing with cult, anthropologists like Jane Harrison have commented on the flawed approach of investigators who start with a general term *religion*, of which they have a preconceived idea, and then try to squeeze into it any facts that come to hand. Instead she proposes no initial definition of religion or religious ritual, but remarks that "we shall collect the facts . . . and see from what human activities they appear to have sprung" (1912: 29). In other words, archaeological inferences about ritual behavior should not begin by formulating a definition of religion, much less biblical religion, but by outlining categories of behavior included in religious ritual and then testing those categories against an analysis of material culture correlates, without prejudging whether a structure or artifacts are "cultic."

When dealing with cultic structures, one should not make the mistake of assuming that all cultic structures were necessarily monumental and official public buildings, set aside exclusively for cultic use. There clearly were temples, sanctuaries, and shrines that were set apart in this way. But, in addition to being able to identify temples, sanctuaries, and shrines, one also needs to recognize that cultic activity took place outside such centralized, formal cult places—i.e., what Renfrew calls "domestic cult," which takes place in domestic contexts. He suggests that two conditions must be met for domestic cult to be identified archaeologically: (1) there must be a specifically defined place that is set aside for ritual focus, and (2) well defined, non-secular forms used for symbolic focus or in offerings must be found there (1985: 22). Gilmour has recently suggested a number of criteria that distinguish household cult from public cult (1995: 16):

— it is not set in an exclusively cultic location, and consequently architecture may not be a contributory identification factor;

— there are fewer and simpler cult-specific artifacts, reflecting its lesser formality;

— it is on a smaller scale;

—there is unlikely to be any continuity from phase to phase or stratum to stratum;

—its religious imagery/votives may focus on popular or folk deities, or on major deities in unconventional forms.

Recognizing that not all cultic sites are temples, sanctuaries or shrines, Gilmour has proposed five types of cult sites in early Iron Age Palestine (1995: 427): (1) temples, (2) secondary shrines, (3) industrial cult corners, (4) open-air outdoor cult places, and (5) extramural shrines. His category called secondary shrines is a covering term for several different kinds of cult places situated within buildings whose functions included non-cultic ones as well. He subdivides this category into: (a) secondary public cult rooms, (b) cult rooms in monumental buildings, and (c) domestic cult corners. He categorizes the Taanach cultic structure as a secondary shrine/ secondary public cult room. He categorizes the nearby, contemporary Megiddo locus 2081 as a domestic cult corner. A cultic installation, as we will use the term in reference to the Iron Age cultic structure at Taanach, is simply any built structure that, although not dedicated exclusively to cultic activities and not necessarily set apart as a public structure, is, nevertheless, one in which cultic activities occur on a recurring basis.

Several strategies for examining cult and its material correlates in a systemic and processual manner have been proposed. The most thorough models, and ones most applicable to an archaeology of cult, are those formulated by the social anthropologist Roy A. Rappaport, and the European archaeologists Colin Renfrew and G. C. Gesell.

Rappaport begins with the observation that most functional studies of religious behavior in anthropology have as their goal the interpretation of events, process, and/or relationships *within* a social unit. He cites Homans as representing the dominant line of anthropological thought concerning the function of religious ritual:

> Ritual actions do not produce a practical result on the external world—that is one of the reasons why we call them ritual. But to make this statement is not to say that ritual has no function. Its function is not related to the world external to the society, but to the internal constitution of the society. It gives the members confidence, it dispels their anxieties, it disciplines their social organization (Rappaport 1984: 2).

Rappaport's main interest, however, is not with the part ritual plays in relationships occurring *within* a social group, but with how ritual affects relationships between a social group and its environment. Of course, simply to state that a people's ritual actions may measurably affect components of their environment is, as Rappaport recognizes, to state the obvious, if not the trivial. If, in order to perform a ritual, a person cuts down a tree, the environment is obviously affected. Or a ritual sacrifice may require that one or more animals be slaughtered. These actions, by any definition, obviously affect the environment. Rappaport, however, observes that ritual is a mechanism, or set of mechanisms, that regulates some of the relationships of a group with components of that group's environment. The use of the terms "regulate" or "regulation" imply a system, and for Rappaport a system is any set of specified variables in which a change in the value of one of the variables will result in a change in the value of at least one other variable. A regulating mechanism is one that maintains the values of one or more variables within a range or ranges that permit/s the continued functioning of the system. Furthermore, systemic relationships are not only regulated, they are self-regulated. The term "self-regulation" is applied to systems in which a change in the value of a variable itself initiates a process that either limits further change or returns the value to a former level. This process, sometimes referred to as "negative feedback," may involve special mechanisms that change the values of some variables in response to changes in the values of others. Thermostats, for instance, are mechanical regulating mechanisms in heating/cooling systems in which measurable quantities of hot or cold air emanating intermittently from a controlled source and the temperature of a surrounding medium are variables (Rappaport 1984: 3, 4). The ways in which religion, through ritual, helps to regulate the social and economic processes of a social system is graphically illustrated in the feedback diagram in figure 1.

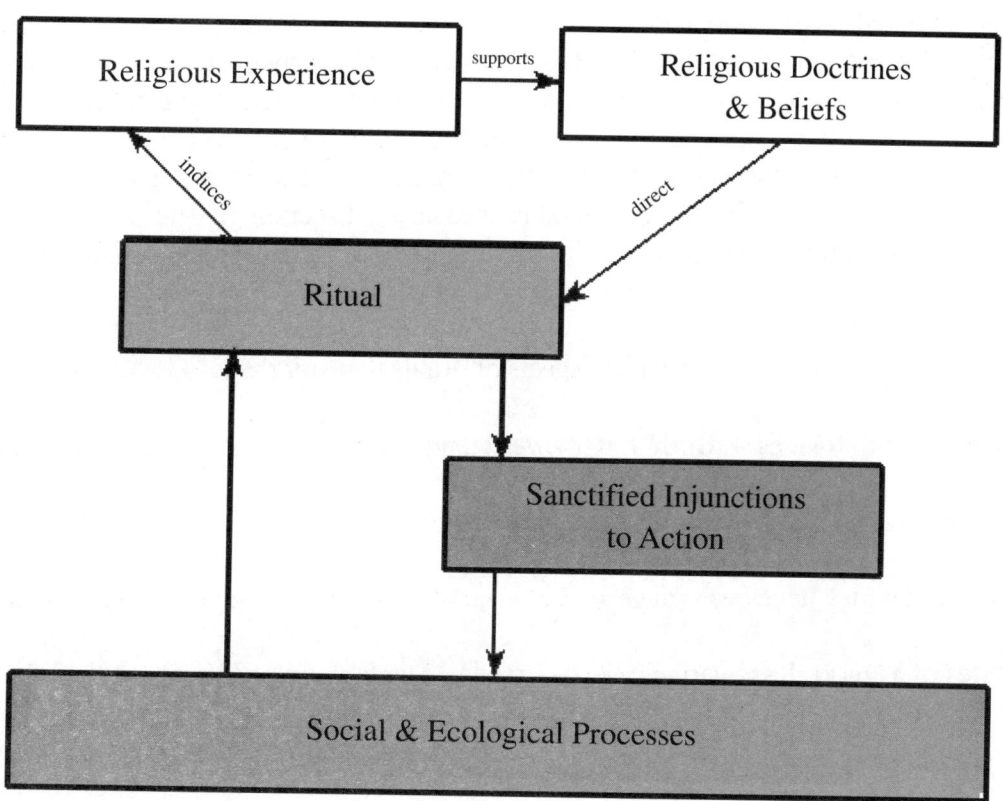

Rappaport's model suggests a relationship between religious beliefs and rituals and also the impact of rituals on a group's environment. Religious activities are primarily part of the informational processes of human societies. Rappaport correctly understands religion as a set of sacred beliefs held in common by a group of people *together with* the more or less standard actions (rituals) that are undertaken with respect to those beliefs. He defines ritual as "conventional acts of display through which one or more participants transmit information concerning their physiological, psychological, or sociological states either to themselves or to one or more others" (1971a: 25). From these definitions, Rappaport proceeds to sketch the outlines of the cybernetic loop represented in figure 1:

> Inasmuch as the religious experience is an intrinsic part of the more inclusive emotional dynamics of an organism, and inasmuch as the emotional dynamics of an organism must be closely related to its material state, it is plausible to assume that religious experiences are affected by material conditions. But the latter are, particularly in primitive societies, in some degree a function of the operation of the control hierarchy which the religious experience itself supports. Thus the willingness, indeed the ability, of the members of a congregation to affirm through religious experience the ultimate sacred propositions which sanctify the control hierarchy may be in considerable measure a function of the effectiveness of the hierarchy in maintaining equilibrium in and among those variables which define their material well-being in the long run, and thus adaptation (1970: 62).

Rappaport also speaks of particular aspects of rituals that suit them to function as homeostats and communication devices. Both the *content* and *occurrence* of rituals are important in communication. Ritual *occurrences* that are not locked into a specific calendrical date may be a "yes-no" signal that may have been triggered by the achievement or violation of a particular state or range of states of a "more-less" variable. (1971b: 63). The *content* of a ritual, on the other hand, is particularly important in the transmission of quantitative or more-less information and is of significance mainly within single systems or subsystems; the *occurrence* of a ritual is especially important in the transmission of information across the borders of separate and unlike systems or subsystems (1971b: 65). Echoing Rappaport's model, Carol Meyers has recently suggested that current modes of interdisciplinary analysis can reveal how the formal aspects of ancient Israel's religious life existed within the context of material reality and also as essential parts of a sociocultural system (1995). However sacrifice may have functioned on a symbolic or phenomenological level as an expression of a particular belief system, Meyers demonstrates, in a particular case, how it was also integrally related to the socioeconomic conditions of ancient Palestine. "Indeed . . . ritual behavior stands in sensitive relationship to environmental factors and is instrumental in sanctioning subsistence patterns that maximized the various ecosystems" (1995: 79). Taken as an aggregate, the material items of the sacrifice discussed by Meyers (that of Hannah in 1 Sam 1:24) represent typical elements of ancient Israelite village food production in villages with a mixed pastoral and agricultural regime: animal husbandry, field crops (wheat), and horticultural activity (in this case, wine).

Rappaport's model suggests that cultic installations are not necessarily monofunctional, but that rituals are often used for other than strictly "religious" purposes as a vital part of informational processes in preindustrial societies. Cultic installations considered in this way may indeed be multifunctional, thus eliminating the need to draw sharp distinctions between cultic, domestic, and commercial activity areas within a site, a distinction that is both artificial and unsupported by the archaeological record in Iron Age Palestine. As suggested above, cultic activities occur not only in large public buildings like sanctuaries or temples, but also in what Yigal Shiloh referred to as "cult corners" in residential locations (149-151), structures which, according to Dever (134, 135), gained popularity during the Solomonic period and retained many domestic functions. Ahlström has made a similar argument regarding "cultic corners" during the Sololmonic period (1982). Rast adopts such a position and modifies it by suggesting that what we may have, in the case of the rooms or parts of buildings at Taanach, Megiddo and other sites, called "cult corners" by Shiloh, are residences belonging to priestly groups that were used to extend the control of a centralized Jerusalem administration. In the centralization of the cult that occurred during Solomon's reign, priestly families in outlying areas were allotted responsibility for the cult and entrusted with cultic materials, which they kept and used, not in shrines set apart for the purpose, but in their residential quarters (1994: 361). Thus the cultic structure at Taanach, contemporary Locus 2081 and Building 10 at Megiddo were probably places where traditional cultic material was stored, repaired, or perhaps even manufactured, either by priests or by craft specialists under their supervision (Rast 1994: 361).

A problem faced by archaeologists that is not addressed by Rappaport, however, is the fact that religious belief systems and their accompanying ritual expressions are not always given expression in material culture. When they are—in what one might call the *archaeology of cult*, defined as the system of patterned actions in response to religious belief—there is the problem, to which Rappaport has alerted us, that such actions are not always clearly separated from other actions, but can be embedded within everyday functional activity. The first task of the archaeologist, therefore, is to recognize the evidence of cult for what it is, and not make the error of labeling as "cultic" any object that cannot be otherwise interpreted.

William G. Dever, an archaeologist who has written extensively on the subject of archaeological correlates of religious ritual in ancient Palestine, concludes that there are four basic types of actions involved in religious ritual: (1) food and drink offerings, (2) various libations, (3) animal sacrifice, and (4) possible incense offerings. He also maintains that there is "no evidence whatsoever for . . . large scale, much less public rituals" (1987: 222-226, 229). Dever has also developed an outline of the material remains of religious ritual that are amenable to archaeological investigation. In this outline he includes five kinds of material remains (1983: 572):

1. <u>Architecture</u>. For Dever this includes monumental structures as well as local shrines, and residential cultic structures. With reference to Taanach in particular, he speaks of a small "household shrine" at 10th-century Taanach, the structure that is the subject of this study.

2. <u>Art</u>. This category includes both monumental art and the "minor" arts—especially pottery and other ceramics such as figurines, plaques, terra cotta stands, temple models, censers, etc.), ivory carvings, seals, and possibly textiles. "In theory at least, no other category of material culture should be so readily accessible or potentially revealing in explicating the cult as works of art" (1983: 572). Again, with reference to Taanach, Dever says "No Israelite statuary or sculpture, large-scale iconographic representations, or paintings are known to us, *save two 10th-century cultic stands from Ta'anach*" (emphasis mine) (573). The pottery types found in the context of these shrines [as in the cultic structure at Taanach] are mostly utilitarian rather than specifically manufactured for cultic use, but in a systemic understanding of cult, that does not rule out the use of such pottery in the cult. As at other sites, ceramic figurines of the so-called "Astarte" (more accurately "Asherah") type, for which the neutral designation †-shaped figurines is employed in this monograph, were found at Taanach. As at other sites, ceramic male figurines of any type are conspicuously absent at Taanach.

3. <u>Artifacts</u>. Dever subdivides artifacts into: (a) generally fixed architectural furnishings (benches, altars, *favissae*, stands, basins, braziers, censers, etc.), and (b) smaller, more portable objects, whether found in temple/shrine contexts or used in everyday life, such as votives of all kinds, human or animal figurines, any "magical" items (such as masks or aids in divination and

incantation), and other *objects d'art*. We will discuss both types of artifacts from the Taanach cultic structure below.

    4. <u>Texts</u>

    5. <u>Burials</u>. No Iron Age burials were found in the Taanach excavations.

Dever's cultic behavior categories have been sharpened further in an evaluation of the evidence from LB Hazor by P. M. Michèle Daviau, who cites the following theory: "The theory to be tested is that cultic behavior . . . included a wide variety of activities, whose specificity can be partly discerned on the basis of artifact classification and whose location can be identified by spatial distribution" (1994: 73). In testing this theory, Daviau focuses on the functional characteristics of artifactual evidence, organized in locus groups and activity sets, as embodying the material correlates of religious behavior patterns. The underlying assumption is that the distribution of finds in any given architectural space may reflect patterned activity. Such patterned activity can be identified once the function of individual artifacts and the possible uses of specific activity sets have been determined. As Daviau suggests, in an ideal situation a set of known material correlates for each precise religious activity should be established as a control for the functional identification of ancient remains. Daviau recognizes, however, that there are problems with establishing suitable analogous materials for this purpose.

Colin Renfrew, a British archaeologist whose fieldwork is in Europe, has developed a comprehensive list of archaeological indicators of ritual. Renfrew's indicators are especially useful as a means of avoiding the imposition of a text-based (i.e., biblical) understanding of religious belief and ritual on archaeological data from Palestine, something that has characterized most histories of Israelite religion, which have dealt almost exclusively with canonical biblical texts and thus reflected the biases of the biblical writers and editors. If archaeological indicators of religious ritual can be recognized without first discerning them with a "biblical" spotter, archaeology can be a powerful tool in aiding the reconstruction of "popular" religion as it was practiced in Iron Age Palestine, not as an ideal entity or "official cult" that was envisioned by a later, elite minority.

Renfrew begins by suggesting that if we are to recognize cultic activities, it is important not to lose sight of the transcendent object of cultic activity. "Religious ritual involves the performance of expressive acts of worship towards the deity or transcendent being" (Renfrew and Bahn 1991: 359). In these acts there are generally at least four main components: (1) focusing of attention (location, light, sounds, smell, etc.) ; (2) boundary zones between the secular and the sacred; (3) symbolic presence of the deity; and (4) participation and offering (movement, eating and drinking, material offerings). From these four main components Renfrew develops the concrete archaeological indicators of ritual that are listed below, some of which will usually be found when rituals occur, and by which the occurrence of ritual may therefore be recognized. The more indicators present, the stronger the inference that religious ritual is involved. Renfrew cautions, however, that only a few of these criteria will probably be met in any single archaeological context.

Archaeological Indicators of Ritual (Renfrew and Bahn 1991: 359, 360):

Focusing of attention:
1. Ritual may take place in a spot with special, natural associations.
2. Alternatively, ritual may take place in a special structure set apart for sacred functions.
3. The structure and equipment used for ritual may employ attention-focusing devices, reflected in the architecture, special apparatus (cultic stands, benches, hearths, lamps, ritual vessels, censers, etc.)
4. The sacred area is likely to be rich in repeated symbols (known as "redundancy").

Boundary zone:
5. Ritual may involve both public display and hidden exclusive acts.

6. Concepts of cleanliness and pollution may be reflected in the facilities (e.g., basins of water) and in the maintenance of the structure.

Symbolic presence of the deity:
7. The association with a deity or deities may be reflected in the presence of a cult image, or a representation of the deity in some form.
8. Ritualistic symbols will often relate iconographically to the deities worshiped and to their associated myth. Animal symbolism (of real or mythical animals) may often be used, with particular animals related to specific deities or powers.
9. Ritualistic symbols may relate to those seen in funerary rituals and other rites of passage.

Participation and offering:
10. Ritual will involve special movements—gestures of adoration—and these may be reflected in the art of iconography of decorations or images.
11. Ritual may employ various devices for evoking religious experience (e.g., dance, drugs, etc.)
12. Sacrifice of animals or humans may be practiced.
13. Food and drink may be brought and possibly consumed as offerings or burned/poured away.
14. Other material objects may be brought and offered (votives). The act of offering may demand breakage and hiding or discard.
15. Considerable investment of wealth may be reflected both in the equipment used and in the offerings made.
16. Considerable investment of wealth and resources may be reflected in the structure itself and its facilities.

Gesell (1985: 2), an archaeologist whose work is in the Aegean area stresses that where architecture and cult objects are not present together [which appears to be the case at Taanach], there are two options: (1) when there is a room without cult objects whose architecture and location within the building are similar to the architecture and location of a positively identified shrine room elsewhere, it is "reasonable" to conclude the room had a cultic function; or (2) where only architecture or cult objects are present, one may only suggest "possibility." She uses the three criteria of architecture, location, and artifacts to identify cultic activity in Minoan contexts where written or pictorial representations are absent. Gilmour (1995: 5) has adopted these same three criteria with the comment: "Particularly appropriate for the southern Levant in Iron Age I is her [i.e., Gesell's] emphasis on the element of probability in archaeological identification [of cult]."

Finally, Michael Coogan has proposed four criteria that can be used to determine if a structure was cultic or not, on the basis of archaeological evidence. The four are: (1) isolation (i.e., separation between the holy and the profane); (2) exotic materials (i.e., material not typical of other contexts); (3) parallels at other sites; and (4) continuity (i.e., a building is dedicated to cultic use through time). Coogan's first two criteria clearly presuppose a kind of either/or, sacred/profane bifurcation—either the building and the artifacts found within it were sacred or they were profane. There is little room in his criteria for a both/and argument—a building and contents that are cultic in the sense that they are an integral part of the socioeconomic workings of society, not detached from society as a sacred abstraction. With regard to Coogan's third criteria, we will certainly draw on analogies from other sites in assessing possible cultic functions of installations and artifacts from the Iron Age "cultic structure" at Taanach. If artifacts found in definite cultic contexts and from contemporary or near contemporary periods elsewhere are also present in our structure at Taanach, we can more confidently conclude that it was used for cultic purposes.

Coogan's fourth criterion concerns continuity in cultic structures. While our analysis of the structure at Taanach will concentrate on period IIB (960-918 BCE), we will also present some evidence that the building may have had a cultic use in earlier periods as well.

In assessing whether the structure at Taanach that has been identified by some as a "cultic structure" was indeed that, we will apply, in what follows, Rappaport's model, Dever's categories of ritual actions, Daviau's activity sets and functional characteristics of artifactual evidence, Gesell's three criteria, Coogan's criterion of parallels, and Renfrew's list of archaeological indicators of ritual to the structure (and its contents) that was excavated in SW 1-7, 1-8, 2-7, and 2-8 at Tell Taanek (= biblical Taanach). As mentioned above, we will concentrate on this structure as it existed in period IIB (960-918 BCE), when its identification as a cultic structure seems clearest. In our conclusion, we will return to the question of whether this installation can justifiably be labeled a "cultic structure."

It is the intent of this monograph to analyze the development of the Iron Age cultic installation at Taanach and explain its contents. A comprehensive catalogue of all the objects found in association with this installation is beyond the limits of the monograph. Appendix C does, however, present a comprehensive list of registered objects from SW 1-7, 1-8, 2-7, and 2-8, with those that can be stratigraphically assigned to particular periods so designated following the registered object number. Appendix D lists those registered objects from SW 1-7, 1-8, 2-7, and 2-8 that can be dated to period IIB (960-918 BCE) with some certainty.

Part II. The Cultic Structure at Taanach in Its Geographical and Archaeological Context

In order to understand the cultic structure at Taanach systemically, it is necessary to place the site in its geographical context. Tell Taannek and its surrounding region is shown in figure 2. As is apparent from the map of Taanach's region, the site is located on the western edge of the central hill country along the southern edge of the Esdraelon Plain. It is thus a site linked to both the central hill country and the Esdraelon Plain, areas which varied in terms of their populations' ethnicity, economic, political, and social organization. Socially and politically akin to the hill country sites to its south, Taanach was more closely associated economically, and most likely ethnically, with the Canaanite cities in the Esdraelon Plain to its north throughout the early Iron Age. As will be seen below, these associations are reflected in the objects found in the cultic structure. In the early Iron Age, the central hill country came to be occupied by a people who were Israelites or proto-Israelites. By contrast, the cities in the Esdraelon Plain, represented especially by Megiddo, were occupied by Canaanites in the early Iron Age, and carried forward the material culture of the Late Bronze Age.

Strategically Taanach commands the road that runs southeast from the coast along the Carmel Ridge, past the sites of Yoqne'am, Tell Qiri and Megiddo (the main route from the coast to the Esdraelon Plain) to Jenin (ancient 'En-Ganim), a route that continues into the central hill country past Ibleam. A secondary route leads southwesterly from Taanach to the coastal plain.

The area around Tell Taannek is agriculturally fertile. The site has no natural water supply in the form of significant springs or streams, but it receives an average annual rainfall of 500 mm., which was stored in a system of cisterns. The soils around the site are predominantly terra rossa, with some patches of Mediterranean brown forest soil. This combination of adequate precipitation

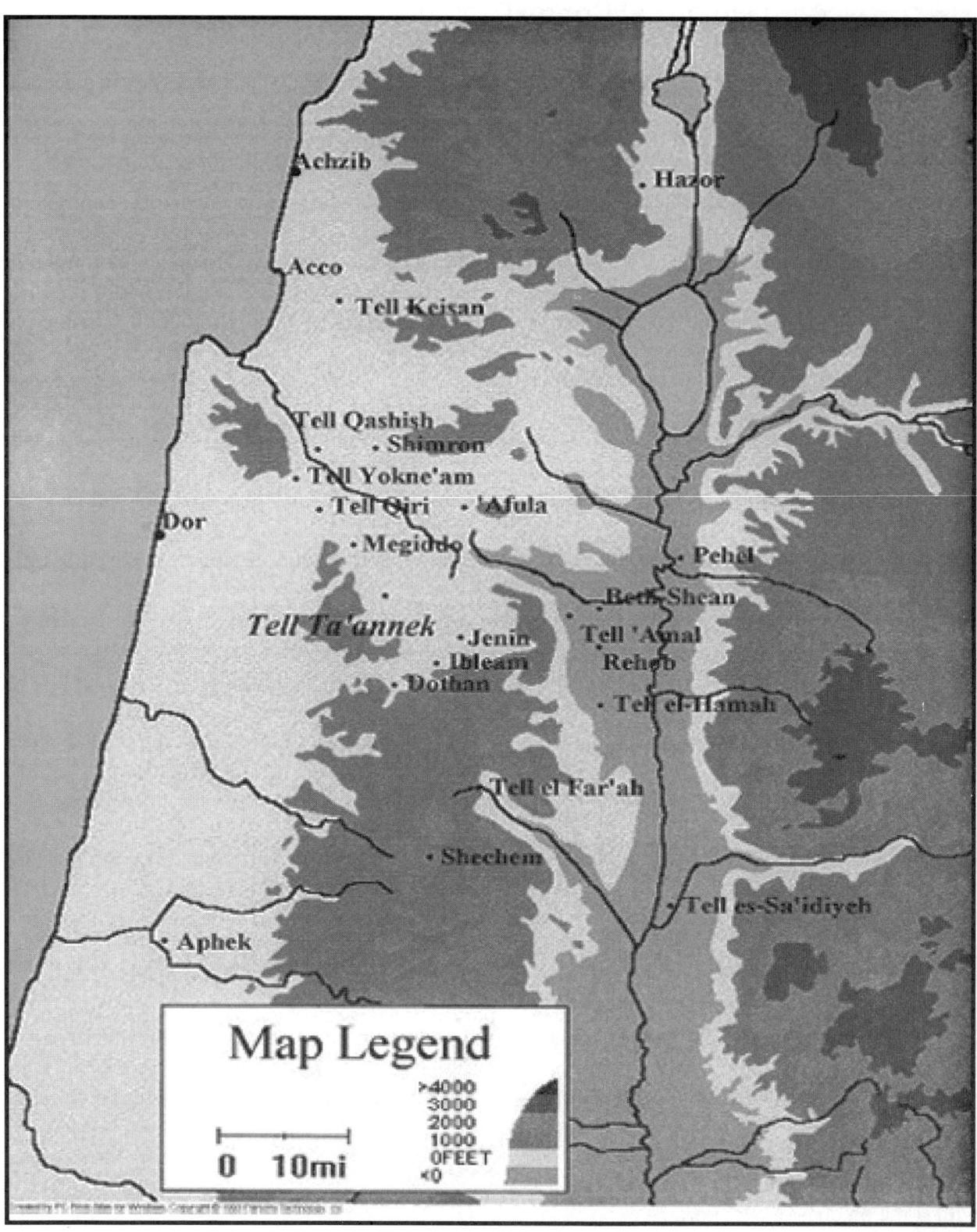

Figure 2: Taanach in Its Regional Setting

and soils supported dependable agriculture as well as abundant grasses for the grazing of sheep and goats. Cereal grains, olives, grapes, and other fruits were the staple crops of the region, and thus would also constitute the offerings presented in the cult, together with offerings from the herds of sheep and goats. As will be noted below in the discussion of installations and artifacts associated with the cultic structure, agricultural produce as well as offerings from herds were represented in the apparatus of the cultic structure, and the cult probably played a role in regulating agricultural production and herd management.

Taanach was affiliated with other sites in its area as part of a three-level site hierarchy. At the top of this hierarchy was the large regional urban administrative center represented by Megiddo, with which Taanach exhibited shifting political and economic affiliations. It would appear that occupational histories of Taanach and Megiddo were interrelated. E. g., during the Solomonic zenith of Megiddo, Taanach was largely deserted. Taanach was a second-level site, a mid-sized, decentralized, agrarian town. Related to Taanach within about a ten-mile radius were also third-level small, unfortified farming villages such as Tel 'Amal. The nature of Taanach's affiliation with sites above and below it in this hierarchy changed during the four major phases of the early Iron Age periods (IA, IB, IIA, and IIB). On the basis of a stratigraphical analysis of early Iron Age materials, Meehl has provided a description of these shifting affiliations in the four phases of the early Iron Age represented at Taanach: IA (ca. 1200-1150 BCE); IB (1150-1125 BCE); IIA (1020-960 BCE); and IIB (960-918 BCE). The summaries that follow are based on Meehl's thorough analysis. Iron I phasing at Taanach, together with comparative stratum designations for other sites in the region is presented in tabular form in Table 1 below.

Period IA

As the 13th century BCE gave way to the 12th, an unfortified new town was built on Tell Taannek. Period IA artifacts from Taanach display a distinctive influence from the culture of the Late Bronze Age found in the contemporary cities in the adjacent Esdraelon Plain. The presence of a metalworking industry at Taanach that could produce the kind of iron implements found is more typical of the urban Canaanite sites in the North, and differentiates Taanach from the villages of the central hill country. The similarity in material culture between the period IA occupation at Tell Taannek and that of Megiddo stratum VIIA indicates that no significant sociopolitical boundaries blocked contact between the two—that the population of neither site was intent on establishing or maintaining the physical markers of a separate cultural identity. As Meehl suggests, one explanation for such a situation is that two different ethnic groups inhabited the sites and shared the same objective markers (physical characteristics), while maintaining cultural conformity and distinctiveness in ways that have not survived in the archaeological record. Ethnic identity may have been demonstrated in areas of culture such as language, shared moral values or beliefs, or political organization. If the biblical evidence regarding the Canaanites in the valleys and the Israelites in the hills is taken at face value, two separate ethnic identities may have become quite polarized in the early Iron Age. Although the moral values, beliefs, and political organization of the Israelites, idealized by the later biblical authors, set them apart from the Canaanites, these distinctions would not be apparent in the archaeological record (Meehl 317). Another explanation for the striking similarity in material culture between Taanach and Megiddo in this period is that people from two different ethnic groups lived in Megiddo and at Taanach, but they were not in competition for the same resources or power. They thus saw no need to establish or maintain internal cultural conformity and distinct cultural markers. In theory, this would mean that the Canaanites at Megiddo were not threatened by the hill country Proto-Israelite occupants of Taanach. A third, and probably the most likely explanation for the similarity in material culture between Megiddo and Taanach is that people of the same ethnic group, in this case LB Canaanites, lived in both places and had basically the same material culture. Differences in political organization and settlement pattern would be due to the adaptation of the Taanach group to the environmental niche of the hill country as opposed to the strategic location of Megiddo in the Jezreel valley straddling major trade routes. Megiddo was a main administrative center and Taanach was a second-level, less developed outpost (Meehl 319).

Table 1: Comparative Iron I Stratigraphy

Taanach	Bethel, 'Ai, El-Jib, Shiloh	Gezer	Tell Qasile	'Ain Shems, Ashdod	Tell el-Far'ah	Deir 'Alla
Pre-Period IA/LBII					VI	
Period IA ca. 1200-1150	Bethel Phase 1 (early 12th cent); 'Ai Phases I and II; el-Jib; Shiloh	3		Ashdod XII (Philistine)	VI	
Period IB 1150-1125	Bethel Phase 2 (late 12th cent)	4	XII, XI	AS III (late 12th-early 11th cent); Ashdod XI (Philistine)	VI	Phases A-D (ca. 1125-1050)
Gap					VIIA	
Period IIA ca. 1020-960	Bethel Phase 3 (11th cent); Bethel 4a (early 10th);	7 (post-Philistine, pre-Solomonic)	X (post-Philistine, pre-Solomonic)	AS IIa (late 11th-early 10th cent); Ashdod X (post-Philistine)	VIIB	Phases E-J (mid-11th-late 10th cent)
Period IIB 960-918	Bethel 4b (Solomonic)	6 (Solomonic)	IX (David and Solomon)	AS IIb (late 10th cent)	VIIB	

Part II—Page 23

Taanach	Tell Beit Mirsim	Megiddo	Hazor	Tell Abu Hawam, Tell Zeror, Tell ʿAmal, ʿAfula	Beth-Shan	Yoqneʿam	Tell Qiri	Tel Kedesh/Tell Abu Qudeis
Pre-Period IA/LBII		VIII			VII	XIX A-B		VIII
Period IA ca. 1200-1150	B1 (12th cent)	VIIB (late 13th-ca. 1175)	XII	TAH V (1st quarter, 12th cent); IVA (ended in mid-12th cent)	Lower VI—beginning with Rameses III, 1182-1151 (Yadin's 4)		IX/VIII	VII
Period IB 1150-1125	B2 (late 12th-most of 11th cent)	VIIA (ca. 1175-1125)	XII (mid-12th cent)	ʿAfula IIIB (last half 12th cent)	Lower VI (beginning with Rameses III, 1182-1151) (Yadin's 4)			VII
Gap		VIB-VIA			Upper VI (Yadin's 3 & 2)	XVIII	VIII	
Period IIA ca. 1020-960	B3 (10th cent)	VI A-VB	XI (11th cent)	TAH IV (late 11th cent); ʿAfula IIIA (late 11th-early 10th cent)	Lower V (Yadin's 2)	XVII-XV	VIII-VII	VI
Period IIB 960-918	B3	VA-IVB	Xb-Xa	TAH II (late 10th cent); TZ (late 10th); TA IV-III	Lower Level V (Yadin's 1)	XIV	VII	VII

Rast, on the basis of the ceramic record, asserts that the period IA inhabitants of Taanach were probably Canaanites (1978: 15). Finkelstein has also stated that the inhabitants of Taanach at this time were probably sedentary Canaanites, but ethnically mixed (1988: 90, 91). On the basis of a comparison with other sites in the area, Meehl concludes that the population of Taanach in this period should be viewed as an extension of the culture of the Jezreel Valley sites that adapted economically, socially, and politically to the environment of the hill country.

The link between Taanach and Megiddo is also evident in the fact that Taanach was destroyed shortly after the destruction of Megiddo VIIA. As long as Megiddo was strong, Taanach thrived. When Megiddo weakened, Taanach declined until the two sites were destroyed at about the same time. Also, when Taanach was put into one of Solomon's administrative districts, according to 1 Kg 4:12, it was included in the same district as Megiddo. Meehl believes that Taanach may have served not only as an agricultural outpost in the hill country, but also as a collection point for agricultural products and perhaps as an administrative center operating on behalf of the urban centers on the plains (1995: 338). The similarity in the material culture between Taanach and Megiddo, as evidenced in objects found in cultic structures at the two sites, may indicate, as suggested earlier, that the cult was a component of the regulatory mechanism of the royal authority that was based in Megiddo and which utilized Taanach as one of its administrative centers.

Period IB

Little change is evident in the archaeological record at Taanach as the period IB town appeared shortly after the structures of IA were abandoned. The population was less than in IA, the sociopolitical organization stayed basically the same, Iron Age types replaced those of the LB in the ceramic repertoire, and the economy remained agrarian, dominated by the cultivation of cereals and olives and by the herding of sheep and goats. Change was evident, however, in increased evidence of social differentiation, involvement in trade, and specialized craft activity (Meehl 1995: 340).

The material culture still closely resembled that of Megiddo, and to a lesser degree Beth-Shan. Many common features and forms in the pottery of Megiddo VIIA and period IB at Taanach point to the continuation of the shared pottery tradition and/or manufacturing center that had begun in the early 12th century. There is also evidence in this period for a technologically advanced metalworking industry at Taanach. Many of the iron objects from Taanach were found in stratified contexts, and they comprise one of the largest groups of closely datable iron objects from ancient Palestine. What is even more significant for this study is the fact that the largest group of iron artifacts found at Taanach came from three of the squares that constituted the location of the cultic structure—SW 1-7, 2-7, and 2-8. The metal objects from the cultic structure will be treated in detail in part IV.H below.

A striking indication of the cult's economic regulatory role comes from this period in the contents of a period IB cooking pot (TT 753) found in L (= locus) 27 of the SW 2-8 square of the cultic building, lying on a plaster floor 28. The contents of this pot included several weights, beads, metal fragments, whelk shells, and a bone stamp seal (TT 702). The contents of this cooking pot (TT 753) will also be discussed in detail in the section below on objects and artifacts. In commenting on the contents of this pot, Meehl says: "Although the precise purpose of the contents of this pot remains unclear, they are *unique and not related to subsistence agriculture, suggesting a specialized activity*" (emphasis mine) (1995: 344).

Taanach's associations during period IB remained closer with the Canaanites to the north than with the proto-Israelites to the south in the central hill country. Megiddo VIIA and Beth-Shan Lower VI went into decline and were destroyed sometime after the middle of the 12th century. Taanach IB suffered destruction ca. 1125 BCE, shortly after the fall of Megiddo and Beth-Shan. Without the presence of the large urban administrative centers, the sites under them in an administrative hierarchy either adapted to the new situation, as did Tell Qiri, or were destroyed, as were Taanach, Jenin, and Tel Kedesh/Tell Abu Qudeis.

Period IIA

After a gap in occupation that lasted about 100 years, a new unfortified village arose on Tell Taannek in about 1020 BCE, which stood for only about sixty years until it was abandoned and partially destroyed ca. 960 BCE. In addition to archaeological evidence for standard subsistence agriculture, the archaeological record at IIA Taanach, including the four "squares" of the cultic structure, includes items indicating trade and craft specialization. Marine and freshwater shells, basalt tools, and items of faience, carnelian, and agate are among the trade goods evident. The presence of unfinished carburized tools, together with iron and bronze slag suggest that there was a sophisticated metal industry at the site (Stech-Wheeler et al. 1981: 253-255).

While IIA Taanach presents the appearance of a large, decentralized agrarian town, similar to what it was in period IA, there was an unequal distribution of basins and storage silos, which when considered with the artifacts from this period, point to increasing social fragmentation. Social differentiation is indicated by the evidence of on-site metal working, the presence of exotic items, and numerous metal artifacts, both utilitarian and non-utilitarian. The standing stones (מצבות) that were found in secondary usage may have been part of a period IIA "cultic corner," and would also be an indicator of increased social differentiation (Meehl 1995: 368).

The material culture of IIA Taanach is paralleled at Megiddo (VIA and VB), Yoqne'am (XVII) and is part of a repertoire found throughout northern Palestine, moving toward a cultural homogeneity that was reached during Solomon's reign in the latter part of the century. While no distinctive ethnic indicators appear in IIA Taanach, the material culture suggests that Canaanite culture, as found in the Esdraelon Valley to the north, held considerable influence over the site during the late 11th century. Meehl proposes that this was the time when David succeeded in subduing his main enemies in the region of Taanach and incorporated it into his expanding empire (1995: 375). Period IIA occupation ended at the site when the town was abandoned and partially destroyed during the transition from David to Solomon in the mid-10th century.

Period IIB

In this period, which lasted from 960-918 BCE, Taanach became, according to 1 Kgs 4:12, an administrative center in one of Solomon's twelve districts. This period also saw increasing specialization and social differentiation, as exhibited by the appearance of another new feature in Taanach's material culture. This new element is related to the cultic structure. Offering stands found in and around the cultic structure suggest that religious rituals were performed in this specific location. The stands themselves will be discussed in section IV.D below, which deals with ceramic artifacts. Under the administrative policies of Solomon, there was a close connection between civil administration and religion, and thus specific "cult corners" were established to serve as branches of the Solomonic cult/administration in regions only recently brought under the control of the Jerusalem-based monarchy. In the case of Taanach, that "cult corner" was in a location that had cultic connections from earlier periods.

In period IIB, Taanach looked like an agrarian hill country village, but socially bore more resemblance to the hierarchical sites in the valleys. With increasing urbanization, the characteristics of the hill country and the valleys intermingled. With the bringing of these areas under a single political administration under Solomon, material culture differences between sites stemmed from their adaptation to micro-environments. During this period the parallels between assemblages from the cultic structure at Taanach and Locus 2081 at Megiddo are especially striking (Loud 1948: 43-46; Rast 1978: 34, 35; table I; Kempinski 1989: 186, 187). Solomonic Hazor also had cultic artifacts (tripod strainers and part of a cultic stand) similar to those from period IIB Taanach (Ben-Tor 1989: 39, pl. 171:16, 17). Cultic artifacts at Tell el-Fâr'ah (VIIb) show close connections with IIB Taanach as well. Among these artifacts at Tell el-Fâr'ah are a tripod strainer, a "tambourine" goddess figurine, a terra-cotta shrine model, and a flagstone basin similar to the one found in SW 1-7 (Chambon, 1984: 31, fig. 12). Regarding the cult of this period at Taanach, Meehl concludes:

> Incorporation into the larger society of the United Monarchy may have meant the imposition of a state religion as well. No religious images appeared in the remains of the Taanach occupations which were dominated by the LB culture. Period IIB Taanach, the Iron Age town connected closely with the United Monarchy and, according to the Bible, its aniconic religion, produced the cult stands with their pronounced Canaanite imagery and the figurine mold. If the site served as an administrative center for the Israelite nation-state as the biblical records report, the cult stand and the figurine mold may be evidence of the close association of cult and administration in the United Monarchy (1995: 421).

Part III. The Architecture and History of the Cultic Structure at Taanach

III.A. Major Excavations of Taanach's Cultic Structure

Taanach has seen two major archaeological expeditions in the 20th century—one led by Ernst Sellin in the early part of the century and the Concordia-ASOR Expedition led by Paul Lapp in the 1960s. Sellin's Austrian expedition conducted three seasons of excavation at Taanach from 1902 to 1904, during which several large areas and numerous probes and trenches were opened. Unfortunately, as a consequence of when it was done, neither stratigraphical excavation methods nor the knowledge of ceramic typology informed Sellin's work to any appreciable extent. What would now be recognized as distinct strata were often simply lumped together into one stratum by Sellin. There is also very little information about pottery in his report.

Sellin divided the tell into quadrants and excavated five-meter-wide trenches, as well as several probes. Trenches were excavated by starting at the edge of the tell and then working toward the center. Most of the digging was done in the 1902 season, which was the one during which the smashed, but complete, "incense stand," "olive press," and a cistern were found in the area of the cultic structure, in what Sellin called the South Trench. The precise find spot of the "incense stand" is unknown; Sellin merely records it as eight meters southeast of the "olive press" (1904: 76). Sellin assigned these finds to his stratum 3a, which included pottery dating all the way from LB I to Umayyad, but which was predominantly 10th century BCE. Both the "olive press" and the cistern found by Sellin were re-excavated by the Lapp expedition and dated to the Iron Age IIB period (960-918 BCE). In the re-excavation of the cistern, the Lapp excavations also found two more cultic stands. Meehl has suggested that the presence of numerous whole pots in the west half of the cultic structure, that were found by Lapp's excavation adjacent to Sellin's "South Trench," indicates that there were structures in that area in the past, but Sellin failed to discover them. Alternatively, he indicates that the whole pots may have been taken out of the buildings and left on exterior surfaces at that time of the buildings' destruction. Since no Iron Age graves were found in the part of the tell excavated by Lapp, it is unlikely that these whole pots were from Iron Age graves.

Lapp's expedition worked at the tell for three seasons: 1963, 1966, and 1968. Prior to digging, based on Sellin's findings, Lapp divided the site into four functionally specific areas—cultic, domestic, industrial, and fortifications. These four areas of the site were sampled using large (5 x 7 m.) "squares" and trenches. Lapp used a judgmental site sampling method, a method which has the highest degree of bias of commonly used sampling strategies. Using the judgmental sampling method, the location of excavation units is directed towards maximizing the recovery of artifacts at a known site. Excavation units are clustered around surface finds in the hope that these artifacts represent buried artifact concentrations. This method of sampling produces a sample that does yield stratigraphic control and detailed artifactual information, but may skew the results.

The Lapp expedition's recovery of Sellin's "incense altar," which was completely shattered into at least 36 pieces, together with the discovery of two other stands in a nearby cistern that had been noted by Sellin, added strength to the thesis that the area of Sellin's South Trench, Lapp's Area B, was either devoted to cultic purposes or that these items were part of an assemblage belonging to a "cult corner" in a residence. Sellin himself believed that the find spot of the "incense stand" (which he called a *Raucheraltar*) was a residence, but, believing that such an artifact must have been associated with a public shrine, he added: "Of course, it remains possible, in and of itself, that the altar once stood in a public sanctuary and was carried off for some reason to this spot" (Hillers 1962: 65). He also reports "later finds of fragments of a similar object, about 30 m. farther south."

Here, we will focus on "squares" that were opened by the Lapp expedition in Area B, which was under the direction of Alfred von Rohr Sauer. Much of what follows in this section is gleaned from von Rohr Sauer's unpublished "final report" on the area. Area B was made up of a total of eight 5 x 7 m. "squares" that were designated on the master grid as SW 1-7, SW 2-7, SW 3-7, SW 1-8, SW 2-8, SW 1-9, SW 3-5, SW 3-6. SW 2-7 was extended eastward 2 m.. and southward 5 m. during the 1963 season, probing into areas that would be included in SW 1-7 and SW 2-8 during the 1966 season. Laid out directly west of Sellin's "south shaft, which measured 14 x 18 m., Site B was directly to the west of Sellin's "south shaft," where he had found the *Raucheraltar* ("incense altar") and what he believed to be an olive press with its crushing stone. The latter was seen by Lapp and his team as a cultic basin and a standing stone (מצבה) (1964: 37). Speaking of this structure in his final report, Sellin says:

> In this shaft . . . I found a stone structure which made me think at first of an altar, but was probably an olive-press . . . . The heavy rounded stone with which the pressing was done still lay nearby, but . . . I did not find a stone hollowed out to receive the liquid. The press was 2.5 m. long, 1.30 m. wide (Hillers 1962: 63).

Sellin reports the discovery of the *Raucheraltar* in this way:

> Eight m. southeast of the press I was to make the find which was probably the most important of the whole first excavation. At first a portion of a winged animal's body of thick clay was found, then at a distance of 2 m. were scattered animal heads, etc. 36 pieces in all. After the area had been thoroughly searched began the reconstruction which yielded an almost complete product; with the help of cement an ancient incense altar rose before our eyes . . ..
>
> There could not be a moment's doubt as to the purpose of the object as a whole: it had no bottom, but on the front side of the bottom were two little rectangular holes, in each side-wall were four medium-sized holes, and in the back, one big hole. The object, which grew narrower at the top, ended in a clay bowl 30 cm. In diameter and thus unquestionably was designed on the same principle as oriental hearths and stoves. The fire was kindled on the ground and the object placed over it. The fire was kept going by the draft which was produced so that it heated the incense which lay in the bowl (Hillers 1962: 63, 64).

It should be noted that Sellin does not mention any marks of burning on the *Raucheraltar*, a fact to which we shall return below in part IV.D, where we will question the interpretation of such cultic stands as "incense altars."

While the choice of the location of area B by the Lapp expedition had considerable potential, it also posed some serious archaeological problems. One might surmise that if there were visible marks of the religious life of the ancient community, these could reasonably be looked for in the geographical context of the "incense altar." But of the eight "squares" in the area, five had already been cut into by Sellin's "south shaft," making it extremely difficult for Lapp's team to determine whether the Austrians had been there before them or not. Although the three westernmost "squares" (SW 3-5, SW 3-6, SW 3-7) were quite removed from the spot in which the Sellin altar had been found, the purpose for including them in the Site B operation was to provide continuity between sites B and D, and also to see how far westward the presumed cultic area extended. In these three squares ground level was fairly even and undisturbed by Sellin. By contrast SW 1-7, SW 1-8 and SW 1-9 generally followed the bottom of the Sellin "south shaft" and were therefore considerably lower. The terrain in the middle square SW 2-7 sloped sharply both from north to south and also from west to east. Four squares were laid out during 1963, SW 2-7, SW 3-7, SW 3-5, and SW 3-6. In the first two of these evidence of Iron I and Iron II occupation was encountered so early and in such volume that digging extended only into the period ±900 BCE in SW 2-7 and to LB II in SW 3-7. An Iron Age structure was exposed in SW 2-7.

In the hope of shedding additional light on cultic activity, four additional squares, 1-7, 1-8, 1-9, 2-8, were opened in 1966. Digging in 1-7, 1-8, and 1-9 indicated that Sellin's "south shaft" had probed as deeply as MB IIC, well beyond the depth of the "olive press"/cult basin in SW 1-7. In the

1968 season the objective was to reach bedrock wherever possible in Site B. This was accomplished in part in 1-7 and 1-8, but in most other squares digging extended only to about 150 cm. above bedrock.

III. B. The Stratigraphy of Area B at Taanach

This section of our study draws on Mark Meehl's 1995 Johns Hopkins Ph. D. dissertation, which focused specifically on the stratigraphic analysis of Iron Age materials from Taanach. Meehl's work is meticulously done, being based on his first-hand study of the excavators' field books, artifacts and pottery, preliminary articles and studies, and other original data such as locus lists and object registry lists. One of Meehl's advisers for this study was Walt Rast, who has published the Iron Age pottery from Taanach. Here, we will utilize Meehl's work, augmenting it and commenting on it where it seems beneficial. As a reference for the reader, section drawings of balks of the four squares in the area from the different seasons of the Lapp excavation have been included as Appendix A. These section drawings, slightly simplified, have been reconstructed by the author from the Lapp expedition field books. Likewise, Appendix B provides tables of the principal loci in the four "squares" (SW 1-7, SW 2-7, SW 1-8, and SW 2-8), which are referred to below as L followed by the number assigned to that locus by the excavators. Appendix C is a list of registered objects, grouped according to the material from which they are made, with designations of the period to which they are to be assigned, the square in which they found, locus and basket numbers, dates of pottery from that locus and basket, and brief descriptions. Appendix D lists those registered objects dated to period IIB (960-918 BCE), the principal period under investigation here.

III.B.1. The Late Bronze Age in Area B (SW 1-7, SW 1-8, SW 2-7, SW 2-8)

In most of the areas of the tell excavated by the Lapp team, the Iron Age period IA village (ca. 1200-1150) rested directly upon the leveled, weather-hardened surface of the brown mudbrick debris of the LB I city, which suffered a catastrophic destruction (Lapp 1969: 5). In Area B "squares" SW 1-9 and SW 2-8, this LB I mudbrick debris was not, however, discovered immediately below period IA remains. Instead, two phases of LB II occupation appeared (Meehl 1995: 70). Remains of the initial LB II occupation were found in SW 1-9 above the typical LB I white-flecked hard brick debris. The only features associated with this phase were three pits (128, 125, and 102). Pit 102 was situated along the east balk of SW 1-9, and the other two pits were in the middle of the square. Most pits, bell-shaped ones like pit 128 in particular, were used initially for storage, and later for rubbish disposal. Artifacts found in pit 128 included:

TT 1157	cup-and-saucer (Rast 1978: fig. 90:1) [dated by Rast to period IA, but also typical of LBII]
TT 1081	rubbing stone
TT 1099	blue paste beads
TT 1105	ceramic zoomorphic figurine fragment
TT 1115	unfinished black bead/weight

In pit 102, the only registered object found was a faience bead TT 1058. Artifacts found in the pit deposits do not, however, provide sufficient information about the specific kinds of activities in the area.

A second phase of LB II occupation in Area B was discovered on top of the deposits that covered the pits and surface of the first phase. In Meehl's analysis, the only features from this second phase, cut or set into the surface, were pit 137, a pile of stones 118 that covered pit 125, and a plaster-lined basin 115 (72). Pit 137 held a stone stopper TT 125 and a basalt grinding stone TT 1738. In the soil inside basin 115 were 13th-century sherds and faience bead TT 1012. Again, these artifacts do not provide sufficient information to enable one to posit a specific function for this location.

A second area of LB II loci was excavated in the southern half of SW 2-8. There, the excavators found two thin layers of soft brown clay above the hard brown LB I brick debris and below the earliest constructions of period IA (Meehl 1995: 74). In these two thin layers the excavators found an incisor from a four-year-old bovine, a †-shaped female figurine torso TT 857, and two left sheep/goat astragali.

The remains of LB occupation in Area B were so scattered and fragmentary that few conclusions about functional areas can be drawn. So few architectural elements remained that no building plans could be reconstructed.

III.B.2. Iron Age Period IA in Area B (SW 1-7, SW 1-8, SW 2-7, SW 2-8)

The excavation of squares SW 1-7, SW 1-8, and SW 1-9 were complicated because Sellin's dig had removed the east part of each of these squares, as well as some of their upper strata. There are, however, some stratigraphical observations that can be made regarding this period in Area B.

In SW 1-9, in the southeastern part of the area south of wall 49, two phases of IA were apparent (Meehl 1995: 80). Belonging to the initial phase was wall 49, an east-west wall running from the west balk to Sellin's trench to the east. Beaten-earth surface 90 south of wall 49 was the location of two deep bell-shaped pits (140 and 152), which were cut into this surface. In the second phase of IA in this area, these pits were covered with a hard, bricky material, which was then tamped into the surface into which pit 120 was dug. No complete artifacts were found in any of the early phases of period IA in 1-9, leading to the conclusion that the deposits were secondary. In pit 152, there was found the right astragalus of a small ruminant, ceramic whorl TT 1304, and flint blade TT 1418. Pit

140 contained iron and bronze slag, a tabun sherd, female figurine fragment TT 1212, and the base of a crucible with bits of copper adhering to it, which suggests a local metalworking industry in Taanach during period IA. However, since the crucible with bits of copper was found in a secondary deposit, this metalworking industry cannot be connected for sure to SW 1-9.

A second location of period IA evidence in Area B is in an L-shaped band of pits and an open area found in SW 1-7, SW 1-8, SW 1-9, SW 2-7, and SW 3-7. This L-shaped space was bounded by wall 31 (SW 2-8) on the west, wall 49 (SW 1-9) to the south, and extended north into SW 1-7, SW 2-7, and SW 3-7 (Meehl 1995: 82). Two construction phases were evident in the southeastern part of this space, just north of wall 49. The beaten-earth surface of the first phase was cut by five pits (91, 105, 108, 111, 129). The deposits covering this first phase were for the most part secondary.

During the second phase of period IA in this L-shaped area, the features of the first phase were covered with bricky material, which was packed into a surface. On top of this leveling soil a plaster surface, 84 (SW 1-9) was laid. Wall 49 was re-used in this phase, and a new east-west wall 93 was built over the top of pit 129 of the earlier phase. Sunk into the plaster surface 84 was a circular, shallow, stone-lined structure 103, which was probably a hearth. Farther north in the southeastern part of the L-shaped area, few significant features appeared since Sellin's excavations had seriously disturbed SW 1-8. West of the beaten-earth surface in SW 1-8 and east of wall 31 (SW 2-8) several layers were found, indicating multiple period IA phases. A large later pit 21 had cut through many of the earlier strata.

The features of the second phase of period IA in the L-shaped area were covered by a secondary deposit of hard gray soil. The contents of the shallow stone-lined structure 103 included two sheep/goat vertebrae, deer teeth, and olive pits, suggesting food preparation around a hearth.

Very few of the deposits found in the open area east of wall 31 (SW 2-8) were described by the excavator. In the earliest period IA deposit in the southeast, small finds included two female figurine torsos TT 830 and TT 831, a set of figurine legs TT 839, and a flint knife or sickle point TT 838. In the lowest layer in the northeast area was an unfired clay loom weight TT 791. Above the last surface in this area was a bone spindle or handle TT 744.

The gray, bricky soil layer continued into SW 2-7 and SW 3-7 where it covered the period IA surfaces and pits. This was leveled and used as the foundation for the occupation in period IB. Although the brick debris was a secondary deposit, some primary deposits, marked by the presence of stone items found on the period IA surface, may have remained (Meehl 1995: 87). Sealed on the surface by the gray soil were a grinding stone and a sherd from an Egyptian faience vessel TT 787, a bone whorl TT 788, three basalt rubbing stones (TT 789, TT 805, and TT 856), a door jamb, and an astragalus—all of which suggest a domestic work area. Two stone drums, TT 115 and TT 116, resemble the stone drums found in the period IIB cultic structure in this square, which may have served as bases for shaped standing stones (מצבות).

The west half of SW 2-8 produced another cluster of period IA remains as well as evidence of a period IA building (Meehl 1995: 90). Parts of this building found in SW 2-8 included wall 31, stone-lined silo 50 with its capstone 36, and several pieces of wall 39, 53, 58, and 59. A sequence of thin soil layers/floors was found in the southwest corner of the square. Stone pavement 55 was bounded on the north and south by walls 39 and 53. Inside the building the only small finds came from pits, which were probably filled with secondary refuse. They consisted solely of items associated with food preparation and consumption—basalt rubbing stone TT 847, fragmentary krater TT 832 (Rast 1978: fig. 89:1), carbonized olive pits, and a left goat astragalus, all recovered from silo

50. Again, the remains of this building are too fragmentary to permit any sound conclusions regarding its function.

The features of the second phase of period IA in the shaped area were covered by a secondary deposit of hard gray soil. The contents of 103 included two sheep/goat vertebrae, deer teeth, and olive pits, suggesting food preparation around a hearth.

III.B.3. Iron Age Period IB in Area B (SW 1-7, SW 1-8, SW 2-7, SW 2-8)

Meehl divides Period IB remains in Area B into four major groups (1995: 47). The first group was discovered between wall 49 (SW 1-9) and wall 6 (SW 1-8). In SW 1-9, two phases of floor construction and the building of walls 49 and 93 belonged to period IB. The leveled debris of period IA was sealed by two successive plaster floors from the first phase of period IB. This, in turn, was covered by a hard brown soil that was a secondary deposit of leveling material for the next phase, which was marked by three successive plaster floors associated with the re-use of walls 49 and 93. The plaster surfaces were used in conjunction with two stone-lined hearths (72 and 75) and a pit 68. Several small finds came from the last phase of period IB in SW 1-9. In the second plaster surface there was a basalt grinding stone TT 817, and in the uppermost one was a left sheep/goat astragalus. Silo 64, which was close to wall 49, held an unfired clay loom weight TT 808.

A second group of features in Area B was associated with the building found mostly in SW 2-8 (Meehl 1995: 149). Apparently, after the area was cleared and leveled, pavement 10 was laid, walls 11, 41, and 63 were constructed, support pillar 12 was raised, and the period IA walls 39 and 53 were cleared and re-used. Wall 11 continued into SW 1-8 as Wall 6. Small finds from this building were found principally in two deposits—ashy material above cobbled pavement 10 and in the cooking pot 27 (TT 753; Rast 1978: fig. 91:1), which rested on plaster surface 28 (Lapp 1969: 34, 35). Set in the plaster floor itself were the legs of a LB female figurine TT 762. On the surface of the floor was a flint fragment and cooking pot TT 753, which was filled with an interesting collection of weights, beads, metal fragments, shells, and a bone stamp seal TT 720. Registered objects found in cooking pot TT 753 include:

TT 643	basalt rubbing stone
TT 701	bone scaraboid
TT 702	bone stamp seal
TT 703	lead bead
TT 704	bronze bead
TT 705	bronze trapezoidal weight
TT 706	bronze trapezoidal weight
TT 707	bronze turtle weight
TT 708	bronze baboon figurine/weight
TT 709	bronze frog weight
TT 710	bronze dome weight
TT 711	bronze dome weight
TT 712	bronze dome weight
TT 713	bronze loaf-shaped weight
TT 714	bronze loaf-shaped weight
TT 715	bronze loaf-shaped weight
TT 716	bloodstone bar weight (?)
TT 717	serpentine dome weight
TT 718	serpentine (?) biconical weight
TT 719	black stone weight
TT 720	biconical black stone weight
TT 721	ovoid black stone weight
TT 722	oval black stone weight
TT 723	pear-shaped black stone weight
TT 724	serpentine egg-shaped weight
TT 725	drum-shaped cylindrical weight
TT 726	iron chisel with three smooth stones (weights?) corroded to it
TT 727	canine incisor corroded to knife handle
TT 728	eleven shell lips and one shell fragment
TT 729	miscellaneous smooth stones

This pot and its contents will be analyzed below in the section on artifacts.

Although the two rooms in this structure appear to belong together, the relationship between them is not readily apparent. The different nature of the small objects found on the cobbled-floor room in the south and the plaster-floored room in the north suggests that an east-west wall may have divided the two areas, but was probably destroyed when the cistern/pit 21 was dug or when it collapsed (Meehl 1995: 152). Contrary to Daviau's observation that cobbled-floored rooms in Bronze Age residences where generally devoid of small finds (1983: 84, 254), numerous small finds were discovered in this room. Meehl (1995: 153) concludes that this period IB building was a domestic structure "belonging to a merchant or an artisan, . . . possessing at least a working or living room and a cobbled area used for storage of items related to food preparation or for food preparation itself." While this building may have indicators that point to a residential function, as suggested above, this does not preclude a cultic function as well. As we will argue below, the collection of weights found in the cooking pot, when considered together with other artifactual finds from the structure, may well be connected to a priestly regulatory function.

Period IB Taanach in Area B consisted of three buildings and a band of open space where pits and silos were located. The building in SW 1-9, which had both underground storage facilities and cooking structures, had been abandoned some time before period IB occupation ended. The northern building also been abandoned when period IB ended. The third building in SW 2-8, which may have been the home of a priest or craftsman, was also abandoned and destroyed at the end of period IB, and was then leveled before period IIA began (Meehl 1995: 160).

III.B.4. Iron Age Period IIA in Area B (SW 1-7, SW 1-8, SW 2-7, SW 2-8)

Period IIA at Taanach commenced after a hiatus in occupation that lasted about a century. Period IIA occupation lasted about sixty years, from about 1020 to 960 BCE. At the beginning of this period, three, perhaps four, structures were built in Area B. These buildings were domestic structures, but because of the brevity of this period, the archaeological remains are scant, and stones from these structures were robbed out by later inhabitants. Consequently, the plans of these structures cannot be determined with any certainty.

The first building was in the southern part of the area, in the northern end of SW 1-9, where period IIA plaster surface 60 covered the leveled remains of period IB occupation. Basin 61 was set into this surface. The body of a 10th-century jug (TT 844) was set in basin 61, forming a catchment basin. Walls 49 and 93, and the stone lined silo 12 (SW 1-8) were re-used from period I. The function of the plaster basin 61 and jug TT 844 set into its surface is unclear. As Meehl suggests (1995: 199), the structure may have been used during some activity for the collection of liquids that were then channeled into the jug below. Such a structure might have been used for libations, one of the basic forms of offerings of agricultural produce in liquid form, especially of wine and olive oil.

The lowest levels of a two-phase building that extended to the east were found in the eastern central part of Area B. Only the western part of the building survived. From its first phase its west wall 89 remains (SW 2-7), part of its north wall 92 (SW 2-7, re-used), an area of stone pavement 95 (SW 2-7), and twelve thin surfaces in SW 1-7. (Meehl 1995: 201). Only a single course of the walls of this building survived. Pit 93 (SW 2-7) was dug into the flagstone pavement, and another pit 88 (SW 2-7) was sunk just south of wall 92. East of these pits were two more pits, 60 and 93, and two puzzling stone-lined features 63 and 72, together with the bottom half of a stone-lined silo 58.

The other feature constructed during the first phase of period IIA was basin 75, a structure that was excavated first by Sellin, who called it an "olive press." This basin and its function will be discussed in more detail below in part IV.A. Here, however, we will concentrate on the stratigraphy associated with this basin. Basin 75 was first built at the beginning of the first phase of period IIA. After a foundation trench had been dug into the hard brown bricky soil of the LBI period, the stones making up the sides of the basin were set up. In some places the bottom of the foundation trench was covered with a thin ash layer or hard yellow-brown clay. The builders then packed hard gray soil around the stone and soil fill. Then a surface was prepared, covering the foundation trench and abutting the basin. No trace of a period II surface was found by Lapp's team, suggesting that Sellin must have removed it when he excavated the basin (Meehl 1995: 202). The latest sherds from the foundation trenches of the basin were dated to ca. 1000 BCE.

The occupational remains from the first phase of period IIA are sparse. In the northern part of the building in which basin 75 was located, there are surfaces from the first phase of period IIA in the form of twelve very thin layers, into which were sunk two stone structures 63 and 72, pit 60 (SW 1-7), and re-used period I pit 93 (SW 1-7). As with nearly all period IIA deposits, it is impossible to determine whether these were primary or secondary deposits. Pit 93 was re-used throughout period IIA, probably for some kind of storage. Pit 60, which was filled in and covered by a wall during the second phase of period IIA, contained an iron armor scale TT 602, olive pits, plaster fragments, and pieces of red dirt. Since most of the deposits in this building are probably secondary, the finds cannot directly point to activities that occurred within it.

The second phase of period IIA saw structural changes in the building where basin 75 was located. During this phase two stone-lined pits 63 and 72 were covered and paved over. A leveling fill of 12th-century material was spread over the area of these pits, followed by the first floor of the second phase of period IIA, on which wall 56 was built (Meehl 1995: 206). A thin layer of what was probably secondary debris covered the final period IIA surfaces in the building in 2-7 and 1-7. The soil covering the laminated surface in the north of SW 1-7 contained a rim fragment of a stone bowl and some pieces of charcoal. The surface south of wall 56 was covered by stone collapse that sealed a bone inlay fragment TT 591 and some carbonized olive pits underneath it. These items are probably primary deposits, as are the items in pit 88. The shallow pit 88 to the west was filled with crumbled brick that included a miniature lamp TT 624, a carnelian bead TT 638, a bone spindle TT 668, and a basalt rubbing stone TT 636. The top of this stone collapse served as the floor for period IIB occupation. There were no signs of destruction in the debris dating to the end of period IIA, therefore one can infer a peaceful transition to the following period.

III.B.5. Iron Age Period IIB in Area B (SW 1-7, SW 1-8, SW 2-7, SW 2-8)

Taanach was re-occupied shortly after the end of the period IIA site, around 960 BCE. The new period IIB town is probably to be associated with the Solomonic administrative district governed by Ba'ana' be 'Ahilud, in which Taanach, together with Megiddo, Beth-Shan, and Jokmeam were key cities, according to 1 Kings 4:12:

> Baana son of Ahilud, in Taanach, Megiddo, and all Beth-shean, which is beside Zarethan below Jezreel, and from Beth-shean to Abel-meholah, as far as the other side of Jokmeam.

Occupation at Taanach in this period ended with destruction, only about forty years after it began, probably at the hands of the Egyptian Shoshenq I (biblical Shishak), a destruction that is probably the one referred to in 1 Kings 14:25: "In the fifth year of King Rehoboam, King Shishak of Egypt came up against Jerusalem."

In period IIB, Area B contained a single building, the cultic structure in SW 1-7, SW 1-8, SW 2-7, and SW 2-8. This building was surrounded by a large open space, which on the west reached to the structures in Area D. The area to the south of SW 1-8 did not include any clearly defined period

IIB features or deposits (Meehl 1995: 242). Only the northwestern part of the cultic structure survived (but see figure 4 below for our tentative reconstruction of the cultic structure as a four-space Iron Age House). Excavation west of wall 16 and north of wall 30 recovered no additional walls. The area to the south and east, which has been tentatively reconstructed in figure 4, had been cleared by Sellin, who reported only the *Raucheraltar*, a stone-lined basin ("olive press"), and a cistern mouth in his trench (Sellin 1904: 75-78; fig. 102, 104, 105; pl. 12, 13). The excavations in the 1960s re-excavated both basin 75 and cistern 69. The walls belonging to the cultic structure, according to the Lapp excavation, were 15, 16, 21, 30, and 38, which seemed to indicate three rooms (Meehl 1995: 244). Within the building the following features were identified: a hearth and re-used period IIA pit 93 (in room 2 north of wall 15), the stone- and plaster-lined silo 16, the re-used basin 75, and the large cistern 69. Silo 12 (in the southeast corner of SW 1-8) was re-used in this period and may have been associated with the cultic structure. The floors in this building, with the exception of plaster floor 20 and the one in silo 16, were all of beaten earth, the leveled and packed down top of period IIA debris. The building was destroyed in a fire that sealed numerous artifacts under and in a stratum of burnt mudbrick debris and ash.

Beneath the artifacts found in rooms 1 and 2 were a flint block in room 1 and a hearth and pit in room 2. The hearth was a low rock platform with a border of small stones, built against wall 30. Pit 93 was the re-used upper portion of a period I bell-shaped silo.

Two silos and a cistern were found in the courtyard around basin 75. Silo 12 was a period I stone-lined cylinder that was re-used throughout Period II. It, however, may not have been associated with the cultic structure, since intervening walls may have been removed by Sellin. Five courses of the plaster-covered stone lining of silo 16 were extant.

Room 1 of the cultic structure was filled with artifacts and nearly a meter of tumbled ashy mudbrick destruction. This room probably served as a storeroom for the artifacts that will be catalogued and discussed below. The registered objects found in room 1, which can be dated to period II B are as follows:

<u>Locus 61</u>

TT 480	bowl (Rast 1978 fig. 42:3)
TT 479	bowl (Rast 1978 fig. 42:4)
TT 352	bowl (Rast 1978 fig. 47:2)
TT 412	bowl (Rast 1978 fig. 47:3)
TT 354	bowl (Rast 1978 fig. 47:4)
TT 411	bowl (Rast 1978 fig. 46:2)
TT 455	bowl (Rast 1978 fig. 46:12)
TT 462	bowl (Rast 1978 fig. 46:4)
TT 353	bowl (Rast 1978 fig. 46:5)
TT 457	bowl (Rast 1978 fig. 46:6)
TT 410	bowl (Rast 1978 fig. 46:11)
TT 461	bowl (Rast 1978 fig. 43:3)
TT 463	bowl (Rast 1978 fig. 48:17)
TT 323	juglet (Rast 1978 fig. 40:9)
TT 458	juglet (Rast 1978 fig. 40:10)
TT 466	juglet (Rast 1978 fig. 40:10)
TT 350	amphora (Rast 1978 fig. 36:3)
TT 372	pyxis (Rast 1978 fig. 40:13)
TT 478	ovoid jar (Rast 1978 fig. 30:1)
TT 477	ovoid storage jar (Rast 1978 fig. 30:3)
TT 474	ovoid storage jar (Rast 1978 fig. 31:1)
TT 469	ovoid storage jar (Rast 1978 fig. 31:3)
TT 482	round-based storage jar (Rast 1978 fig. 34:1)
TT 475	round-based storage jar (Rast 1978 fig. 34:4)
TT 459	round-based storage jar (Rast 1978 fig. 34:5)
TT 460	hole-mouth jar (Rast 1978 fig. 35:2)
TT 489	8-handled krater (Rast 1978 fig. 41:1)
TT 454	jug (Rast 1978 fig. 38:1)
TT 470	jug (Rast 1978 fig. 38:2)
TT 351	cult stand (Rast 1978 fig. 51:4)
TT 388	loom weight fragments (at least forty-eight)
TT 389	round stone base
TT 390	round stone base

TT 391	round stone base
TT 324	limestone rubbing stone
TT 392	basalt rubbing stone
TT 393	basalt rubbing stone
TT 394	basalt plano-convex saddle grinder
TT 395	basalt quern
TT 373	socketed stone / mace head

Locus 63

TT 386	juglet (Rast 1978 fig. 40:3)
TT 468	jug (Rast 1978 fig. 39:2)
TT 481	ovoid storage jar (Rast 1978 fig. 31:2)
TT 397	bone spatula

In the next section to the south of room 1 (a section opened up with the removal of the balk between SW 2-7 and SW 2-8), the following registered objects were found:

TT 356	basalt saddle grinder
TT 306	juglet (Rast 1978 fig. 40:5)
TT 327	juglet (Rast 1978 fig. 40:5)
TT 465	bowl (Rast 1978 fig. 46:1)
TT 415	bowl (Rast 1978 fig. 45:4)
TT 467	juglet (Rast 1978 fig. 36:1)
TT 490	side-spouted jug (Rast 1978 fig. 36:2)
TT 414	jug (Rast 1978 fig. 39:4)
TT 456	cooking pot (Rast 1978 fig. 50:1)
TT 472	cooking pot (Rast 1978 fig. 50:2)
TT 476	jar (Rast 1978 fig. 30:2)
TT 483	round-based storage jar (Rast 1978 fig. 31:1)
TT 1866	round-based storage jar (Rast 1978 fig. 35:1)
TT 320	quartzolite rubbing stone
TT 355	bone spatula
TT 398	bone spatula
TT 430	shaped limestone standing stone (מצבה)
TT 431	shaped limestone standing stone (מצבה)
TT 432	shaped limestone standing stone (מצבה)
TT 409	non-carburized iron arrowhead
TT 387	2 carburized iron knife blades fused to a dagger / spearhead

The following registered objects were found in the northernmost 90 cm. of room 1:

TT 73	pyxis (Rast 1978 fig. 40:14)

TT 439	krater (Rast 1978 fig. 42:2)
TT 83	jug (Rast 1978 fig. 39:6)
TT 440	jug (Rast 1978 fig. 37:2)
TT 62	juglet (Rast 1978 fig. 40:7)
TT 63	juglet (Rast 1978 fig. 40:1)
TT 441	bowl (Rast 1978 fig. 46:8)
TT 443	bowl (Rast 1978 fig. 48:3)
TT 448	bowl (Rast 1978 fig. 48:2)
TT 78	serpentine pendant /weight
TT 79	basalt dome weight
TT 81	loom weight
TT 116	basalt quern
TT 117	limestone rubbing stone
TT 71	fragments of non-carburized iron knives or sword (3 pieces)
TT 64	tripod censer or strainer (Rast 1978 fig. 51:3)
TT 89	lamp (Rast 1978 fig. 51:1)
TT 65	cooking pot (Rast 1978 fig. 50:3)
TT 488	pyxis (Rast 1978 fig. 40:12)
TT 445	bowl (Rast 1978 fig. 45:2)
TT 442	bowl (Rast 1978 fig. 46:13)
TT 444	bowl (Rast 1978 fig. 48:16)
TT 446	bowl (Rast 1978 fig. 42:1)
TT 447	bowl (Rast 1978 fig. 48:15)
TT 449	bowl (Rast 1978 fig. 47:1)
TT 450	bowl (Rast 1978 fig. 46:7)
TT 451	bowl (Rast 1978 fig. 43:2)
TT 452	bowl (Rast 1978 fig. 46:14)
TT 453	bowl (Rast 1978 fig. 46:3)
TT 464	bowl (Rast 1978 fig. 45:6)
TT 416	bowl (Rast 1978 fig. 45:3)
TT 487	bowl (Rast 1978 fig. 44:4)
TT 103	jug (Rast 1978 fig. 37:1)
TT 88	juglet (Rast 1978 fig. 40:6)
TT 98	limestone rubbing stone
TT 100	figurine mold
TT 86	foamy basalt rubbing stone
TT 87	oval stone stopper or weight
TT 107	loom weight
TT 91	non-carburized iron plowshare point
TT 108	iron scythe or sickle blade
TT 322	carburized iron scythe or sickle blade fragment

In the debris from this part of room 1 a large assemblage of sheep/goat astragali were found, all of which were charred, and some of which were pierced and worked in some way. Their find spot in room 1 was near a stone protruding from wall 38. We will return to a discussion of the functions of astragali in a cultic setting in IV.B below. The astragali in room 1 are significant in such a context at Taanach especially since a similar, even larger quantity of astragalus bones was found in locus 2081 at Megiddo. As at Megiddo, some of the astragali from room 1 had been worked.

The pottery types found in room 1, including the number of restored vessels as well as the number of pots of which large parts were found, can be summarized as follows (Meehl 1995: 249):

1	censer
1	multi-handled krater
1	hole-mouth jar
1	collared-rim storage jar
2	lamps
2	amphora
3	large bowls
3	pyxides
4	round-based storage jars
4	cooking pots
8	ovoid storage jars
9	juglets
10	jugs
39	bowls

Meehl correctly concludes that room 1 must have been a storage room, based on the observation that the finds in this room were too closely packed to permit any activity. He also asserts that "This assemblage of goods represented a great deal of wealth, and could have belonged to members of a social elite—a wealthy family, the central authority, or a cult" (1995: 250). Certainly, the high proportion of bowls with red slip and burnish is indicative not only of the date of the assemblage, but perhaps of its comparative wealth as well.

The floor and features in room 2 of the cultic structure were covered by more ashy tumbled mudbrick debris. Destruction debris had fallen into pit 93, which contained juglet TT 902, a baking dish fragment, and part of a lamp, along with other large pieces of pots, suggesting that the pit was empty at the time of the building's destruction. The floor, features, and artifacts in this room were covered with ashes, although this room did not contain nearly as many objects as did room 1. Found on the floor in this room, west of the hearth, were a female figurine fragment TT 1842, a large bowl, three smaller bowls including TT 486, and pieces of two storage jars. From just above this debris layer came two large bowls (including TT 484), a large storage jar, and two plow points or ends of goads TT 132 (Meehl 1995: 250). Sherds from deep bowl TT 471, mended with sherds from the destruction debris near the floor south of wall 38, were found mostly near wall 30. South of the hearth were found four small bowls, and a lamp fragment TT 473. East of the hearth were two ovoid storage jars, one round-based storage jar, one large bowl, and two small bowls. Meehl summarizes the pottery finds for room 2 as follows (1995: 251):

1	round-based storage jar
1	juglet
1	lamp
2	ovoid storage jars
3	storage jars of unspecified shape
4	large bowls
12	small bowls

A large room or open courtyard lay to the southeast of room 2. Sellin had removed most of the period IIB deposits. The only remains of a surface found by the Lapp expedition were a plaster floor 20 around silo 16. Basin 75 continued to be used in period IIB, but any deposits that had covered the basin had been removed by Sellin.

South of basin 75 was cistern 69. The bottom of the cistern was covered with a layer of silt, in which were found various bones, a black stone loom weight TT 1652, bronze pieces including a handle fragment TT 1651, two astragali, fragments of basalt tripod bases TT 1625 and TT 1716 (from different bowls), an ivory rod or spindle TT 1655, a basalt grinding stone TT 1671, a horse head figurine spout TT 1540, a bronze piece and tabun fragments. These small finds were deposited during period IIB or at the time of the cultic structure's destruction (Meehl 1995: 254).

A layer of material from the end of period IIB or shortly thereafter covered the silt at the bottom of the cistern, from which was recovered the pieces of two cultic stands TT 1500 and TT 1830 (Rast 1978 fig. 54:1), flint blades TT 1463 and TT 1483, a juglet TT 1465, a bronze rod TT 1478, a female figurine torso TT 1486, and a chalice TT 1853 (Rast 1978 fig. 53:5).

Meehl reconstructs the sequence of events relating to cistern 69 and the cultic stands as follows (1995: 255, 256). The cistern was either dug or cleaned out in the 10th century, when it provided water for the cultic structure and accumulated a thin layer of silt containing period IIB potsherds. When period IIB ended, the cultic stands and other period IIB pottery were thrown into the cistern. Part of the roof of the cistern collapsed some time after period IIB, sealing part of the cistern's floor. Other material fell into the cistern and filled its shaft during the 7th century, when people re-used the cistern, resulting in a mixture of 7th-century sherds and earlier deposits not covered by ceiling collapse.

In addition to the two cultic stands found in cistern 69 by the Lapp expedition, Sellin's *Raucheraltar* also was probably associated with the cultic structure.. According to Sellin's report, it was in this part of his South Trench that he found the smashed remains of the *Raucheraltar*, i.e., 8 m. southeast of the basin or "olive press" (Sellin 1904: 76). It thus seems likely that all three stands belonged to and were used in the cultic structure, contributing to its interpretation as a "cult corner" used as an extension of the regulatory machinery of the United Monarchy (Ahlström 1982: 44, 46, 47), but reflecting popular religious practice as well.

Directly east of wall 21 was a stone-lined silo 16. This silo, with a capacity of about one cubic meter, was probably used for storage of grain and other staples by the occupants of the cultic structure, who also stored grain in store jars in room 1.

Because most of the period IIB deposits had been removed by Sellin's excavation, the nature of the space surrounding basin 75 must be assessed mostly on the basis of the basin's features, in the context of the finds in rooms 1 and 2. In our reconstruction of the cultic structure as a four-space house, the basin is located at least partially in the courtyard, extending into a space that opened onto the courtyard, probably through the stone pillars typical of such structures. This courtyard was a central work space of the building. Whether or not the courtyard was covered cannot be determined. Since, however, archaeological evidence indicates extensive burning in the basin, the courtyard was probably open.

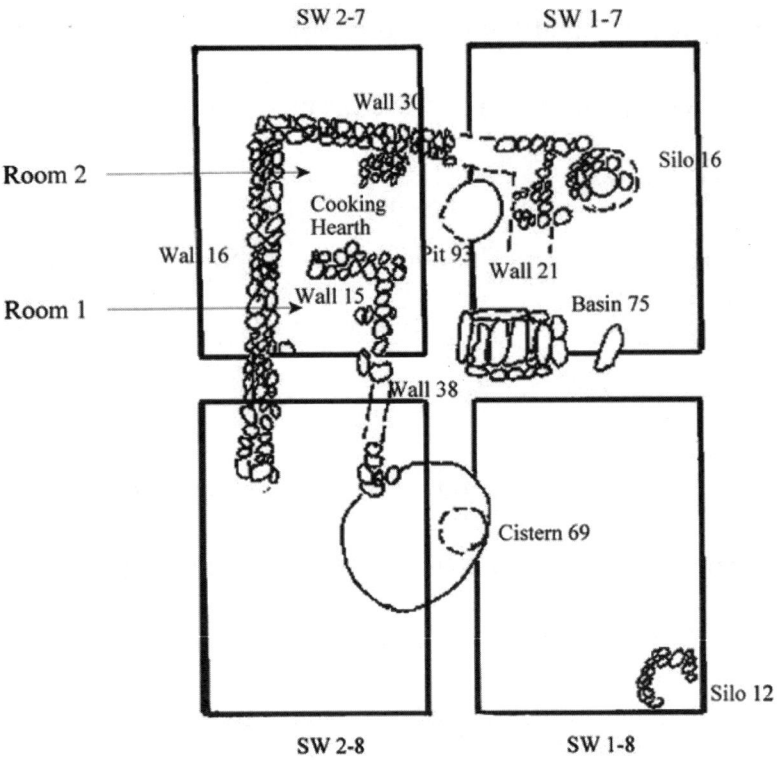

Figure 3: The Cultic Structure in Area B (SW 1-7, SW 2-7, SW 1-8, SW 2-8) in Period IIB

Figure 4: A Reconstruction of the Cultic Structure in Period IIB As a Four-Space Iron Age House

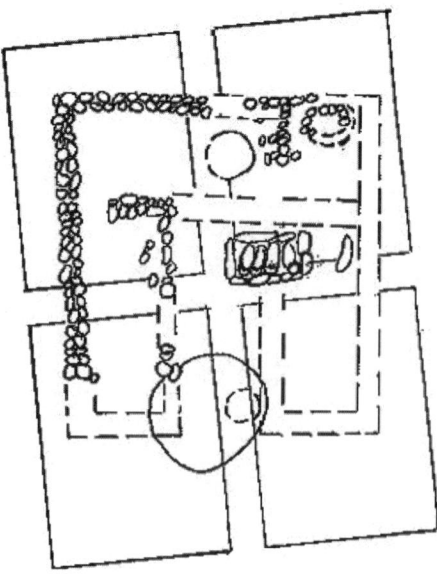

To sum up this section: What came to be called the "cultic structure" was a tenth-century structure that measured about 8.4 x 4.6 m with two rooms that appeared to have quite different purposes, at least in the interpretation of the excavators (see the top plan of this structure in figure 3). The walls in this structure were two stones wide and well built in their early phases. Walls were preserved on the west and north (walls 16 and 30); those on the east and south were destroyed either by ancient predators or by Sellin's excavation. The south room, room 1, was separated from room 2 in the north by an interior wall 2 stones wide (wall 15). In its original form this cross wall may have extended much farther east (see figure 4, which reconstructs the structure as a four-space Iron Age house). Similarly, the north wall (30) must originally have extended farther to the east. The east wall of room 1 (wall 38—an inner wall bordering the courtyard in the reconstruction) was preserved in a single stone width; beyond a break it emerged again in the south, parallel to the west wall of room 1 (wall 30). With respect to artifacts, squares 2-7 and 2-8 certainly lived up to the excavators' expectations, as will be demonstrated below in part IV.

Given Taanach's close association with nearby Megiddo, it is not surprising that there is a close parallel to its cultic structure there. In area A-A at Megiddo, west of the gate, is a structure that is illustrated in figure 5 and is based on the plan of a four-room house.

According to Kempinski (1989: 126, 127), the core of building 2081 is a four-room house unit: the central room, with an entrance that had two decorative pillars. The back room is divided into smaller rooms. The side room 2163

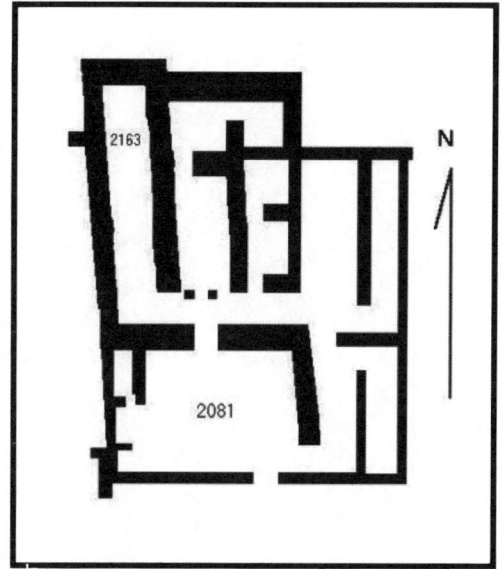

Figure 5: Iron Age House 2081 at Megiddo

should be compared with the two cells on the other side of the main central room. To the east of the core unit are four storeroom units. The front (south side) of the building is built as an enclosed court (room 2081 on the plan) with two cells on its west end. One of these cells was, according to Kempinski, " a cult cell." The two pillars at the entrance of the main room suggest that the long, plastered corridor in front of it was not covered with a roof, and served as a long rectangular light shaft. The size of the house (without the front court) is about 160 square meters. Kempinski believes that this house "belonged to a well-to-do personality who was also engaged in official activities" (187). One of these "official activities" was a census of animals, which might help explain the large number of astragalus bones found in this structure (see the discussion of astragalus bones and their use in a cultic context in part IV.B below).

Part IV. Objects and Artifacts Associated with the Taanach Cultic Structure

In the following multi-part section the focus is on objects and artifacts associated with the cultic structure, grouped either by functional type or by the kind of material of which they are made. Not every object and artifact found in association with the cultic structure will be discussed, but exemplary types will be selected that can be connected, in some way, to ritual activity. References will be made to more detailed descriptions that have been done by others or are in process.

IV.A. Basin 75 in SW 2-7

Basin 75 was first excavated by Sellin and was re-excavated by the Lapp expedition. It consisted of limestone slabs laid on edge lining a rectangle. These upright stones rested on a rectangular stone base that measured ca. 1.2 x 1.85 m. The tops of the upright stone sides stood about .77 m. above the base. The area in which the basin was located had been badly cut up by Sellin's trenching, so the stratigraphic relationship of this structure to the floors of rooms 1 and 2 of the cultic structure could not be determined by the Lapp expedition. By its level, however, Lapp believed it likely that the basin should be associated with the floors of rooms 1 and 2 (1964: 29). Lapp reported that if the same levels as in the cultic structure were operative here, the side walls of the basin would have extended "a few centimeters above the floor (1967a: 30). This structure shows evidence of having been in use for a long period. Its use, however, apparently changed through its several phases.

In the preliminary report of the 1963 season of the Lapp excavations, the basin was given a definite 10th-century cultic interpretation, largely on the basis of the shaped standing stones (מצבות) found inside it (for a photograph of basin 75 in its late 10th-century phase after excavation by the Lapp expedition see figure 17 in Lapp 1964: 32). The shaped stones (מצבות), however, may have been placed in the basin by Sellin. In the 1966 season it was discovered that the foundation of basin 75 had been cut into SW 1-7 L 68, a thick, hard, bricky layer that overlies the LB I occupation levels in many areas of the tell, a layer containing 12th-century sherds. A thin, dark-red, bricky layer 91 with 12th-century pottery served as make-up for the basin, resembling the make-up for pavement L 58. It also became evident that the 20-26 cm. thick paving stones on which the shaped stones (מצבות) rested did not constitute the basin's original floor. When these paving stones were fully exposed, it was discovered that they were 5-20 cm. too short to fill out the basin floor. When they were removed, a make-up layer of hard, brown fill was uncovered. It was set into a layer of black ash, L 86, that was 2-20 cm. thick and extended throughout the basin floor. This ash layer contained late 11th-century sherds. Beneath the black ash another pavement was discovered that consisted of a single slab of limestone extending the full width of the basin, a slab that had been worked like the stones of the side walls. There were indications of burning within the basin. The fact that part of the surface of the slab was damaged at some point, and that the chip, upon removal, showed clear signs of burning, suggests that the burning took place within the basin. This lining slab sloped slightly to the southwest, where a 35.5 cm. deep plastered catchment hole was cut into it . A loosely-fitting beveled stone lid was found *in situ* on top of the catchment hole. The bell-shaped catchment hole was cut into the base slab, which was about 35 cm. in diameter on the surface, extending to a diameter of about 51 cm. below the surface of the slab. Apparently the base and sides of the basin had been originally plastered, as the lower slab had some plaster traces on it, and there were also remnants of a plaster lining on the south wall of the basin. Inside the catchment hole were LB I sherds.

According to the excavators, the function of basin 75 passed through three phases:

<u>Phase One—12th century</u>. In its first phase the plaster-lined basin was used to catch liquid and drain it off into the bell-shaped catchment hole in the southwest corner. The fact that both basin 75 and pavement L 58 had the same kind of dark-red, bricky make-up suggests that the basin and pavement may be associated, even though the pavement was some 30 cm. below the lower slab of the basin. If it was free-standing, the basin would have been rather precarious, and the west side was apparently supported by stones standing against it.

<u>Phase Two—11th century</u>. In this phase the basin's use for gathering liquids was replaced by its use for some type of burning. The catchment hole was not used, but its cover was left in place, so that the catchment hole showed no signs of burning. A layer of ash and charcoal 5-15 cm. deep accumulated during this phase. The burning was sufficient to discolor the stones and catchment hole cover and to cause chipping from the lower slab. Associated with this phase was a limestone mortar TT 837, which was laid inside the basin on top of the ash and other artifacts in the southeast corner, and was filled with black, ashy dirt. Objects in the ash included grinding stone TT 819, an iron plow point TT 820, a rubbing stone TT 803 and an unfinished iron object TT 1879. The basin's east end was repaired with two large stones. Any deposits that had covered the basin were removed by Sellin. The sherds were late 11th century (period IIA).

<u>Third Phase—10th century</u>. In the basin's third phase the secondary pavement of four large stones (disused מצבות ?) was set on a hardish-brown fill mixed with the black ash of the second phase. This paving was not carefully fitted to the basin, being from 5-20 cm. too short to fill the basin's width, but carefully arranged as to avoid the mortar. The four stones of this secondary paving were 20-25 cm. thick. According to Sellin, a shaped standing stone (מצבה) found nearby

belonged to this phase, but its connection with the basin is uncertain. The sherds from this third phase were 10th century (period IIB). Judging from the construction and the many supporting stones in the make-up outside, the basin was intended to go with a ground-level close to its full height.

As Meehl (252, 253) has observed, the stones lining the bottom of the basin are enigmatic. In their final use, at the time of the destruction at the end of period IIB, they made up the bottom of the basin and were used to make it shallower. There are two probable interpretations of their earlier function. The stones may have been quarried with the intention of being used only as building blocks or paving stones. Alternatively, because of the cultic character of the assemblage found in SW 2-7, which, as we shall see, included other shaped standing stones (מצבות), these stones may also have been shaped standing stones (מצבות) (Lapp 1967: 30).

In order to assess basin 75 it is helpful to compare it to other similar structures. A structure somewhat analogous to basin 75 at Taanach is one that was excavated by James Pritchard at the site of Sarepta in present-day Sarafand, Lebanon. Throughout the Iron Age almost the entire area of 600 square meters chosen for excavation had been used for industrial purposes. Pritchard discovered a one-room building in the northwest corner of the excavated area that he identified as a shrine having two phases. While a thorough description of this Iron Age shrine and its features is beyond the limits of this study, a structure found at its west end deserves consideration as a parallel to basin 75 at Taanach, and may help us understand the function of basin 75. Pritchard described this structure as

Figure 7: The "Offering Table" in Shrine I at Sarepta

"an offering table or altar" (16), and this structure is shown *in situ* in figure 7. This structure measures 1.02 x .92 m. Its sides were built of ashlar blocks set about 30 cm. below the plaster floor. In the center of the "table" was a well-cut block. The top of the structure was missing, but fragments of plaster on its east side (at the bottom of the photograph in figure 7) still extended about 20 cm. above the remaining foundation stones. Hence it can be inferred that the top of the structure was higher than the remaining stones on its sides. In front of the structure (at the bottom of the photo in figure 7) there is what looks like a step. To the south of this "step" (left in the photograph) were found impressions of two stones that had once been set in the plaster floor. East of the joint of the two missing stones there is a slight channel or depression in the floor, which is in line with an aperture in the east face of the "table." A layer of 3-4 cm. of dark ash and carbon covered the area around the offering table, but nowhere else within the room was this burnt deposit detectable. The fill inside the "table" contained a stone at the northwest corner (upper right in the photo) with a system of channels, the entire surface of which was plastered over so that there was no indication from above of the system of drains below. In assessing the function of this "table" Pritchard says: "It is impossible to conjecture . . . what functions this object had. It is obvious that the channels served to divert a liquid from the smaller rectangular depression into the circular depression, from which it would have been drained" (17).

About 20 cm. to the east of the "step" in front of the "table" there is a break in the plaster floor that measures about 50 by 60 cm. This depression was filled to a depth of 20 cm. with yellow clay and stone chips. Below this layer there was a thin dark stratum of dark carbonized material on the fill of the plaster floor. Pritchard believes this to have been a socket for a standing object, "probably a stone betyl [i.e., a מצבה] or possibly an incense altar" (18) which broke the plaster floor when it was removed. He does not comment on the layer of ash that surrounded the table but was absent elsewhere in the shrine.

While there are details of the Sarepta "table" and basin 75 at Taanach that are dissimilar, there are two things worth noting in positing the Sarepta "table" as an analogue to basin 75. The first is that this shrine was located in an area of Sarepta utilized for industrial purposes, yet Pritchard has no hesitation in identifying it as a shrine. This speaks to the issue of an unnecessary either/or identification that is present in so much literature dealing with archaeology and cult—either a structure/artifact is cultic or it has an industrial or some other utilitarian function. This divorcing of cult from its social context, for example, is evident in the first of Michael Coogan's criteria for characterizing a site as cultic. His first criterion is that a cultic site is architecturally isolated. Yet, the shrine at Sarepta, and other structures about whose cultic identification there is little doubt, fail to meet this criterion. The separation of the cultic from other aspects of the socioeconomic system has also been thrown into question by the work of Gitin at Tel Miqne-Ekron. In his analysis of cultic elements at Ekron, Gitin observes that the industrial zone of the 7th-century BCE city included more than 100 olive oil structures, making Ekron the largest known industrial center for the production of olive oil in the ancient Near East (249). The cultic objects excavated by Gitin included three major elements: 1) limestone altars; 2) storage jars with dedicatory inscriptions; and 3) painted and petal-decorated chalices. Altars were present in industrial, domestic, and elite zones of occupation in the city, but, as Gitin observes: "It is . . . significant that with one possible exception, the altars were not discovered in what would be regarded as a traditional cultic context, i.e., in a temple, shrine or cult corner" (1993: 250). Thus, there is a linkage between cultic activity and industry rather than a separation between them.

Lapp cites several parallels to basin 75. The closest parallel, according to Lapp, comes from Tell el-Far'ah (N) *Niveau 2* (8th century BCE) (1964: 30, 31). De Vaux reported that this basin in the Iron II B-C gate area was considered to have cultic significance (De Vaux 1951: 428, pls. 6, 8). The basin at Tell el-Far'ah (N) had sides of large stone slabs and a stone base. Its dimensions were similar to basin 75. The standing stone found in the stratum above the basin at Tel el-Far'ah and the socket found in the stratum below it led De Vaux to interpret it as a libation basin at the entrance to the city. Lapp also mentions a parallel structure at Arad, dating to the 10th century BCE. Here again there was a plastered basin with a stone sub floor, accompanied by a standing stone. Other similar basins were discovered both by Sellin (filled with burnt olive pits) (1904: 67-68) and Lapp (1964: 33, figs. 16, 17), to which no cultic function was ascribed.

One of the most convincing arguments for a connection between religious ritual and the everyday concerns of industry has been advanced by Stager and Wolff (1981) in their discussion of an installation within the sacred precinct at Tel Dan. The excavator at Dan, Avraham Biran, interpreted this installation as a place for water libation rites:

> At first sight it seemed to be part of an oil-press. But this idea was dismissed: the bottom of the basin, which was not plastered, would allow valuable oil to seep through. The complete absence of olive pits, and the tremendous quality of gray ash and burnt bone fragments in and around the basin, suggested some sort of animal sacrifice. The large stones lying around the installation may have served as tethers or weights. However, the lack of drainage provisions precluded any activity involving large quantities of blood. The most logical explanation is that the liquid in question must have been water—readily available and ritually significant. . . . It seems that the archaeological excavations at Tel Dan have now uncovered installations connected with water libation ceremonies from the end of the 10th- beginning of the 9th centuries B.C.E. (177, 181).

Stager and Wolf, however, have interpreted this basin at Dan as an olive press. The main features of this installation include a sunken plastered basin having a capacity of about 1.5 cubic

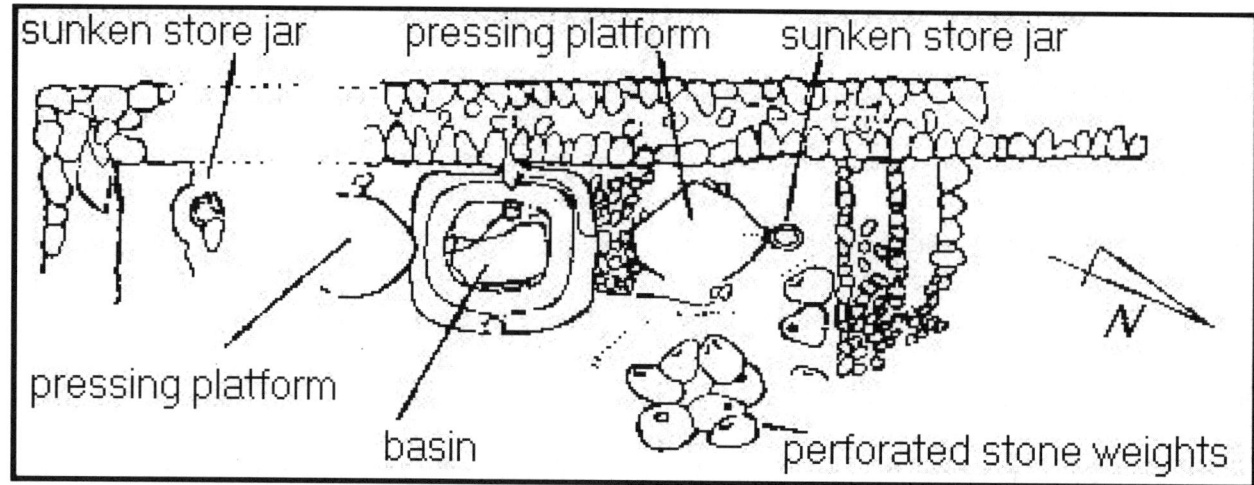

Figure 8: Installation in the Sacred Precinct at Tel Dan

meters, with a bottom lined with stone slabs. This basin was flanked on two opposite sides by basalt slabs that slope gently towards sunken store jars (see the plan of this installation at Tel Dan in figure 8). The installation was situated in a courtyard, and several perforated stones were found just to the northeast of the basin. Biran, in his explanation mentions these stones, but does not offer any explanation of their function in the context of any specific kind of activity, libation or otherwise.

There are, of course, several ritual uses for olive oil, as Stager and Wolff observe: (1) anointing, (2) fuel for lamps, and (3) offerings (97). In connection with the third use, offerings, biblical references mention libation offerings (Gen 28: 18; 35: 4) and the cereal offering (מנחה), which, according to priestly biblical traditions, consisted of finely-ground flour mixed with olive oil (Num 28: 4, 5; Ex 29: 40). Although the proportion of flour and oil in cereal offerings probably varied (due in part to agricultural yields), olive oil, because of its combustible properties was probably always a principal ingredient. Following a recipe for ingredients in the cereal offering in Num 28: 4, 5 and Ex 29:40, which denotes two parts flour to one part olive oil, Stager mixed the flour and the oil into a paste and formed it into cakes. When placed over a gas flame these cakes ignited readily and burned until the cakes were reduced to a charred mass of solid, but brittle residue (Stager and Wolff 100). Stager and Wolff go on to suggest that priests at Dan produced an "approved" olive oil within the *temenos* that worshipers could purchase for libations or burnt grain-offerings.

In the context of their discussion of other examples of the production of cultic commodities within sacred areas in ancient Palestine, Stager and Wolff mention several examples from Taanach, including the figurine mold (TT 100) found in room 1 of the cultic structure. They also suggest that "Spinning and weaving were among the activities that took place in and around the 'Cultic Structure' at Ta'anach. From the same storeroom . . . that produced the figurine mold (as well as astragali and several storejars filled with grain) came at least 60 loom weights and numerous spindle whorls (Lapp 1964: 26-28; 1967b: 25; 1969: 47)" (243). Stager and Wolff have the following to say about basin 75:

> In the 10th century B.C. 'Cultic Structure' at Ta'anach, Lapp completed the excavation . . . of a slab-lined basin. Lapp rediscovered a large monolith . . . resting inside the vat (Phase 3) and concluded that it was a sacred pillar. . . . Sellin's crew had actually found the monolith lying nearby, not in the vat and later placed the slab in the basin (Sellin 1904: 76; cf. Lapp 1964: 35, n. 52). Sellin correctly identified the basin and the monolith as an "olive press." The Germans excavated three other 'presses' in this part of the mound, one of which contained the essential clue to its identity: 'hundreds of burnt olive pits'" (Sellin 1904: 67-68) (99).

Stager and Wolff conclude their study with the observation that "At Dan and Ta'anach we find the olive presses in cultic precincts" (100). In our discussion of the ceramic mold TT 100 (in part IV.D. below) we will suggest types of cultic activity that may be suggested by the discovery of mold TT 100 together with items associated with olive oil production, grinding stones, and a hearth in the period IIB cultic structure.

A methodological concern that complicates the interpretation of the function of basin 75 at Taanach is the way in which floral remains were gathered by the Lapp expedition. Neither floral nor faunal remains were systematically collected. They were simply recovered by workmen whenever they were noticed. There was no routine screening or flotation to recover organic remains. As a consequence, much of the information needed to make a definitive interpretation of what activities might have been associated with basin 75 is missing. In the period IIB phase of the basin's use, with the four standing stones (מצבות) or paving blocks and the limestone mortar TT 837 that were laid inside the basin on top of the ash and artifacts from period IIA, hard soil and small stones were packed into the interstices. In this hard soil some carbonized olive pits were found. Whether these were associated with olive oil production in the basin or the burning of offerings in which olive oil and olives were a principal ingredient cannot be determined.

What do basin 75 and the installations at Tel Dan and Sarepta have in common? While there are obvious differences in their design, all three, in one or more of their phases, show evidence of being associated with the pouring out of liquids and of burning. Their interpretation as olive presses might explain the features associated with pouring of liquids. It does not, however, explain the presence of the ash layers and the evidence of considerable burning in and around the basin. The fact that grain and olive oil were principal agricultural products in ancient Palestine, and thus the stuff of offerings, leads us to suggest that basin 75, as part of an assemblage of objects in the cultic structure at Taanach, had a cultic function that was directly connected to priestly involvement in a system of offerings and sacrifices that were, in turn, one of the ways of monitoring agricultural production.

Part IV. B. Astragali

A striking feature of the archaeological record at Taanach is the large number of astragalus bones that were recovered, mostly from small ruminants (sheep and goats) and gazelles. As Gilmour has reported, the largest cache of astragali in the Levant come from Megiddo and Taanach, both dating to the 10th century BCE (1997: 168). Although our primary interest here is in the 10th-century specimens, the astragalus bones found at Taanach represent a full range of archaeological periods, from the Early Bronze on. Some were found singly, others were in groups. Most were completely preserved, but some were charred. Some have been modified with cut marks, being flattened on the proximal and/or medial side, polished, or by perforating or partially drilling one or more holes through the bone and filling the hole or attaching it to a bronze, copper, iron, or lead fragment.

One of the more unusual finds in the cultic structure was a large cache of astragali (for the precise number, which varies in different reports due to mending, see the discussion below). Of these astragalus bones, originally counted as 140, there were two groups, including 76 and 44 bones, that were found in SW 2-7, L 27, basket 45, a locus dating to period IIB (960-918 BCE). A third group that was part of the 140 was one of 20 bones that was found in SW 2-7 L 60, basket 160, which is also a period IIB locus. This locus was a hard, brown clay layer with a black ash intrusion at an earlier east balk of room 1. Lapp, in his preliminary report on the 1963 season, refers to these bones as pig astragali, and says that they were "The first clearly cultic material excavated in the cult area" (1964: 35). For Lapp there was apparently a close connection between the identification of these astragali as coming from pigs and their interpretation as cultic: "It is difficult to conceive of a noncultic function which would require the exclusive use of pig astragali, and there is clear evidence that the pig was associated with cult in Palestine" (1964: 35). Beyond this suggestion, however, Lapp offered no other explanation for regarding these astragali as cultic, and, according to subsequent studies done, these astragali are almost all from sheep and goats, not pigs. Hesse reports (1990: 214, 215; 1995: 224) that he and Paula Wapnish examined the Taanach cultic structure astragali and determined that they are not from pigs, but predominantly from sheep and goats, with a few (21) being from gazelles and/or roe deer and three from fallow deer. Muhammad M. Al-Zawahra, a faunal analyst at the Palestinian Institute of Archaeology, has done a detailed study of the astragalus bones found during the 1963-1968 excavations at Tell Taanek, which forms part of his forthcoming volume on the animal bones from these excavations. The interested reader should consult his work for specific taxonomic and zoological information. In a private communication Al-Zawahra (1997) reports that he found a total of 193 sheep/goat astragali from various time periods. According to his analysis 93 of them are from sheep and 69 are from goats. 95.1% of them are from the Iron Age and most of them are from area B. Here, we offer observations dealing with astragalus bones as part of a cultic assemblage.

Certainly Taanach is not alone in having a large number of astragalus bones as part of its archaeological record. Gilmour (1997) offers a comprehensive, up-to-date summary of astragalus bones from archaeological contexts. He believes that the widespread distribution of astragali in space and time casts doubt on cultural diffusion alone as an explanation for this distribution. He thinks it more likely that certain characteristics pertaining to the bone itself are the reasons for its selection as a special object by societies that are both temporally and spatially distant from one another. Once selected, the cultural associations pertaining to the bone were passed on from generation to generation, and via cultural diffusion (1995: 254). Gilmour also reports that astragali have been found in other early Iron Age cultic contexts that are the subject of his study (1995: 248). At Tel Qasile, e.g., 20 specimens come from different loci in the cult area, dating to the 12th and 11th centuries. One specimen is reported from Lachish room 49, a small room with possible religious significance dated to the 10th century, and an unspecified number of astragali were found in room 406 in the western complex. No mention is made of any modification of the specimens from these two sites. Although from an earlier period, there was "a very large number" of astragali found near the altar in Fosse Temple I at Lachish (Tuffnell et al. 1940: 94). At Tell el-Hammah an unstated number of astragali were found in room 406, dating to the 10th century. Gilmour's last citation comes from Tel Miqne-Ekron, where during the 1994 season a cache of about 40 sheep/goat astragali were uncovered in an 11th-10th -century context. Figure 9 pictures four of the astragali from Tel Miqne-Ekron that show cutmarks and smoothed surfaces.

Figure 9: Four Astragali from Tel Miqne-Ekron (11th/10th century BCE) showing cutmarks and smoothing (photograph courtesy of Garth Gilmour)

Astragali have been copied in metal, glass and stone, and have been found in burials all over the Mediterranean. Guy and Engberg (1938: 59, 177, pl. 115.11) report that at Megiddo, 70 goat astragali came from MB II tomb 251, of which two were rubbed and polished. In the Baq'ah Valley, 16 goat astragali were found with burials in Cave B3, dated to LB II. Three of the 16 had smoothed sides, and two had cut marks. The cut marks in this case were superficial, and were probably made during the skinning of the animals (Foster 1986: 317-319).

At nearby Megiddo a huge cache of 684 astragali, dating to the 10th century BCE and having characteristics similar to the 10th-century cache from Taanach was found in a krater in L 2081.

Although the krater is not pictured in Loud's report (1948, fig. 101) where the find spots of those artifacts found in a niche in the southwest corner of the locus are plotted, it does appear in fig. 102, suggesting that the astragali were probably related to the numerous cultic artifacts found in the locus, which was a niche in the southwest corner of the courtyard. In their study of the Megiddo locus 2081 astragali, Hesse reports that he and Wapnish discovered that 135 specimens, about 20 per cent, had cut marks, shave marks, or had been polished, 11 had been drilled or perforated, and 2 had copper or bronze metal fragments attached (Hesse 1988:14).

Clearly, astragali were and are used as gaming pieces throughout much of the world. In fact, this is the most common modern anthropologically observed use for them. Hesse and Wapnish (1985: 56) suggest that this is one reason for their numbers in the archaeological record. Indigenous modern archaeological workers, familiar with the use of astragali as gaming pieces, may recognize them as something worth saving—thus their numbers in the archaeological record. It is also clear that astragali were used as gaming pieces in the ancient world. The 12th Dynasty Egyptian game "Hounds and Jackals" used a game board made of ivory and ebony veneer, which used ivory pins with the heads of dogs and jackals as game pieces (cf. Pritchard 1954: fig. 213). These game pieces were moved up and down the board according to the cast of knucklebones, i.e., astragali, which substituted for dice. In many cases astragali are found that have been ground or trimmed to create more planar surfaces and a more cuboid shape, suggesting their use as gaming devices. Lead-weighted examples of astragali may be suggestive of this function, as one of the anthropologically observed games uses a heavier bone to scatter other unweighted ones (Schaeffer 1962: 103). Some gaming pieces have incised marks on one side or another. As Gilmour observes, these cuts range

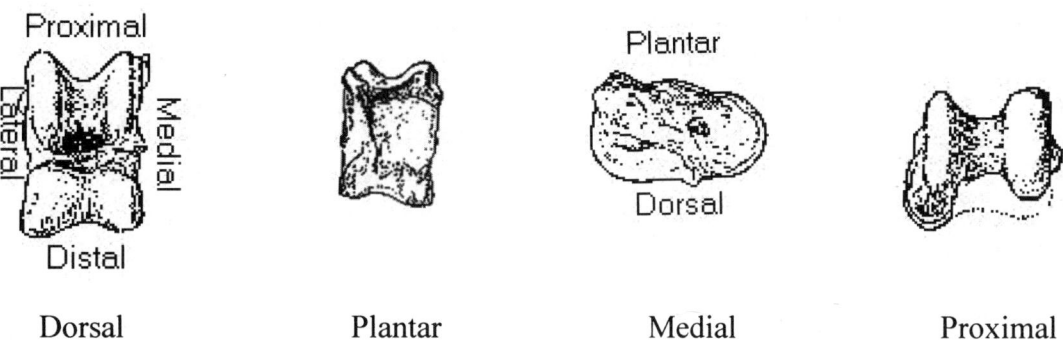

Dorsal   Plantar   Medial   Proximal

Figure 10: Four Aspects of a Male Sheep Astragalus Bone

from deep deliberate incisions, as on the astragali from Tel Miqne, to light superficial marks, like those on specimens from the Athenian Agora (Foster 1984b: 80).

Pigs (*Sus Domesticus*), sheep (*Ovis Aries Linné*) and goats (*Capra Hircus Linné*) belong to the mammalian order Artiodactyla. A defining anatomical characteristic of artiodactyls is the astragalus, an ankle bone that supports the tibia in mammals, has rounded articulations (areas of contact with connected bones) and no constricted neck, instead of simply having one rounded articulation above a neck, as is the case in other mammals. The artiodactyl astragalus also has an articulation on its rear surface for the calcaneum (heel bone). The three articulations are in nearly parallel planes, allowing the astragalus to rotate vertically (see figure 10 for drawings of a male sheep astragalus bone from its dorsal, plantar, medial, and proximal aspects). Since the publication by Boessneck et al. (1964) of morphological distinctions in the adult skeletons of domestic sheep (*Ovis aries*) and goat (*Capra hircus*), experience with European samples has shown that some of these distinctions can be used to differentiate between sheep and goat quite successfully, others less so. Prummel and Frisch (1986: 574) have summarized these distinctions:

> (1) The protuberance on the medial-anterior face of the astragalus is much more pronounced in goats than in sheep. (2) In goats the medial condylus ends proximally in a point; in sheep the shape of this part of the bone is auriculate to rectangular. (3) The capsize test . . . is based

on the number of points of support of astragali lying on their lateral side . . . . Sheep astragali have two points of support in that position: one on the distal end and one on the posterior rim of the lateral side of the bone . . . . In goat astragali an extra point of support, that of the distal end of the lateral condylus, gives more stability. If you put a goat and sheep astragalus down on their lateral side and press down with equal force on the proximal end of the medial condylus . . ., the goat astragalus wobbles, but stays in the same position, whereas the sheep astragalus capsizes to the posterior face of the bone.

The astragalus bones found in the cultic structure SW 2-7, locus 27.45 and locus 60.60 have been studied by zoologists at the Tel Aviv Institute. One group of astragali from 27.45 was assigned lab number 3299/N and identified as "63 charred astragali, *Capra*" (L. Glock). The second group from 27.45 was given the lab number 3271/N and noted as "capra/ovis astragali, 32 plus 23 fragments" (L. Glock). The count, however, when these astragali were received from the Tel Aviv laboratory was 35 astragali and 21 fragments, suggesting that some mending had been done. Other envelopes of single astragali designated by Alfred von Rohr Sauer as 45A were given the following lab numbers and identification in Tel Aviv:

Laboratory Number	Identification
3285/N	*Capra*, charred astragalus
3286/N	*Capra/Ovis*, charred right (R) astragalus
3288/N	*Capra/Ovis*, part, astragalus
3290/N	*Capra* astragalus
3291/N	*Capra* charred R astragalus
3292/N	*Capra/Ovis* L astragalus
3294/N	Small ruminant, 2 charred astragali
3295/N	*Capra/Ovis* charred astragalus
3296/N	*Capra*, 2 astragali, 1 charred
3298/N	Small ruminant astragalus with hole

A revised total for basket 45 thus appears to be 98 plus 21 fragments.

Locus 60, basket 160 was described by Lapp as being "a third group of 20 [astragalus bones] ... found in a jug of cooking ware [TT 456] 90 cm. southwest of the [flint] block" (1964: 35). This group was assigned the laboratory number of 3272/N in Tel Aviv, and identified as "*Capra/Ovis* 16 astragali." Of these, eight were charred, and eight were uncharred (L. Glock). Thus, instead of the 140 astragali initially reported by Lapp, the total astragali from the three groups found in the cultic structure appears to be as follows: 122 *Capra* or *Capra/Ovis*; 22 *Capra* or *Capra/Ovis* fragments; and 3 small ruminants.

The Taanach astragali also have been studied by Giraud V. Foster, M.D., Ph.D. In August of 1984 Foster examined and measured them and compared their measurements to a standard reference collection of over 100 astragali of sheep and goats of known species, sex, and age. Applying partial function discriminate analysis, Foster claimed that he could make reasonable determinations of the number of sheep and goat astragali in the Taanach sample, their distribution by sex, and their age at the time of slaughter (1984a). Foster examined about 400 astragalus bones and concluded that almost all of them were from male sheep and goats of about two months of age. While only about 80% of the bones were classified as male by Foster, he claimed that "Since the method of determining age [sic, presumably this should read "sex" instead of age] is only about 80% accurate this means that the assemblage of animals was probably initially 100% male" (Foster 1985). In the "cult room," Foster says that goat astragali predominated over sheep in a ratio of 4:1. Thus, Foster's determination is that the astragali from the cultic structure represented animals that were predominantly goats, male, and about two months of age.

The concentration of astragali in groups and the special treatment given to some of them certainly implies that this particular animal bone had some distinctive significance and uses. As we have noted, ethnographic studies have made it clear that astragalus bones have been used widely as gaming pieces. Thus, an important consideration here is whether astragali also had distinctive uses in a cultic setting or were used only for games. A study of types of games has shown that unlike games of physical skill or strategy, games of chance, where chance is present and both physical skill and strategy are absent, appear to be associated with religious activities in the ethnographic record (Roberts, Arth and Bush 1959). In these "games" of chance, outcomes are attributed to the intervention of a magical or supernatural force.

As mentioned above, concentrations of astragali have been found in the ethnographic and historical record in many different parts of the world (e.g., Italy, Siam, Cyprus, Egypt, North America, the Levant, etc.) and in both ancient and modern times, where they have been and are used as gaming devices. In a study of astragalus bones used as dice in the late Mississippi period in the Lower Mississippi Valley in the United States, most astragalus specimens that have been recovered archaeologically show some distinctive features (Barry, 1988). They show a strong luster or polish from use, no bias in selection of right or left astragalus for dice, and occurrence as burial goods at 12 of 19 sites studied.

Given the particular characteristics of these bones, however, it is our contention that there is a distinct possibility that their use in religious ritual and their use as gaming devices need not be mutually exclusive. Just as there is considerable ethnographic evidence for the use of astragalus bones as dice, so there is archaeological evidence for their cultic use. At Paestum in Santa Venera, Italy, a quantity of astragalus bones were recovered, all worked and found in a sanctuary context

(Pedley, 1993). Aaron Brody has recently completed a dissertation on the religious beliefs and practices of Canaanite and Phoenician sailors. According to Brody, sailors tried to find out about the future through divination, which coincides with evidence about soothsayers on board Phoenician ships, the casting of lots in the book of Jonah (1:7), etc. (Brody, 1996). Bass (1967: 132, fig. 143, 133) reports that a single astragalus bone was found in the underwater excavation of the Bronze Age Cape Gelidonya shipwreck in Turkey. Although he does not specify the type of bone, judging from his subsequent comments it is a sheep astragalus. He comments:

> A single knucklebone, from area G, was the only large animal bone found on the ship and was, therefore, probably not from a sheep slaughtered for food. . . . Astragalomancy, in which the fall of the bone indicated divine will, was a later form of divination particularly associated with Hermes, patron of cleromancy, a god with Mycenaean origins in Greece, and, at the same time, god of merchants. . . . What more suitable talisman was there than a knucklebone for a merchant captain in a time when the sea was feared? We know that divine guidance was sought by the captain before he chose the route he would sail (1997).

In order to facilitate further analysis, a table has been formulated that appears as Appendix E. This table combines data from Foster, the Tel Aviv laboratory, and this author's own examination, relating to the astragali found in the cultic structure. Beginning with the left column, the table assigns a serial acquisition number to each astragalus. In succeeding columns there are the numbers assigned by Foster and the Tel Aviv laboratory. These numbers are followed by the date of associated pottery, locus and basket numbers, whether it is a left or right astragalus, sheep or goat (or other) classification, an indication of sex, and descriptive comments where relevant. Appended to the end of this table is a brief one describing worked astragali from other locations on the tell. A second table appears as Appendix F, and provides data regarding astragali from the entire site. Beginning with the left column this table lists a serial acquisition number, the Tel Aviv laboratory number, a left/right indication, Foster's sheep/goat determination, Foster's male/female determination, measurements of circumference and longitudinal diameter, and finally, indications of whether the astragalus is burnt, unburnt, cut, or polished, with descriptive remarks where relevant.

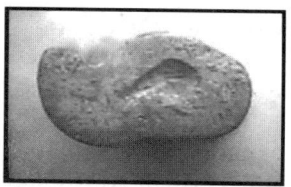

Figure 11: Polished Astragalus from SW 2-7

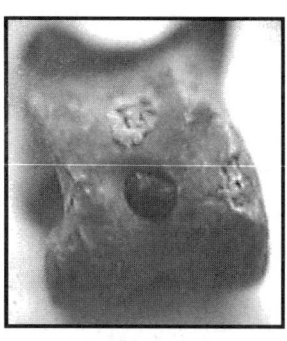

Figure 12: Astragalus with Metal Insert from SW 2-7

Figure 13: Astragalus that has been incised and repaired

A pertinent observation about astragali at Taanach is that almost half, about 49%, of all astragali found at the site were found in the four "squares" associated with the cultic site, SW 1-7, 1-8, 2-7, and 2-8. Almost all the worked astragali were found in these four squares. Some 15 of the 191 astragali from the cultic structure show signs of having been worked in some way: several have been polished on the lateral and/or medial face, several have had one or more holes with a diameter of about 4.0 mm. drilled in them, in which traces of metal oxide coloring remain. Many have incised marks on them, and most are charred from burning. Figure 11 shows an example of an astragalus from the cultic structure that has been polished on both its lateral and medial faces (acquisition number 1/Foster number 140 in Appendix E—from SW 2-7, 140). Figure 12 is an example of an astragalus that has had a hole drilled in it and a piece of metal inserted (acquisition number 2/Foster number 112—from SW 2-7, 60.160—one of the 16 astragali from pot TT 456). This hole was then plastered over so that the metal could not be seen. When this astragalus was first inspected and photographed by the author in 1987, the piece of metal, as well as a piece of the plaster that covered it, was visible. In 1995, both were missing. Several other astragali apparently had similar metal inserts in them, given the metal oxide stains in the holes drilled in them. Figure 13 is an example of an astragalus with visible incised marks and indications that it has been repaired (acquisition number 34/Foster number 77—from SW 2-7, 27.45). Figure 14 shows an astragalus from a square adjoining the cultic structure (Foster number137/laboratory number 697—from SW 1-9, 41.85) that has three holes drilled through from its plantar to dorsal face. None of these worked astragali show any signs of burning.

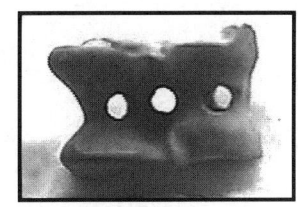

Figure 14: Astragalus with 3 Drilled Holes from SW 1-9

Astragali, both modified and unmodified, may well have been used as dice or as divination devices in a cultic setting. Reese (1985: 388, 389) suggested this use of astragali at Kition on the basis of their presence in the sacred area in association with other probable divination tools such as liver and kidney models and incised bone scapulae. An interpretation of astragali as divination tools is supported by Tuffnell in her discussion of the astragali from Fosse Temple I at Lachish (1940: 94) and by Dever (1991: 111). Gilmour (1995: 258) cites later textual evidence from Greece and Asia Minor that support the use of astragali in divination and concludes: "Although there is no firm evidence in Bronze or Early Iron Age contexts of the use of astragali in divination, the evidence of later periods lends support to this proposal."

In addition to their documentation as gaming devices in the ethnographic record, Gilmour points out (1995: 254) that in southern Africa, anthropological research among several groups has shown that astragali are the most common element of "witch doctor" divining sets. Here too the bones are modified in several ways, most commonly by polishing the sides flat, and by attaching copper wire (Plug 1987: 57, 58).

The feature of astragalus bones that facilitates their use as gaming and/or divination devices, is the fact that like dice, when they are cast they come up on one side or the other. Grinding or

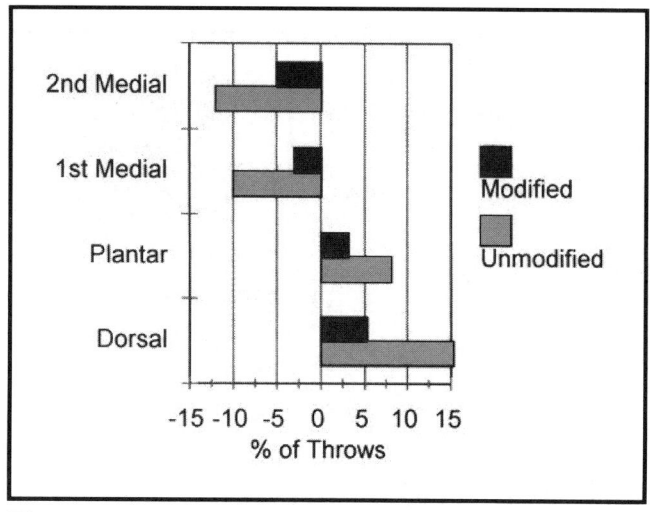

Figure 15: Outcomes of Astragalus Throws (after Lorenson)

polishing on one or may faces of the astragalus may have been done to change the odds affecting the outcome of a die throw. Lorenson counted the outcomes of 200 throws each of modified and unmodified astragali from an American Indian site in the Lower Mississippi Valley from the Late Mississippi period. His results show that the outcome of a throw of an unmodified astragalus bone is biased toward the dorsal and plantar sides of the die and against the two medial sides. The effect of grinding on the odds can also be seen as randomizing the outcome, with no particular side having a distinct advantage. The results of Lorenson's experiment are graphically illustrated in figure 15. Gilmour has suggested that there may have been special symbolic status attached to astragalus bones:

> What was the nature of the symbolism attached to the astragalus? It seems that in different areas and perhaps periods astragali played different symbolic roles. The presence of individual astragali, often perforated, in some sites suggests that they were used as amulets or talismans, while the presence in some cultic contexts of larger quantities suggests they served as offerings. These offerings may relate to the sacred symbolism pertaining to the astragalus itself, or may incorporate an aspect of personal identity of the owner of the astragalus. In the latter case, the presence of large caches of worked astragali, which in other contexts may have been identified as gamepieces, suggests that prior to being offered these items were the personal possessions of the offerer, or in the cases of burials, the deceased (1995: 257).

It is our suggestion that astragalus bones may have served multiple functions in their cultic context at Taanach. They may, as Gimour suggests, have been related to a system of offerings and/or animal sacrifice. Multiple sets of these bones may have been kept by functionaries in the cultic structure for use in divination, with different astragali used for different incidents. Following Lorenson's results, examples of astragali that have been ground would produce one set of more-or-less randomized results, those that were not modified would produce more biased outcomes, and those with holes drilled in them may have been the equivalent of "loaded" dice—with metal inserts put in the drilled holes and plastered over, which would cause the astragalus always to land on the same face, eliminating any element of chance.

In addition to their use as divination devices, given the large number of astragali found in the cultic structure that show signs of incised marks and burning, astragali also may have been used as counting devices in a system of herd management that was administered, at least in part, through ritual means. It is a widespread misconception that sheep and goat pastoralism is a simple subsistence strategy, one that was adopted when all else failed. On the contrary, sheep and goat pastoralism requires both substantial capital investment in stock and a delay before the investment pays off in the form of meat, milk, and fiber. It is a subsistence strategy that requires constant attention to herd management.

While all the minutiae of how the large cache of astragalus bones at Taanach can be worked into Wapnish's model of sheep and goat husbandry cannot concern us here, the model deserves consideration as a possible way of understanding large caches of astragalus bone in a cultic context. Paula Wapnish (1993) has produced a model for dealing with the integration of faunal data with archaeology that works with data from two early Iron Age phases at Tel Dan. She begins by determining that the ratio of sheep to goats remains constant in her sample, but then observes that there is a significant change in the animals selected for slaughter. The shift is from animals less than a year old to animals one to two years of age. The data is presented in tabular form as follows (Wapnish 1993: 431):

Age of Animals Slaughtered	Early Phase (D+C)	Late Phase (B+A)
0-1 year	34%	25%
1-2 years	10%	20%
3 years and over	56%	55%

This change, according to Wapnish, suggests a re-orientation of sheep and goat husbandry towards meat production, which could have occurred in two ways: (1) Local producers could have shifted from subsistence-oriented dairy production towards market-oriented meat production; or (2) Meat production could have been supplemented by outside producers while local husbandry continued to focus on milk production, though at reduced levels. Wapnish offers this conclusion:

> The animal bone evidence from Tel Dan suggests that the following processes of community development occurred between the earlier and later phases of the early Iron Age. Plow-based agriculture became more significant in the economy. The additional investment in land suggests that this asset took on greater value as a medium for social interaction. The use of cattle would have allowed households to redirect human labor to other purposes. The sheep and goat sector of the pastoral economy became partially decoupled from the community at Dan. In addition to the animals slaughtered as part of local milk production, with a husbandry operating at less intensity than in the earlier phase, meat was being provided by outside producers in the form of market-age animals brought to Tel Dan and obtained by households through a redistributive or market system. Social units larger than the household would have taken on greater significance (1993: 432, 433).

A social unit with a control function may have been centered in the cultic structure at Taanach.

A key indicator of herd management can be seen in the pattern of the age of animals selected for slaughter, since choosing animals for the cull is one of the crucial decisions a pastoralist makes. As Wapnish (1993: 437) points out, ethnographic examples and computer simulations show that even slight adjustments to the age composition of the cull produce sharply different levels of production among the three products of sheep and goat husbandry—meat, milk, and fiber.

Since the three significant age categories are 0-1, 1-3, and >3 years of age, culling patterns can be portrayed on a triangular plot, as represented in figure 16. A single dot placed anywhere on the triangle can simultaneously represent the proportion of each age group in the cull. If the relative proportions are plotted for several periods, then the historical pattern of pastoral strategy (whether viewed as production or marketing) at a site can be represented by a trajectory of points. In the main body of the triangle lie those strategies that are both productive and protective of herd integrity. Points nearing any of the corners of the triangle represent unsound herd management or the record of a site where animals were marketed rather than produced. In a production model, a dot near the top of the triangle indicates increasing numbers of animals killed at less than one year of age; too near the top and there would not be sufficient survivors to keep

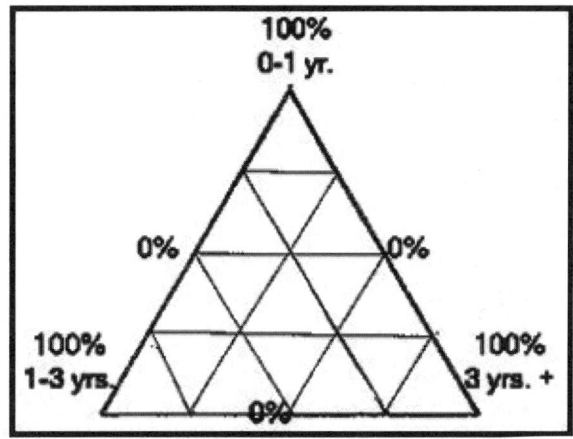

Figure 16: Plot of Culling Strategies in Herd Management

the herd going. If the dot lies near the bottom left corner, the reproductive capacity of the herd would also be disastrously reduced. A mortality pattern near the bottom right corner is also implausible. If Foster's conclusion that almost all of the astragali in the Taanach sample were from male sheep and goats of about two months of age, the collection of these bones in the cultic structure may have been a means of keeping tabs on, by sacrifice or some other means, and limiting the number of animals culled from the herd at the pinnacle of the triangle, so as not to endanger the herd.

Part IV.C Stone Objects

The registered stone objects from the cultic structure at Taanach can be categorized by type/function as follows:

Registered Stone Objects from Iron Age Loci in SW 1-7, SW 1-8, SW 2-7, SW 2-8

Object Type/Function	Registered Object No.
Weights	79, 87, 419, 716, 717, 718, 719, 720, 721, 722, 723, 724, 725
Rubbing/Pounding Stones	86, 98, 117, 320, 324, 392, 393, 503, 597, 636, 667, 729, 803, 856
Querns/Grinders and Mortars	116, 356, 357, 358, 394, 395, 578, 632, 633, 732, 906
Standing Stones (מצבות) and Bases	430, 431, 432, 359, 389, 390, 391

Miscellaneous
  Bead
  Pendant
  Figurine
  Legs from base of tripod bowl
  Mace head (?)
  Loom weights (?)
	
	509
	78
	623
	1625, 1716
	373
	81, 1652

IV.C.1 Weights

The first category of stone objects from the cultic structure is stone weights. Appropriately enough, weight pieces are called "stones" (אבנים) in the Hebrew Bible (e.g., Lev 19:36; Deut 25:13, 15; Prov 11:1; 16:11) as they were in Akkadian (*abnu*), reflecting a tradition that probably goes back to the Early Bronze Age, with stone being the preferred medium for weight standards throughout the Bronze Age. Thousands of weight stones, that together suggest a multitude of different norms, have been recovered in archaeological excavations throughout the ancient Near East. No comprehensive, scientific study of them exists, however. Most surviving weight stones are small, and deviation from a hypothetical norm increases as the size of the weight increases. Powell has suggested that one should reckon with the possibility of a ± 5 percent variation (1997: 340). In the Hebrew Bible, the shekel is regarded as the primary unit of weight metrology. One norm, deducible from marked specimens recovered in Palestinian archaeological excavations, would put the shekel in the 10 gram range. Other norms for the shekel are elusive, but Powell (1992: 906) concludes, based on extant specimens that there was a heavier norm that fluctuated from 11 to13 grams.

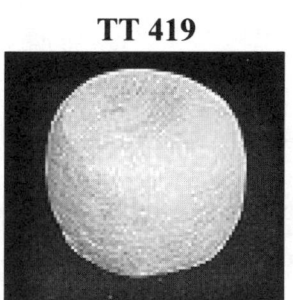

TT 419

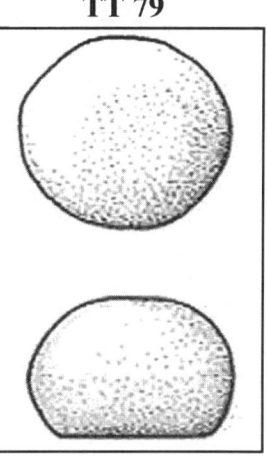

TT 79

Pritchard reports that a weight stone weighing 51.585 grams, with a mark indicating that it represented 4 [shekels] was found at Gibeon (el-Jîb) (1959:30), which would represent a shekel of 12.9 grams. TT 419, a drum-shaped limestone weight of 50 grams from L 67, basket 249 in SW 2-7, found in association with pottery dating ±900, is the heaviest weight found in the cultic structure at Taanach. While unmarked, if it like the weight from Gibeon represents 4 shekels, the resulting shekel weight would be 12.5 grams. TT 79, a basalt dome weight (H=2.2 cm; D=2.5 cm), also found in SW 2-7 (locus 26, basket 37) in association with pottery dating ±900, is the next largest weight from the cultic structure, weighing 22 grams. It may represent 2 shekels of 11 grams, at the bottom of the range of Powell's heavier shekel. TT87, a cylindrical stone weight (H=1.4 cm; D=2.1-2.3 cm) found in locus 27, basket 46 of SW 2-7 with pottery dated to ±900 weighs 13 grams, which would put it at the top of the range for the heavier shekel. All other stone weights from the cultic structure were found in a single locus and basket (27.90) in SW 2-8 inside a period IB (1150-1125 BCE) cooking pot (TT 753) on plaster floor 28. In addition to the weights, the contents of TT 753 included beads, metal fragments, whelk shells, and a bone stamp seal (TT 702). The precise use to which the contents of this pot were put is unclear, but it is unlikely that they were associated with ordinary domestic or agricultural activities. The presence of a collection of weights, in association with other items in the assemblage, implies a specialized activity associated with a regulatory function of cultic activities carried on in the structure, if the structure was used for cultic purposes in period IB.

Weights from SW 2-8, Locus 27, Basket 90

Registered Object No.	Size	Weight	Description
TT 716	W=1 cm; L=2.2 cm; H=1 cm	10 grams	Rectangular bar weight; bloodstone
TT 717	H=20 mm; D=19 mm	13 grams	Dome weight; serpentine
TT 718	W=10 mm; L=20 mm; H=8 mm	14.4 grams	Biconical weight; serpentine(?)
TT 719	W=9 mm; L=27 mm; H=10 mm	8.2 grams	Cylindrical weight; flat base and flattened ends; black stone
TT 720	W=14 mm; L=32 mm; H=17 mm	11 grams	Biconical weight with flat base; black stone
TT 721	W=20 mm; L=30 mm; h=17 mm	18.5 grams	Ovoid weight with flat base; black stone
TT 722	W=31 mm; L=30 mm; H=25 mm	undetermined	Oval weight; undetermined black stone; unweighed because corroded to bronze fragment
TT 723	W=18 mm; L=23 mm; H=16 mm	12 grams	Pear-shaped weight with flat base; black stone
TT 724	H=9 mm; D=15 mm	6 grams	Egg-shaped weight; serpentine

| TT 725 | H=9 mm; D=15 mm | 5.1 grams | Drum-shaped weight; serpentine |

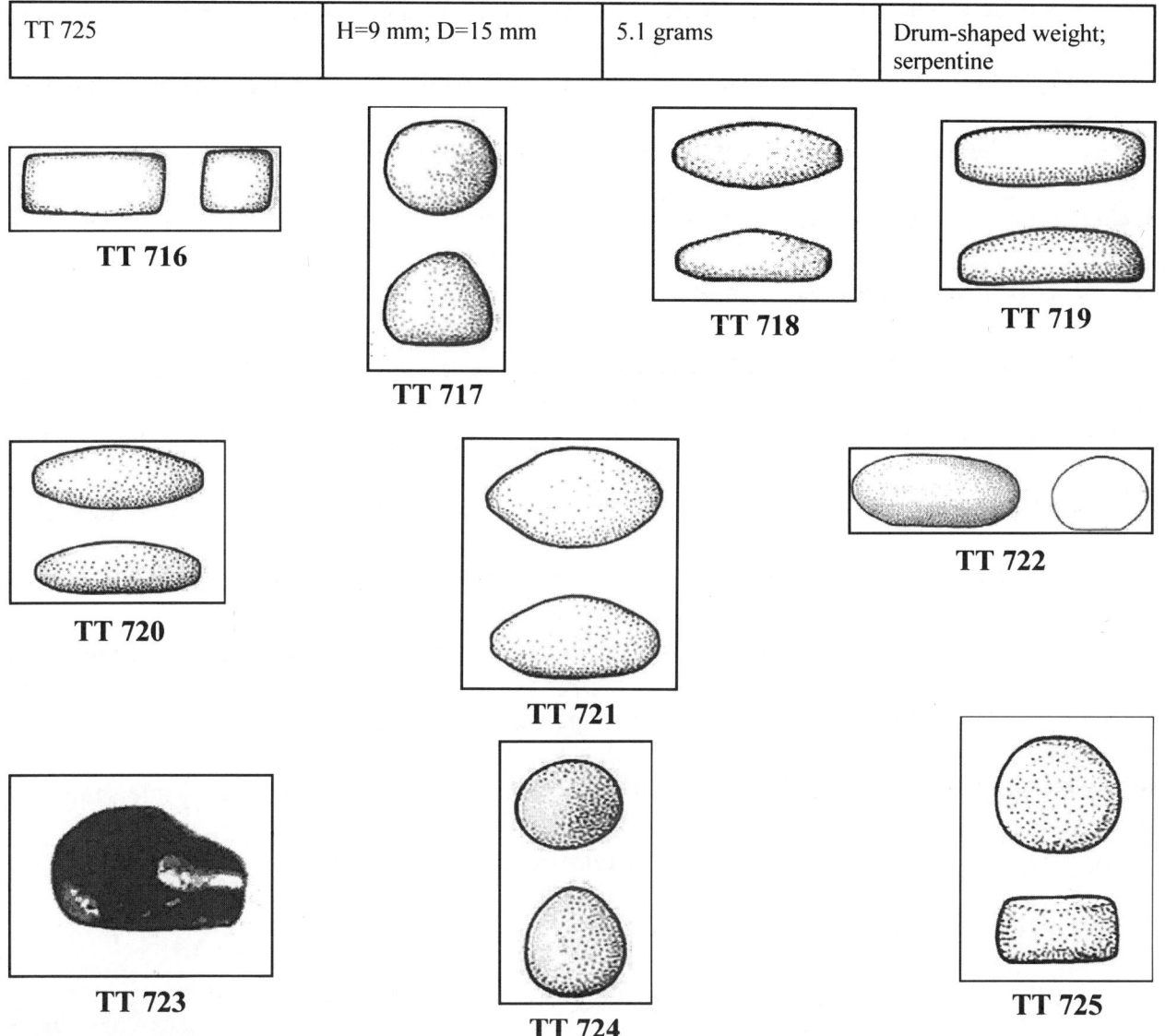

If one concedes that both a lighter and heavier shekel norm existed in early Iron Age Israel, with a 10-13 gram range (± 5 per cent), four of the weights from SW 2-8, L 27.90 may represent shekels (TT 716, TT 717, TT 720, TT 723). TT 718 and TT 721 are beyond even + 5 percent of the top end of the heavier norm. TT 719 is below even - 5 per cent of the lighter norm. Three other weights from this collection whose weights can be determined may represent fractions of a shekel. TT 724, which weighs 6 grams, and TT 725, which weighs 5.1 grams, may represent half shekels.

TT 719, which weighs 8.2 grams may represent a *pym* (פים). While the meaning of *pym* is uncertain (it occurs in the Hebrew Bible only once, in the corrupt 1 Sam 13:21), the New Revised Standard Version translates it as "two thirds of a shekel." A weight of 8.2 grams would qualify as .67 of a shekel in the 11-13 gram range.

IV.C.2 Rubbing/Pounding Stones

An assortment of rubbing/pounding stones was found in the cultic structure. The rubbing/pounding stones were made of various kinds of stone and were in different shapes. The different kinds of stone from which these stones were fabricated and their various shapes may suggest that certain kinds of stone and specific shapes may be related to particular tasks, but these tasks cannot be discerned with any specificity. In non-cultic contexts, such stones were used for various domestic/cultic tasks related to cottage industry-type tasks. The rougher stones, such as foamy basalt, would have been the equivalent of a file, rasp or coarse sandpaper, while smoother stones, such as those that are a part of TT 729 may have been used to seal the pores of clay before firing, i.e., to burnish the surface of the clay.

TT 86, a neatly-shaped pyramidal rubbing stone of *basalt scorie* (foamy basalt), with gas bubbles forming a very rough surface, was found in SW 2-7 (27.46) in a period IIB locus. TT 117, TT 320, TT 324, TT 392, and TT 393 were also found in SW 2-7, all in period IIB loci. TT 117 (26.38) is an oval rubbing stone of undetermined stone found in the same locus as TT 78, the pierced serpentine

TT 86

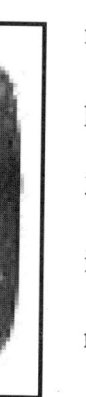
TT 117

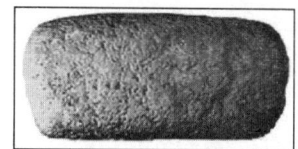
TT 320

pendant/weight described below under miscellaneous objects. TT 320 (59.149) is a rectangular rubbing stone made of light, porous, quartzolite with one flat surface. TT 324 (61.164) is a semi-spherical rubbing stone made of limestone, with visible lines of smoothing. It was found in the same locus as TT 322 an iron sickle or scythe fragment), TT 358, (a broken and incomplete quartzolite quern), and TT 359 (a round limestone base (?)). TT 392 (61.203) is a rubbing or pounding stone of basalt of which no one surface shows any more wear than others. It was found in the same locus as TT 324, TT 358, TT 359 and TT 393 (a basalt rubbing stone whose base is worn smooth). TT 393 was found in L 61.203. TT 503 (74.268) is a basalt rubbing stone with a flat bottom, found with pottery dating to the 10th century. TT 636 (88.300) is a basalt rubbing stone found with pottery dating to the 11th century. TT 667 (88.285) is a rectangular rubbing stone with a perforated handle of *basalt scorie* (foamy basalt) that was found with mixed pottery dating from the LB all the way to the Abbasid periods.

TT 729 is a collection of some 49 miscellaneous burnishing stones, three of which were found fused to an iron knife handle. This assortment of stones was found in SW 2-8 (27.90). The final example of a rubbing stone from the cultic structure is TT 856, which is a rubbing stone made of fine-grained basalt that was found in SW 2-7 (117.352) in association with pottery that suggests it belongs to period IA (ca. 1200-1150 BCE).

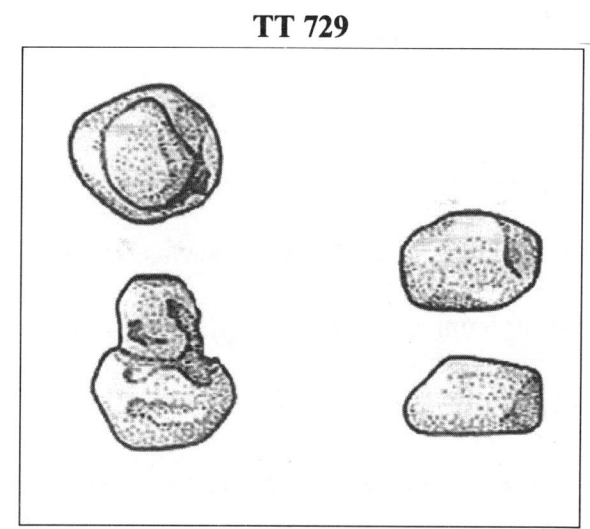

TT 729

IV.C.3 Querns/Grinders and Mortar

TT 632

TT 633

TT 856
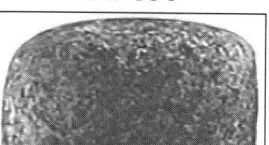

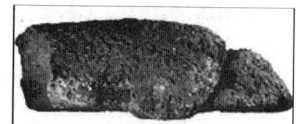
TT 356
TT 357

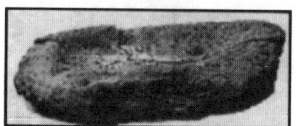

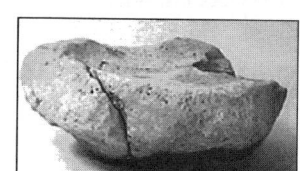
TT 358

TT 394

TT 395
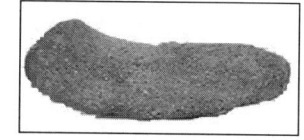

TT 578

Four querns and two saddle grinders were found in SW 2-7, all probably belonging to period IIB. Presumably these were used for grinding grain, perhaps to prepare cakes that ould be burned as cereal sacrifices (see the iscussion of TT 100 in section IV.D. on ceramic bjects below). TT 116 (26.38) is a coarse-textured basalt quern with an ashy spot on its base. It was found in the same locus as TT 71 (fragments of iron swords), TT 78 (a serpentine pendant), TT 79 (a basalt dome weight), TT 83 (a jug), and TT 117 (a rubbing stone). TT 356 (55.141) is an incomplete limestone saddle grinder that was found in the same locus and basket as TT 357, a broken but complete quern made of porous basalt. TT 358 (61.169) is a broken and incomplete quartzolite quern. TT 394 (61.203) is a plano-convex saddle grinder made of coarse-textured basalt that was found in the same locus and basket as TT 395, a basalt quern that resembles TT 357. TT 578 is a limestone mortar that was found in SW 1-7 (35.?), belonging to period IIA. TT 632 (87.302) and TT 633 (88.300) are both saddle grinders made of porous basalt that were found in SW 2-7. TT 632 and TT 633 both should probably be assigned to IIA. Finally, TT 732 (87.321), also from period IIA, is a medium-grained basalt saddle grinder found in SW 2-7.

IV.C.4 Standing Stones (מצבות)

Shaped standing stones (מצבות in the Hebrew Bible) are ubiquitous in ancient Palestinian sites, where they probably served as aniconic representations of deities. The Hebrew noun מצבה derives from the root נצב, which means "to stand." The noun is used in the Hebrew Bible to refer to shaped standing stones that were used for different purposes. Occasionally they served as burial markers (cf. Gen 35: 19-21; 2 Sam 18:18). They could also be set up as witnesses to an agreement between two parties (cf. Gen 31: 29-32; Exod 24: 3-8). The most frequent use of the term, however, is in a clear cultic context. One of the most thorough studies of shaped standing stones in ancient Palestine is that of Carl Graesser (1972). It is sometimes difficult to determine whether a shaped stone or standing pillar represents a god, has a funerary or monumental function, or was erected as a symbolic substitute for the worshiper. Nevertheless, there are enough examples to make a strong case for the cultic use of shaped standing stones in ancient Israel and among her neighbors. Mettinger (1995) makes a case that such material aniconism was a hallmark of northwest Semitic religions in general and pre-Deuteronomic Israelite beliefs in particular. In official Israelite religion, as it is represented in the Hebrew Bible, however, material aniconism (the use of a shaped standing stone to represent the deity) was prohibited together with anthropomorphic or zoomorphic representations. While there was thus a likely reduction in the number of shaped standing stones in the official monotheistic Israelite religion, there was probably no essential change in aniconism in cultic settings. The practice of setting up shaped standing stones was widespread in the ancient Near East, documented by Mettinger as having been done from as early as the 11th millennium B.C.E. in the

Negev and continuing in Iron Age Judah and Israel, Syria and Lebanon of the late second millennium B.C.E., in the Punic colonies and their Phoenician homeland, and on to the pre-Islamic Arabs. The identification of מצבות in the archaeological record is, however, sometimes problematic and while one can certainly exclude pillars that have a structural function in a building, the identification of other shaped standing stones as cultic artifacts depends, to a large degree, on the context in which they are found.

Shaped standing stones are represented in the cultic structure at Taanach by TT 430, TT 431, and TT 432, all of which were found in SW 2-7 in the same locus and basket (57.228),

TT 430 (l), TT 431 (c) and TT 432 (r)

| **TT 430 (reverse)** | **TT 431 (reverse)** | **TT 432 (obverse)** |

dating to period IIB. TT 430 and TT 431 are approximately the same size, about 26 cm. tall and 18 cm. wide. Both are made of limestone. Both are tapered in width as well as thickness, being wider at the base than at the top. Both are partially coated with plaster and show marks of having been shaped, perhaps with a coarse basalt rubbing stone.

TT 432 is smaller than TT 430 and 432, being only 17.7 cm. tall and 14.5 cm. wide. It has an average thickness of about 11 cm., but like TT 430 and TT 431, it also tapers from its base to its top. Unlike TT 430 and TT 431, TT 432 is made of basalt. The fact that these three shaped standing stones were found together may suggest that they represented three different deities. Perhaps the difference in types and sizes of stones is significant in symbolizing male and female deities.

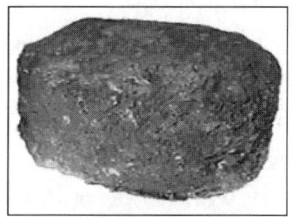  

TT 389 **TT 390** **TT 391**

Strengthening the case for the interpretation of TT 430, TT 431, and TT 432 as shaped standing stones is the presence of three stones that could have served as bases for such stones—TT

389, TT 390, TT 391—all of which were found in SW 2-7, L 61, a dark, hard clay stratum that covered the entire southern part of room 1 of the cultic structure, a locus that dates to period IIB, and one that was rich with artifacts (see Appendix B). All three of these worked stones were carved from limestone. They were flat on one side and irregular on the other, and show the same kinds of smoothing marks and traces of white plaster as do TT 430 and TT 431.

IV.C.5 Miscellaneous Stone Objects

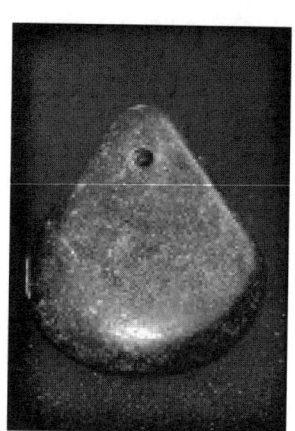

TT 78

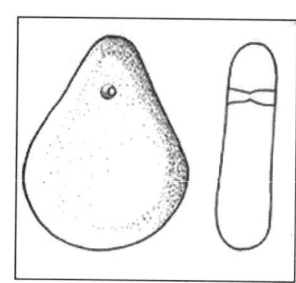

TT 78

The first of the miscellaneous stone objects found in the cultic structure to be catalogued in this section is TT 78, a pierced, finely-polished serpentine pendant. Serpentine is a form of hydrated magnesium silicate that is suitable for carving and takes a fine polish. It is now used mostly in carving as a substitute for nephrite jade, for which it is sometimes mistaken. TT 78 was found in SW 2-7 (26.37) and dates to period IIB. This object weighs 36 grams, which if it was used as a weight would represent 3 shekels in a system in which the shekel would weigh 11-13 grams. If this object was used as a weight, as were all of the other serpentine objects found in the cultic structure, the hole may have been used to hang it on some sort of balance. Otherwise, the hole would make it possible to wear it as a status object on a cord around one's neck. In this same locus were found the stone objects TT 79, TT 116, and TT 117, as well as the pottery objects TT 62, TT 63, TT 73, TT 83, TT 439, TT 440, TT 443, and TT 448 (all of which are rather ordinary domestic pottery types), and TT 71, fragments of two iron swords. Other serpentine objects found in the cultic structure are the weights TT 717, TT 718, TT 724, and TT 724 that have been described above. The nearest significant occurrences of serpentine are in Italy and Russia, which suggests that it was a long-distance trade object, and thus at least a semi-precious stone that would most likely have been in the possession of a member of the elite, perhaps functionaries who managed the cultic activities in this structure.

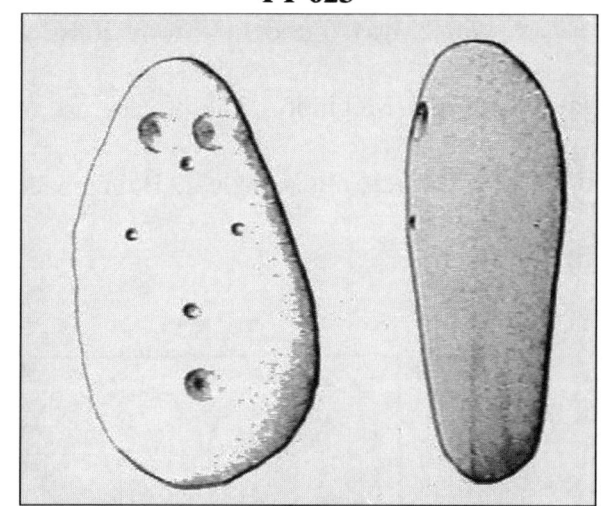

TT 623

The second miscellaneous stone object from the cultic structure to be mentioned here is TT 623, which is the sole stone figurine found in the cultic structure. Even though it does not date to period IIB but comes from a locus with pottery dating to MB IIC, LB I, and the 12th century BCE, we mention it here because not only is it the only stone figurine found in the structure, it is also without parallel in any of the clay figurines that will be discussed below. This stylized figurine apparently represents a female figure with no details other than carved-out depressions, two large ones for eyes, one smaller one for a nose/mouth, two for breasts, one for a navel, and a larger one representing a vulva. It may represent an earlier version of the clay female figurines that will be discussed in the following section.

Two pieces of legs, TT 1625 and TT 1716, from two different basalt tripod bowls were found in SW 2-8 in 171.404, dating to period IIB. TT 1625 is a leg from the base of a tripod bowl that originally stood ca. 17 cm. tall. TT 1716 is slightly larger.

TT 1716

Basalt Tripod Bowl No. a 732 from Room 2081 at Megiddo

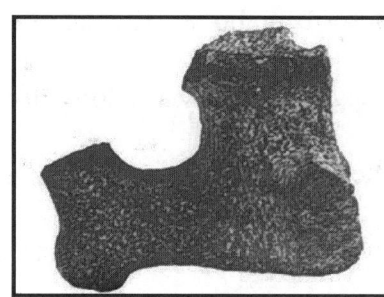

TT 1625

Both are made of fine-grained basalt, and are apparently from bowls resembling No. a 732, which was found in Room 2081 of stratum VA-IVB at Megiddo. The precise use to which these bowls were put is unclear. Being made of fine-grained basalt, they would, however, be more durable than a clay bowl, and could thus have been used over a longer period of time.

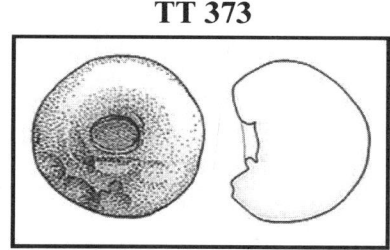

TT 373

Another stone object from L 61 (basket 205) in SW 2-7, the period IIB locus in which the stone objects TT 389-TT 395 were found is TT 373, a curious socketed stone made of undetermined stone. It has a height of 3 cm. and a diameter of 3.8 cm. The closest parallels suggest that it may have been a mace head, although the socket seems too shallow to attach the stone to a shaft. Most stone mace heads have a hole drilled completely through their length, and are more pear-shaped than TT 373.

TT 1652

The final two stone objects from the cultic structure to be described here, both from period IIB, are TT 81 and TT 1652. These two stone artifacts, are labeled tentatively as loom weights, largely on the basis of their size and shape, although most loom weights are made of clay rather than stone. TT 81, found in SW 2-7 (26.37; the same locus and basket as TT 78 above) is 2.7 cm. long, has a diameter of 2.8 cm, and is made of undetermined stone. TT 1652 is from SW 2-8 (171.352) and is made of black stone. It is 2 cm. long, has a diameter of 2.5 cm., and has a hole through it that is neither round nor centered. The use to which this object was put cannot be determined. We will return to a discussion of the function of ceramic loom weights in the following section.

Part IV.D Ceramic Objects

The subject of this section is selected ceramic objects found within SW 1-7, SW 1-8, SW 2-7, and SW 2-8. While the list in the table below is complete, we exclude from detailed discussion here those classes of ceramic objects that have been, or will be, the subject of special studies by others. These studies include:

- Common Iron Age pottery types. The Iron Age pottery has been published by Rast (1978).

- Ceramic loom weights. These are to be published in a forthcoming volume, *The Loom Weights*, by Glenda Friend. Friend's volume will be dedicated to the analysis of those objects involved with textile production. In addition to loom weights it will treat bone spatulas used as pattern weaving tools. The monograph will include a complete catalogue of loom weights as well as other related objects.

- Seal impressions on ceramic objects. These are to be published in a forthcoming volume, *Die Glyptik*, by Othmar Keel. This volume will contain all the scarabs/stamp seals, cylinder seals, and seal impressions.

- Beads. These are to be published in a forthcoming work by Nan Broedern.

Ceramic Objects (excluding common pottery types) from SW 1-7, SW 1-8, SW 2-7, and SW 2-8
(Those positively dated to period IIB in **boldface**)

Type of Object	TT Registered Object Number
Pottery and faience objects	**64**, **489**, 624, 639, 787, 854, 997, 1087, 1108, 1127, 1143, 1190, 1204, 1393, 1648, 1836, 1838, 1884
Figurines and figurine fragments	94, 253, 515, 527, 641, 669, 754, 755, 759, 760, 761, 762, 830, 831, 839, 855, 857, 882, 895, 900, 974, 991, 999, 1027, 1048, 1051, 1100, 1101, 1112, 1130, 1167, 1202, **1486**, **1540**, 1642, **1842**
Mold	**100**
Cultic stands	**351**, **1500**, **1830**
Loom weights	**107**, 313, **388**, 583, 763, 791, 1193, 1231, 1232, 1233, 1234, 1235, 1236, 1237, 1310, 1311, 1312, 1313, 1314, 1320, 1322, 1323, 1376, 1377, 1378, 1455, 1587, 1631, 1632, 1633, 1634, 1636, 1673
Miscellaneous Fasteners or whorls Disks Stoppers Mask fragment Wheels Button Tablets	421, 646, 1089 423, 531, 549 538, 548 965 1045, 1126 1308 1848, 1849
Seal impression	566

IV.D.1 Pottery

Iron Age pottery from the cultic structure has been published by Rast (1978), who has categorized the pottery by commonly employed types: jars (figs. 3-36); jugs (figs. 37-39); juglets and pyxides (fig. 40); krater (fig. 41); large bowls (figs. 42-44); medium and small burnished bowls (figs. 45-48); cooking pots (figs. 49-50); and lamps, censers, and stand (fig. 51). In the same volume, Rast also includes the Iron Age pottery from the two cisterns, Cistern L 69 in SW 2-8 and Cistern L 74 in SW 6-2. It was probably in this area that Sellin discovered the cultic stand mentioned previously. It was in the bell of this cistern L 69 that the Lapp expedition, during the 1968 season, found the fragments of cultic stand TT 1500, probably the best-known single artifact from Taanach. The stratigraphic relation of the cistern to the cultic structure could not be determined with any accuracy, however, since the Sellin excavation had destroyed the relevant evidence. However, as Rast observes, the cache of pottery from Cistern L. 69 belongs typologically to the same horizon as the period IIB pottery from the cultic structure, and it is probable that the cistern was part of the cultic structure complex (1978: 23).

With respect to the various period II pottery types presented by Rast, the cultic structure contained many complete as well as partially complete large storage jars, which were found mostly in room 1 of the cultic structure, the only exception being two rim pieces that were found in L 28.47 in room 2. Some of these storage jars still contained traces of grain. Jugs of various types are represented, as are juglets and pyxides, some of which have close parallels in Locus 2081 and Building 10 pottery at Megiddo (see the table at the end of this section on Cultic Structure Pottery Parallels to Locus 2081 and Building 10 Pottery at Megiddo).

Rast describes the large multi-handled krater, TT 489, as "the most spectacular vessel to come from the Cultic Structure." The krater has eight handles that are attached from nearly the bottom of the rim to the carination of the shoulder. The rim is thickened and flattened and overhangs on both the interior and exterior of the vessel. There is a collar on the shoulder midway between the carination and the rim, and the vessel sits on a heavy ring base. Rast cites as the most striking parallel to TT 489 one from contemporary building 10 at nearby Megiddo (Lamon and Shipton 1939: Pl. 21:125). Another parallel, although from several centuries earlier (LB II), is a large krater found in a cultic context at Hazor (Yadin et al. 1958-1961: Pls. 122:1, 4; 280:12; 303:9).

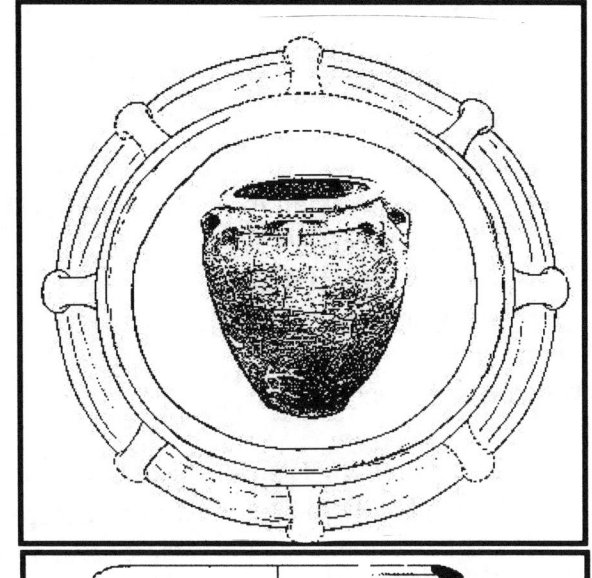
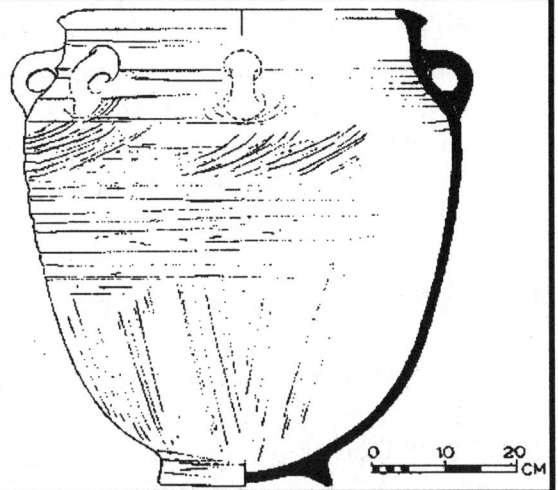

TT 489 (after Rast 1978: fig. 41)

The Hazor krater was found in the "Holy of Holies," L 2113 in Area H, ascribed to Stratum 1A and dated to the end of LB II. It was found in association with other cultic equipment such as an altar, a basin, and a basalt libation table. In her analysis of traces of cultic behavior at Hazor, Daviau assigns the more than 100 items found in L 2113 to function classes as follows (Daviau 1994: 85-86):

Items	Functional Class
28+ bowls	food preparation/food offerings/consumption
1 cooking pot	food preparation/food offerings
2 baking trays	food preparation/food offerings/consumption
1 jug	food preparation/food offerings/consumption

1 krater	food preparation/libation
2 kraters (1 w/drain)	food preparation/libation
1 chalice	consumption/libation
4 goblets	consumption/libation
6 juglets	multipurpose/libation
1 basalt tray w/multiple depressions (H 143)	libation?
2 basalt trays (H 137, H 138)	libation?
1 basalt krater (H 136)	food preparation/consumption/libation?
1 basalt basin (H 135?)	libation?

Daviau concludes:

> The remaining rooms [of Stratum 1a in Area H] contained few finds, none of which would point to additional cultic actions except for a kohl stick from the middle room (L 2115). The use of cosmetics in the temple setting may suggest some sort of cultic drama. . . . There are no finds which point to animal sacrifice. It appears that a significant change in cultic action took place following the destruction of Stratum 2. Extensive animal sacrifice was replaced by large scale food offerings and libations. A similar range of activities, consisting of items for cosmetic use, cutting, food consumption, libation, and votive offerings, were represented by the artifacts in the rooms (L 2115 and 2107) fronting the main room and in the outer porch (L 2118) (1994: 84-86).

It thus appears that the krater in the Hazor assemblage appears, as does its counterpart in the cultic structure at Taanach, as part of an assemblage of pottery that covers a variety of repetitive functions, ranging from food preparation, offering and consumption, to libation. This suggests that the cultic structure at Taanach may have served both as a residence and a cultic structure.

The next type of pot in Rast's analysis is large bowls, for which he again cites parallels from Locus 2081 and Building 10 at Megiddo (cf. Lamon and Shipton 1939: Pl. 29:110, Pl. 89:14, and Pl. 30:116). The cultic structure also contained a large group of medium and small bowls, almost all of which had been hand burnished, again with close parallels from Locus 2081 and Building 10 at Megiddo.

Gilmour (1995: 240-243) has observed that the inventory of artifacts from the cultic area at Tell Qasile makes possible an evaluation of the types of artifacts from specific loci. It is thus significant that a majority of vessels in each of the strata XII-X temples were bowls. To support this conclusion, Gilmour offers the following data from Tell Qasile:

Temple	# of bowls/# of vessels	percentage of bowls
stratum XII Temple 319	31/50	62%
stratum XI Temple 200	157/237	66%
stratum XI Pit 125	278/422	66%
stratum X Temple 131	166/312	53%
stratum X Shrine 300	12/28	43%

Data published from the Fosse Temples at Lachish (Tuffnell et al. 1940: 79), although not representing the entire excavated pottery corpus as at Tell Qasile, appear to agree with the Tell Qasile numbers. The proportion of bowls as a total of the registered vessels from each temple at Lachish is as follows (Gilmour 1995: 241):

Temple	# of bowls/# of vessels	percentage of bowls
Fosse Temple I	422/533	81%
Fosse Temple II	615/798	77%
Fosse Temple III	769/845	91%

Preliminary quantitative data from two buildings in the 7th-century industrial area in Field III at Tel Miqne-Ekron (Gitin 1989: 37, 38, tables 1-4) also show a high proportion of bowls in the restorable vessels:

Building & room	# of bowls/# of vessels	percentage of bowls
Building 1, room 15 (oil pressing room)	75/108	69%

Building & room	# of bowls/# of vessels	percentage of bowls
Building 1, room 14 (adjacent inside room)	26/88	29%
Building 2, room 26 (oil pressing room)	20/39	48%
Building 2, room 27	66/142	40%

Utilizing Rast's publication of the Iron Age pottery from Taanach (1978), it appears that there are a total of 82 vessels from the cultic structure that date to period IIB (excluding loom weights and cult stand fragments). Of these 82, there are 35 bowls, representing 42.7% of the total, a figure on the lower end of the range of percentages in the tables above representing data from Tell Qasile, Lachish, and Tel Miqne-Ekron. While Gilmour (1995: 242, 243) cautions that more data of this sort incorporating quantitative analysis is needed to confirm the relevance of such numbers, he thinks that is a possibility that a high proportion of bowls may be seen as a potential cultic indicator, and can suggest the possibility of cultic activity that would need to be supported by other artifactual or architectural evidence. Two types of cooking pots were found in the cultic structure (Rast 1978: figs. 49-50), both of which have parallels in Locus 2081 and Building 10 at Megiddo.

While Rast (1978) published only two lamps from the cultic structure that date to period IIB, they are typical for the end of Iron I and have close parallels at Megiddo. Gilmour (1995: 238) points out that a fair quantity of lamps have been found in early Iron Age cultic contexts, most notably at Tell Qasile XII-X, the southern temple at Beth Shean, and at Lachish room 49. While lamps obviously were not limited to ritual contexts, they just as obviously played a significant role in ritual.

In cultic contexts, lamps such as TT 89 (Rast 1978, fig. 51:1) and TT 473 (Rast 1978, fig. 51:2) may have been placed on top of cult stands.

TT 64 is an unusual vessel that Rast groups with lamps and a stand. According to Rast, this vessel belongs to "a class of small, perforated cups set on a tripod base. . . . Many parallels are present at other sites, and these may be classified in two types with or without handles. The Taanach vessel belongs to the latter type" (1978: 33). Rast goes on to suggest that the use of such vessels has posed a problem for which the Taanach example may suggest a

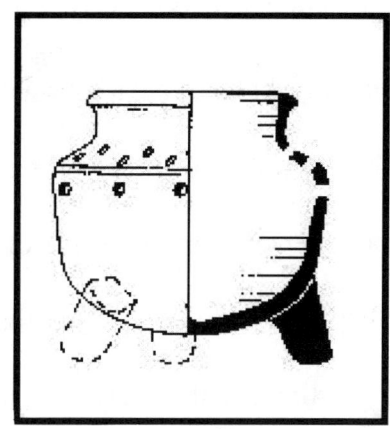

TT 64

solution. At Hazor, Yadin suggested that such vessels were strainers. At Tell el-Fâr'ah (N), De Vaux suggested that they were used in cheesemaking. As Rast observes, however, had they been used as strainers, one would expect the perforations to be nearer the base, whereas in the Taanach example and its parallels, the perforations are almost uniformly near the shoulder and neck. Crowfoot, on the basis of her study of vessels of this type from the Aegean area, has proposed that they should be interpreted as censers (as cited by Rast 1978: 35) and could have been used for some sort of cultic purpose. Rast concludes: "The Taanach example lends support to this explanation in that its context is more probably cultic than not, and an interpretation of this vessel as a censer would fit well with other contents of the building from which it came" (1978: 35).

TT 351

Finally, TT 351 is described by Rast (1978:35 and fig. 51:4) as a "jar stand." Like so many other cultic stands this "jar stand,"

so-called due to its open top, which could have been the resting place for a round-bottomed vessel, is characterized by fenestrations, in this case two irregular squarish "windows" on opposing sides at the shoulder of the vessel. The function of these fenestrations cannot be determined with any certainty, but they are a constant feature of cultic stands in Palestine from the Chalcolithic period on. The suggestion that they provided ventilation to support the burning of incense is not supported by sooty deposits on the inside of this or most other stands. The fact that in this case, and in some others, the "windows" are above the center of gravity and opposite one another, leads to the suggestion that they may have been put in the vessel so that a rod could be inserted through them to move the vessel if it could not be touched for some reason. That the windows are symbolic of actual windows in large structures is a distinct possibility, but seems to be more likely in larger square cultic stands that may represent miniature shrines, as we shall see below in the discussion of TT 1500.

Before proceeding to the discussion of ceramic figurines, the following table, adapted from one in Rast (1978: 34), itemizes pottery parallels between Taanach, locus 20811 and building 10 at Megiddo.

Cultic Structure Pottery Parallels to Locus 2081 and Building 10 Pottery at Megiddo

Cultic Structure at Taanach	Megiddo Locus 2081 (Loud 1948: 43-46)	Megiddo Building 10 (Lamon and Shipton 1939: Fig. 6, P-Q 13)
Jars (Rast 1978: figs. 30-32) TT 478, TT 476, TT 477, TT 36, TT 474, TT 481, TT 469		Pl. 21:123
Jars (Rast 1978: fig. 34:4-5) TT 475, TT 459		Pl. 20:120-121
Jars (Rast 1978: fig. 36:1-2) TT 467, TT 490		Pl. 19:106
Amphora (Rast 1978: fig. 36:3) TT 350		Pl. 19:113, 22:130-131

Cultic Structure at Taanach	Megiddo Locus 2081 (Loud 1948: 43-46)	Megiddo Building 10 (Lamon and Shipton 1939: Fig. 6, P-Q 13)
Jug (Rast 1978: fig. 37:1) TT 103		Pl. 7:174
Juglets (Rast 1978: fig. 40:4-6) TT 327, TT 306, TT 88		Pl. 5:126
Juglet (Rast 1978: fig. 40:8)	Pl. 88:13	
Juglet (Rast 1978: fig. 40:11) TT 484		Pl. 5:121
Krater (Rast 1978: fig. 41) TT 489		Pl. 21:125
Bowls (Rast 1978: fig. 42:1-4; fig. 43:1-2) TT 446, TT 439, TT 480, TT 479, TT 471, TT 451		Pl. 29:110
Bowl (Rast 1978: fig. 44:3) TT 461	Pl. 89:14	
Bowl (Rast 1978: fig. 44:5)		Pl. 30:116
Bowl (Rast 1978: fig. 45:1) TT 485		Pl. 30:126
Bowl (Rast 1978: fig. 45:2) TT 445		Pl. 30:120
Bowls (Rast 1978: fig. 45:5-7) TT 464		Pl. 28:98
Bowl (Rast 1978: fig. 45:8)		Pl. 28:106
Bowls (Rast 1978: fig. 46:3, 7, 12) TT 453, TT 450, TT 455	Pl. 89:10	
Bowl (Rast 1978: fig. 47:1) TT 449	Pl. 147:8	
Bowls (Rast 1978: fig. 47:2-3) TT 352, TT 412	Pl. 89:9	
Bowls (Rast 1978: fig. 47:4-5) TT 354		Pl. 30:130
Bowls (Rast 1978: fig. 48:1		
Bowls (Rast 1978: fig. 48:15-19) TT 447	Pl. 89:11	
Cooking pot (Rast 1978: fig. 50:1) TT 456		Pl. 5:119
Lamps (Rast 1978: fig. 51:1-2) TT 89, TT 473	Pl. 90:9	Pl. 38:19

IV.D.2 Figurines

While the registered object list for the four "squares" of the cultic structure includes 35 figurines, partial or complete, only 11 can be dated to the Iron Age with any certainty. These 11 are:

Period IA (ca. 1200-1150 BCE)	TT 830, TT 831, TT 839
Period IB (1150-1125 BCE)	TT 755, TT 761, TT 762
Period IIA (ca. 1020-960 BCE)	TT 641, TT 754
Period IIB (960-918 BCE)	TT 1486, TT 1540, TT 1842

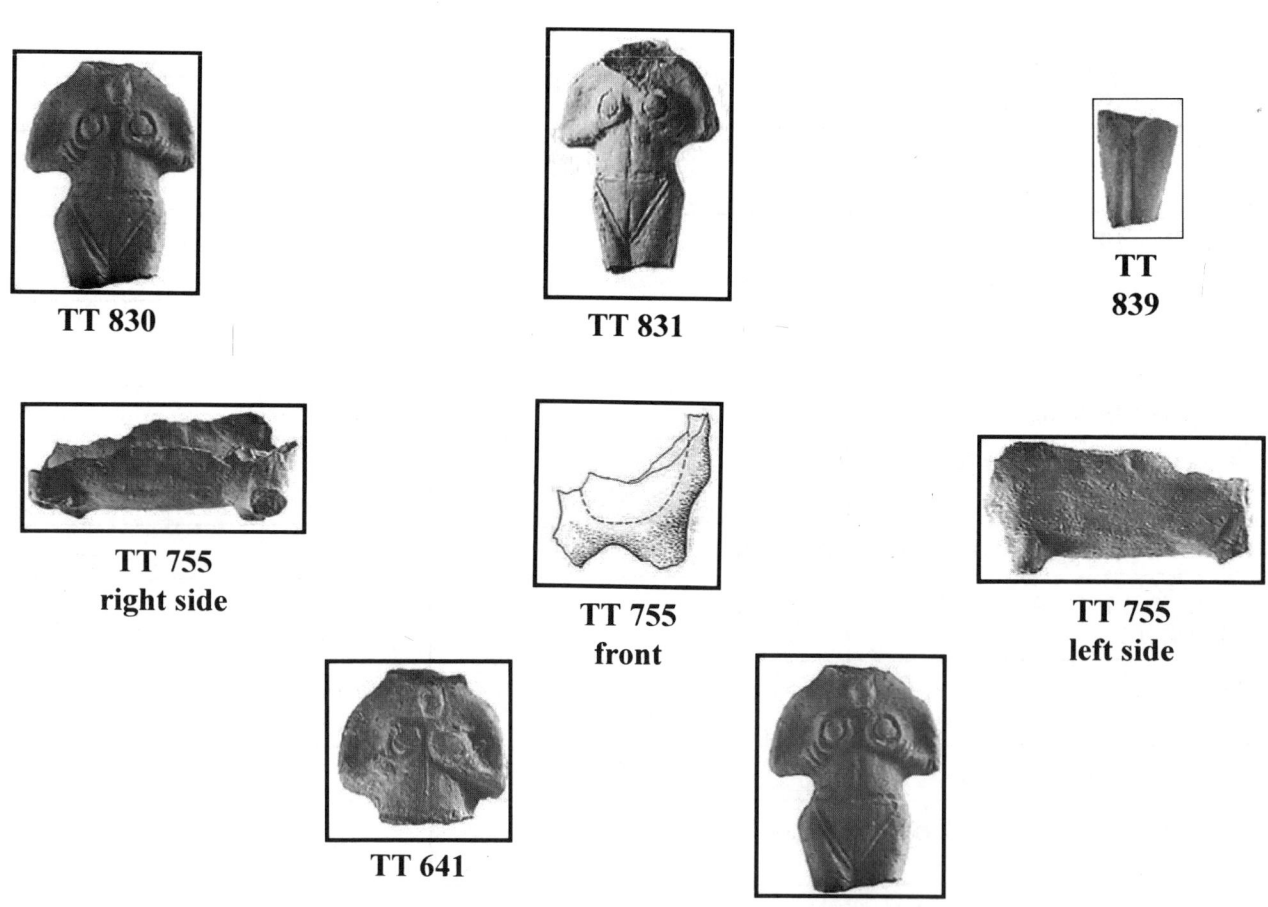

As is apparent from the thumbnails above, all of these figurines, with the exception of TT 755, are of the same type, a type which in Holland's typological scheme of Palestinian Iron Age baked clay figurines is classified as Type C: female plaque figurines in which both hands clutch the breasts (1977: 122). A composite description of this type, as represented in the specimens mentioned above would be that of a nude female, whose pubic triangle and cleft are emphasized. She is wearing bracelets on her ankles, a girdle of some sort that does not, however, cover her genitals (perhaps made of three strands of beads), and a "ball" necklace. The back of these figurines is nearly flat except for the hair which is in a single braid down the center of her back to the waist.

TT 755 belongs to Holland's Type H: hollow hand-modeled animal figurines that are not spouted (1977: 123). Under this type he includes the following sub-types: horses, horses with riders, birds, bovinae, horned family, and not classified. The majority of examples of this type come from coastal and northern Palestinian sites. Because TT 755 is only partially preserved, it is difficult to determine which of Holland's sub-types it represents. In the registered objects list it is described as a "bovine." Holland (1977: 125) observes, however, that the horse is represented more than any other animal in Iron Age figurines. If TT 755 represents a horse it may be an early Iron Age (period IB) example of the horse symbolism that appears in period IIB in TT 1540 and on the top level of TT 1500, the cultic stand.

Although it comes from a context (SW 2-7; locus 24, basket 42) that is not assuredly, but probably to be dated to the early Iron Age, we include TT 94 here because of its unique nature. The locus in which TT 94 was found was in a trial trench between wall L 16 and the west balk in SW 2-7, a locus that contained mixed potsherds dating from Late Bronze through Iron II, with some Abbasid sherds as well. It is a fragment of a nude female figurine with one, three-dimensional leg, that is appliqued to a fragment of a cylindrical stand that had a diameter of ca. 18 cm. Parts of four small rectangular fenestrations show on the fragment that is about 6.1 x 7.5 cm. in size. There are traces of a red slip on the figurine.

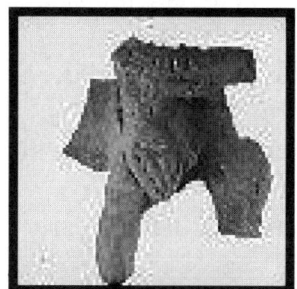

TT 94 (front)
[note fenestrations on bottom and upper rt.]

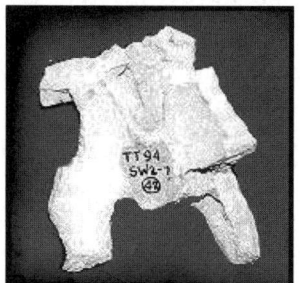

TT 94 (back)
[note fenestrations on bottom and upper lt.]

The low number of figurines found in the period IIB cultic structure is not unusual. Gilmour (1995: 244, 245), observes that figurines are present in small numbers at two high probability cultic sites, Beth Shean (one in the Northern Temple and three in the Southern Temple) and Tell Qasile Stratum XI. They also occur in small quantities at seven other early Iron Age cultic sites that Gilmour analyzes and evaluates as cultic sites.

While figurines had some cultic identity, they are most often found in non-cultic contexts. Gilmour suggests that the fact that the vast majority of clay female figurines are found in non-cultic areas "must provide strong support for the interpretation of this particular type of figurine as personal charms or talismans owned by individuals for private use" (1995: 245).

TT 1486

TT 1486 is a plaque-type female figurine of the same type as discussed above, that was found in SW 2-8 (156.292). It is 8 cm. long and represents a nude female torso from neck to the knees, with hands clasped over the breasts and the pubic triangle and cleft emphasized. It has a single braid in the back and is made of pink-tan ware. This type of figurine, represented from other periods in the cultic structure, typically has a "ball" necklace and bracelets on the ankles.

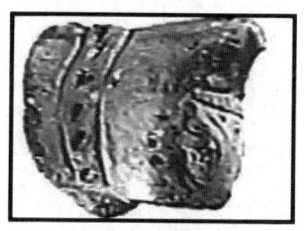

TT 1540 (side view)

TT 1540 (front view)

TT 1540 may be related to the iconography of the cult stand TT 1500, especially if one accepts Taylor's (1993: 24-37) interpretation of the quadruped below the winged sun disk on the top register of the stand as a horse, given the prominence of horses in relation to a cult involving the sun. TT 1540 is a horse head figurine spout, with some mane marks visible. It is made of gray wadi clay with a tan slip. It has botanical, basalt, and micro-fossil inclusions. It is 6 cm. long and has a diameter of 5.2 cm.

TT 1842 is the only other period IIB figurine from the cultic structure. It is a fragment of a human figurine, probably female, but a fragment representing the knees to the ankles only. It appears to be from the same type of figurine as represented in the plaque-type female figurines discussed above.

TT 1842

IV.D.3 Mold

TT 100 is a ceramic mold measuring 7.3 x 18.6 cm. that was found in SW 2-7 in a period IIB context, L 27 (basket 49), which was the area adjoining the south balk of L 26, the area east of wall 16 and south of wall 15—room 1 of the cultic structure where so many objects appear to have been stored. The mold apparently was designed to produce in quantity representations of a female who is nude except for an elaborate headdress, a belt, and bracelets on both wrists and ankles. Hillers (1970) considered the mold to be for the purpose of producing cheap sacred objects connected with private cult, with folk religion. The female is holding a disc over her left breast with both hands. The vulva, navel, and one exposed breast are depicted with a small, circular indentation in all three cases. The object produced by the mold would be in high relief on the front and flat on the back, as is apparent in the plaster casting from the mold. The rear of the mold is semi-circular with incised lines running both horizontally and vertically. The combination of the shape of the back of the mold, together with the incised lines, may have been to facilitate holding it in the palm of one's hand while pressing the substance to be molded into the hollow on the front of the mold. The purpose of the incised line may have been to prevent the mold's slipping in one's

Rear of TT 100 (approximately ½ size)

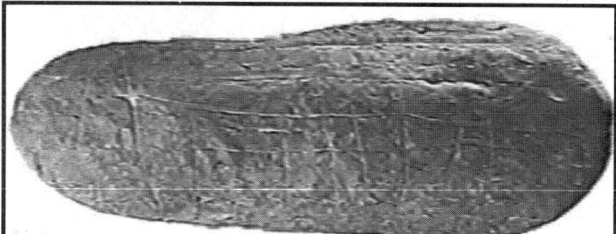

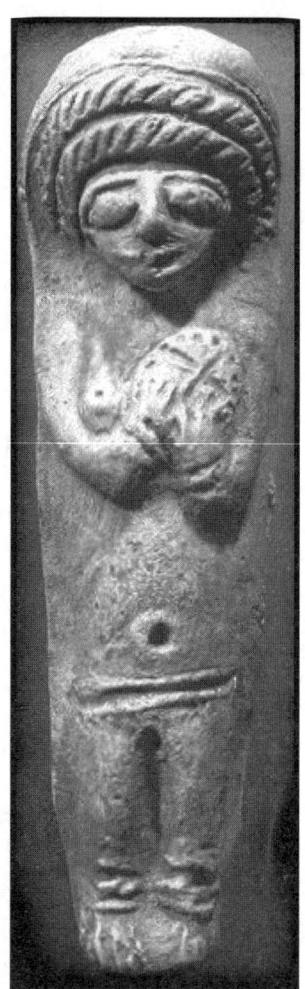

A plaster casting from TT 100

hand. While the actual mold has not been available for inspection, the author has seen a plaster casting from the mold and photographs and drawings of it.

Pritchard (1943), more than twenty years before the discovery of TT 100, devised a classification system for a corpus of nearly 300 small figurines and plaques depicting nude females. He divided them into eight types, of which only about 5% were assigned to his Type V, "Figurine Holding Disc," the category to which TT 100 would belong. Pritchard, however, made no attempt to identify what these females were holding. The controversy as to what the object represents, however, began before Pritchard and has not receded. That controversy has existed at least since figurines of this type were discovered in L 2081 at Megiddo. May commented on this as early as 1935:

> A vexatious issue is the identification of the disks held by some of the female figurines. . . . Are they tambourines or cakes? The writer is tempted to affirm that sometimes one, sometimes the other, is intended; for while sometimes the object is obviously a tambourine, in other instances it is held in a position not suitable for a tambourine and at times is too small and crude and may represent a cake. There is, of course, no conclusive evidence (May 1935: 32).

In a more recent study of a different sub-type of disc-holding female figurines that takes the Taanach specimen into consideration, Meyers (1987: 118) observes that scholars' attaching labels to the disc has brought confusion to the discussion of disc-holding female figurines. It has been labeled as a sun disc (Amiran 1967) and a plate (Van Buren 1930). With express reference to TT 100, the disc has been identified as a musical instrument (Hillers 1970) or as a cake or round loaf (Lapp 1964). In an attempt to bring clarity to the discussion about the identity of the disk, Meyers (1987) divides Pritchard's Type V into two groups and describes some of the critical differences between them. One group, to which TT 100 belongs, consists of nude or partially nude females. Their fingers are represented individually, and the discs they are holding are often marked with pebble-like impressions or scalloped borders, as is TT 100 (see figure 16, which is a detail of the disc and the female's hand holding it). Most of them wear elaborate headdresses, as does TT 100. The discs are positioned parallel to the body, pressed against the left breast, as is the disc in TT 100.

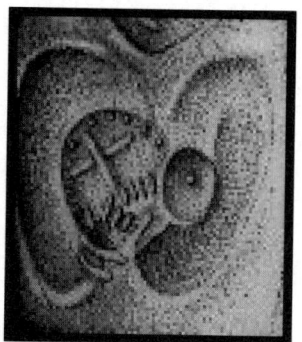

Figure 16: Detail of female's hand holding disc in drawing of TT 100

By contrast, the second group of disc-holding terra cottas under Pritchard's Type V depicts women who are clothed with gently flared, almost cylindrical skirts. Their headdresses, probably their own hair, consist of simple loose or loosely-braided tresses. Their fingers are not individually modeled. Finally, what Meyers (1987: 120) regards as the most important distinction involves the discs themselves. Unlike those of the group to which TT 100 belongs, in this case the discs are held at right angles to the body, or nearly so. The discs of this group are undecorated, except for a thin ridge that appears around the circumference of most examples. The identification of the disc of this second group seems certain, as does the human rather than the divine identity of the female holding it. The object is a frame-drum, not a tambourine, since none of the discs in this group are decorated with any objects resembling the metal discs that are set into the rim of a tambourine. Furthermore, tambourines are usually played by shaking them or by hitting them with the knuckles; neither gesture is suggested by the rendering of the arms and hands of the women represented in this group. Thus, while Meyers does not specifically identify the disc in TT 100 as bread or a cake, her discussion of the characteristics of the two types of disc-holding females appears to rule out the identification of it as tambourine or frame-drum.

The disc in TT 100 is decorated with seven small perforations on the part of its rim that is exposed (as is evident in figure 16). The surface of the disk is also marked with an incised, off-center

X-shaped mark. Goodenough (1956: 62-76) discusses the depiction of bread or cakes as "round objects" in Jewish art and in its Greco-Roman period and Near Eastern antecedents. While he does not document a "round object" that is decorated like TT 100, many of the "round objects" he discusses are clearly loaves of bread or cakes (the two are indistinguishable). In other cases in the Near East, "round objects" represented the solar disc, but Goodenough adds:

> It is probably with the double meaning of sun and bread that this became the form of Egyptian ceremonial cakes for burial offerings. . . . Sayce and Macalister may have been right in implying that the "round objects" on jar handles and images came into primitive Canaanite syncretism from Egypt (1956: 66).

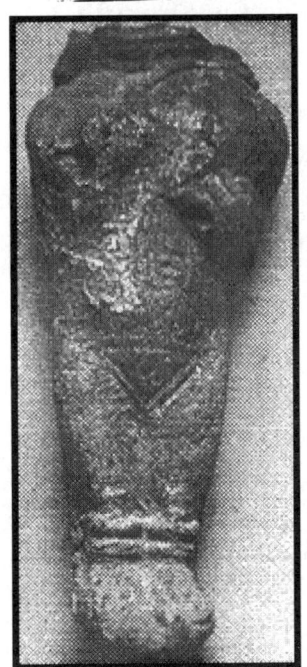

Megiddo 36.958 (front view)

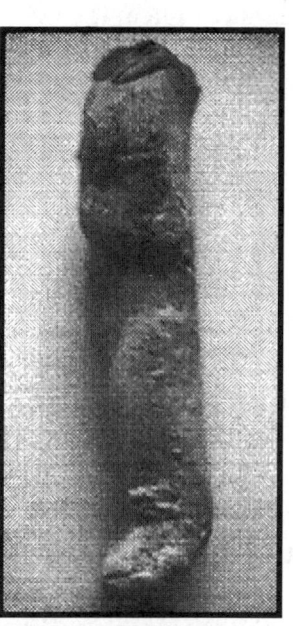

Megiddo 36.958 (side view)

There are several contemporary figurines from neighboring Megiddo made from molds resembling TT 100. One of these is 36.958, a near contemporary of TT 100, which was found in the Stratum IV filling but probably belongs to stratum V (L R9=lime floor 1693). This casting is made of brown ware, with a grey core and a red slip. It is 12.1 cm. tall, but is missing its head, so it may have been made from a mold approximately the same size as TT 100. The right breast is exposed and pierced, as it is in TT 100. The disk is held over the left breast and, as in TT 100, the fingers of the hand holding the disc are fully molded. The Megiddo 36.958 casting also has bracelets on wrists and ankles and an obscure girdle. In the Megiddo example, the disc is being held in both the female's hands (although the right hand has been broken off), as in TT 100. The navel and pubic area areas in the Megiddo 36.958 are treated differently, however, than in TT 100, as is the disc. The high-relief front and the flat back of Megiddo 36.958 suggest that it may have been made from a mold similar to TT 100.

One of the striking facts about TT 100 is that not a single casting made from it was found in the Taanach excavations. There are two possible explanations for this: (1) no clay castings made from TT 100 survived in the archaeological record for some reason (which seems unlikely); or (2) castings from TT 100 were made of a substance that was perishable and thus did not survive as part of the archaeological record. It is the opinion of this author that the absence of clay castings from TT 100 strengthens the suggestion that the disc held was a loaf of bread or cake. TT 100 was used to make cakes of flour and oil, representing Asherah or Astarte holding a cake, which were then offered up as a cereal offering, perhaps on the cooking hearth in room 2 of the cultic structure. This explanation combines both "official" and popular ritual practice and helps make sense of the assemblage of artifacts and structures that includes TT 100 together with basin 75 (used for the production of relatively small quantities of olive oil), the hearth in room 2, and the several grinding stones that were used to process flour. There are numerous references in priestly biblical traditions to a cereal offering (מנחה), which consisted of flour mixed with olive oil (Ex 29:2, 23, 40; Lev 2:1, 2, 4; Num 7 (passim), etc.). Although the proportion of flour and oil in cereal offerings probably varied (due in part to agricultural yields), olive oil, because of its combustible properties, was probably always a principal ingredient. Given the variability of grain yields, the number of such cakes offered may have been another way of monitoring the carrying capacity of the agricultural system in any given season. As mentioned above in part IV.A., following a biblical recipe for ingredients in the cereal offering of two parts flour to one part olive oil, Stager performed a replication experiment in which he mixed the flour and the oil into a paste and formed it into cakes. When placed over a gas flame these cakes ignited readily and burned until the cakes were reduced to a charred mass of solid, but brittle residue (Stager and Wolff 100). In the "official" religious ritual of ancient Israel, as reflected in the biblical book of Leviticus, flour was presented in the form of cakes: "When you present a grain offering baked in the oven, it shall be of choice flour: unleavened cakes mixed with oil, or unleavened wafers spread with oil" (Lev 2:4). As an expression of a prophetic critique of popular religious practice, there are two references in Jeremiah that are relevant here: "The children gather wood, the fathers kindle fire, and the women knead dough, to make cakes for the queen of heaven; and they pour out drink offerings to other gods, to provoke me to anger" (7:18). "And the women said, 'Indeed we will go on making offerings to the queen of heaven and pouring out libations to her; do you think that we made cakes for her, marked with her image, and poured out libations to her without our husbands' being involved?'" (44:19). In these condemnations of popular rituals the prophet refers to the practice of making burnt cereal offerings and libations to "the queen of heaven."

While the precise identification of "the queen of heaven" is in doubt, Susan Ackerman has suggested that she is "a syncretistic deity whose character incorporates aspects of West Semitic Astarte and East Semitic Ištar" (1989: 116, 117). The references to "the queen of heaven" in Jeremiah (which are the only ones in the Hebrew Bible) suggest that this otherwise unidentified deity was worshiped in Judah during the 7th and 6th centuries BCE, and possibly earlier and in Israel as well. It is particularly significant that Jeremiah 44:19 mentions that the cakes made as offerings to the queen of heaven were "marked with her image," suggesting something like the cakes that would have been produced by TT 100. Biblical scholars who have commented on the biblical cult of the queen of heaven generally have been puzzled by the phrase "cakes in her image" (להעצבה). Ackerman (1989:

115, 116) observes that those who hold that the queen of heaven is Ishtar often explain "in her image" by pointing to several clay molds found in the palace kitchen at Mari. These molds portray a nude female figure, so it has been suggested that the molds represent Ishtar, and that they were used to shape cakes baked in the image of the goddess. These cakes were then offered to Ishtar as part of her sacrificial cult (cf. Rast 1977: 171-174). It is probable that both TT 100 and TT 1500 with its symbols representing Asherah (which will be discussed below) were associated particularly with women's rituals, suggesting that popular religion offered an alternative to the marginal status of women in the official Yahwistic cult as represented in the Hebrew Bible

IV.D.4 Cultic Stands

Without a doubt, cultic stand TT 1500 is the single artifact from Taanach that has received the most attention. It has appeared in numerous publications, is on the dust jacket of two recent books (J. Andrew Dearman, *Religion and Culture in Ancient Israel*. Peabody, MA: Hendrickson, 1992 and Mark S. Smith, *The Early History of God,* San Francisco: Harper Collins, 1990), and has been the subject of numerous scholarly articles. TT 1500 is, however, only one of three cultic stands found at Taanach in association with the cultic structure. Here, we shall provide only a brief description of these stands, their greater archaeological context in the ancient Near East, their archaeological context at Taanach, and references to some of the more important studies that have been done of them (principally of TT 1500).

Cultic stands have a long history in the ancient Near East that has been thoroughly documented by Meyers (1976: 57-93). In ancient Palestine their number increases significantly in the Late Bronze Age, but it is in the early Iron Age, and then especially in the Jezreel and Beth Shean valleys, that the numbers of three types of cult stands, cylindrical, box- or house-shaped, and the

Figure 17: Distribution of Early Iron Age Cult Stands by Type (after Gilmour 1995: Map 10). ○ = cylindrical; □ = box- or house-shaped; Δ = "Taanach Type"

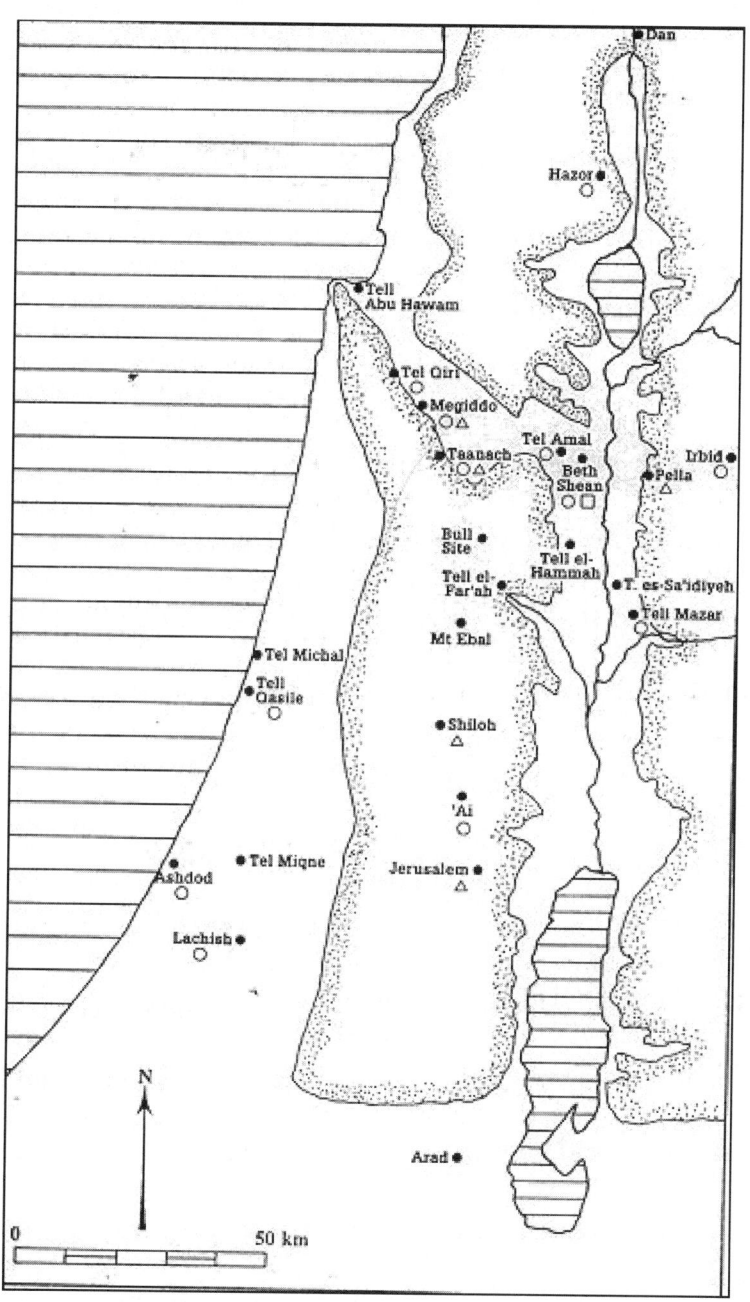

"Taanach type" reach a peak (Gilmour 1995: 227, cf. figure 17, adapted from Gilmour, map 10). By "Taanach-type" Gilmour means a kind of stand with multiple layers of iconographic decoration, with one layer on top of another. The cylindrical type of stand has a long history in the ancient Near East, with extant specimens dating back to at least the third millennium BCE. These cylindrical stands are depicted on Mesopotamian cylinder seals, usually in cultic contexts, being used for libations, as pots for trees, and possibly as burners with flames. As mentioned above, fenestrated stands appear already in the Chalcolithic period in Palestine. Within the three types there are also variations in decoration. By the early Iron Age fenestrations were oval, rectangular, or triangular in shape, plastic molding of different kinds was attached, animals and human figures appeared in some variety, and painted decorations ranging from a simple red slip or wash to elaborate bi-color, red and black painting appeared. While MB and LB stands were found almost exclusively in temple contexts, in Iron I they appear in a variety of contexts, including temples, secondary cult sites, and workshop areas. The appearance in the early Iron Age of box- or house-shaped stands and the "Taanach-type" stands appears to be restricted to sites in the Jezreel and Beth Shean valleys, except for two sherds from a possible square stand from Shiloh (Gilmour 1995: 232). "Taanach-type" stands, other than TT 1500 and Sellin's stand, have been found at Megiddo ("pottery shrines" 2985 and 1986; May 1935: pls. XIII, XIV, XV), at Pella, where a fragmentary stand of this type dated to an 11th-10th-century context (Potts 1985: 204; pl. XLII; 1992: 98-100; pl. 71), and probably at Shiloh and Jerusalem (Gilmour 1995: 233).

While the definite function of cult stands in the early Iron Age is unclear, they most likely were not "incense stands," as they are so often referred to in archaeological literature. The use of incense in antiquity is documented in the Bible, in ancient Near Eastern, and classical sources, all of which testify to its rarity and costliness as an import from the southern and southeastern end of the Arabian peninsula and from what is today the northern end of Somalia. As Haran (1993: 240) observes, "It is hardly imaginable that in biblical times people in Judah and Israel took the trouble to erect altars in a variety of places in order to burn incense brought from distant southern Arabia upon them." In other words, the burning of incense would be totally unrelated to the regional ecology, and would have little meaning as the stuff of sacrifice for the bulk of the population. Haran (1993) has examined some 39 so-called "incense stands" from the Iron Age and found no remains of organic material or traces of burning on them. The conclusion seems clear—these cult stands were not altars for burning at all, let alone burning incense. He suggests that three main kinds of offerings could have been offered on these cult stands: meat, liquid (i.e., libations), and grain offerings. In addition to the use of these stands for presenting offerings, they could have served as holders for other objects or as stands for lamps (Meyers 1976: 77).

Sellin reports the discovery of the stand found during his excavations in the following manner:

Eight m. southeast of the press [Basin 75] I was to make the find which was probably the most important of the whole first excavation. At first a portion of a winged animal's body of thick clay was found, then at a distance of 2 m. were scattered animal heads, human heads, etc., 36 pieces in all. After the area had been completely searched began the reconstruction, which yielded an almost complete product: with the help of cement an ancient incense altar rose before our eyes . . . which to date is probably the only one of its kind. It was exactly 90 cm. high, the four sides at the bottom each 45 cm. long, the walls were 5-2 ½ cm. thick (Hillers 1962: 63).

According to Sellin's description, the find spot of the stand would have been near or perhaps slightly south of Silo 16 in SW 1-7 (cf. Figure 3 in Part III above). Since Sellin's report included no stratigraphic information, however, there is no way of stratigraphically relating this stand to other artifacts and structures from the cultic structure. The decorative features of the stand, and the fact that it was found in the general area of SW 1-7, make it likely, however, that it was connected with the cultic structure.

The cult stand found by the Lapp expedition in 1968 (TT 1500) was found in the lower part of Cistern 69 (cf. Figure 3 in Part III above) within the bounds of the cultic structure (Lapp 1969: 42-44). Due to the soft layer of silt beneath it, the stand fragments survived the ten-meter-fall down the cistern shaft and the subsequent deluge of collapsed bedrock. On the basis of associated pottery, this stand was in use during period IIB. This stand, like Sellin's, was almost certainly associated with the cultic structure.

A third stand, TT 1830, badly damaged and less elaborate than the other two, also was found in Cistern 69 (Rast 1978: 36, fig. 54). Unlike Sellin's stand and TT 1500 this one is not one of

Gilmour's "Taanach-type" stands but a cylindrical one. Its top is not preserved. It has two rows of down-turned tabs each protruding from a ridge. The ridges are placed one below the other with the lower ridge serving as a shoulder as the vessel gradually narrows from this shoulder to the top. There are two loop handles below the second row of tabs. There is a third ridge below the handles, just above a plain, cylindrical base. Other than the tabs, this cult stand is undecorated.

One of the most through and recent studies of the stands found by Sellin and Lapp, with a detailed discussion of their construction, composition, iconography, and relevant parallels, is that of Pirhiya Beck (1994). Other substantive discussions of TT 1500 include Dever (1990: 135-137); Hestrin (1987); Lapp (1969b); and Taylor (1993: 24-37).

The front and both sides of the Sellin stand, which is now housed in the Istanbul Museum, are pictured in figure 18 (adapted from Beck 1994: 353). This stand, which is 90 cm. tall and has a square base that measured 45 cm. tapers to a basin on its top. On its sides are five pairs of winged sphinxes, one on top of the other. On the right side, which is more poorly preserved

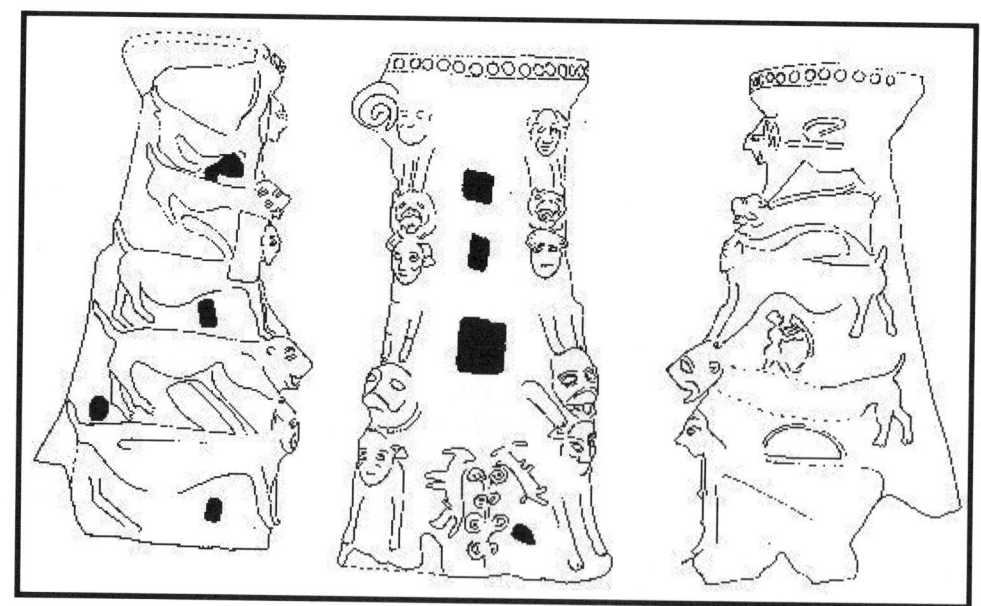

Figure 18: Front and sides of Sellin's stand (after Beck 1994)

than the left, between the lioness in the second level from the bottom and the sphinx in the third level, a person holding a serpent is depicted. A volute appears on the top left side. On the front side of the stand there are rectangular fenestrations on the second, third and fourth levels from the bottom, and two oval ones on the bottom level, the left one of which is damaged . Fenestrations also appear on the left side, with small rectangular ones on the first level and above the lioness on the second level, a round one behind the lioness on the second level, and an irregular one between the figures on the fourth and fifth level. A stylized tree with four volute-shaped branches (the tree of life?) appears in the center of the front on the bottom level, with two animals, ibexes or goats, standing upright, facing the tree on either side. While Beck nowhere represents the rear of Sellin's stand, she reports that there is a window (of undescribed shape) in its center and a larger square fenestration in the lower part of the back (1994: 355). She reports no soot remains on the stand.

TT 1500, like Sellin's stand, is also square with multiple levels topped by a basin which, also resembling Sellin's stand, is decorated on all but the back side with a row of applied button-like discs. A different scene appears on each level, and TT 1500's iconography resembles, in part, that of Sellin's stand. The three lower registers each contain a pair of lions or sphinxes arranged so that their heads and forelegs are modeled on the front and their bodies are shown in a striding position on the sides of the stand. The sides of the top level have winged griffins, which unlike the creatures on the lower level, are fully represented.

There is a large rectangular fenestration on the front of the stand on the second level and irregular ones to the front, rear, and between the legs of the animal on the top level. The fenestrations

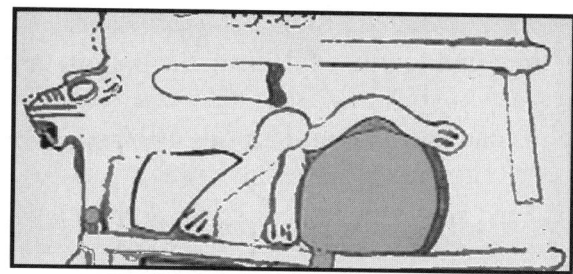

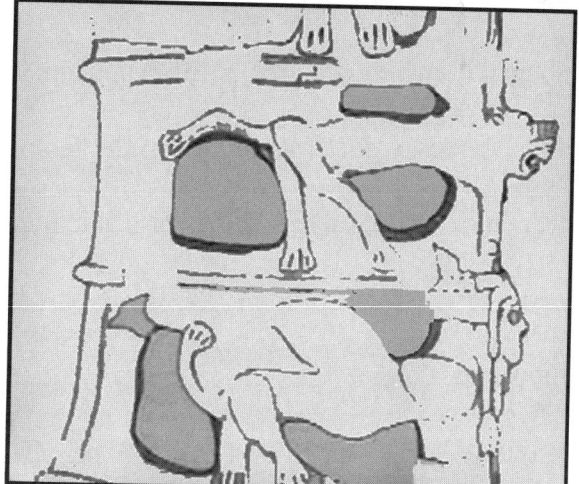

Figure 19: Drawings of Right Side (top) and Left Side (bottom) of TT 1500 Showing Fenestrations

on the sides are irregular in shape and between the creatures' legs, above or below their bodies (cf. figure 19). There is also a large, rectangular window in the center of the back, which is opposite the one on the second level and extends above it.

As is apparent in figure 20 below, a different scene appears on each level on the stand's front. We offer here a brief description of each level,

TT 1500: First or Bottom Level

beginning with the bottom one, level one. The bottom level displays a frontally-facing nude female who grasps the ears of lionesses on either side of her with her fully-molded fingers. She has an over-sized head, applied eyes, and a coiffure that extends above the line marking the upper limit of the level, accentuating her importance as dominating the lionesses. There is an incised circle of unknown significance between the female and the lioness to her left.

The second level depicts winged sphinxes or cherubim with female heads with hairdos having inward-turning curls at their tips. Between the two is a large rectangular fenestration.

TT 1500: Second Level

TT 1500: Third Level

The third level from the bottom pictures a stylized tree with three pairs of voluted branches. It is flanked by goats standing on their hind legs nibbling on the tree. The goats are themselves flanked by lionesses that are essentially the same as those on the bottom level. The scene of the animals flanking the tree closely resembles the scene on the bottom level of Sellin's stand.

Figure 20: TT 1500 (view from front right)

An animal, whose identification has been disputed, appears in the center of the fourth or top level. Above this animal, there is a winged sun disc. Flanking the animal is a pair of volutes, probably representing free-standing columns. Beneath these volutes are two grooved stele-like small objects with bent tops that were interpreted by Lapp as cult stands (1969: 2). They might also represent the trunks of trees that have been cut down, or even snakes (Hestrin 1987: 76).

TT 1500: Fourth or Top Level

In the case of "Taanach-type" cult stands, it seems clear that the fenestrations represent actual windows, not smoke vents. These stands with their square shapes are probably models of shrines, with the superimposed levels representing either different floors of a multi-storied building, or the artist's attempt to depict different aspects of a one-story structure. This understanding of what the stands represent as a whole provides an important clue for the interpretation of their individual elements. E.g., Taylor (1993: 28) correctly observes that the free-standing voluted columns on the top tier, which flank the quadruped and sun-disk on the top level, are clearly architectural elements that establish a pattern for understanding the lions or cherubim in the same flanking position in the tiers below. They should also be seen as architectural features of temple architecture, an interpretation clearly supported by the fact that both free-standing pillars and large animal orthostats characteristically mark entrances in Syro-Palestinian temple architecture. The pillars, lionesses and sphinxes on the various levels of TT 1500 thus mark the entrance to shrines "housing" the deities represented in the central space on the front of the stand: the nude female holding the lions on the bottom level, the open space or fenestration on the second level, the goats and tree on the third level, and the quadruped and solar disc on the top level. Beck (1994: 358) concludes that the Taanach stands functioned "either as pedestals for statues of the goddess, or perhaps, as the house of the deity," basing her argument on analogies from Anatolian seal impressions.

Controversy about TT 1500's iconography has centered mainly on the identification of the deities represented on the stand. One argument calls for symmetry in seeing two deities represented on the stand, with levels one and three representing one deity and levels two and four representing the other. While there has been consensus that level one with the nude female and level three with the goats and tree represent Asherah, the identity of the deity represented on the second and fourth levels has been more controversial.

The animal on the fourth or top level has been identified as either a calf (Lapp 1969:2; Hestrin 1987; Beck 1994) or a colt (Glock 1975; Taylor 1993). If the animal is identified as a calf, it is intended to represent or is an attribute of the Canaanite storm god Baal-Hadad, whose association with a bull is well attested in Near Eastern iconography. This interpretation would tend to support an identification of the stand as Canaanite. If, however, the animal is to be identified as a young horse, which seems to be more likely (cf. the discussion of Taylor 1993: 30-33; cf. also the description of the horse head figurine spout TT 1540 above), and the horse is coupled with the solar disc on the same level, the deity in question is identified as Yahweh. The association of a horse or horses in relation to a cult involving the sun is suggested in the Bible as part of the description of Josiah's reform program: "He removed the horses that the kings of Judah had dedicated to the sun, at the entrance to the house of the LORD, by the chamber of the eunuch Nathan-melech, which was in the precincts; then he burned the chariots of the sun with fire" (2 Ki 23:11). Taylor (1993: 31, n.2) adds, however, that even if the animal were identified as a calf, an association with Yahweh would not be ruled out, since Yahweh's animal symbols, especially in the northern kingdom, were calves. Taylor (1993) thus favors a symmetric interpretation of the stand in which there are two levels dedicated to one deity and two to another, in this case Asherah and Yahweh. This symmetric gestalt probably influences the idea that since the deity represented on level four is Yahweh, then the deity represented on level two must also be Yahweh. Taylor cites several reasons for supposing that the upper level is a cultic scene in which Yahweh is represented by the sun, ending with the observation (1933: 34): "...A final means of testing the interpretation of the top tier is offered by the griffin [there are griffins on either side of the top level], the animal chosen to complete the scene with horse, temple entrance and sun. Are the mythological connotations associated with the griffin consistent with the view that the top tier represents a deity with a solar character?" He then proceeds to offer an overview of the griffin in ancient Near East iconography and concludes by saying (1993: 36): "If my interpretation is correct that the top tier portrays a deity with solar traits, a griffin is precisely the kind of animal that we might expect to complete the cult scene on the top tier."

Given the argument from symmetry that suggests that Yahweh is also represented on the second tier, how should the iconography of this tier be understood. This level is the exception to the pattern displayed on the other three levels, in that there is no figurative representation between the two architectural features. Beck, who is otherwise quite comprehensive in her discussion of the stand's iconography says nothing about the gap in the center of the second level, except for the simple comment: "A different scene appears on each register, except for the second-from-bottom tier, which is hollowed out" (1994: 355). In this lack of comment on any significance of this hole, she is joined by most who have commented on the stand. In other words, whereas there is something in the center of the other three levels, in level two there is nothing—the deity one expects to find between the two cherubim is conspicuously absent. Taylor (1993: 29) adds: "Moreover, as a close examination of the stand reveals, the central deity is not just missing, but in fact was never portrayed." In other words, the fenestration between the sphinxes on the second level is part of the stand's original design and execution, not a hole that was carved out at a later point. The question then is this: Does this nothing represent nothing, or does this nothing represent something? Hestrin (1987: 71) suggests that the nothing is precisely that, a hole flanked by guardian sphinxes. While she acknowledges that "One scholar . . . says the empty space represents the new Israelite concept of the incorporeal God Yahweh," she interprets this rectangular fenestration on the front of the stand as "the entrance to the shrine"(1991: 58). She adds: "The figure of a deity may have been placed inside the hollow stand to be seen through the opening (1987: 71). Taylor (1993: 29), on the other hand, thinks that this particular nothing represents something—an "invisible" deity posed between two cherubim. From this assertion it is only a short leap to the conclusion that the deity in question is none other than "Yahweh of hosts who dwells on (or between, over) the cherubim" (1 Sam 4:4; 6:2; Isa 37:16), which Dever labels Taylor's "one original—and excellent idea" (1995: 43).

There has been a greater consensus when it comes to the identification of the deity represented on the first and third levels, but there is not total agreement. Kantor (1962: 100) points out that in ancient Near Eastern iconography the lion (or lioness) is associated with goddesses of fertility, such as Ishtar and Kybele. Beck (1994: 368) observes that in Mesopotamia, however, these female deities are always clothed, not nude as on level one of TT 1500. According to Dever (1984: 33) there is growing evidence that the female figure here is none other than the Mother Goddess Asherah, one of whose principal epithets was "the Lion Lady." Dever adds that in Egypt, she is often portrayed nude, astride a lion. From Palestine, Dever (1990: 136) notes several 12th-11th century BCE arrowheads from el-Khadr which bear a Proto-Canaanite inscription with names of archers and a dedication to "the Lion Lady." As additional evidence connecting Asherah to lions, Dever (1990:36) mentions a perfectly preserved skull of a lioness found on the altar of an early Iron I temple at Jaffa and several lion-headed masks and drinking vessels representing lions that were found in a contemporary temple at nearby Tell Qasile. Yadin, however, associated the skull from Jaffa and the lion rhyta from Tell Qasile with Resheph, whom he identified with Nergal. The lioness, according to him, is "the Lion Lady," the companion of Resheph (1985). Hestrin (1987: 71) has suggested that "the naked female here represents the mother goddess Asherah, accompanied by two lions."

The figures of the sacred tree and the goats on the third level and the nude female with the lionesses on the first level are two common ways of representing Asherah. Especially significant in this light is a sacred tree flanked by two goats in conjunction with a lion painted on a pithos from Kuntillet 'Ajrûd, since Asherah is mentioned in an inscription on the same vessel (Dever 1984). Taylor (1993: 29) observes that "although the sacred tree (clearly Asherah) and the nude female might independently represent different deities (in the case of the nude female, Astarte, for example), the only deity likely to be represented as *both* nude female and sacred tree, in each case flanked by virtually identical pairs of lionesses, is Asherah." Beck (1994: 360) points out that the stands from Taanach are the only known ones from Palestine on which lions and winged sphinxes appear together. Similarly, although horned animals on either side of a tree is a familiar, venerable motif in the ancient Near East, such a grouping is quite rare on cult stands and is probably not accidental. Although this motif is generally seen to be related to fertility, it has no direct link to any specific deity. The fact that an entire level is devoted to the tree and goats emphasizes the importance of this motif.

Is this stand Canaanite or Israelite? If one follows the suggestion made above that levels one and three represent one deity while levels two and four represent another, then the stand represents a male-female pair of deities. Those who understand the animal on the uppermost level to be a calf, a symbol of the Canaanite storm god Baal-Hadad, would see the stand as a Canaanite artifact (cf. Beck 1994 and Hestrin 1987, 1991). In Beck's case (1994), while she discusses most of the stand's details, she never discusses why she calls this creature a calf rather than a young horse. Those who would see Baal-Hadad as the male deity to whom this stand is dedicated characteristically do not comment specifically on the significance of the large rectangular fenestration between the sphinxes on the second level of the stand, but consider it together with the other fenestrations (cf. Beck 1994 and Hestrin 1987).

Those who see the animal on the top level as a horse and the accompanying solar disk imagery on the top level as representing Yahweh (cf. Taylor 1993) thus label the stand as an Israelite artifact. They also see the large rectangular opening between the cherubim on the second level as an iconographic attempt to symbolize a deity who cannot be imaged (thus Taylor 1993 and Dever 1995). Thus, a pair of major Israelite deities is portrayed on TT 1500: Asherah, personified both as a nude female holding lionesses, and in the form of a sacred tree, and Yahweh, represented with horse-solar disc imagery and a void that stands in place of an image of a deity who cannot be imaged. Taylor's conclusion seems to be a reasonable one (1993: 36, 37):

> In my judgment . . . the iconography of the Taanach cult stand is an early monarchic representation of Yahweh and Asherah, the form of whom is conveyed alternatively by means of an invisible deity posed between two cherubim, classical imagery of the temple in biblical tradition, and by means of the sun along with one of the horses that drew it in a chariot, imagery reluctantly admitted by DH (but to its credit) for the temple of Yahweh in 2 Kgs 23.11. . . . The cult stand . . . apparently bears witness to yet another cult of Yahweh and

Asherah, this time at a large-scale cultic center which perhaps functioned under (at least indirect) royal administrative sanction during the reign of Solomon.

IV.D.5 Loom Weights

As mentioned at the beginning of this section on ceramic objects, ceramic loom weights from the cultic structure will be published in a forthcoming volume by Glenda Friend. Friend's volume will provide a complete catalogue of loom weights and will also analyze other objects involved with textile production, including bone spatulas used as pattern weaving tools. Here we offer only a brief discussion of the place of loom weights in the cultic structure. The ceramic loom weights included among the registered objects from the four "squares" of the cultic structure from period IIB are TT 107 and TT 388. TT 107 is from SW 2-7, L 27, basket 49. This locus was one rich with artifacts (cf. Appendix B), including TT 100, the ceramic figurine mold. L 27 was an area adjoining the south balk of L 26, which was the area east of wall L 16 and south of wall L 15. TT 388 was also found in SW 2-7, L 61, baskets 219-222. Locus 61 was a dark hard clay stratum covering the entire southern extension of room 1 of the cultic structure. TT 388 consisted of fragments of about 48 loom weights of two types. One type (a) had a diameter of ca. 9.2 cm. and a height of 6.7 cm. The other type (b) had a diameter of ca. 10.2 cm. and a height of ca. 5.3 cm. These loom weights were found in association with the multi-handled krater TT 489, as is evident in the photograph of the

Figure 21: SW 2-7 (looking N) with TT 489 in situ near Wall 16 on the left

excavation of SW 2-7 shown in figure 21. Although the loom weights appear to be inside TT 489, this was not the case, but is the result of the angle at which the photograph (which appeared in Lapp 1964: 28, fig. 13) was taken. This cache of loom weights was actually found on the far side of the krater, which was empty except for a small juglet (TT 458, Rast 1978: pl. 40:9). Since the krater was found broken, however, the loom weights originally may have been inside it. Figure 22 shows the loom weights of TT 388 after restoration. In commenting on this hoard of loom weights, Lapp (1969: 47) said that most of them "were unbaked, extremely fragile, and could hardly have served as loomweights." He

Figure 22: TT 388 (restored)

suggests an alternative interpretation: "Groups of these 'doughnuts' may have been used to absorb heat in connection with the burning of sacrifices. Perhaps the large eight-handled crater in which the Taanach hoard was found was also associated with sacrifice." Lapp's suggestion does not account, however, for the fact that they were unbaked and very fragile. Gilmour (1995: 261) also favors a sacrificial interpretation, suggesting that the loom weights were synecdochical offerings, perhaps to obtain the favor of the deity. His interpretation sees them as real or at least "virtual" loom weights. The most straightforward interpretation appears to be one that sees these objects as loom weights that were used with a vertical warp-weighted loom, as suggested by Sheffer (1981).

It is obvious that loom weights are indicators of weaving and other textile-related enterprises. While they are indicators of cottage industry, they are also known in cultic contexts. Gilmour (1995: 260-261) catalogues several such contexts that are both geographically and chronologically close to the cultic structure at Taanach. At Beth Shean, four loom weights were found in the Northern Temple, one from the Southern Temple and two from rooms between the two temples. A single loom weight came from the first phase of Temple 30 at Tell Abu Hawam, and 26 were found in stratum X at Tell Qasile, 15 from room 204 and 11 from building 225, both of which were in the area to the south of the temple. There were 20 unbaked and unperforated loom weights found in room 350 at Tel Miqne-Ekron Field IV, which was adjacent to rooms B and C where cultic activity was indicated. At Tel Miqne-Ekron the loom weights were found alongside olive presses, as is the case in the cultic structure at Taanach, if one sees basin 75 as an olive press. Commenting on this juxtaposition of loom weights and olive presses, Gitin, the excavator of Tel Miqne-Ekron, suggests that the buildings that housed the presses were used on a seasonal basis both for olive oil production and textile manufacture. The presses were used for about four months of the year for pressing olives, with textile production taking place in the buildings for the other eight months of the year (Gitin 1990: 38). Ceramic loom weights have also been found in an Iron II cultic context at Kuntillet ʿAjrûd, as well as more than 100 examples of linen and woolen textiles (Meshel 1978: 16, 17).

While it is not possible to determine precisely what kind of activity related to the cult is indicated by the presence of loom weights and other objects related to textile manufacture, they do suggest some relationship between textile manufacture and the cult. Perhaps the presence of loom weights, spindle whorls, and other textile-related artifacts indicates their use for the making of special priestly garments. Given the Asherah symbolism on cult stand TT 1500, it is tempting to connect the loom weights and other apparatus connected with textile production to biblical references that relate textile manufacture and the Asherah cult. One such reference is found in the account of Josiah's cultic reforms in 2 Kings 23: 7: "He broke down the houses of the male temple prostitutes that were in the house of the LORD, where the women did weaving for Asherah." The Hebrew text of this verse is problematic, as reflected in the Septuagint translation. The Hebrew Masoretic text reads *'ōrĕgôt šām băttîm,* [the women] "wove there houses/temples," which appears to be nonsensical, unless one sees the word *băttîm* to mean something like tent-shrines. The Septuagint, however, reads *chettiin* for *băttîm,* and the Lucianic recension reads *stolas*, both of which are Greek terms meaning "garment" or "tunic." The Hebrew term the Greek versions translate may have been *kĕtōnet*, "tunic," "priestly garment." Dever (1994: 150) asks:

> "Which is the superior text? Is it the LXX, in which case one might argue that the "vestments" were being woven for a wooden or metal image of the goddess . . . ? Or is it the MT, in which case woven tent shrines—perhaps in the ancient (and modern) Near Eastern desert tradition—were being erected as pavilions for Asherah in the Temple precincts (alongside the *băttîm* of the "consecrated ones" in the same verse)?

In any case, the cultic connection of textile manufacture seems clear and is another illustration of the crossover between the domestic and cultic.

IV.D.6 Miscellaneous Ceramic Objects

In this section dealing with miscellaneous ceramic objects, most are common and occur in such small numbers as to add little to our understanding of the Iron Age cultic structure. None of these miscellaneous objects can be dated with certainty to period IIB. We catalog and briefly describe most of these objects here without interpretive comment.

TT 646, and TT 1089 are common ceramic spindle whorls, and thus are related to the kind of textile production discussed above. TT 646 was found in SW 2-7 (87.299) and dates to period IIA. It has a diameter of 2.8 cm. and a height of 1.2 cm. TT 1089 was found in SW 2-8 (89.198) with pottery dating to MB IIC and LB I. It has a diameter of 2.5 cm. and a height of 1.2 cm. TT 421 (SW 2-7, 69.256), although shaped like a spindle whorl, given its size (diameter of 1.9 cm; thickness of 3 mm.), is probably some kind of fastener. The pottery associated with it dated from LB through Persian.

TT 423, TT 531, and TT 549 are small, flat, ceramic disks. TT 423 is from SW 2-7 (68.251), and was associated with pottery dating to ± 900 BCE. It measures 8.5 cm. in diameter and 2.5 cm. in height. It has an impression of fabric on it, so it may have been connected in some way with textile manufacture. TT 531 is a perforated ceramic disc that is 4.2 cm. in diameter with a thickness of 8 mm. It has been broken and mended. It was found in SW 2-8 (8.40) in association with mixed pottery dating from MB IIC all the way the the 7th century BCE. TT 549 is also a perforated disc, closely resembling TT 531. Its diameter is 3.4-3.6 cm. with a thickness of ca. 7 mm. It was also found in SW 2-8, locus 8, but in a basket (50) in which the pottery dated from the 10th -7th centuries BCE. The function of such discs is unknown.

There are two jar stoppers in this miscellany of ceramic objects: TT 538 and TT 548. TT 538 is an irregularly shaped jar stopper with a diameter of 4-5 cm. and a height of ca. 3 cm. that was found in SW 2-8 (9.43), associated with pottery dating from the 10th-7th centuries BCE. TT 548 is a chipped, unbaked jar stopper that was found in the same place as TT 549 (SW 2-8, 8.50).

TT 965 is an unusual object that deserves additional consideration. Even though it was not found in one of the four "squares" of the cultic structure, but in the one that abuts SW 1-8 to the south, i.e., SW 1-9, because of its proximity it may have been associated with the cultic structure in period IA or period IB (the pottery of this locus, 92.168, is mixed, containing sherds from MB IIC, LB I, and down through the 12th century BCE). As the two graphics indicate, TT 965 is an approximately life-size human ear (ca. 3.3 x 6.5 cm.), that was possibly part of a mask similar to one found in a LB shrine at Hazor (Yadin 1958-1961: I, pl. 163; II, pl.183). The fragment is finished off behind

TT 965

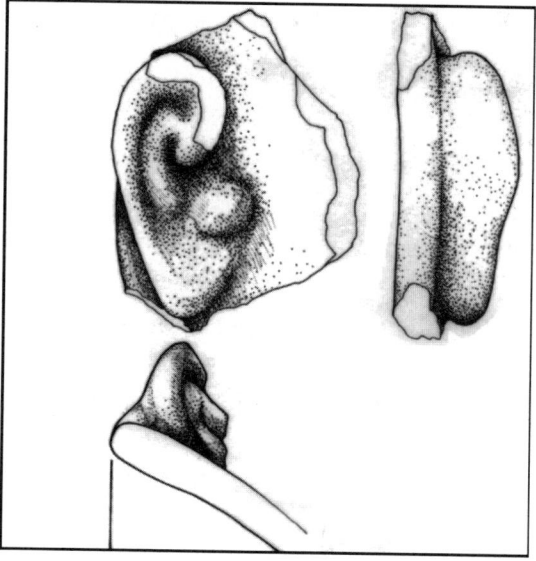

TT 965 (3 views)

the ear like the rim of a vessel, with marks made by the potter on the wheel running inside the length of the ear. The ware is orange-red in color. Because of the fragmentary nature of this object, it is impossible to determine whether it was, in fact, part of a mask that was used in the cult, worn either by a human being or placed on the image of a deity. It is, however, difficult to imagine what other use such an object might have had.

TT 1045 and TT 1126 are wheels. TT 1045 is made of coarse ware, and is broken and incomplete. It was found in SW 1-7 (125.288), in association with late MB IIC potsherds. It has a diameter of ca. 6.8 cm., is 2.1 cm. thick at the hub and has broken edges. TT 1126 is a wheel of about the same size as TT 1045, having a diameter of ca. 6 cm. Like TT 1045 it is made of coarse ware. TT 1126 was found in SW 2-8 (77.185) with LB I and 13th century potsherd.

TT 1308 is a ceramic button with two holes. It has a diameter of 3 cm. and a thickness of 5 mm. It shows considerable wear. It was found in SW 1-8 (53.186) with EB and MB IIC potsherds.

TT 1848 and TT 1849 are blank rectangular unfired "tablets." The dimensions of TT 1848 are 8.5 x 6.5 x 2.5 cm. It has one surface smoothed and was found in SW 2-7 (74.270) with 10th-7th century and Abbasid pottery. TT 1849 was also found in SW 2-7 (87.296) and probably dates to period IIA. It is about the same size as TT 1848, measuring 8-8.5 x 5.5 x 2 cm. These objects are called "tablets" because they may have been used as tablets to be written on with ink and stylus.

IV.D.7 Seal Impression

We conclude this discussion of ceramic objects with mention of TT 566, which is an X-shaped seal impression on a jar handle having a diameter of 1.3 cm. It was found in SW 1-8 (8.44) in a locus with pottery dating  from MB IIC through the 7th century BCE. The jar handle on which the impression is made, however, typologically resembles Iron I jars. While we refer

TT 566

the reader to the forthcoming work of Othmar Keel that was mentioned at the beginning of this section for a comprehensive discussion of all seal impressions from Taanach, we reproduce here, without comment, the one seal impression found in the context of the cultic structure.

Part IV.E Calcite Items

There are only two calcite objects that were found in the four "squares" comprising the cultic structure. Neither of them, however, date to period IIB.

TT 644 was found in SW 1-8 (19.84) in association with mixed pottery from MB IIC, LB I, LB II, LB IIB, and Iron I to the 8th century BCE. Stratigraphically it can probably be assigned to period IA. It is a calcite unguentarium stand in which some traces of material on its grinding surface were still present when it was excavated. It has a height of 3.2 cm. and is 3.5 cm. in diameter at its base, flaring to a diameter of 4.4 cm. at its rim. As the name given this object implies, it was used for cosmetic preparation.

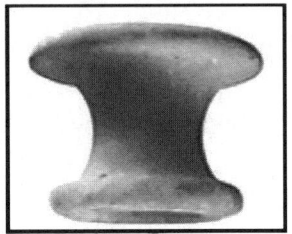

TT 644

TT 1869 was also found in SW 2-8 (20.64). While there are no datable potsherds recorded in association with TT 1869, stratigraphically it can be assigned to period IB. It is a vessel sherd with a diameter of ca. 6 cm., a height of 6 cm. and a thickness of 1 cm.

Part IV.F Shells

Two collections of shells were found in the four "squares" of the cultic structure: TT 728 and TT 1699. Neither of them came from period IIB. TT 728, found in SW 2-8 (27.90) dates to period IB and consists of 11 complete shell lips and one fragment that were found inside cooking pot TT 753 as part of a cache with other objects TT 643 and TT 701-729, which are as follows:

TT 643	Basalt rubbing stone
TT 701	Scarab with hunting scene
TT 702	Dome-shaped bone stamp seal picturing a gazelle and scorpion
TT 703	Bronze bead or whorl*
TT 704	Fluted bronze bead*
TT 705	Bronze trapezoidal weight*
TT 706	Bronze trapezoidal weight*
TT 707	Bronze turtle weight*
TT 708	Bronze baboon weight*
TT 709	Bronze frog weight*
TT 710	Bronze dome weight*
TT 711	Bronze dome weight*
TT 712	Bronze dome weight*
TT 713	Loaf-shaped bronze weight*
TT 714	Loaf-shaped bronze weight*
TT 715	Loaf-shaped bronze weight*
TT 716	Rectangular bloodstone bar weight**
TT 717	Serpentine dome weight**
TT 718	Serpentine biconical weight**
TT 719	Cylindrical black stone weight**
TT 720	Biconical black stone weight**
TT 721	Ovoid black stone weight**
TT 722	Oval black stone weight** (corroded to bronze fragment)
TT 723	Pear-shaped black stone weight**
TT 724	Egg-shaped serpentine weight**
TT 725	Cylindrical serpentine weight**
TT 726	Iron chisel with three smooth stones (perhaps weights) corroded to it*
TT 727	Canine (?) incisor corroded to TT 726
TT 729	49 Miscellaneous burnishing stones**

* See section IV.H below   ** See section IV.C.1 above

While this section is concerned with shells, and although the seals found in TT 753 will be discussed more thoroughly in the forthcoming work by Othmar Keel on glyptics, we mention here the two seals that were part of the cache of objects that included TT 728, the shells.

TT 701

TT 701 is a scarab with a hunting scene. This bone scarab has detailed dung beetle markings on its back and sides, and is 9 mm. wide, 11 mm. long, and has a height of 8 mm. As is evident in the photograph, it has a hole bored through it lengthwise for a cord. It pictures two animals with a hunter wielding a bow facing them. Because they are rendered in "stick figure" style with little detail, it is impossible to determine what kind of animals are represented. It is also impossible to say whether the artist's intention was to represent an actual hunting scene or a contest scene, which was so common in ancient Near Eastern glyptic art, in which humans or superhumans were pitted against animals and monsters, representing the eternal conflict between civilization and those forces that would destroy it. The scene carved on this scarab from Taanach should be compared to that on a seal from Lachish pictured in Tuffnell and Harding (1953: pl. 43:49) and one from Beth Shan in James (1966: fig. 109:8).

While TT 701 may or may not be an attempt to represent a mythic scene, TT 702 almost certainly is, combining as it does two creatures that do not constitute a natural pair. When

TT 702

found it was lime-encrusted and its surface was chipped. TT 702 is a dome-shaped bone stamp seal that pictures a nursing gazelle and a scorpion.

This seal had a height of 18 mm. and a diameter of 15 mm. at its base. As is apparent from our photograph, it had a hole bored through its length for the attachment of a cord. It has close early Iron Age parallels from both Megiddo and Lachish. The Megiddo example, 36.1891 is a brown sandstone dome seal that was found in Level VA (Lamon and Shipton 1939: Pl. 69.22, 40). It is a deeply-incised rendering of a gazelle standing, facing to the left, with its head turned backwards toward the scorpion on the right side of the seal.

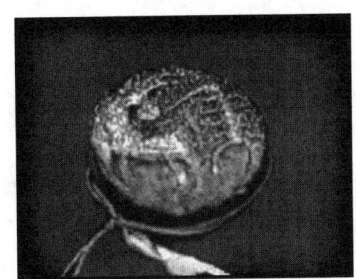
Megiddo Stamp Seal 36.1891

There are two seals from Lachish that should also be considered as parallels to the Taanach example (Tuffnell and Harding 1953: Pl. 44: 91, 92). In no. 91 from Lachish, a scorpion and gazelle are clearly represented, but in no. 92, the scorpion appears to have become a plant. In both cases, a hole has been bored through the seals for the insertion of a cord.

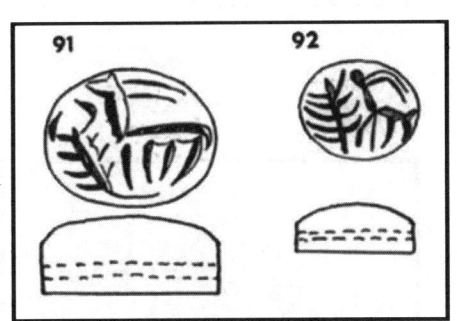
Lachish stamp seals 91 and 92 (after Tuffnell and Harding 1953: Pl. 44: 91,92)

What is the mythological significance of the scorpion? In the Egyptian pantheon, Selket was a scorpion-goddess, represented as a beautiful woman with a scorpion posed on her head. Her creature, the scorpion, struck death to the wicked, but she was also prayed to to save the lives of innocent people stung by scorpions. Selket was also viewed as a helper of women in childbirth. Although the scorpion appears elsewhere in the ancient Near East, e.g. on Babylonian boundary stones, its precise symbolism remains unclear.

Shell lips such as those in TT 728 have been the subject of a study by Reese (1989), who catalogs the occurrence of the lips of *Phalium* shells in archaeological sites in the Near East and Mediterranean Basin. The thickened outer, palatal, or apertural lips of two species of Mediterranean helmet shells (Superfamily Tonnacea, Family Cassidae, Genus *Phalium*), often water-worn, were collected on beaches, often pierced with a hole, and used as ornaments. They have been found at the following archaeological sites: Jericho, Ghassul, En-Gedi, Hadidi, Beth Shan, Mari, Hancilar, and the Abri Pataud, where all examples were pierced with one hole except for one from pre-pottery Neolithic Jericho and Chalcolithic Ghassul (Reese 1989: 38). Lips as well as whole shells are also known from graves at Yiftah'el (unholed), Hadidi (both holed and unholed), Tawi (unholed) esh-Sharqi (unholed), and T. el-Far'ah (S.) (unholed), T. el-Far'ah (N.) (whole), Reidan (whole), T. es-Sa'idiyeh (whole), Kourion (whole), Amathus (whole), Paros (whole), Vroulia (whole), Kameiros (whole), and Patrizi (whole) (Reese 1989: 38). Reese also documents the presence of cassid lips and whole shells at several sanctuaries, including: En-Gedi, Beth Shan, Mari, Kourion, Kommos, Kition, Juktas, Syme, the Corycien cave, Lindos, and Paestum (1090: 38). Reese correctly concludes, concerning the presence of these shells: "Many of the *Phalium* are found far from the sea; and this, along

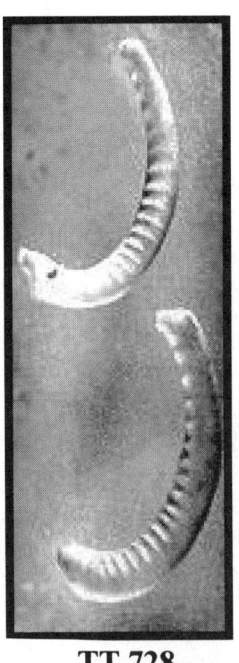

TT 728

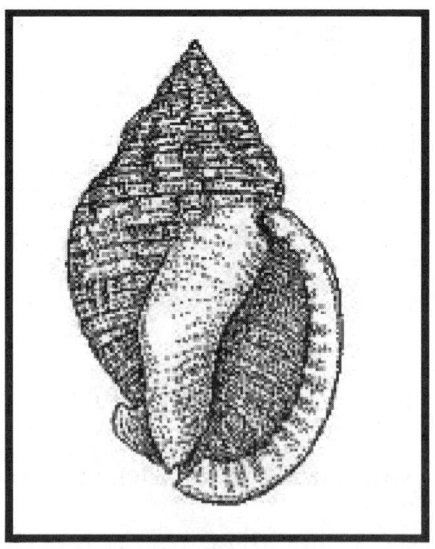

Phalium granulatum undulatum

with their presence in graves and sanctuaries, and their often modified condition, suggests that helmet shells were given special attention in the Near East and Mediterranean basin over a very long period of time."

TT 728 includes at least two shell lips, one of which (the upper one in the photograph) has clearly been pierced, from the species *Phalium granulatum uundulatum*, which were called "shell sticks" by Lapp (1967a: 34, 35, fig. 24; 1967b: 25-27). The two specimens from TT 727 pictured above beside the *Phalium* shell are ca. 6.5 cm. long.

Why might shells, especially *Phalium* shells, have been part of such an assemblage? While the evidence for the structure in area B under discussion having a cultic function in period IB is not as strong as in period IIB, the presence of these shells, and the assemblage of which they were a part, which contains several relatively valuable objects, at least suggests ownership by a person or group of relatively high status, who may have exercised some control functions that were located in a structure that, in a subsequent period, came to be used even more for cultic purposes. Meehl (1995: 152) believes that the shells may have been used in the manufacture of perfume.

The other group of shells from the "squares" comprising the cultic structure is registered as TT 1699. This collection of shells was found in SW 1-7 (194.423) on bedrock in a locus including pottery dating to EB II-EB III. There are 37 cockle shells in this group, 30 of which are small, six somewhat larger, and one that is completely worn smooth. All of them are perforated at the hinge, perhaps for stringing and use as jewelry.

Part IV.G Bone and Ivory Objects

The registered bone and ivory objects found in the four "squares" comprising the cultic structure include the following, with those from period IIB in boldface type:

TT 355	**bone spatula**
TT 397	**bone spatula**
TT 398	**bone spatula**
TT 420	bone spindle whorl
TT 591	bone inlay fragment (period IIA)
TT 601	bone button
TT 626	polished bone bead
TT 668	bone spindle (period IIA)
TT 727	canine (?) incisor (period IB; corroded to TT 726)
TT 788	bone spindle whorl (period IA)
TT 968	ivory inlay/plaque
TT 1016	bone button
TT 1031	worked astragalus*
TT 1109	bone inlay
TT 1114	bone whorl
TT 1129	bone spatula (period IA)
TT 1172	bone inlay
TT 1244	bone handle and haft
TT 1295	bone tool fragment
TT 1372	bone whorl
TT 1459	astragalus*
TT 1475	bone awl
TT 1502	ivory comb
TT 1653	bone whorl or button
TT 1655	**ivory rod/handle/spindle**
TT 1689	bone spatula or tool

* see section IV.B

Here we will categorize and provide brief descriptions of these objects, remembering that the bone spatulas and other objects related to textile production will be discussed in more depth in the forthcoming volume by Glenda Friend.

IV.G.1 Bone spatulas (TT 355, TT 397, TT 398, TT 1129, TT 1689 [?])

Three bone spatulas from the cultic structure date to period IIB: TT 355, TT 397, and TT 398. TT 355 was found in SW 2-7 (60.160). It is broken and incomplete, pointed at one end and round at the other (like TT 397, which is pictured below). Its measurements are 1.5 x 12.2 cm. TT 397 was also found in SW 2-7 (63.236). It was found complete, but broken into three pieces and charred. It length is 20.7 cm. and its width is 2.4 cm. TT 398 is a third spatula from period IIB that was found in SW 2-7 (57.228). When found it was broken into four pieces, leading to the suggestion that what is registered as one object may actually be parts of two spatulas. The four pieces together measured 14.5 x 2 cm. One piece was encrusted with a powdery substance when it was found. Its shape approximates that of the other two period IIB spatulas, being round at one end and pointed at the other. These three spatulas from the period IIB phase of the cultic structure, when taken together with the loom weights and other evidence, point to the fact that weaving went on in the cultic structure during period IIB.

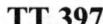

TT 397

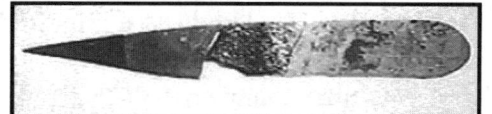

TT 398

One or maybe two other bone spatulas were found within the boundaries of the cultic structure: TT 1129 was found in SW 2-8 (44.143) with pottery from as early as MB IIC and as late as the 12th century BCE, and should stratigraphically be assigned to period IA. This example has a surface that is highly polished, but it is broken and incomplete. The fragment found measures 3.8 x 1.9 cm., and has a thickness of 1 mm. TT 1689 is a fragment of a bone spatula or tool that cannot be identified with any certainty. The fragment measured 5.8 x 1.8 cm., with a thickness of 3 mm. It was found in SW 1-7 (219.434) in connection with late EB II-early EB III potsherds.

IV.G.2 Spindle whorls (TT 420, TT 788, TT 1114, TT 1372, TT 1653)

Also associated with spinning and weaving are bone whorls. Five whorls appear in the registered objects list that were found in the area of the cultic structure, dating from different periods. TT 420 was found in SW 2-7 (69.256) in association with pottery dating from the LB through Persian periods. It has a height of 8 mm. and a diameter of 2.6 cm. TT 788 was also found in SW 2-7 (108.333) and belongs to period IA. It has a height of 5 mm. and a diameter of 2.9 cm. TT 1114 was found in SW 2-8 (94.208) in association with potsherds from MB IIC and LB I. Its height is 8 mm. and its diameter is 2 cm. TT 1372 was also found in SW 2-8 (138.268), in a locus with no datable pottery. It measures 7 mm. in height with a diameter of 3.2 cm. Finally, TT 1653 appears in the registered objects list as a "spindle whorl or button." While it resembles a whorl in its shape, its dimensions are quite different than the other whorls, measuring 2 cm. in height with a diameter of 4.2 cm. It was found in association with potsherds from MB IIC.

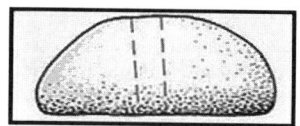
TT 1653

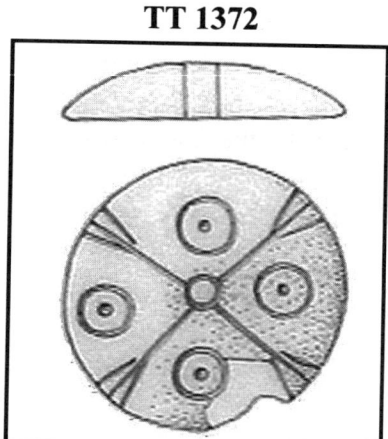
TT 1372

IV.G.3 Buttons (TT 601, TT 1016)

Two bone buttons are in the registered objects list for the four "squares" of the cultic structure: TT 601 and TT 1016. TT 601 was found in SW 2-7 (78:281) in association with pottery from the 12th-10th centuries BCE. It had scratch marks from its original shaping and polishing and measured 5 mm. in thickness with a diameter of 3.5 cm. TT 1016 was found in SW 1-7 (132.261) in a locus with pottery dated from as early as EB and as late as the 13th century BCE. Its diameter is 2.1 cm. and its thickness is 7 mm.

IV.G.4 Inlays (TT 591, TT 968, TT 1109, TT 1172)

TT 591 is an ivory inlay fragment belonging to period IIA that was found in SW 1-7 (46.90). This fragment has a length of 4 cm. and a thickness of ca. 2 mm. While the fragmentary nature of the object makes its identification uncertain, it appears to represent a palmetto or lotus. TT 968 is an ivory inlay or plaque with an Egyptian motif that was also found in SW 1-7 (121.246) in association with LB I pottery. It was broken, incomplete, and dark brown in color. It is 6.2 cm. long, varies in width from 2.9=3.6 cm., and has a thickness of 1-4 mm. Its back is unmarked. TT 1109 was found in SW 2-8 (91.201) with MB IIC and LB I potsherds. It was found in two pieces, both of which were incomplete. One piece measured 3.7 x 1.9 cm., with a thickness of ca. 1 mm.; the other was 2.5 cm. long and had a width of 9 mm. TT 1172 is another bone inlay from SW 2-8 (117.233), a locus with MB IIC pottery. It was also broken, incomplete, and discolored. It measures 7.6 cm. in

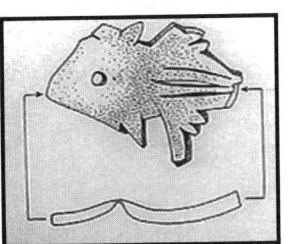
TT 591

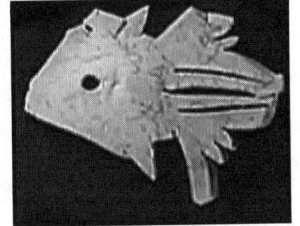

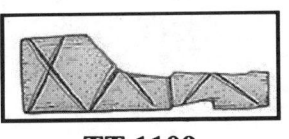
TT 1109

TT 1172

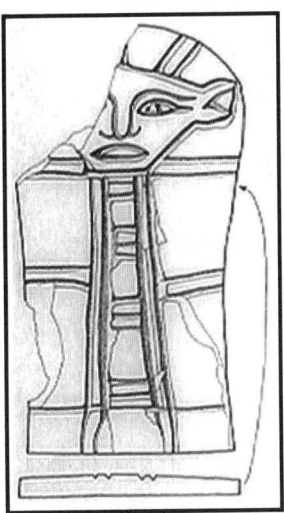
TT 968

length with a varying width of 1.2-1.5 cm. It is ca. 2 mm. in thickness.

None of these inlays date to period IIB, and thus do not have any direct relevance to our analysis of the early Iron Age cultic structure in that period. They do, however, as imported elite items, suggest that the structure or structures of which they were a part in the earlier period were the residence of an upper stratum of Taanach society.

IV.G.5 Miscellaneous Objects (TT 626, TT 688, TT 727, TT 1144, TT 1295, TT 1475, TT 1502, **TT 1655**)

To conclude this section on bone and ivory objects we include miscellaneous objects from the registered objects list. The first of these is TT 626, a polished bone bead with a length of 2.3 cm. and a diameter of 1.2 cm. It was found in SW 2-8 (21.84) with pottery dating from as early as MB IIC and as late as the 10th century BCE. TT 668 is a carved, broken, and incomplete spindle that resembles a similar object from Megiddo (Loud 1948: pl. 197: 8, 9). It was found in SW 2-7 (88.300) in a context with MB IIC and 11th century BCE pottery. Its length is 7.5 cm. and it has a diameter of 8 mm. TT 727 is a canine (?) incisor that was part of the period IB cache found in SW 2-8 (27.90) referred to in the previous section. It was found corroded to TT 726, an iron chisel. This tooth was ca. 3 cm. in length. TT 1244 is a bone handle and haft. The handle is broken into four pieces and has a diameter of ca. 2.5 cm. It was found in SW 1-7 (117.269) in a locus having no datable potsherds. TT 1295 is a broken fragment of what appears to be some kind of bone tool. Its

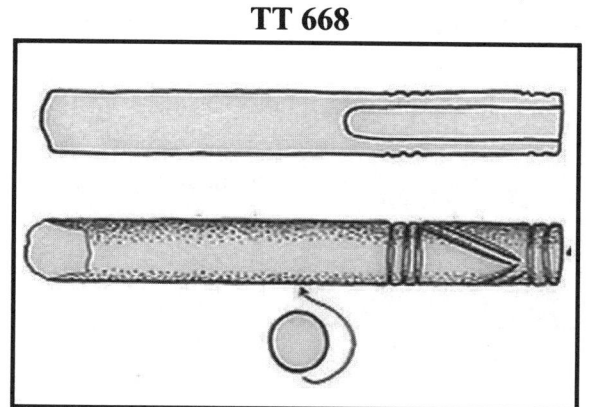

TT 668

find spot was SW 1-7 (147.357), where it was found with EB and MB IIC pottery. It measures 1.4 x 8 cm., with a thickness of 2 mm. TT1475 is a complete but broken bone awl that was found in SW 1-7 (197.415) with potsherds from EB III. It measures 13.8 cm. in length when mended. TT 1502 is a fragment of an ivory comb that was found in the same locus as TT 1475. It measures 3.5 x 6 cm., with a thickness of 2 mm.

The final object in this miscellany comes from period IIB. TT 1655 is a fragment of an ivory object that has been described as a rod, a handle, or a spindle. It was found in SW 2-8 (171.367) and measures 11 cm. in length with a diameter of 5.5 mm. Few ivory objects have been found from the early Iron Age and the presence of objects like TT 1655 in the cultic structure at Taanach at this time certainly represents a luxury item that was in the possession of some elite person or group.

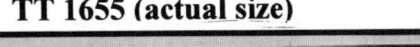

TT 1655 (actual size)

Part IV.H   Metal Objects

Numerous metal objects were found in the cultic structure, dating from various periods. Some of these objects were made of copper or bronze, while others were made of iron, both carburized and non-carburized. The metallurgical aspects of eleven iron objects from the cultic structure at Taanach have been the object of a study by Stech-Wheeler, Muhly, Maxwell-Hyslop and Maddin, in which they acknowledge that since many of the iron objects from Taanach are from stratified contexts, "They thus comprise one of the largest groups of closely datable iron artifacts from Palestine" (1981: 247). They add: "The largest group of iron artifacts comes from the two rooms which comprise the 'cultic building' (Area B, SW 2-7/8) and from the courtyard east of the building (SW 1-7)" (1981: 248). Stech-Wheeler et al. also offer an interpretation of Basin 75 (see above, part IV.A) on the basis of the iron objects found in its fill:

> The fill in the basin is stratified so the two iron artifacts found therein can be closely dated. . . . The iron artifacts from rooms 1 and 2 include three plowshares, two pointed ends of goads, two hoe-shaped plowshare scrapers, one knife blade, one sickle blade, one scythe blade and one sword blade. From the square in which the basin was found come a piece of scale armor, a chisel, a sword and a plowshare (TT 820); the last two objects were found in the basin in the black ash layer attributable to the late tenth century destruction. Preliminary examination of materials associated with metalworking from these three squares (including tuyères, a broken copper tool, copper spillage most likely from melting and casting operations, copper ore and corroded amorphous bits which may also be spillage) suggests that metallurgical activities were taking place there. These by-products of metalworking, the comprehensive nature of the iron finds (while many can be classified as agricultural or military, there are also an iron toggle pin and a fine piece of scale armor) and copper finds (a collection of elaborate weights, a bead and a tool) and the two unfinished iron objects from SW 1-7, when taken together, suggest that this area may have been in part a smith's work area, or at least a smith's storage area. The random nature of the iron finds and the lack of evidence for installations in which metallurgical procedures actually took place, may be interpreted as indications of the collection of broken or damaged artifacts for later repair" (1981: 249).

This author has argued elsewhere that in preindustrial societies, smiths had to be familiar with many technical procedures, the knowledge of which was handed down and guarded jealously from one generation to the next (Frick 1971, 1992). When smiths were among agriculturalists, as they were at Taanach, they probably held a prestigious position in society. A particular kind of religious lifestyle was one way in which smiths safeguarded their technical secrets and passed them down through endogamous family lines. Thus, the association of smiths with the cultic structure at Taanach is a logical one, with one social elite, metallurgists, living in close proximity to another, priests. We shall return to this association at the conclusion of this section.

While we will not set forth here a detailed metallurgical study of the metal objects, we will catalogue and categorize them. The following table lists and categorizes all metal objects that were registered by the Lapp excavations (with those dated to period IIB in boldface type and those studied by Stech-Wheeler et al. in italics) from the four "squares" of the cultic structure):

Type of Object	Registered Object Number
Armor Scales	*TT 408*, TT 497, *TT 602*, TT 1095, TT 1798, TT 1799
Arrowheads	**TT 409**, TT 600, TT 1028, TT 1095, TT1443
Blades	**TT 71**, TT 90, **TT 387**, *TT 1880*
Fibulae/Toggle Pins	TT 258, TT 259, TT 342, TT 1404
Nails	TT 44, TT 572, TT 1094
Needles/Pins	TT 671, TT 1131, TT 1154, TT 1192, TT 1195, TT 1210, TT 1227, TT 1659, TT 1685
Plowshare Points/Goads	***TT 91***, **TT 132**, ***TT 820***
Scythes/Sickle Blades	**TT 108**, *TT 322*
Spear Points	TT 1243, TT 1891
Weights	TT 705, TT 706, TT 707, TT 708, TT 709, TT 710, TT 711, TT 712, TT 713, TT 714, TT 715

Other Tools	TT 598, *TT 726*, TT 1030, TT 1215, T 1651, TT 1679, **TT 1879**
Miscellaneous	TT 703, TT 704, TT 1008, TT 1216, TT 1223, TT 1415, **TT 1478**, TT 1507

IV.H.1 Armor Scales

Five armor scales or amor scale fragments were found within the area of the cultic structure, two of which were examined by Stech-Wheeler et al. The five are: TT 408, TT 497, TT 602, TT 1798, TT 1799, with TT 408 and TT 602 having been studied by Stech-Wheeler. None of these armor scales date to period IIB.

TT 408 comes from SW 2-7 (66.243), a locus which was a pit in the midst of the southern extension of room 1. The associated pottery is indicated in the field books as simply being "Iron." TT 408 is an iron armor scale with two perforations. It is totally

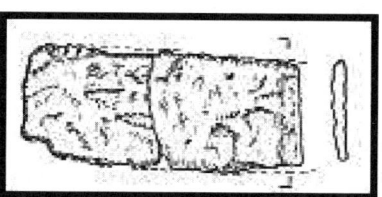
TT 408

corroded and measures 3.3 x 8.4 cm., with a thickness of 4 mm. Stech-Wheeler et al. (1981: 251) removed a sample 1.2 cm. long from the rounded end, performed various tests on it, and concluded that it was carburized and worked moderately after carburization.

TT 497 is a bronze armor scale that was found in SW 2-8 (1.2) in association with mixed pottery from LB I, Iron 1, Iron 2, Hellenistic, and Abbasid periods. It measures 2 x 6.2 cm., has a thickness of 1.5 cm., and was found corroded.

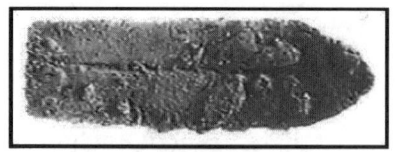
TT 497

TT 602

TT 602 is another iron armor scale. It was found in SW 1-7 (60.97) and stratigraphically can be assigned to period IIA (ca. 1020-960 BCE). It measured 3 x 6.3 cm., had a thickness of 2 mm.,

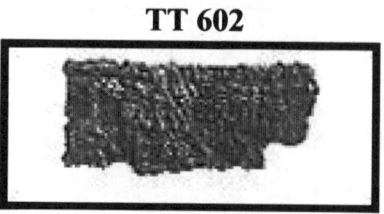

and was totally corroded. It was examined by Stech-Wheeler et al. (1981: 253), who removed a sample 1.1 cm. long from one end. No optical microphotographs of this scale were taken because no evidence for carburization was detected.

TT 1798 represents two bronze armor scales corroded together that were found in SW 2-7 (70-.260) in a locus with Iron 2, Persian, and Abbasid pottery. One scale is broken but complete; the other one corroded to it is incomplete. The dimensions of the two corroded together are 2.2 x 6.5 cm., with a thickness of 1.5 mm.

TT 1799 is a fragment of a bronze armor scale that was found in SW 2-7 (70.262) in association with Iron 2, Persian, and Abbasid potsherds. It measures 1.9 x 4.8 x 1.5 mm.

IV.H.2 Arrowheads

The registered object list has five arrowheads whose provenance is the area of the cultic structure. TT 409 is the sole example from period IIB. It is a leaf-shaped arrowhead with the

TT 409

tang missing. It was found in SW 2-7 (57.218) and was badly rusted. When found it was fused to TT 387, two iron blades that will be discussed below. It is 8.2 cm. in length, its width varies from 0.8-1.7 cm., and its thickness ranges from 0.5-0.6 cm. Stech-Wheeler et al. removed a sample 2.0 cm. long from the tip and concluded that no evidence of carburization could be perceived—it was simply forged from bloomery iron, i.e., the first product of the smelting of iron ore in charcoal, which is a relatively pure iron containing small amounts of slag (1981: 251, 252).

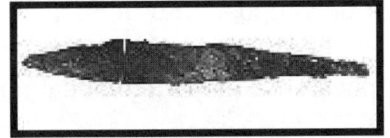
TT 600

TT 600 is a bronze arrowhead broken into four pieces that was found in SW 2-7 (78.281) in association with pottery dating to the 12th-10th centuries BCE. It measures 1.3 x 10.3 cm.

TT 1028 is another bronze arrowhead. It was found in SW 2-8 (76.178) with LB pottery. It was corroded and measured 1.7 x 8 cm.

TT 1095 is also a bronze arrowhead that was found slightly corroded in SW 1-8 (24.93) in a context with MB IIC pottery. It measures 1.7 x 7.3 cm.

TT 1443 is yet another bronze arrowhead that was found bent and corroded in SW 2-8 (21.285), in association with pottery dating to EB, MB IIC, and LB I. It measures 1.8 x 8 cm.

IV.H.3 Blades

A variety of blades were found in the area of the cultic structure. Four are found in the registered objects list: TT 71, TT 90, TT 387, TT 1880. Two of these date to period IIB (TT 71 and TT 387), and three of the four were examined by Stech-Wheeler et al. (TT 71, TT 387, and TT 1880).

TT 71 consists of three corroded tip and tang fragments, probably of two blades. One tip fragment is 15.5 cm. long, has a width that varies from 1.1-3.2 cm., and a thickness of 0.8-1.0 cm. Stech-Wheeler et al. (1981: 249) removed a sample 2.0 cm. in length from the tip end of this fragment and some evidence for the existence of a slight pearlite was found optically (pearlite is the product formed when austenite, a solid phase of carbon in iron, is more slowly cooled, causing the austenite to decompose into an array of alternate platelets of ferrite and cementite, which has a pearly appearance under an optical microscope). This small amount of pearlite may have been the result of an unsuccessful carburizing operation, or it may have been introduced unintentionally from the bloom or during forging. The second and third fragments were both 14 cm. long.

TT 90

TT 90 is an iron knife that was found in two pieces in SW 2-7 (27.45, 49) with pottery dated to ± 900 BCE. It was so badly corroded as to preclude any metallurgical analysis by Stech-Wheeler et al. Together, the two pieces were 24.8 cm. long and measured 5 cm. wide at the widest point.

TT 387 is a curious mix of several implements that have corroded together, probably one goad and two blades or share scrapers. This aggregate was found in SW 2-7 (57.228) with pottery dating to ± 900 BCE, and is stratigraphically assigned to period IIB. Stech-Wheeler et al. identify the two socketed, triangular, blades as share scrapers, which were probably hafted at

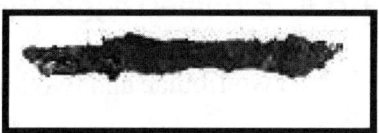
TT 387

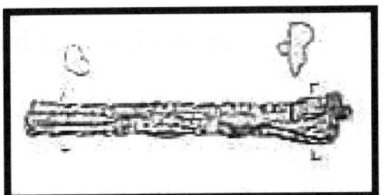

one end of the shaft of an animal goad and used to dislodge earth from plow points. They point out that the shape of the scrapers is similar to that of TT 986, a scraper that was found in SW 7-7 (2.8) in a mixed context. The earlier TT 387 is, however, larger, being 16 and 11 cm. in length as compared to 7.4 cm. for TT 986 (1981: 251). In their optical examination of this conglomerate, Stech-Wheeler et al. observed surviving carbides in the form of a network, and pearlite. The distribution of the pearlite indicates that carburization was fairly homogenous. They conclude that the object was forged into shape, carburized, and after carburization reforged at a temperature around 700° C., the final operation perhaps to sharpen an edge or to correct deformation that might have come about during carburization (1981: 251).

TT 1880 is an unfinished iron blade with tang that was found in SW 1-7 (93.1783), in a context in which no datable pottery was recorded. It has a veneer of surface corrosion and a metallic core. It measures .3-2.1 cm. in width, is 2.4 cm. long, and has a thickness that varies from .1-.7 cm. Stech-Wheeler et al. (1981: 252, 253) removed a sample 1.5 cm. long from the tip for their examination. They concluded that this unfinished object was deliberately carburized and worked to a certain extent after carburization, at temperatures around 700° C. The manufacturing process was interrupted before the tool was completed.

IV.H.4 Fibulae/Toggle Pins

Two fibulae and two toggle pins were found in the area of the cultic structure. None of them date to period IIB.

TT 258 is a bronze fibula that was found in SW 2-7 (46.110) in a context with 10th-6th century BCE, Persian, Hellenistic, and Abbasid pottery. It measures 25 x 41 mm.

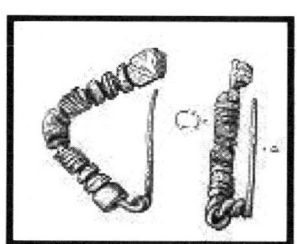
TT 258

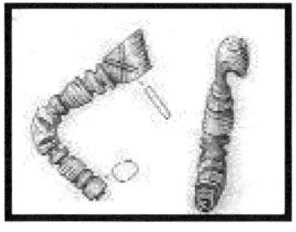
TT 259

TT 259 is also a bronze fibula with a badly-rusted iron pin that both closely resembles TT 258 and had the same find spot (SW 2-7, 46.110). It is, however, slightly larger than TT 258, measuring 32 x 51 mm. It is similar to an Iron Age example from Lachish (Tuffnell, Inge, and Harding 1953: Text, p. 93, pl. 56:37). These elaborately-made fibulae were probably used by members of the elite.

TT 342 is an iron toggle pin that was found rusted and broken into two pieces in SW 2-7 (61.185) in a locus with pottery dating to ± 900 BCE. It is 6.5 cm. long.

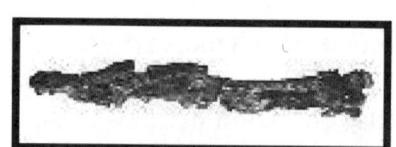
TT 342

TT 1404 is a bronze toggle pin that was broken, incomplete, and corroded. It was found in SW 2-8 (147.277) in a context showing pottery from EB and MB IIC. Like TT 342 it is 6.5 cm. long.

IV.H.5 Nails

Three nails or nail fragments were found in the area of the cultic structure: TT 44, TT 572, and TT 1094. TT 44 is an iron nail that was found in SW 2-7 (17.23) in association with Iron 2 and Abbasid pottery. It was corroded and measures 6.4 cm. in length with a head that was 2.33 cm. in diameter.

TT 572 is also a corroded iron nail, with a square shaft and a round head. It was found in SW 1-8 (7.42) in association with pottery dating from the 12th-7th centuries BCE and from the Persian period. It is 10.8 cm. long and its head has a diameter of ca. 2.3 cm.

The third nail found in the cultic structure area is TT 1094, a bronze nail (perhaps a toggle pin) that was found in SW 2-8 (93.204) with LB I and late 15th century BCE pottery. It is 17 cm. long and has a diameter of ca. 3 mm.

IV.H.6 Needles/Pins

Numerous needles, pins, or fragments thereof were found in the cultic structure's four "squares." None of them dates to period IIB. TT 671 is a bronze needle or pin that was found in SW 1-8 (15.71), broken into two pieces and incomplete. The pottery in this locus dates to MB IIC, LB, and Iron 1 and 2. It has a length of 6.8 cm.

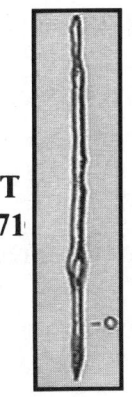

TT 671

TT 1131 is a bronze needle that was found in SW 2-8 (94.209) with pottery from MB IIC and LB I. It was broken, bent, encrusted, and the eye was incomplete. It is ca. 9 cm. long.

TT 11154 is a bronze pin that was found in two pieces in SW 2-7 (169.444) with potsherds dating from EB, MB IIC, and LB I. Its length is 7.8 cm.

TT 1192 is another bronze pin that was found in two pieces, corroded at its large end. Its find spot was SW 1-7 (167.326), where there was pottery from EB, and MB IIC-1500 BCE. It is 15 cm. in length.

TT 1195 is also a bronze pin that was found broken and incomplete, with both ends missing. It was found in SW 2-8 (104.255) in association with MB IIC and LB I potsherds. It is 6.5 cm. long.

TT 1210 is an incomplete, broken bronze needle or pin found in SW 1-7 (108.328) with MB IIC and LB I pottery. It is 8 cm. long.

TT 1227 is a corroded, incomplete bronze pin that was found in SW 1-8 (47.161). Associated pottery is from EB and MB IIC. It measures 10.5 cm. in length.

TT 1659 is an incomplete, bent bronze pin that originated in SW 2-7 (288.675). The pottery in this locus dates to EB III. The pin fragment is 6.2 cm. long and has a thickness of 2.5 mm.

TT 1685 is a bent bronze needle that is 10.2 cm. in length and has a thickness of 2.5 mm. It originated in SW 2-7 (290.687) in a locus with pottery dating to EB III and MB IIC.

IV.H.7 Plowshare Points/Goads

Three plowshare points, all from period IIB, come from the area of the cultic structure. Two of the three have been studied by Stech-Wheeler et al.. The terms "point" and "plowshare" can be used to denote the detachable iron-socketed implement of iron or bronze that was drawn over and attached to the wooden beam of the plow. As Stech-Wheeler et al. observe, confusion has arisen over the use of the term "plowshare," which is identified as the metal moldboard on a modern plow that is designed to throw the earth away from the furrow made by the point. There is no such device on primitive wooden plows where this function is performed by the wooden beam. The Taanach plow points were probably used with a type of plow that was designed for use on light soils in semiarid climatological zones. It was kept in position by a plowman pressing his foot on the heel of the wooden sole to which the point is fixed (Stech-Wheeler 1981: 250).

In examples from contemporary agriculture in developing nations, the shape of the plow point is either a beaked or a slightly curved type that is straight from socket to tip. The slightly curved type is used when a deeper furrow is desired. At Taanach, TT 91 is of the beaked type, while TT 820 is of the curved type. Stech-Wheeler et al. (1981: 250) catalog Iron Age plow points that are comparable to the Taanach examples.

TT 91 is a badly corroded plow point that was found broken into five pieces. Its find spot was SW 2-7 (27.49), a period IIB locus that was rich with artifacts, including extensive pottery and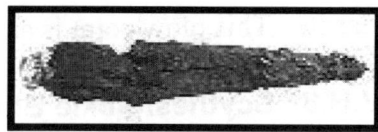

TT 91

TT 100, the ceramic figurine mold discussed above. In their examination of this plow point, Stech-Wheeler et al. (1981: 250) found no evidence of carbides. They concluded, therefore, that it is likely that TT 91 was simply forged from an iron bloom, and no attempt was made to carburize it. This point is ca. 5 cm. wide and 21 cm. long.

TT 132 is another iron plow point from SW 2-7 (28.47) from a period IIB locus. As found, it consisted of two points corroded together, both broken into two pieces. The tip of one piece was missing. One piece is 20.8 cm. long; the other is 20.6

TT 132

cm. This point should be compared to ones pictured in Tuffnell, Inge, and Harding 1953: pl. 177:2-5. It was too badly corroded for metallurgical analysis by Stech-Wheeler et al.

TT 820 was found in Basin 75 in SW 1-7 (75.160) in a period IIB locus. It was broken into four pieces and three small fragments, was incomplete, and badly corroded (cf. Lapp 1967a: fig. 18). Its length is estimated to have been ca. 24.2 cm. The shaft hole has a diameter of 1.7-3.1 cm.

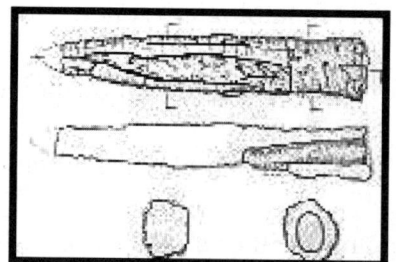

TT 820

Stech-Wheeler et al. (1981: 253) report that this plow point shows evidence of a regular carbide network and some surviving carbides. The carbide network exists in several places in the form of pearlite. This plow point is an object that has been deliberately and successfully carburized.

IV.H.8 Scythes/Sickle Blades

TT 108 is an iron scythe or sickle blade that was found corroded and in two pieces, but nearly complete. It was found in SW 2-7 (27.49), the artifact-rich locus from period IIB (room 1)

TT 108

that was mentioned above. It was too badly corroded to be the subject of metallurgical analysis by Stech-Wheeler et al. It is 11 cm. long.

TT 322 is also an iron sickle blade or scythe fragment that dates to period IIB. It was also found in SW 2-7 in two loci (27.85 and 61.164)—room 2. It was found in three pieces consisting of a tip or tang that was 2.3 cm. long, a middle section that was 4.1 x

TT 322

10.8 cm., and an end section that was 2.3 cm. It was corroded, but not so much as to preclude analysis by Stech-Wheeler et al. (1981: 250) who report that the evidence for manufacturing technique for this object comes only from SEM replication study, since little of the microstructure was visible in the optical microscope. They concluded that there was good evidence of deliberate carburization in the form of fine pearlite in a slightly worked condition. Therefore, it is apparent that the blade was forged into shape, carburized, and forged further after the carburizing treatment, probably at a temperature in the 600-650° range.

IV.H.9 Spear Points

TT 1243 is a bronze spear point that was found complete, except for a chip at the point. It was lime encrusted and slightly corroded. It was found in SW 2-8 (119.241 and 123.241) in association with pottery dating from MB IIC to 1500 BCE. The length of the blade is ca. 17.5 cm. and that of the haft ca. 9 cm. The diameter of the haft is 2.7 cm. and its thickness is 2 mm. The blade is 4.2 cm. wide at its widest point and is ca. 1.1 cm. thick.

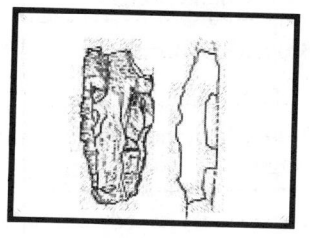

TT 1891

TT 1891 is a fragment of an iron spear point (?) that was found in SW 2-8 (51.40). Neither dimensions nor associated pottery for this object are recorded in the Lapp excavation records.

IV.H.10 Weights

One of the more unique metal object finds from the cultic structure is a collection of metal weights, TT 705-TT 715, all of which were found in SW 2-8 (27.90) and can be dated to period IB. This concentration of weights was part of a concentration of small finds (including the stone weights, shells and bone stamp seal TT 720 discussed above) found in cooking pot TT 753, which was found lying on plaster floor 28 (Lapp 1967a: 34, 35). Before proceeding to a discussion of individual weights, we offer a table, in the same format as the one in the discussion of stone weights in part IV.C.1 listing them all:

Metal Weights from SW 2-8, Locus 27, Basket 90

Registered Object No.	Size	Weight	Description
TT 705	L=16.5 mm.; base = 7 x 9 mm.	4 grams	Bronze trapezoidal weight
TT 706	L=11 mm.; base=5 x 9 mm.	3 grams	Bronze trapezoidal weight
TT 707	W=1.3 cm.; L=2.2 cm.; Th=6 mm.	6.2 grams	Bronze turtle weight
TT 708	H=3 cm.	41.6 grams	Bronze baboon weight
TT 709	W=8 mm.; L=1.5 cm.; Th=ca. 7 mm.	2.3 grams	Bronze frog weight
TT 710	H=8 mm.; D=10 mm.	4.3 grams	Bronze dome weight
TT 711	H=10 mm.; D=13 mm.	7 grams	Bronze dome weight
TT 712	H=15 mm.; D=15 mm.	19 grams	Bronze dome weight
TT 713	W-10 mm.; L=222 mm.; H=10 mm.	8.1 grams	Bronze loaf-shaped weight
TT 714	W=12 mm.; L=24 mm.; H=9 mm.	8.6 grams	Bronze loaf-shaped weight
TT 715	W=16 mm.; L=32 mm.; H=14 mm.	24.8 grams	Bronze loaf-shaped weight

In the following discussion, we assume, as suggested in part IV.C.1 above following Powell , that one should reckon with the possibility of a ± 5 percent variation (1997: 340) in weights. One norm for the shekel in ancient Israel, deducible from marked specimens recovered in Palestinian archaeological excavations, would put it in the 10 gram range. Using a ± 5 percent variation, this would suggest that a shekel weight would weigh 9.5-10.5 grams. Other norms for the shekel are elusive, but Powell (1992: 906) concludes, based on extant specimens, that there was a heavier norm that fluctuated from 11 to13 grams. In the Hebrew Bible there are several references to "the shekel of the sanctuary" as consisting of twenty gerahs (Exod 30:13, Lev 27:25, Num 3:47; 18:16, Ezek

45:12), where the *gerah* may represent the weight of a bean, probably a carob bean, which if a shekel weighed 10 grams would make the weight of a bean .5 gram.

TT 705 and TT 706 are bronze trapezoidal weights. The former weighs 4 grams, and the latter 3. A 4 gram weight could represent 1/3 of the heavier shekel while a 3 gram weight would be on the light side of 1/3 of a shekel of the lighter norm.

TT 705

TT 706

TT 707, TT 708, and TT 709 are bronze weights in the shape of animals—a turtle, baboon, and frog respectively. Why these particular zoomorphic types were used for weights is unknown. There are, however, analogues for TT 708, the baboon, at Gezer (Dever 1970: 76, fig. 22), Lachish (Tuffnell, Inge, and Harding 1953: pl. 35:31), and Megiddo (Loud 1948: pl. 206.62). TT 707 weighs 6.2 grams, which may represent a *pym* (פים) or 2/3 of a shekel in the range of 9.5 grams.

TT 707

TT 708

TT 708 is in the form of a baboon with its paws over its mouth. It is the heaviest of all the weights in this assemblage, weighing 41.6 grams, which could represent 4 shekels at the heavy end of the 9.5-10.5 norm for the shekel.

TT 709 is in the shape of a frog, and is the lightest of all the weights in this assemblage, weighing only 2.3 grams. It may represent 1/4 of a shekel in the 9.5-10.5 gram range. While no metal analogues to this weight can be cited, a carnelian frog was found at Megiddo (Loud 1948: pl. 206.62).

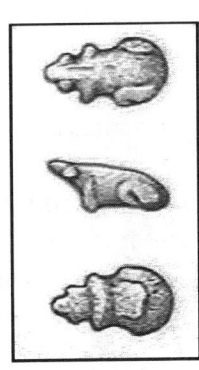
TT 709

TT 710, TT 711, and TT 712 are bronze dome weights that weigh 4.3, 7, and 19 grams respectively. 4.3 grams may represent 1/3 shekel of a 11-13 gram norm shekel. TT 711 at 7 grams may be an example of a *pym* (פים) or 2/3 of a 10.5 gram shekel. TT 712 at 19 grams may represent 2 shekels of a weight of 9.5 grams.

TT 711

TT 712

TT 713, TT 714, and TT 715 are loaf-shaped bronze weights. TT 714 is corroded and split, while TT 715 is cracked.

TT 713

TT 713, with a weight of 8.1 grams may represent a *pym* (פים) or 2/3 of a 12 gram shekel. TT 714, with a weight of 8.6 grams may also represent a *pym* (פים) or 2/3 of a shekel at the top end of the heavier norm, a shekel weighing almost 13 grams.

TT 714

TT 715

TT 715, at 24.8 grams represents a weight about three times as heavy as TT 713. If TT 713 represents 2/3 of a shekel, then TT 715 would be a 2-shekel weight, representing a shekel at the heavier end of the 11-13 gram norm.

As suggested above in Part IV.C.1, the precise use made of the contents of cooking pot TT 753 is unclear, but it is unlikely that these objects were associated with common domestic or agricultural activities. Given the number of weights and the assemblage of which they were a part, they appear to indicate a specialized regulatory activity that was carried on in this place by an elite group.

Why weights of both stone and metal and of so many different shapes? The only suggestion that comes to mind is that different kinds of weights were used for weighing different kinds of things. The substantial variation in the weight of these weight stones and metal weights reminds one of the lack of standards for weights and measures that led to the dishonest business practices bemoaned by the prophet Amos: "We will make the ephah small and the shekel great, and practice deceit with false balances" (8:5)

IV.H.11 Other Tools

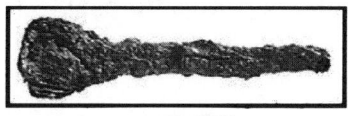
TT 598

The area of the cultic structure also produced an assortment of other tools. TT 598 is an iron chisel (?) with a "head" that is solid and globular. It was found totally corroded and in two pieces in SW 2-8 (21.69), in association with pottery from Iron I, Iron II, and Abbasid periods. It is 8.5 cm. long.

TT 726 is an iron chisel with three smooth stones (perhaps weights) and an incisor (canine?) corroded to it. Its tip is missing. It was found in SW 2-8 (27.90), the same locus as the bronze weights and other objects discussed above and thus dates to period IB. It measures .9 x 7.8 cm. with a thickness that varies from .8-1.2

TT 726

cm. Stech-Wheeler et al. (1981: 252) removed a sample 1.3 cm. long from the broken working end of the chisel for their examination, which concluded that no signs of carburization were present.

TT 1030 is a bronze wire pick or pin that was found broken off at both ends, but not badly corroded. It comes from SW 1-7 (145.276), a locus with pottery dating to ± 1500 BCE. It is 8.6 cm. long and has a diameter of 1 mm.

TT 1215 is a bronze handle or chisel that was found corroded but in fair condition in SW 1-7 (173.334) in association with pottery from the EB and MB IIC periods. It is 11 cm. long.

TT 1651 is a bronze handle fragment that was found with a pin or nail fragment. It is pierced with a .5 cm. round hole and measures 1.9 x 3.8

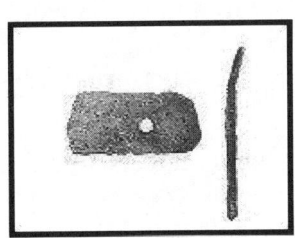
TT 1651

cm., with a width that varies from 1-2 mm. It was found in SW 2-8 (170.350) in a locus that is dated to period IIB.

TT 1679 is a bronze axe or adze blade that was found corroded and incomplete in SW 1-8 (118.284) with EB III potsherds. It measures 3.9 cm. in length with a width that varies from 2.9-3.6 cm. and a thickness of 4 mm.

TT 1879 is an unfinished iron object, potentially an axehead, that was found in SW 1-7 (86.156), a locus that is assigned to period IIB. It is 7.9 cm. in length, has a width of 1.0-2.9 cm., and has a thickness of .2-1.7 cm. This object was examined by Stech-Wheeler et al. (1981: 252) who removed a sample 3.1 cm. long from the tip. Optical study of this sample revealed a rim of carburization. The carbon content of the remaining metal was estimated to be ca. 0.8%, but it is likely that the carbon content of the outer layers, now lost to corrosion, was higher. They conclude that the object was deliberately carburized and worked to a certain extent after the carburization process was complete. Working probably took place at a temperature around 700° C. They add the comment: "The manufacturing process seems to have been interrupted before its completion, perhaps by the conflagration in which this level ended" (1981: 252).

IV.H. 12 Miscellaneous Objects

We conclude this part of our study of artifacts from the cultic structure with a discussion of miscellaneous metal objects. The first miscellaneous metal object recorded in the registered objects list is TT 703, a bronze whorl or bead in a rosette motif with about 18 ridges. It was found encrusted with lime, corroded, and chipped in SW 2-8 (27.90), as part of the collection of objects in cooking pot TT 753, dating to period IB. It has a

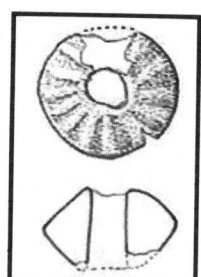

TT 703

diameter of 2.1 cm., a thickness of 1 cm., and weighs 15 grams. It is probably from a piece of jewelry.

TT 704 is also a bronze bead that was probably part of a piece of jewelry. It is fluted and measures 8 mm. in height with a diameter of ca. 10 cm. It was part of the same collection as TT 703.

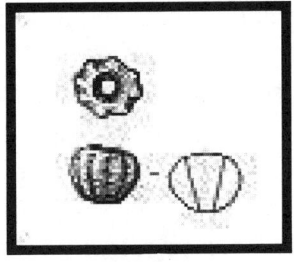
TT 704

TT 1008 is a bronze ring that was found badly corroded in SW 1-7 (133.262) in association with pottery dating to the 15th century BCE. Its diameter is ca. 2.2 cm. It is possibly not an item of jewelry but a fastener of some sort.

TT 1216 is a bronze crescent that was possibly part of a pin or handle. It was found in SW 2-7 (211.495) in association with potsherds from EB, MB, and LB I. Its length is ca. 4.5 cm.

TT 1223 is a bronze wire loop that was found broken and incomplete in SW 1-8 (61.168) in a locus with EB and MB IIC potsherds. It is ca. 4.6 cm. long.

TT 1415 is possibly a bronze weapon haft that was found slightly bent and corroded. It comes from SW 1-7 (195.393), and was found with EB and MB IIC. pottery. It is 7.3 cm. long and has a thickness of 4 mm.

TT 1478 is a bronze rod or scriber from a locus in SW 2-8 (156.305) that is assigned to period IIB. It is 6 cm. long and has a thickness that varies from 4-5 mm.

TT 1478

TT 1507 is a bronze hook, somewhat corroded, that was found in SW 2-7 (274.637) in a locus with EB and MB IIC pottery. It is 3.7 cm. long and has a thickness of 3 mm.

IV.H.13 Metallurgy and Cult

The one remaining concern to be addressed in this section has to do with the correlation of metal objects and a cultic site in the early Iron Age. What can be said about metallurgy at Taanach and its relation to the cult?

Stech-Wheeler et al. have suggested (1981: 254) that the iron artifacts from Taanach with a 10th-century *terminus ante quem* have sufficiently consistent characteristics to allow some general conclusions about their manufacturing process. First, these objects are made of well forged bloomery iron, with little sponginess or slag visible. The well forged condition is attributable to careful working of the bloom to eliminate air holes and extrude slag and/or prolonged forging to shape, either during the manufacture or repair of the objects. A second conclusion offered by Stech-Wheeler et al. is based on evidence for the deliberate manipulation of the iron to produce steel. Of the eleven pieces they examined from a 10th-century context, six showed consistent detectable carburization (1981: 254). They conclude that this evidence suggests that steel was being consciously produced by the 10th-century BCE. Stech-Wheeler et al. also make observations about the organization of iron working activities in 10th-century BCE Taanach that support our thesis regarding the regulatory functions of cult. They report (1981: 256, 257) (emphasis mine):

> The existence of similar collections [of iron artifacts] at Taanach and Megiddo supports the contention that iron working may have been a seasonal activity or that iron smiths may not have resided at each site.
>
> There are indications that smithing or the collection of tools to be repaired at Taanach may have taken place in a common area, in a bazaar-like setting, perhaps under some sort of religious auspices. A similar organization of metallurgical activities has been suggested for Cyprus of the Late Bronze Age and Early Iron Age. . . .
>
> *The control of an income-producing industry like metalworking was probably undertaken for economic reasons rather than purely religious ones and can thus provide some insight into the entities which exercised political and economic control. Although in the ancient world the distinction between secular and religious bodies was much less*

rigorous that it is now (and may in many instances have been non-existent), our perception of these organizations has tended to enforce the differences, rather than recognize the similarities. It seems likely that the Medieval monastery at Lythrodonda offers the best analogy for the way in which Bronze Age and Early Iron Age metalworking industry functioned in Cyprus—the administration controlling the industry was based in religious organizations, with leaders who had functions in both spheres of activity. . . . Although there is no evidence from Taanach to prove that such a situation prevailed there, the apparent concentration of metallurgical remains in one area which has cultic connections suggests that it might have.

Conclusions

Meehl was certainly not engaging in hyperbole when he said: "The Cultic Structure with its plethora of small finds was an unusual building. It produced a large number of artifacts in a primary context, with many of these items such as the figurine mold [TT 100] and the well-crafted incense stands [sic.] being unusual and rare in character" (1995: 258). He then goes on to raise a series of questions that provide the focus for our conclusions:

> Was this the only structure that had not been looted at the end of the period [IIB] and so presented the excavators with a treasure trove of finds due to the vagaries of the looters? Had all of the period IIB structures at Taanach once been as full of items before they were plundered? Would these unusual artifacts appear more frequently if other period IIB structures that had not been looted were found, or were they truly unique to the context of the building in 2-7? (1995: 258)

Certainly the answers to these questions, and others like them, are critical in deciding whether or not what we have called the cultic structure throughout this study did indeed serve that function. Those who have rejected the Tannach cultic structure as cultic such as Yeivin (1973) and Fowler (1984) do so out of lack of a controlled method of identifying cultic activity outside centralized, formal, cultic sites such as temples, sanctuaries, and shrines. Even Lapp did not base his contention that the Taanach structure was cultic on the architecture of the building, much of which had already been destroyed by Sellin's trenching, as noted above. Furthermore, Lapp's "cultic structure" label for the structure does not necessarily settle the question of how to understand its function. Moreover, nowhere did Lapp ever claim that the cultic structure was a temple or sanctuary. In one both Yeivin and Fowler are correct; the cultic structure at Taanach was not a formal cultic site in that unlike a temple, sanctuary, or shrine, it was not exclusively dedicated to the "sacred, but dealt with the "sacred" in a "profane" context.

As we have hopefully demonstrated in this presentation of evidence from Taanach, the question of whether or not a structure can be called a cultic structure is more complex than any conclusions based solely on specific artifacts or particular architectural plans. Rather more systemic issues regarding the role of cult in society and the nature of cultic assemblages must be addressed. The 12th to 10th centuries BCE were, as Gilmour has persuasively demonstrated (1995), a period of decline in centralized, formal, ritual, and there is abundant evidence to suggest an increase in decentralized ritual activity in domestic and workshop contexts. As Rast maintains:

> The very fact of almost identical assemblages in the 'cult corners' at Megiddo and Taanach suggests the management of cult and religion by the emerging state society of the tenth century, whose integrating power also brought this aspect of social life under strong national influence, if not direct control (1994: 361).

We would add that this integrating power also used cultural elites associated with the cult to extend different kinds of socioeconomic control of localities, using mechanisms associated with the cult.

In order to recognize the material correlates of less formal cultic activity, it is simply inadequate to rely on a kind of yes-no methodology that presupposes a certain form of architecture and distinct types of artifacts as cultic. Gilmour is certainly correct when he says that in this area, arguments of probability are unavoidable. On one end of the spectrum are those sites or loci which most scholars would not hesitate to identify as cultic. Temples and shrines that retained the same plan relatively unchanged over a long period of time, meeting Coogan's (1987) criterion of continuity, raise few questions for most. On the other end of the spectrum are all those sites or loci that clearly have no cultic associations. In between these two poles, however, are those sites and loci, like the structure at Taanach, for which there is some evidence, but no certainty about formal cultic activity or significance. As suggested, the identification of such sites calls for an analytical evaluation of artifacts that might have been part of a cultic assemblage. As we have observed, the presence of domestic pottery types such as cooking pots, bowls, jars, etc. in what may have been, on the basis of other evidence, a cultic context, strongly suggests that these "profane" domestic vessels may have been used for "profane" tasks such as the preparation and consumption of food in a cultic setting. The presence of such "profane" artifacts is definitely *not* a counter-indicator of a site's cultic function, as it appears to be for Yeivin (1973) and Fowler (1984), when they observe that the ceramic types found in the Taanach cultic structure are simply examples of ordinary household pottery.

We are in fundamental agreement with Rast (1994: 361) in his conclusion that what we have in the cultic structure and L 2081 at Megiddo were places where traditional cultic material was stored, repaired, and manufactured, either by priests themselves or by artisans allied to them. The fact that rooms 1 and 2 of the cultic structure at Taanach may have been used for storage, or room 2 as a "kitchen," as some have suggested does not negate their cultic function, since both storage space and facilities for the preparation of food were needed for cultic structures. Together, the cultural elites associated with such sites exercised different kinds of regulatory/control functions that were both sensitive to the particular microenvironments in which they were located and also an extension of the control functions of the emerging state society of the 10th century BCE.

It is hoped that this work will be of some help in addressing the complex questions associated with identifying cultic activity in archaeological contexts. As Gilmour concludes, these questions become even more difficult when domestic or other decentralized activity is involved. (1995: 16). As he says:

> The likely absence of two . . . key variables . . ., architecture and continuity, render it unlikely that many domestic cult corners will rate highly on the probability continuum. Nevertheless the circumstances prevalent in the early Iron Age provide a good opportunity for testing the methodology [for identifying cultic sites archaeologically that he develops in his dissertation], for the overall collapse of authority saw a proliferation of several types of decentralized secondary cult sites and loci (1995: 16, 17)

It is also our hope that this work will provide a stimulus for more work using the kind of method developed here and outlined in Gilmour's dissertation, particularly with respect to sites that are excavated with state-of-the-art techniques. Certainly the more work of this kind that is done, the more sophisticated will be our ability to identify the material correlates of cultic activity in the archaeological record. In an area where presuppositions regarding the nature of biblical religion and the role of cult too often go unexamined, this kind of systemic and structural approach would be welcomed by all who seek to use the results of archaeology to reconstruct, as fully as possible, the lives of real people in antiquity.

Appendix A
Section Drawings of SW 1-7, SW 1-8, SW 2-7, and SW 2-8

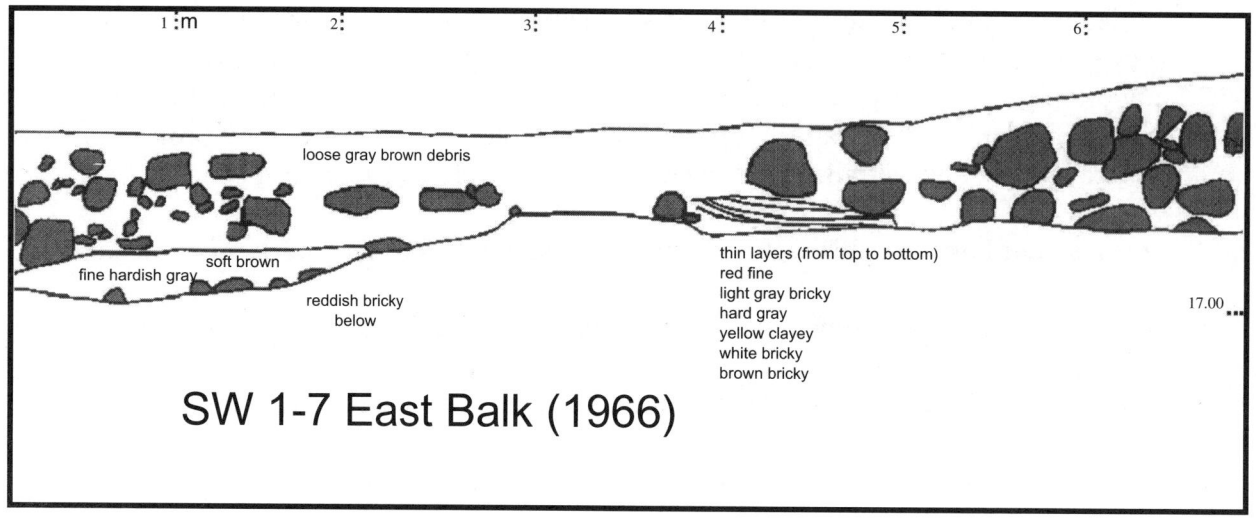

SW 1-7 East Balk (1966)

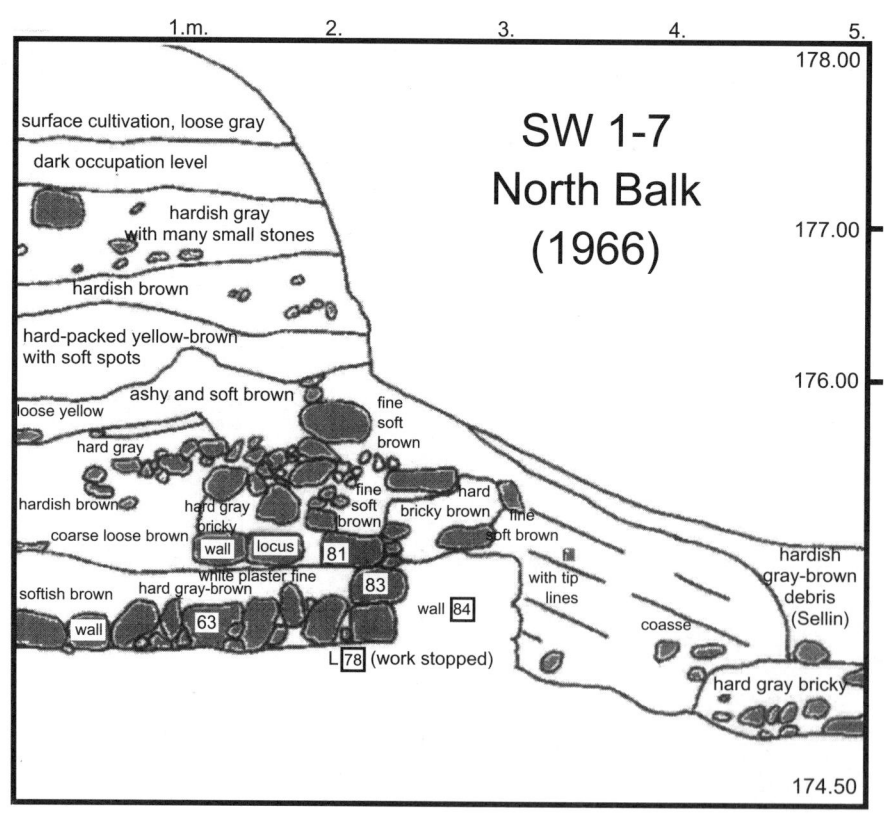

SW 1-7 North Balk (1966)

Appendix A-173

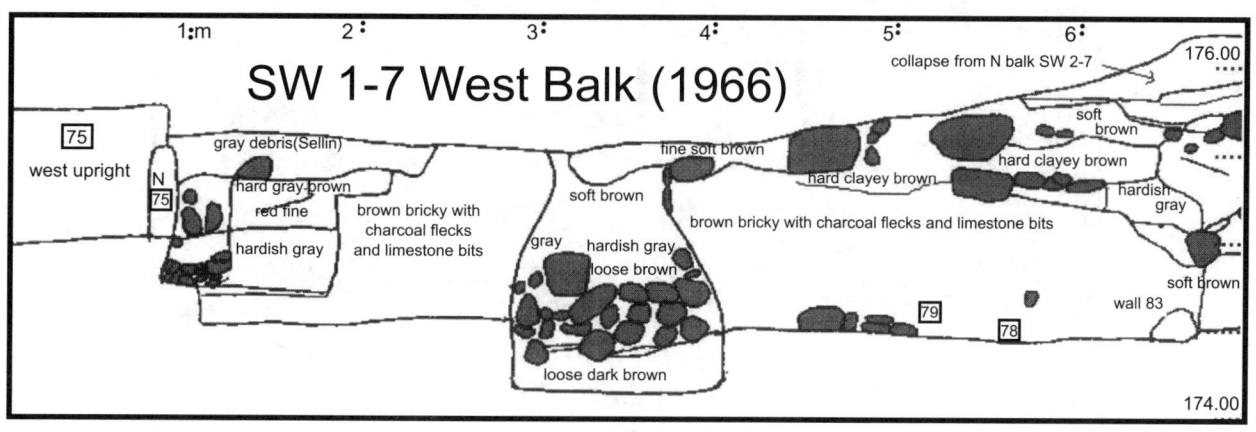

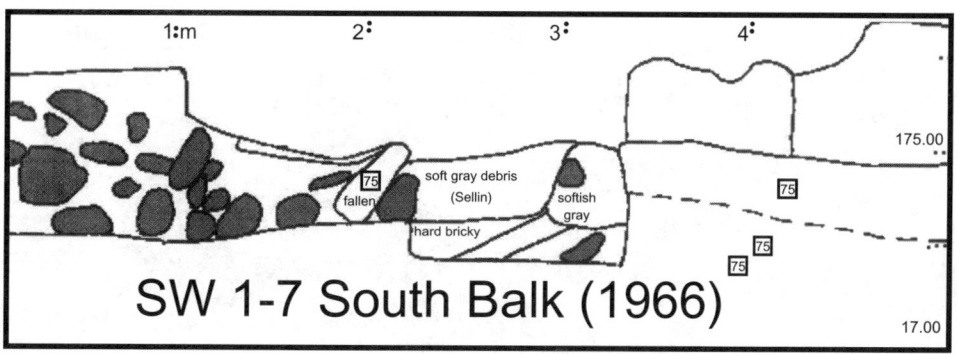

Appendix A-174

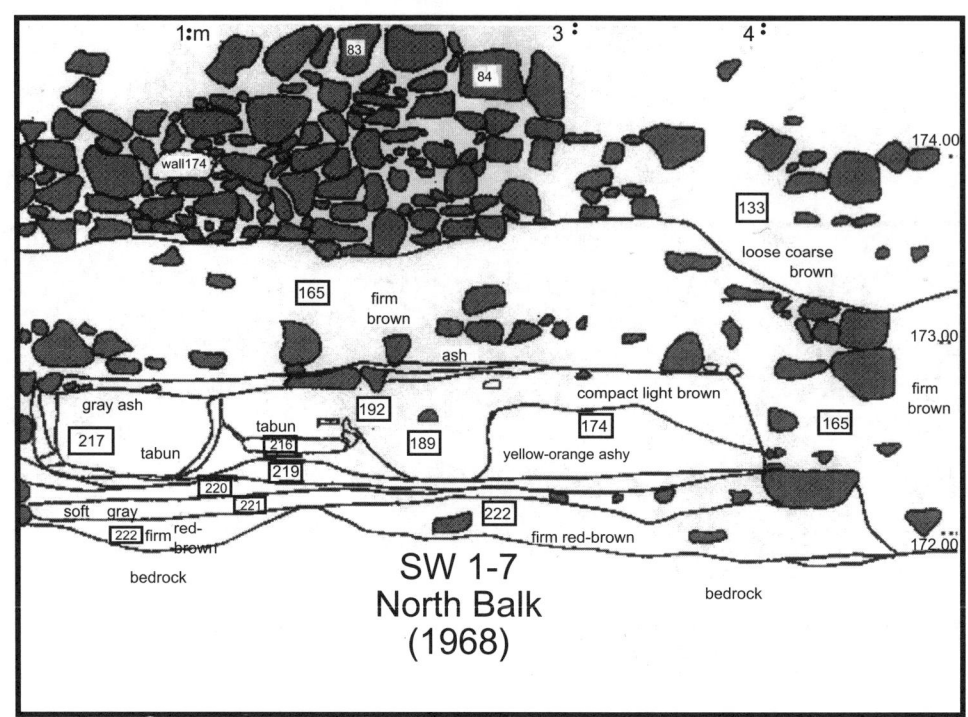

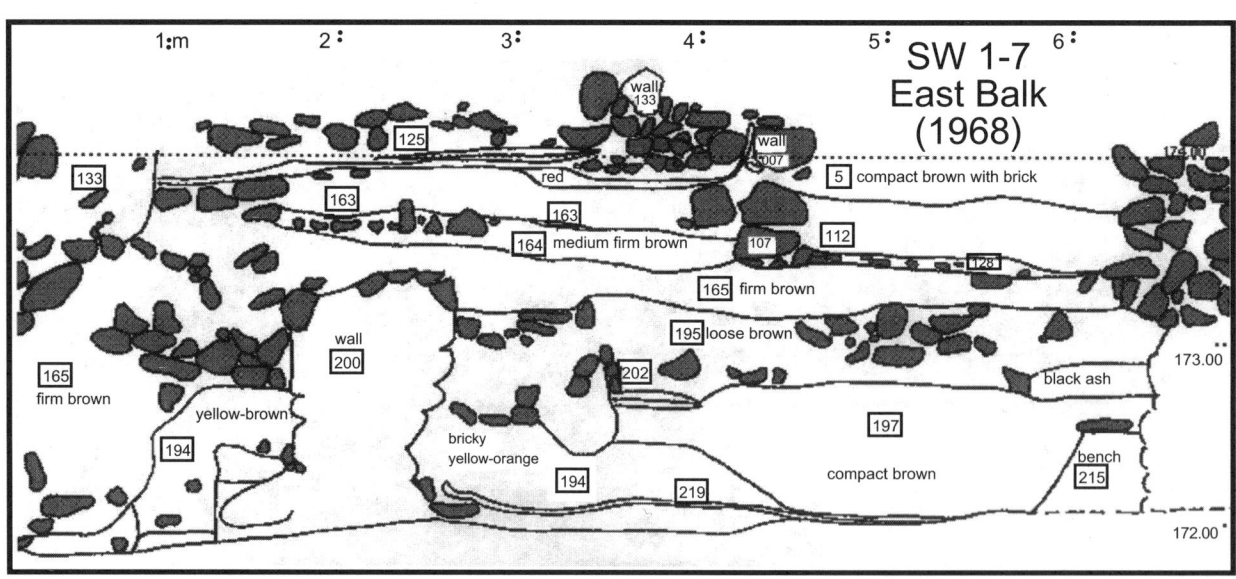

Appendix A-175

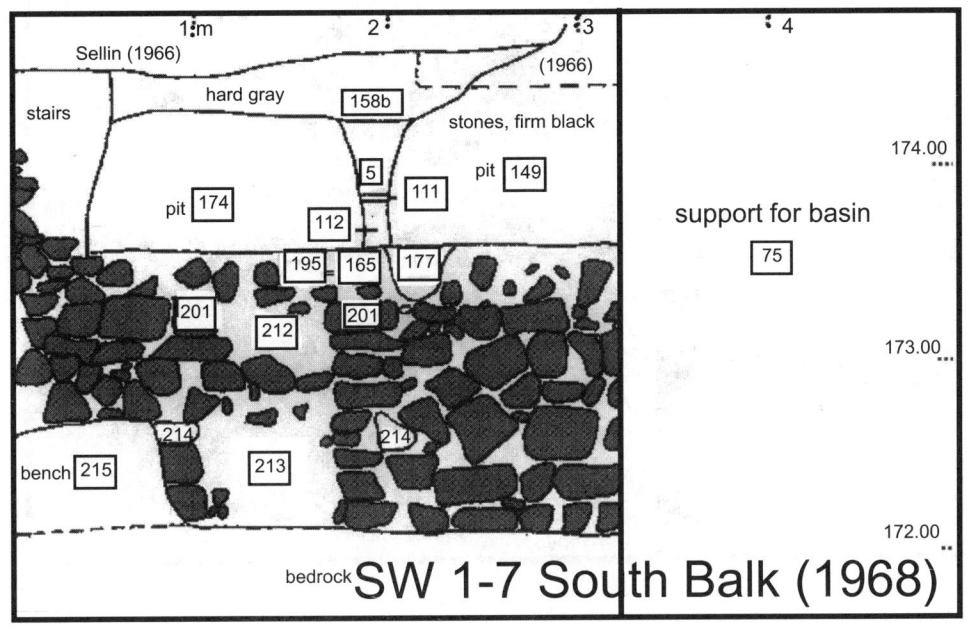

SW 1-7 South Balk (1968)

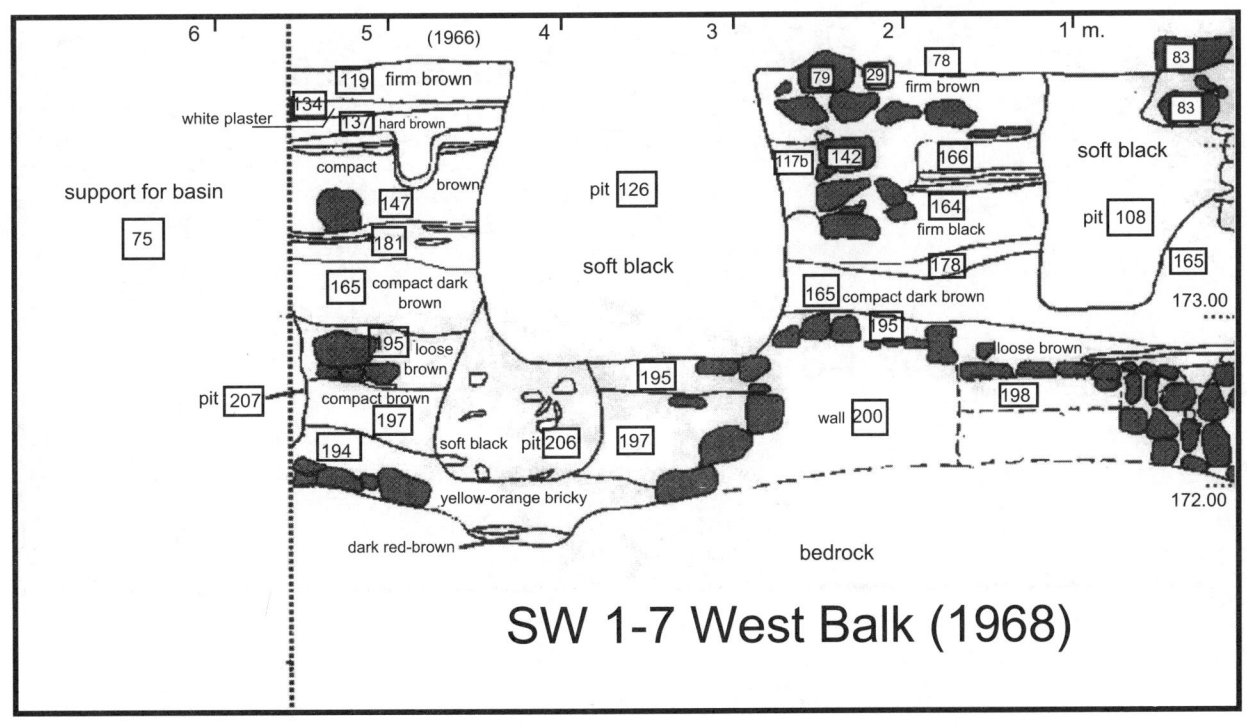

SW 1-7 West Balk (1968)

Appendix A-176

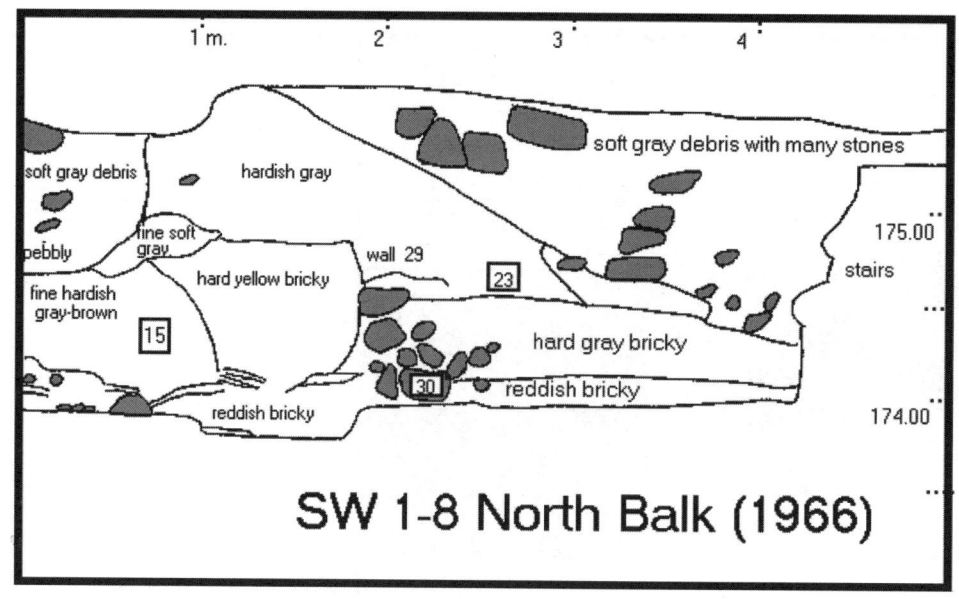

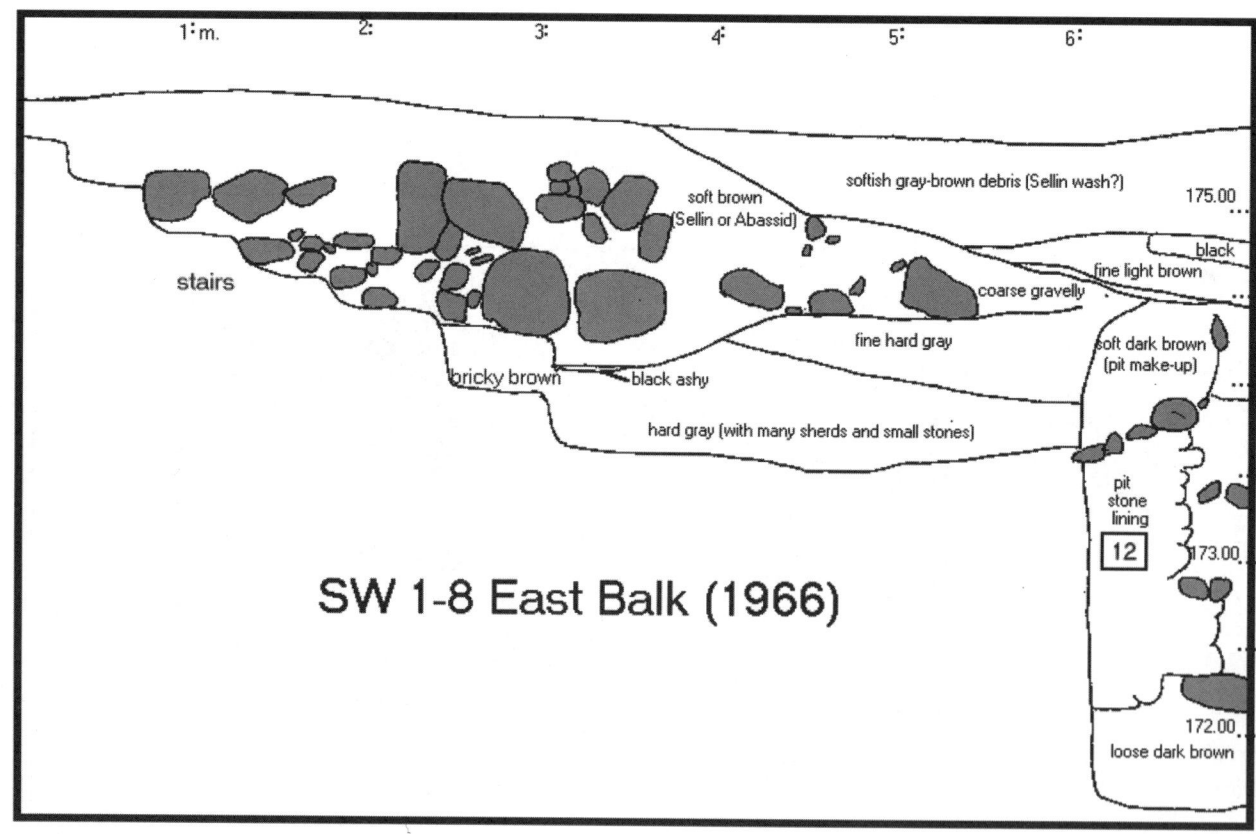

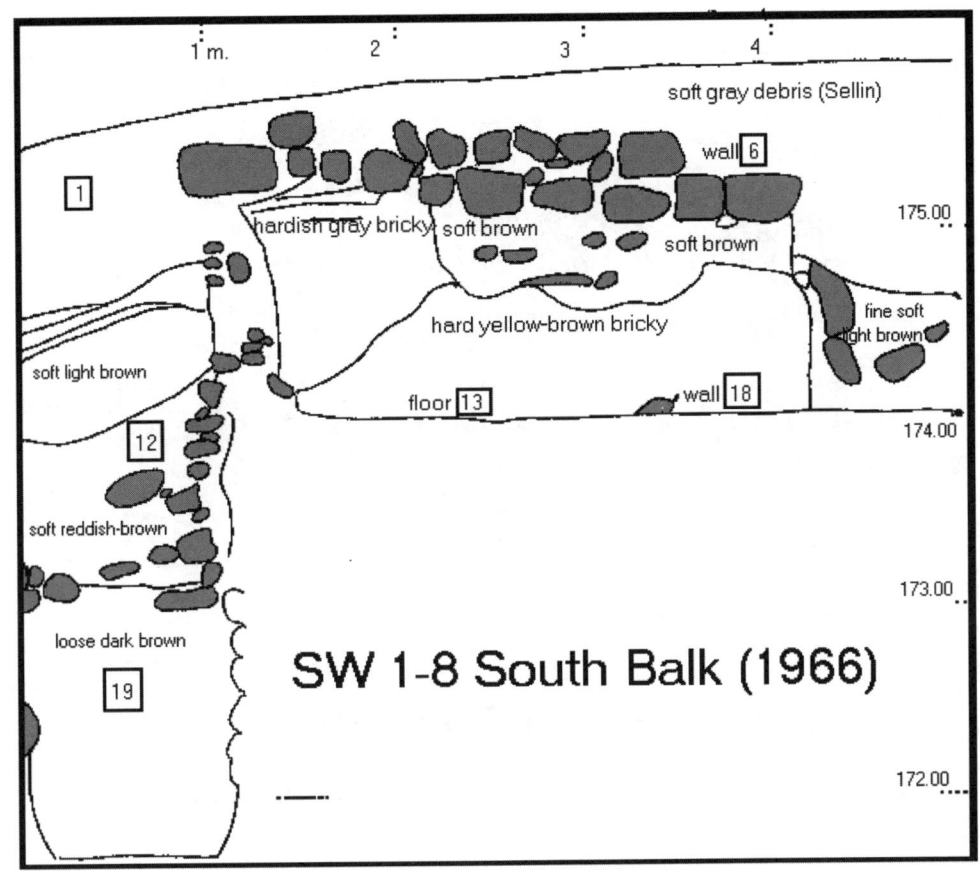

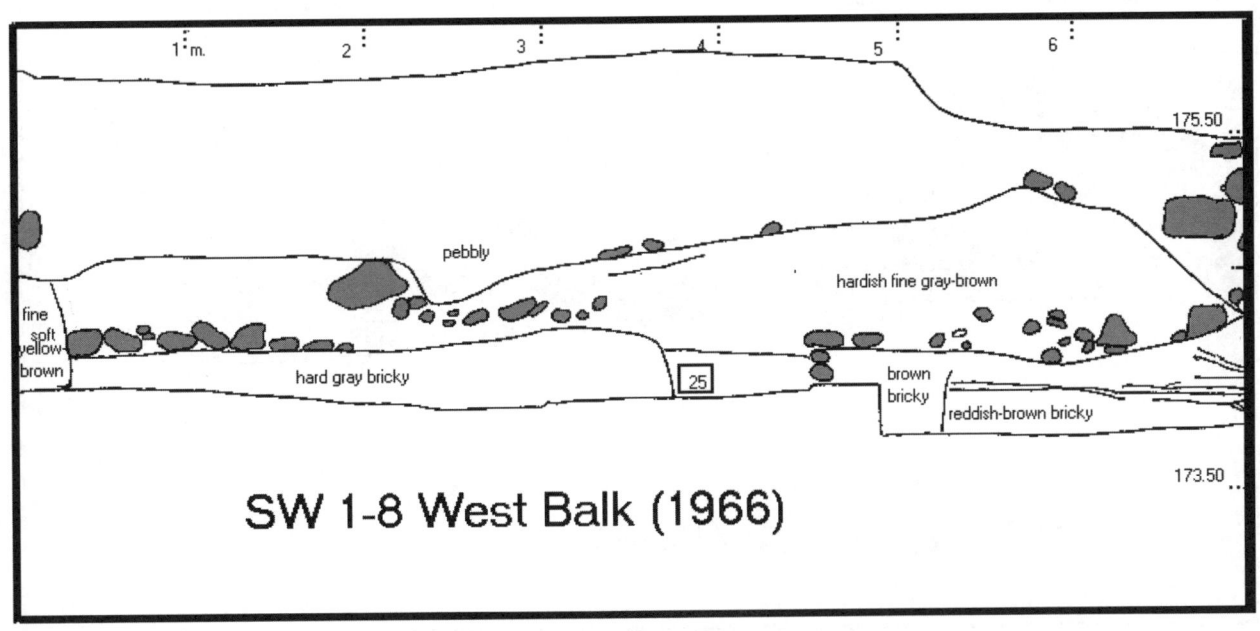

Appendix A-178

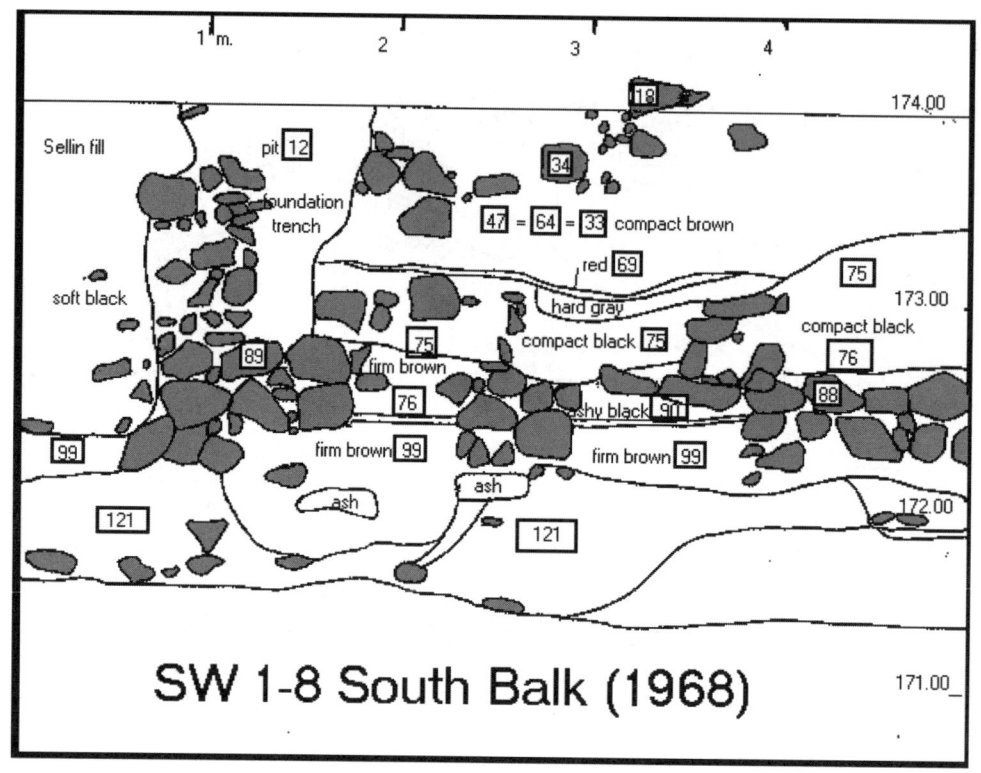

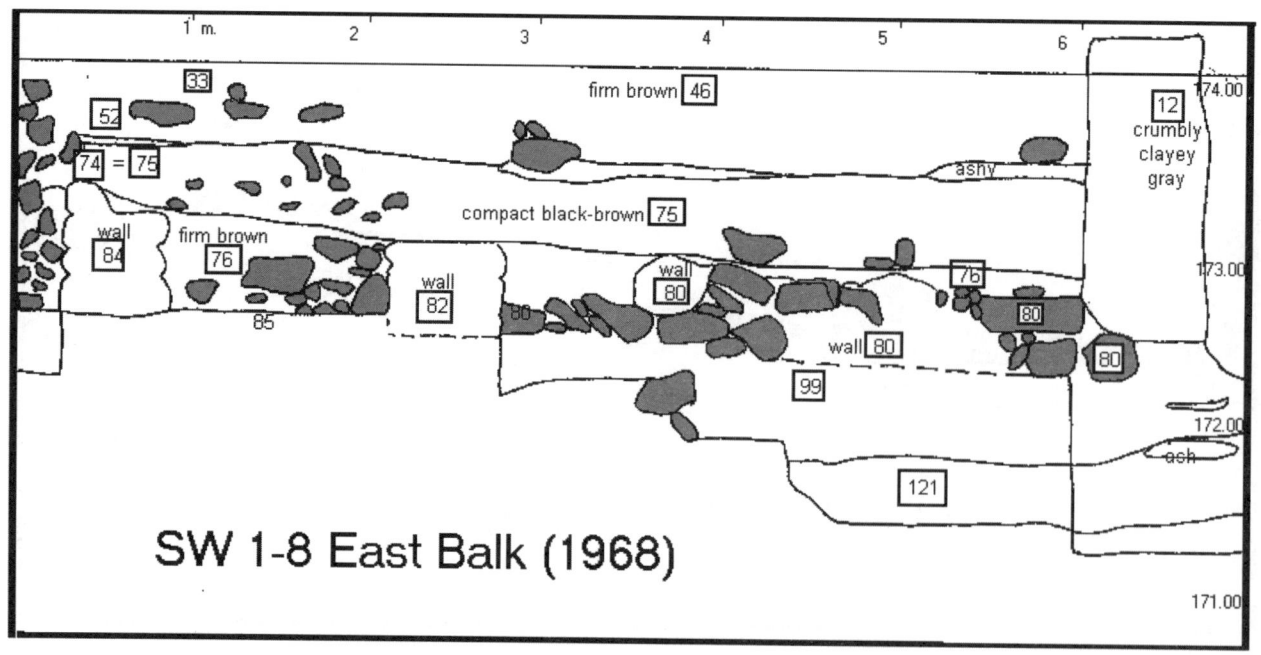

SW 1-8 West Balk (1968)

SW 1-8 North Balk (1968)

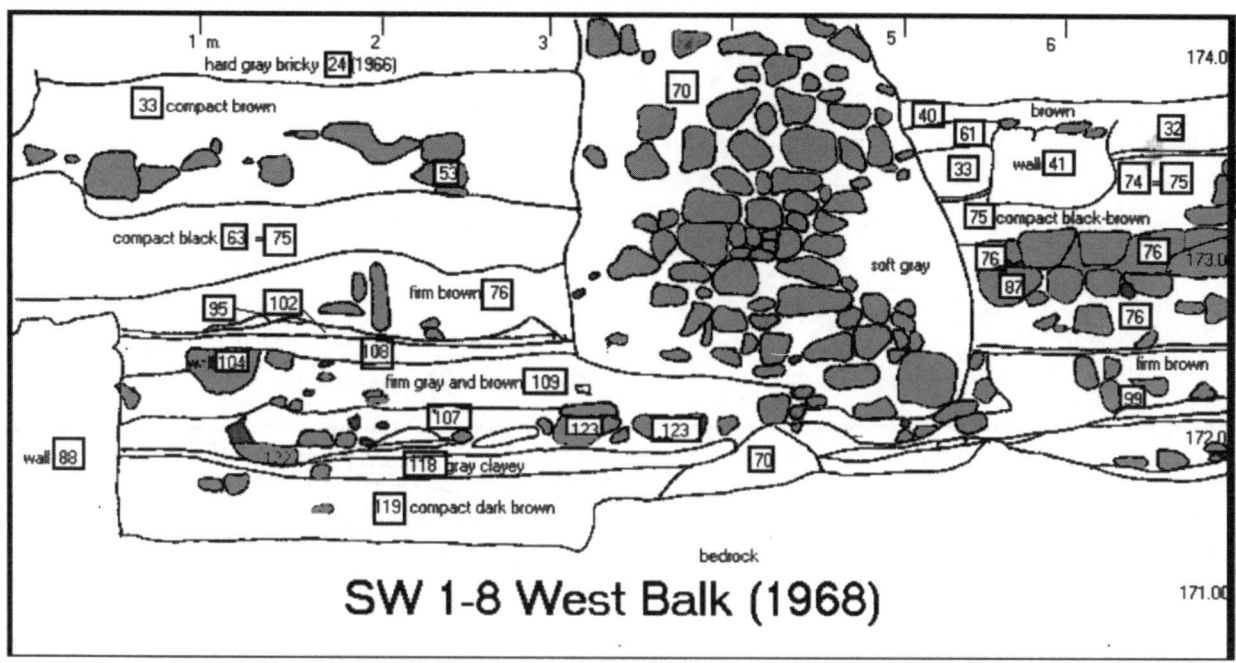

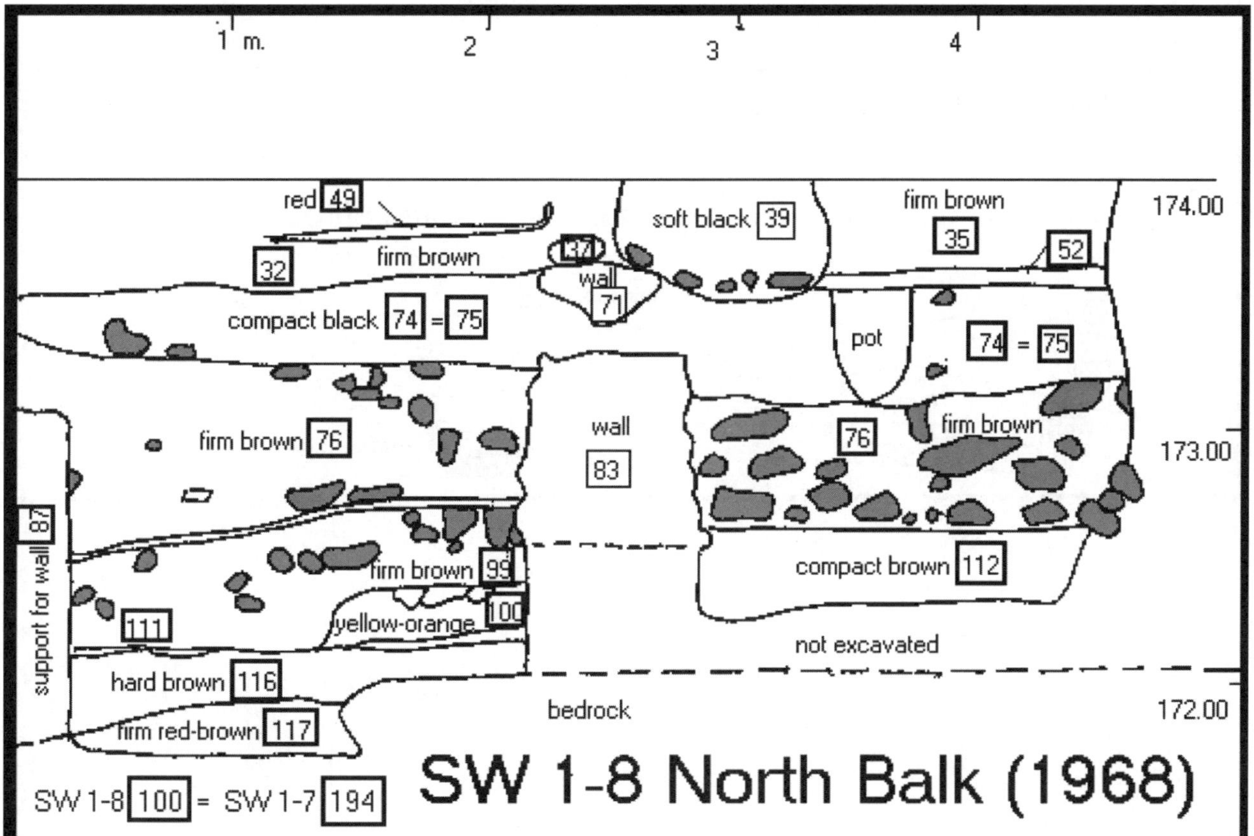

Appendix A-180

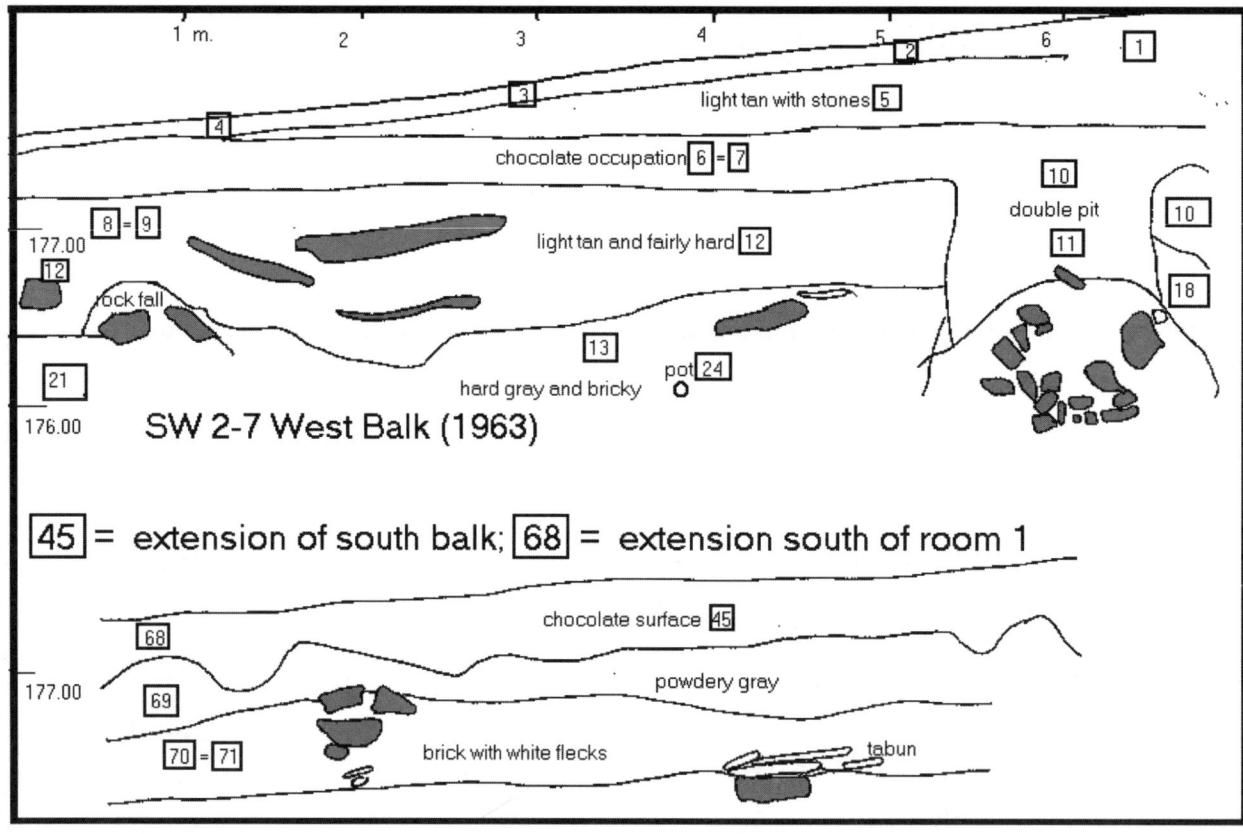

Appendix A-181

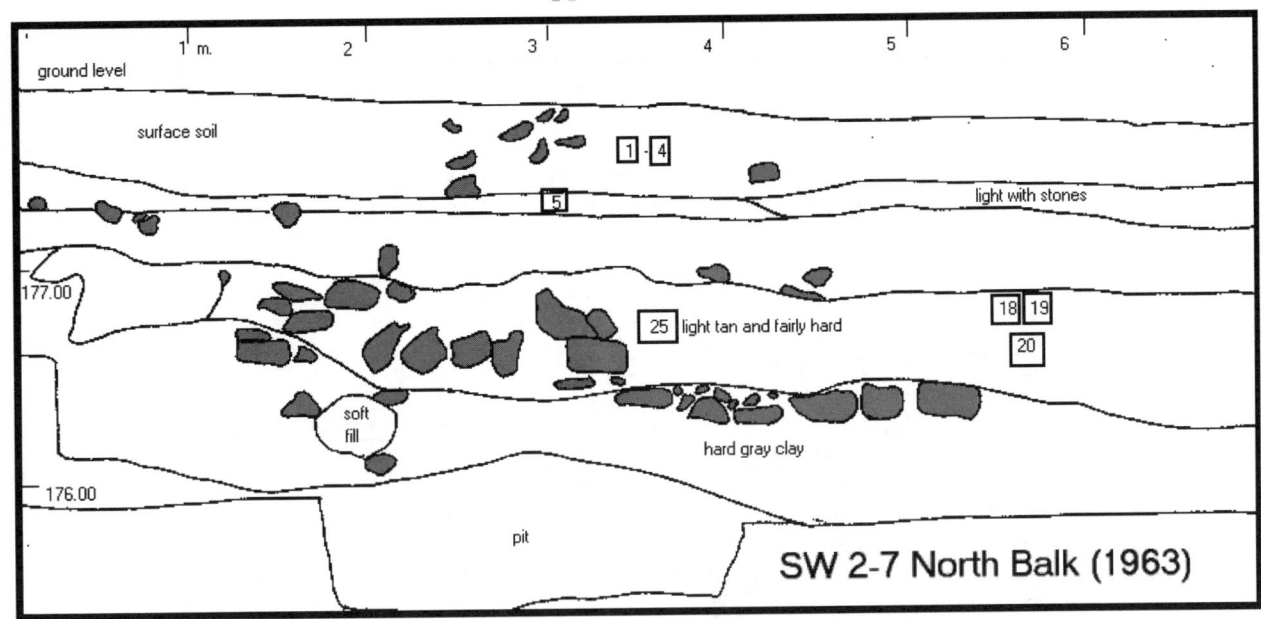

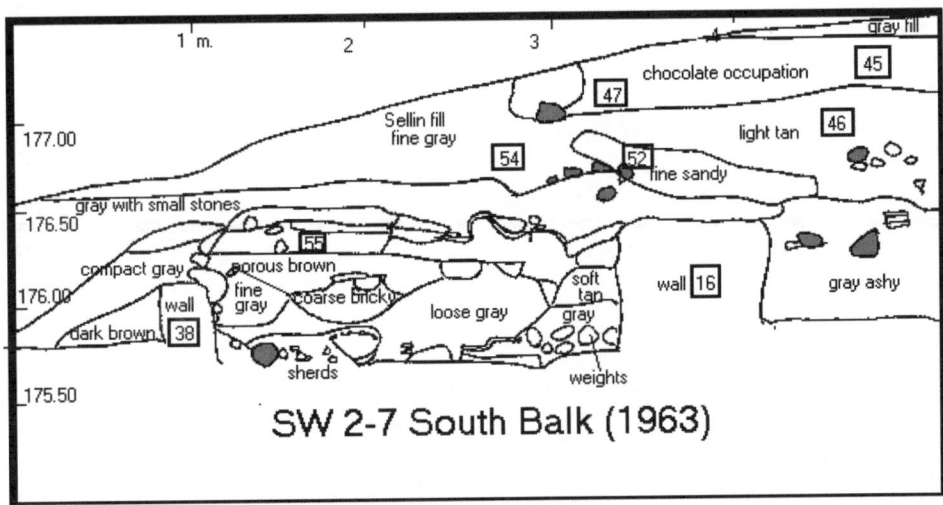

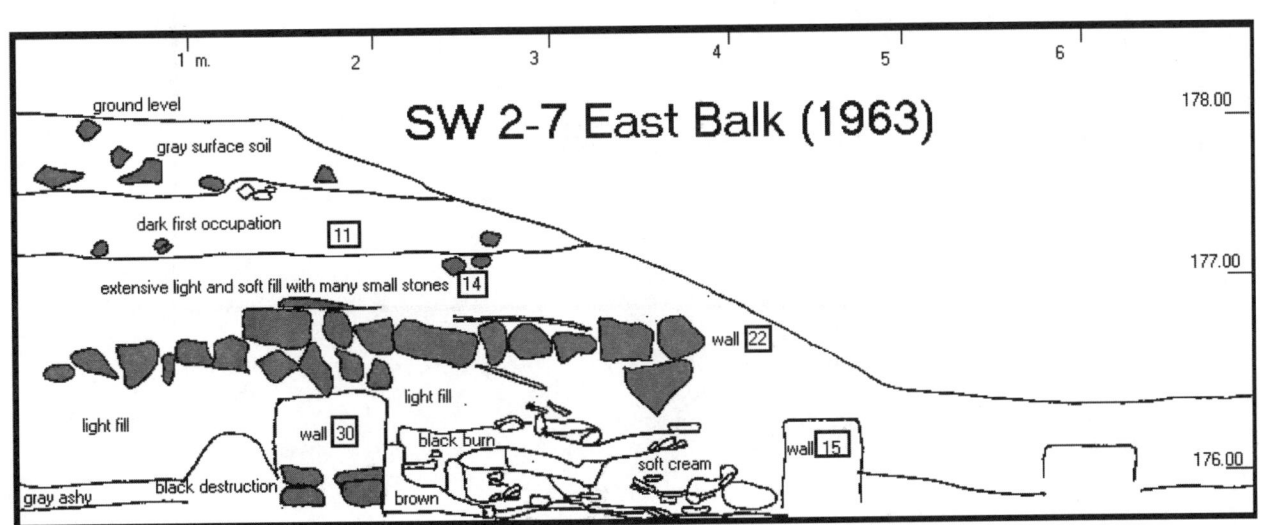

Appendix A-182

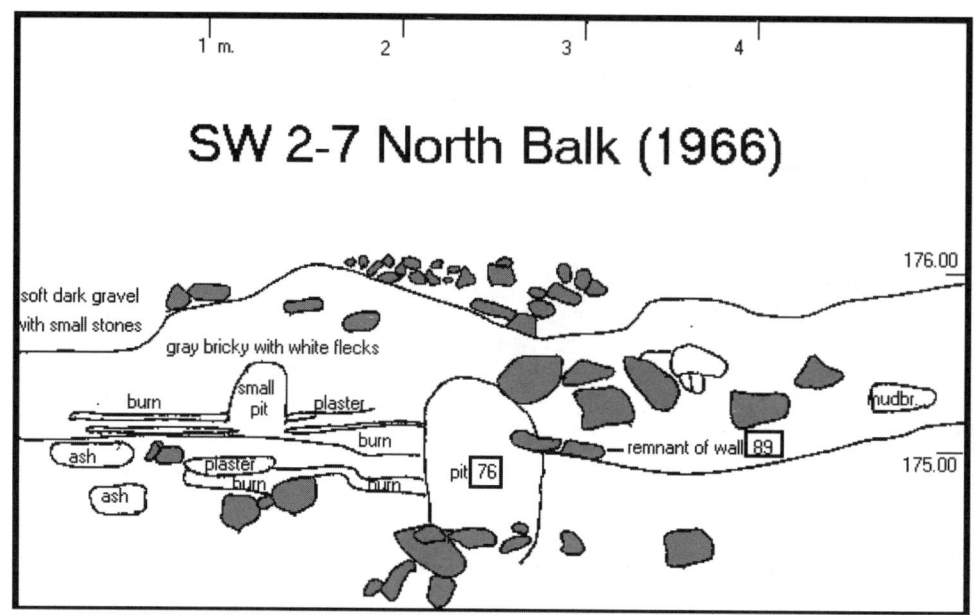

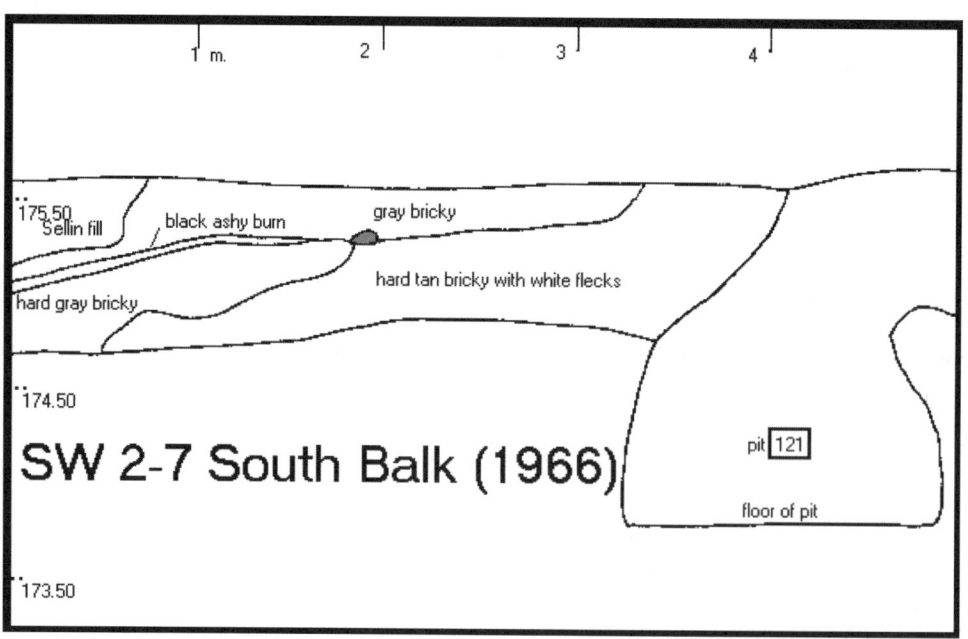

Appendix A-183

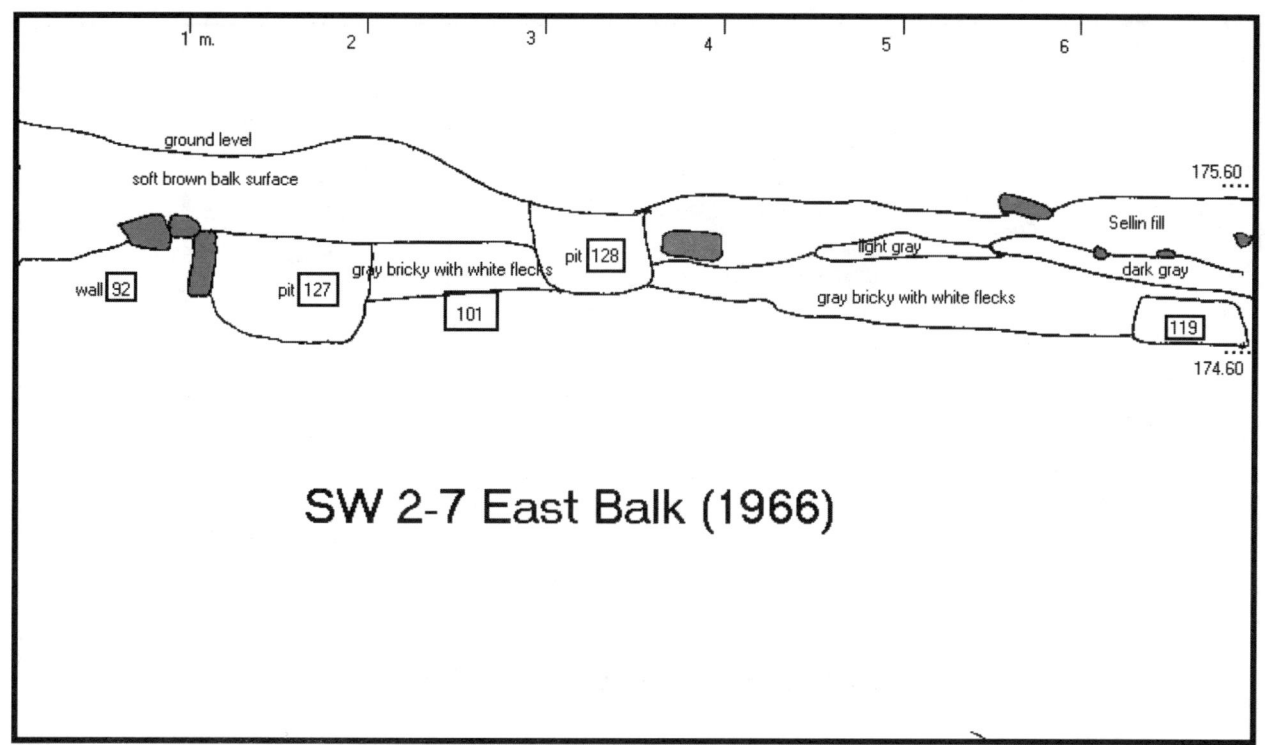

SW 2-7 East Balk (1966)

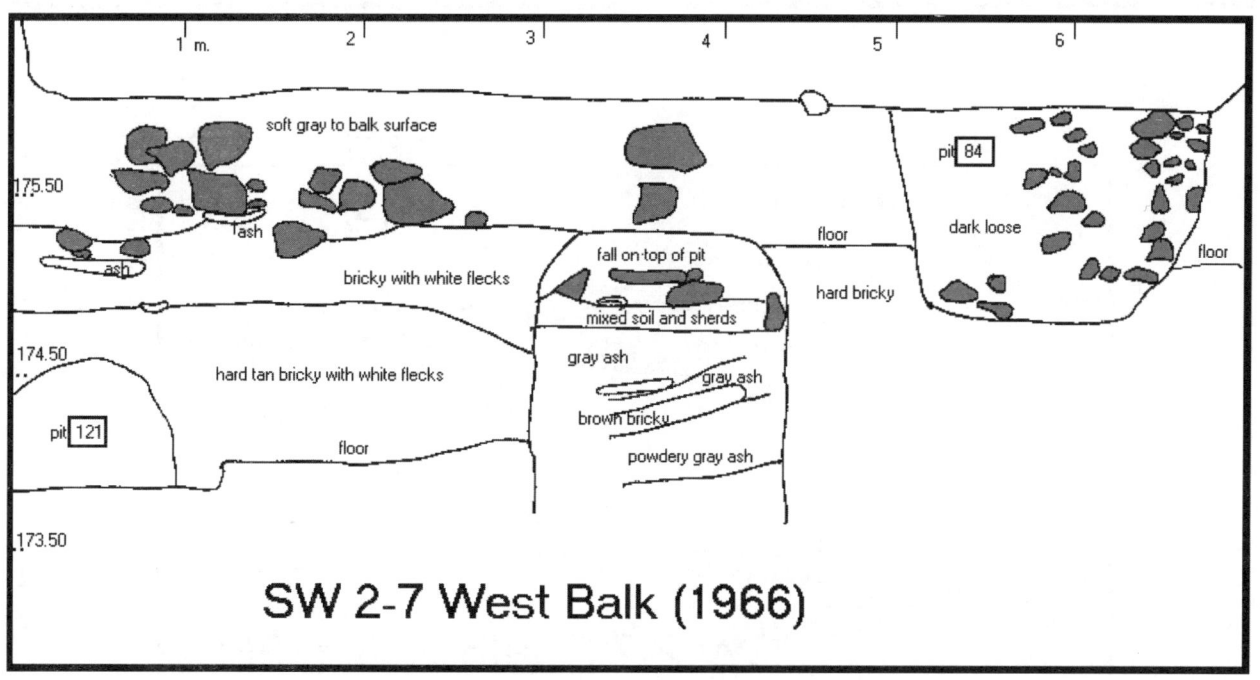

SW 2-7 West Balk (1966)

Appendix A-184

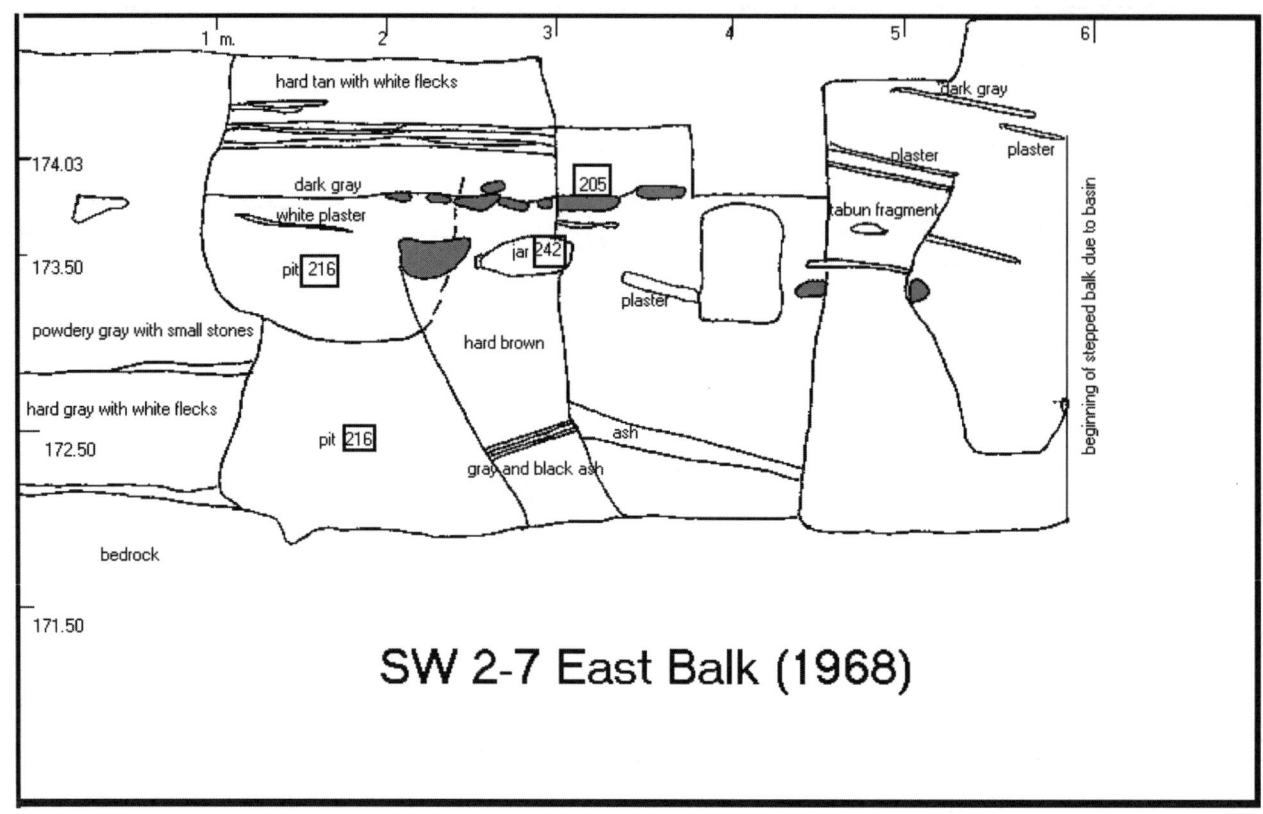

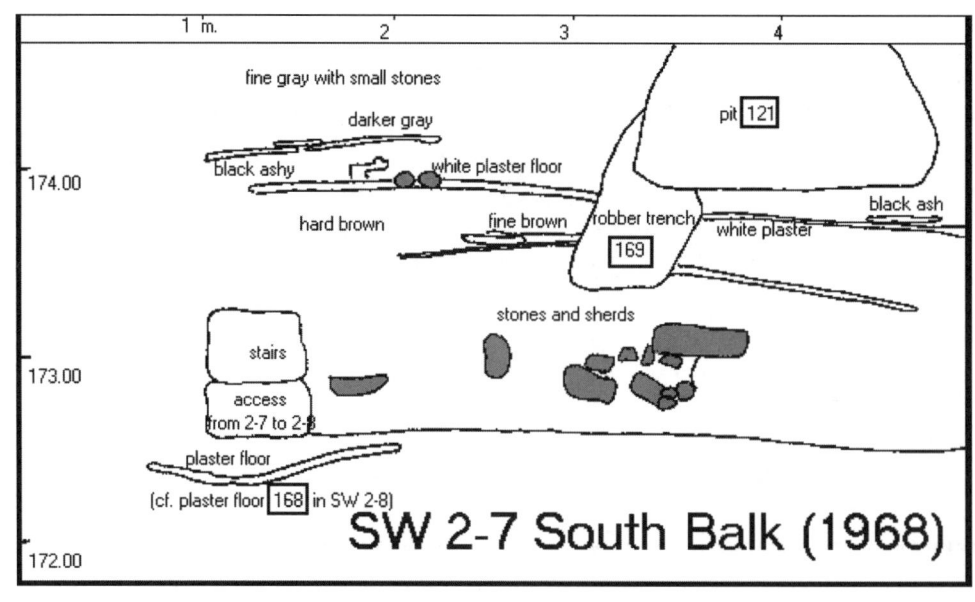

Appendix A-185

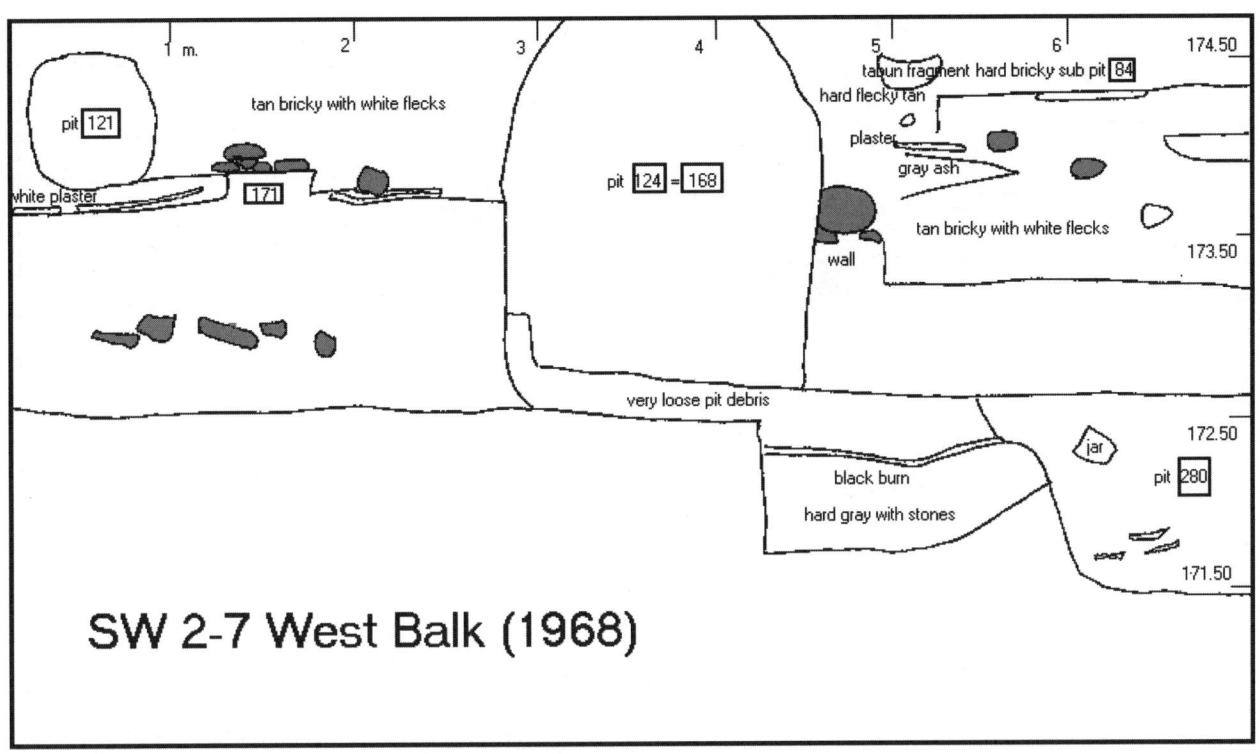

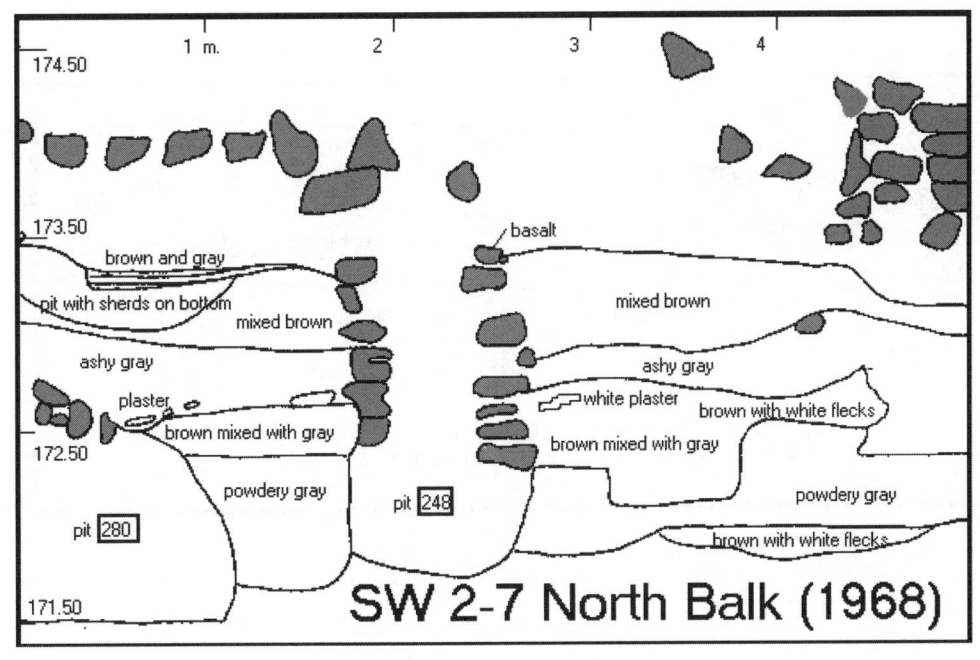

Appendix A-186

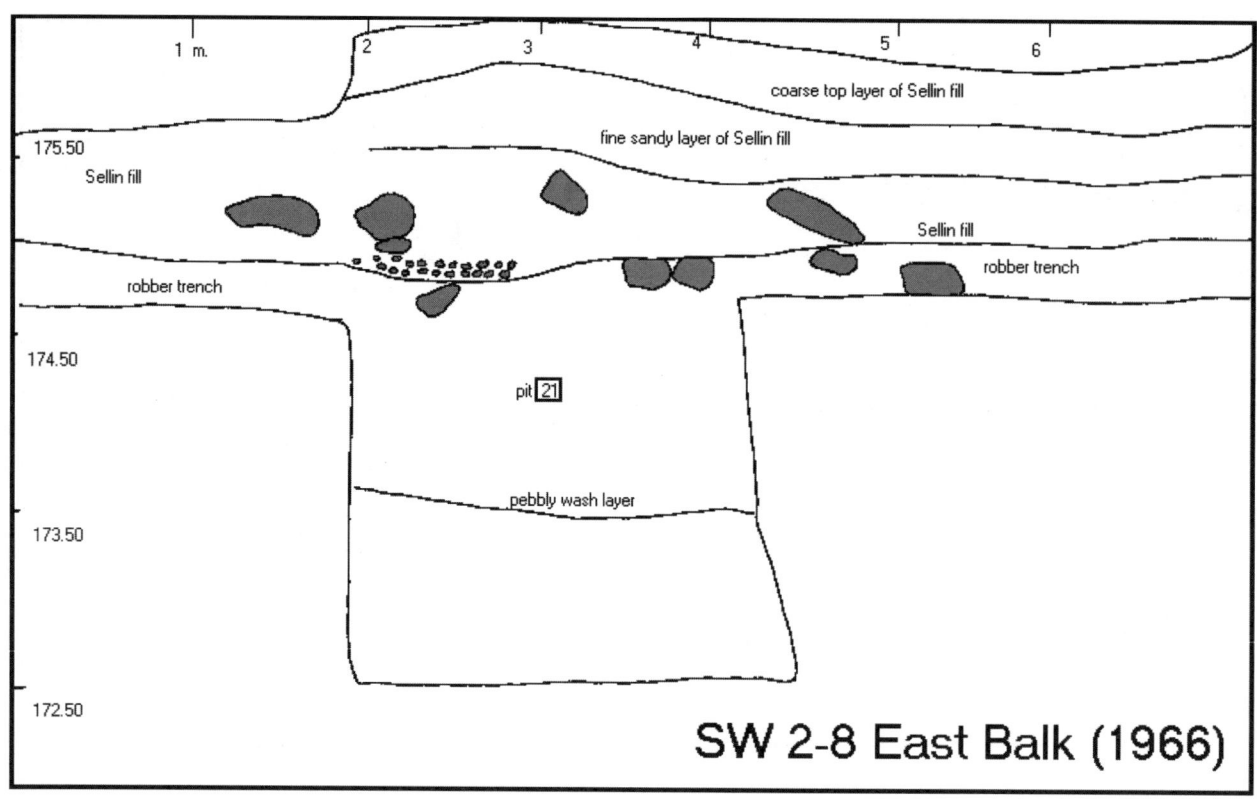

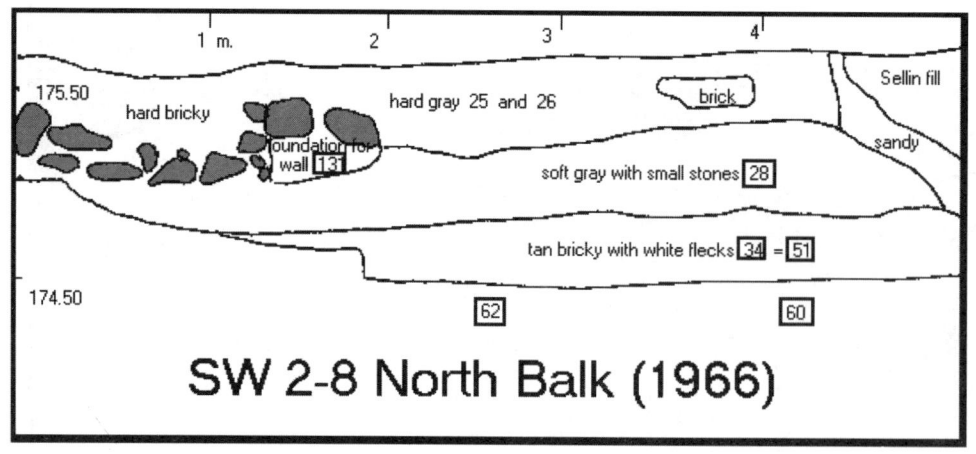

Appendix A-187

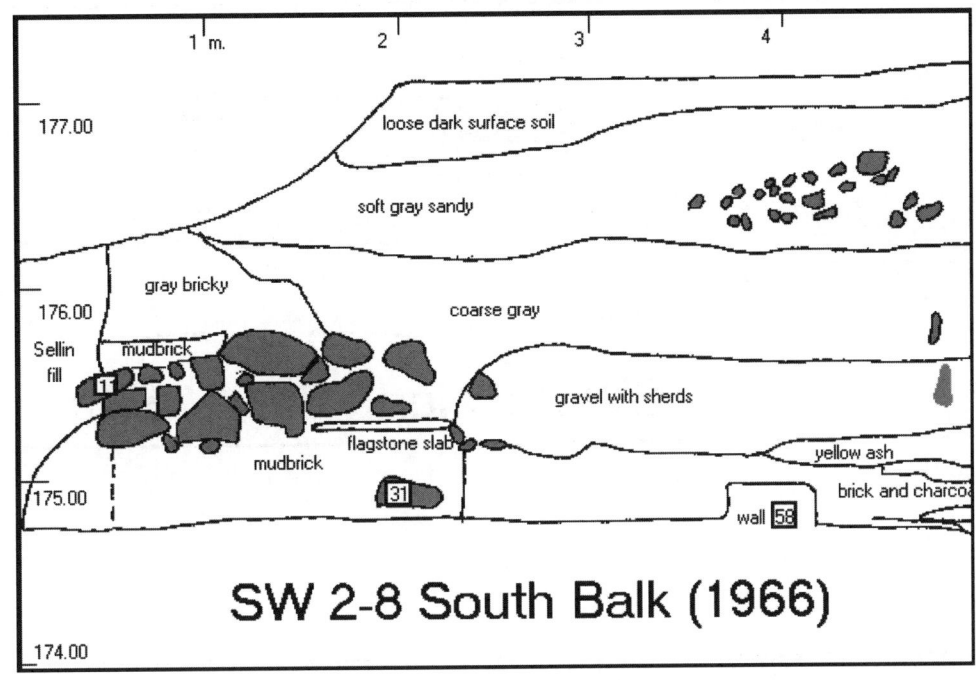

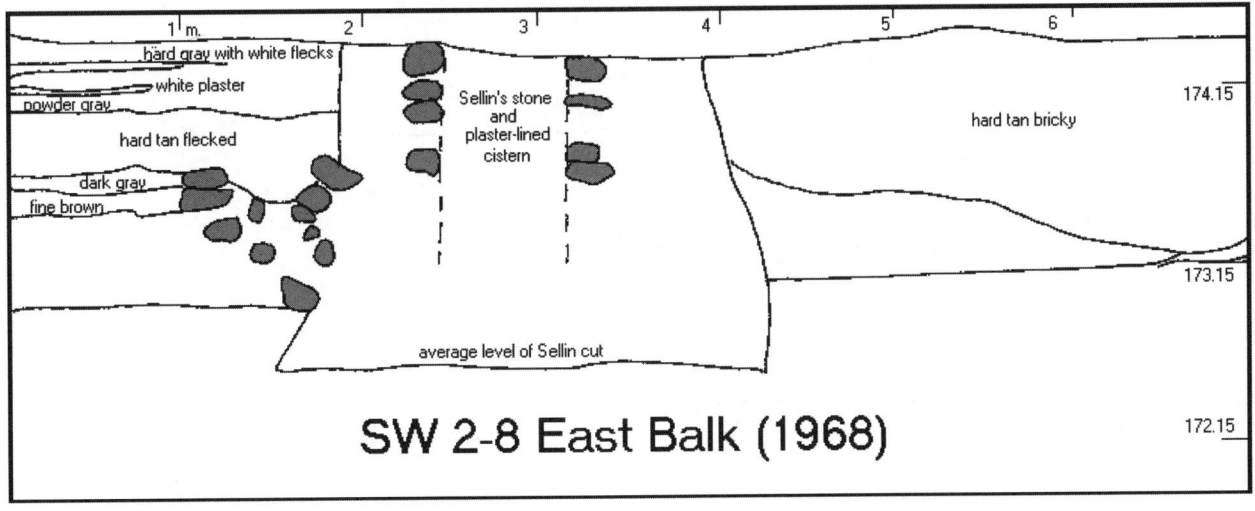

Appendix A-188

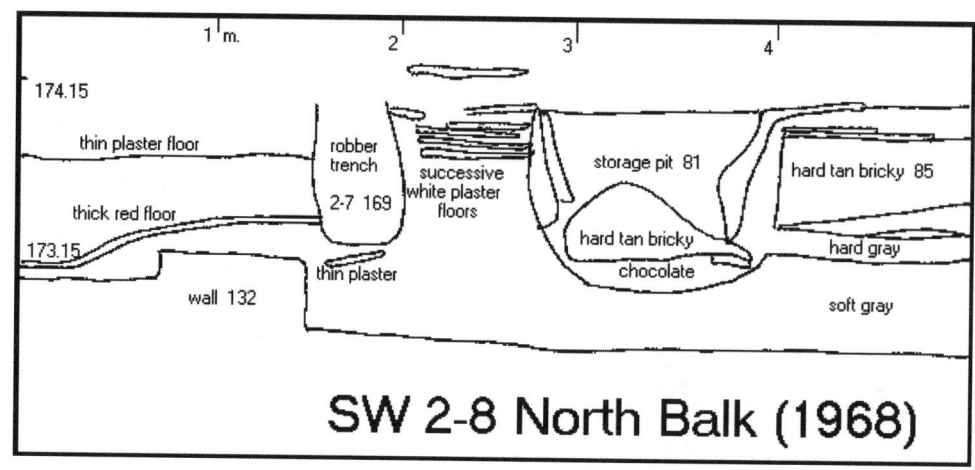

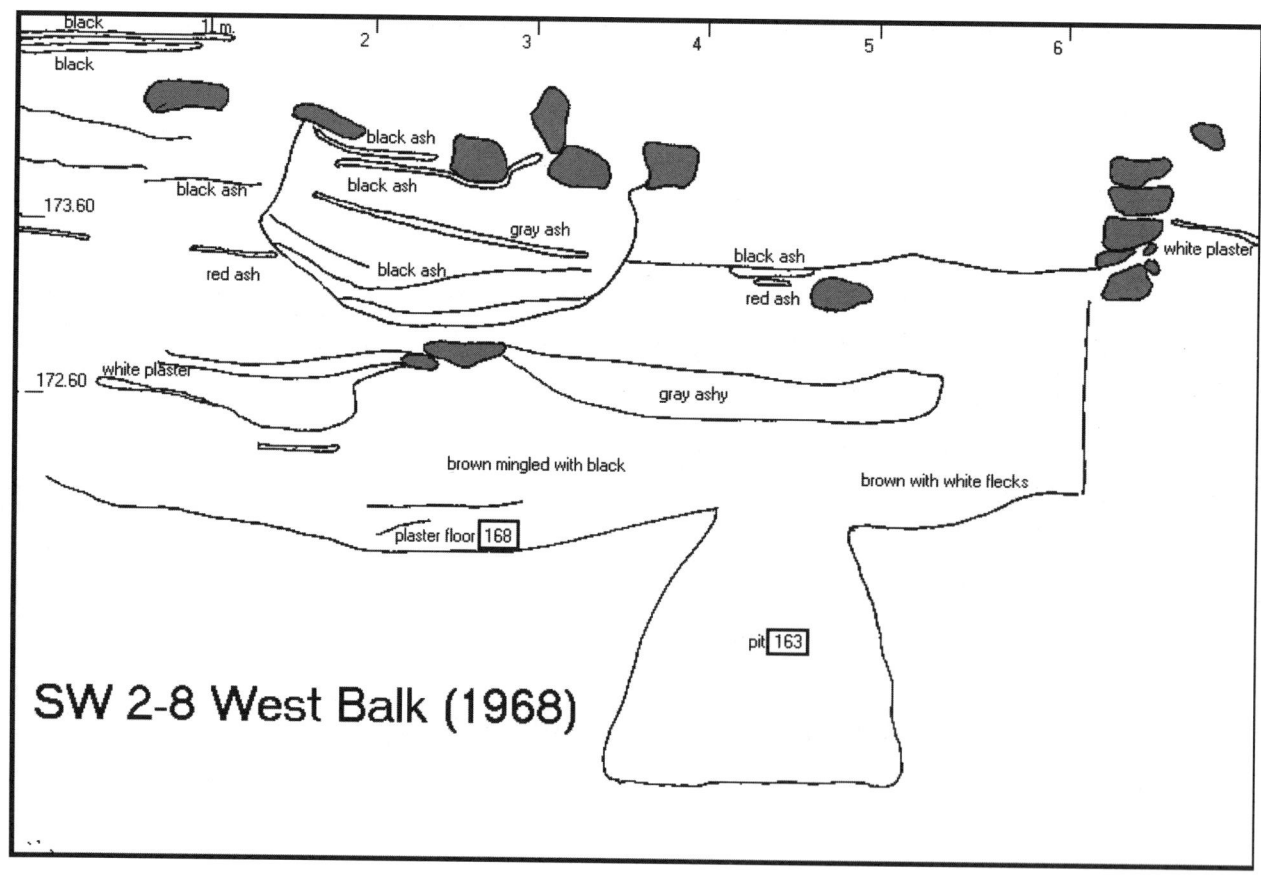

Appendix A-189

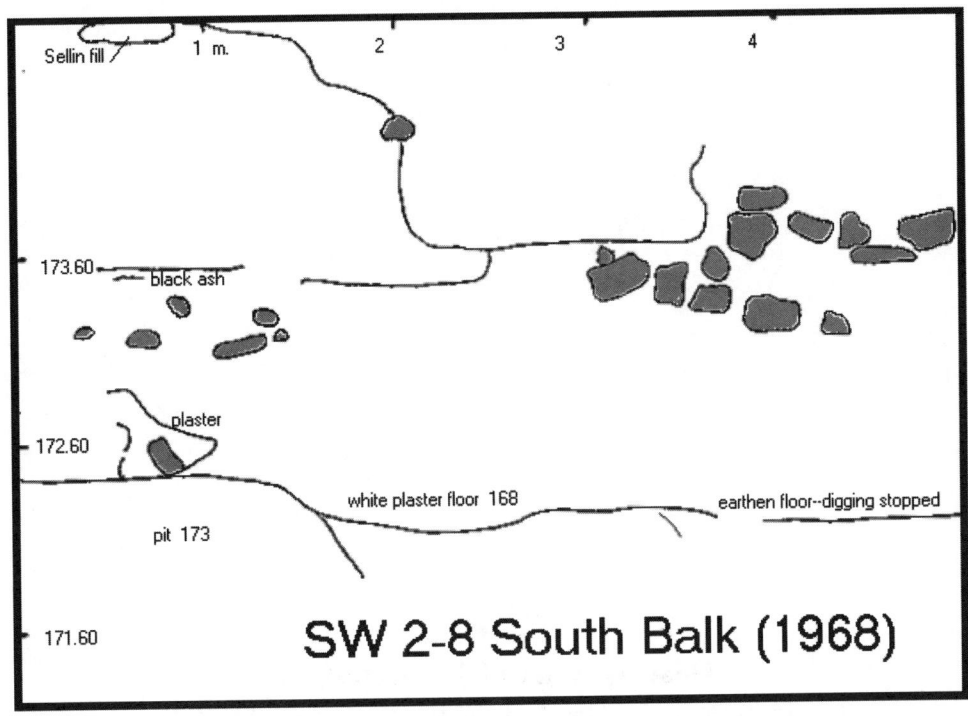

Appendix B
Descriptions of Principal Loci
in SW 1-7, SW 1-8, SW 2-7, and SW 2-8

Principal Loci in SW 1-7
(with Registered Objects)
Published Pottery from Rast 1978 in Parentheses

Locus number	Basket number/s	Pottery dates	Locus description	Registered Objects
1	1, 38, 45, 51, 177, 208, 209	LB I, I_1-I_2, P, A,	Debris from fall of N/NE balk from SW 2-7 extended 1 m into SW 1-7	
2	2	I_1-10th cent	Surface cultivation, 60 cm from ground level of SW 2-7	
3	3	I_1-10th-9th cent-I_2, A, O	Dark occupation level, but no floors; ca. 35 cm thick; sub L 2	
4	4, 5, 13, 16	I_1-10th-9th cent-I_2, P, EH	Hard and soft gray fill with many small stones; perhaps make-up for L 3; no floors observed	TT 503, Basalt rubbing stone
5	6-11, 14, 21, 22, 24, 27, 30, 32-37, 39, 41, 43, 58, 65, 68, 72, 75, 81, 86, 89, 91, 94, 95, 130, 138, 139, 184, 186, 189, 194, 198, 203	EB, MB IIC, LB I, LB II, I_1-10th cent, I_2, P, EH, O, A	Debris from presumed edge of Sellin trench; loose gray and brown soil (brown perhaps undisturbed from pit; cf. L 6); goal was to remove the 1963 balk and edge out the Sellin trench, some borders of which were found	
6	12	12th cent	Light brown from edge of possible circular pit bordering Sellin trench (cf. L. 5); from -144 cm extending ca. 80 cm down	

Locus number	Basket number/s	Pottery dates	Locus description	Registered Objects
7	15	10th-8th cent	Hardish brown in 1963 balk (from -165 cm); perhaps part of a mixed fill with L 4, as appeared to be the case at the N end; bottomed with small stones	
8	17, 18, 25, 99, 104, 215	MB IIC, I₁-7th cent	Hard-packed yellow-brown layer with soft spots; sub L 4 and L 7 in 1963 balk; from -185 cm; found N of wall L 11 and includes foundation trench (30 cm wide) for L 11; extends under L 11 suggesting possible robbing out of wall L 30 of SW 2-7 extended	TT 906, Basalt grinding bowl
35	none	none	Mortar installation associated with floor L 33; fourth of a sequence of twelve floors S of wall L 11 and SW of pit L 16; squarish stone with worked depression filled with black ashy dirt; set into floor L 41 = ninth floor in the sequence of twelve floors; cf. L 46[1]	TT 578, Limestone mortar
46	74, 90, 98	12th-10th cent	Stony area N of sequence of twelve floors (L 18, 31, 32, 33, 36, 37, 38, 40, 41, 43, 44, 45); soft brown dirt; sub L 4 and L 7; borders L 5	TT 591, Bone inlay fragment
60	97, 102	12th-10th cent	Circular pit; soft brown dirt; D=120 cm under ashy layer sub L 46	TT 602, Iron armor scale (?)

---

[1] Levels and locus numbers for the sequence of twelve floors: floor 1 (175.72; L 18); floor 2 (175.67; L 31); floor 3 (175.62; L 32); floor 4 (175.59; L 33); floor 5 (175.57; L 36); floor 6 (?; L 37); floor 7 (175.52; L 38); floor 8 (?; L 40); floor 9 (175.48; L 41); floor 10 (?; L 43); floor 11 (?; L 44); floor 12 (175.42; L 45).

Locus number	Basket number/s	Pottery dates	Locus description	Registered Objects
68	114, 116-119, 122, 124, 128, 129, 132, 136, 137, 141, 143, 144, 146-148, 150-152, 157, 159, 162, 163, 170-172, 178, 179, 180, 185, 192, 196, 197, 206, 207	MB IIC-LB I	Hard bricky layer sub twenty-third floor in a sequence of floors that began with L 18; = L 64	TT 882, Ceramic female figurine torso TT 895, Ceramic female figurine legs
74	134	MB IIC, LB I, 12th cent	Hardish gray-brown layer sub L 68; characterized below L 74 by a thin strip of layers not continuing in the W (where they abut L 68) along the edge of the Sellin trench; layers possibly cut by robber trench for wall L 84 continuation	
75	135, 154, 160	MB IIC, LB I, I₁	= SW 2-7, L 53; the center paving stones, ranging from 20-26 cm in thickness associated with the quern was black ashy dirt (inside the quern and throughout the basin); below the large paving stones, which did not extend the width of the basin, is an earlier paving of stones comparable in working to the siding stones	TT 820, Iron plow point
78	--		Red, clayey floor sub L 68 in NW of square, from 174.39	
79	--		Small stone circle in floor L 78	
81	--		Section of E-W wall at N balk, rebuild of wall L 83; at N end extends only ca. 110 cm, but wall L 83 below continued into W balk	
83	--		Section of E-W wall at N balk	

Locus number	Basket number/s	Pottery dates	Locus description	Registered Objects
84	216	--	Section of N-S wall from N balk, forming corner with wall I 83	
93			See L 113	
103	221, 231	MB IIC	Hard sunbaked gray layer sub L 78; from 174.49 to ca. 174.35	
107	338	EB, MB IIC, LB I	Wall, one course wide and five courses deep sub L 5; from L 174.37 to 173.42; red floors L 109 and L 109b run up against the top two courses, as does red floor L 111 on the S face; floor L 112b runs up to the bottom course; L 107 is cut by robber trench L 132	
108	226, 328	MB IIC, LB I, I₁	= L 104; Soft brown pit cutting wall L 184; sub L 103, sub L 78, sub L 68 , S of L 83; removal later continued when it was determined that it had not been entirely cleaned out at bottom	TT 1202, Ceramic female figurine
109			Red floor sub L5 between walls L 107 and L 124 running up against N face of wall L 107 under wall L 158 in E balk	
111	232	MB IIC	Red floor sub L 5 S of wall L 107; running up to wall L 107 and wall L 157 creating a corner; cut by pit L 154 on S and robber trench L 132 on W; runs up against E face of wall L 150b and runs out at S balk edge (N balk of SW 1-8; 173.84	
112	233, 351, 356	MB IIC	Very compact brown sub L 111; = L 105; sub floor L 109; also = L 147 at ca. 173.74	
113	234	12th cent	Pit equaling L 93 of 1966 season; later divided into 2 pits, L 113 and L126	
117b	269	EB, MB IIC, 15th cent	Compact brown fill between wall L 136 and L 142 sub L 123	
119	242, 245, 249	MB IIC, LB I	Sunbaked firm brown surface; sub L 78, sub L 68; thick plaster floor at 174.29	TT 974, Ceramic female figurine
121	246	LB I	Thick white plaster floor not connected to any structure	
122	247	LB I	Hard brown dirt sub L 121 in middle of plaster L 123	
123	258	± 1500	Hard white plaster floor sub L 119, L 122 at 174.33; broken by robber trench	
125			= L5	

Appendix B—194

Locus number	Basket number/s	Pottery dates	Locus description	Registered Objects
126	248	MB IIC, LB I	Pit separated from pit L 113, cutting walls L 136, 180, 184, as well as plaster floors L 121 and L 123	
129	253	MB IIC, LB I	Minute floor levels sub L 103; cut by pits L 108 and L 126	
133	262, 277, 283	EB, MB IIC, 15th cent	Loose coarse black layer with stones; probably Sellin sub L5 in NE corner	
134	--		White plaster floor sub L 119 at 174.30	
136	--		Wall sub L 137 2 courses wide and 2 deep with floor L 144a running up against it; 174.15 to 173.81; earlier wall L 180 below it	
137	266	15th cent	Hard brown layer between white plaster layers, L 134 and L 144a	
138	270	15th cent	Ashy floor sub L 129; =L 130	
139	271	15th cent	Ashy floor sub L 138 down to firm brown	
140	272	15th cent	Firm brown layer sub L 139 down to pavement L 144 and wall L 142 at 174.11	
142	--		Wall sub L 140 1 course wide and 3 courses deep; from 174.24 to 173.44	
144a	302, 304	MB IIC, LB I	White plaster floor sub L 137; may equal L 17 in SW 1-8	
144b	305	EB, MB IIC, LB I	Black charred floor sub L 144a	
147	357	EB, MB IIC	Compact brown fill	
149	282, 294, 295	EB, MB IIC-12th cent	Pit sub L 119 (1966 season); loose black and compact brown, cutting L 150, L 150b, L 159, and L 144a	

Appendix B—195

Locus number	Basket number/s	Pottery dates	Locus description	Registered Objects
150	--		Wall sub L 119; 2 courses wide and 1 course deep with L 144A running up against it; cut by robber trench L 132 and rests on L 150b; 174.21-174.00	
150b	323	EB, MB IIC	Wall sub L 150; 173.95-173.65; cut by L 132 with L 111 and L 159 running up agnist it = wall L 57 in SW 1-8	
154	291	EB, LB I	Very soft black pit sub L 158b cutting red floor L 111 and walls L 157 and L 150	
157	--		Wall sub L 5 cut by pit L 154; plastered next to L 111; 2 courses wide and 3 deep; 174.26-173.63	
158	297	LB I	Wall in E balk sub L 5 on floor L 109 which runs between walls L 107 and L 124; not bonded to wall 107	
158b	297, 298	LB I	Hard gray layer sub Sellin (1966, L5) in S balk	
159	--		Red floor sub L 147 running up against wall L 150b on W at 173.84 = L 49 of SW 1-8	
163	318	EB, MB IIC	Thin red-brown floor layer patches sub L 105 probably going with lower L 107	
164	319, 344, 381	EB, MB IIC	Firm black fill layer between pits L 108 and L 126	
165	322, 334, 335, 339, 340, 343, 346, 347, 349, 350, 352, 354, 355, 359-364	EB, MB IIC	Compact dark brown layer sub L 164, fill layer across entire square = L 195	
166	325	EB, MB IIC	Patchy red and brown layer sub L 144 not running up to wall L 142, but cut by it	

Locus number	Basket number/s	Pottery dates	Locus description	Registered Objects
167	326	EB, MB IIC, 1500	Compact brown layer sub L 166	
168	327	MB IIC	Gray floor layers sub L 167 with some orange patches	
170	330	EB, MB IIC	Compact red-brown layer sub L 168	
174	--		Wall in N sub wall L 83, which is an upper rebuild; from 174.20 to 173.51; goes with floors N of wall L 142	
177	342	MB IIC	Plaster surface and circular hole sub L5; 173.58	
178	345	EB, MB IIC	Black sherdy layer sub L 164	
181	358	EB, MB IIC	Series of packed earth floors sub L 147, indistinguishable from one another	
186	372	EB	Ashy burn and soft black layer, local only	
187	373	EB III	Soft cream brown layer, local only; sub L 186	
189	376, 379, 386	EB, EB III	Compact light brown sub L 187 = L 197	
192	382	EB III	Thin red layer localized near N balk sub L 189 and related to tabuns L 217 and L 216	
194	421-423, 427, 432	EB II, EB III	Yellow-orange bricky burn layer with ash sub L 189 (= L 197)	
195	385, 387, 388, 391, 393, 394, 398, 420	EB, EB III, MB IIB, MB IIC	Stones in loose brown layer ; = L 165	TT 1100, Ceramic female figurine torso
197	376, 392, 412, 414, 415, 418	EB, EB III	Compact brown layer sub L 195	

Locus number	Basket number/s	Pottery dates	Locus description	Registered Objects
198	--		Pavement sub L 189 = L 197	
200	--		Wall sub L 195 founded on bedrock, joining wall L 218, 172.94, 2 courses wide	
201	--		Wall against S balk with doorway L 212; 173.30	
202	--		Wall against E balk joins wall L 203 resting on floors 209; 173.36-172.70	
206	406-410	EB, EB III, MB IIC	Pit to bedrock sub L 165 and L 126, soft black sherdy	
207	411	EB III	Pit sub L 165, soft black, most of which is sub basin L 75	
209	417	EB III	Compact brown and white floor pieces sub wall L 202	
212	--		Doorway sub L 195 in wall L 201 in S balk	
213	--		Doorway sub L 212 in wall L 214 sub wall L 201	
214	--		Earlier phase wall sub L 201 founded on bedrock	
215	--		White plastered bench sub L 197 and against wall L 214	
216	439	EB III	Tabun against N balk sub L 165	
217	438	EB III	Tabun against N balk sub L 165	
218	--		Wall sub L 165 founded on bedrock, joining with wall L 224 (early phase of L 200) and wall L 214; floor L 219 goes up to it	
219	434, 435, 441	EB III	Ashy black floor sub L 194 connected; 172.13 = L 111 of SW 1-8	
220	436	EB	Firm gray floor sub L 219 N of wall L 200	
221	437	EB III	Soft gray layer sub L 220 N of wall L 200	
222	440	EB III	Firm red-brown layer down to bedrock sub L 221 N of wall L 200	

Principal Loci in SW 1-8
(with Registered Objects)
Published Pottery from Rast 1978 in Parentheses

Locus number	Basket number/s	Pottery dates	Locus description	Registered Objects
1	1-7, 87, 99	MB IIC, LB, I_1-I_2, P, H, A	Soft gray debris as L 1 in SW 2-8 extending from surface 175.94 to arbitrary level of 175.64	
6	--		2-course wall with covering of mudbrick extending along S balk and discernible in S balk of SW 2-8	
8	44-53	MB IIC, LB IIb, I_1-7th cent, P, EH, A, O	Loose brown fill lying above floor in N part of square	
12	76, 80, 98	MB IIC, LB I, 12th cent; 10th-7th cent	Stone-lined pit in SE corner of square	
13	112	--	Floor with white plaster in part at 173.96 sub L 24 and floor L 20	
15	70-73, 77	MB IIC, LB, I_1, I_2	Hardish gray-brown fill sub L 1, perhaps part of L 1	
17	78, 79, 81, 83, 86, 110, 115	EB, MB IIC, LB	Hard, bricky brown layer with charcoal flecks and limestone bits sub L1; adjoins L 15	
18	--		Section of N-S wall associated with floor L 13	

Appendix B—199

Locus number	Basket number/s	Pottery dates	Locus description	Registered Objects
19	82, 84, 90-92, 102, 107	EB, MB IIC, LB I, I₁-I₂, P	Loose, dark brown layer in pit L 12 from -70 cm ; stone lining of pit ends at ca. 172.20 in a hardish brown bricky layer under floor L 23	TT 644, Calcite unguentarium stand
20	96, 97	MB IIC, LB I	Apparent floor sub L 8 in NW corner of square at 174.08; above L 23 in part	TT 760, Ceramic figurine legs
23	100, 103-106, 108, 109, 114	MB IIC, LB I	Plastered floor in NW corner of square sub L 17, sub L 20 at 174.06; continues into extreme NW corner of square, but partly broken; in the extreme NW corner there were 3 successive plaster floors; the uppermost just barely appearing out of the balk; the second was only in the corner for ca. 60 cm, then broken and continuing in S going under L 29 wall stump from N balk; NW corner has several repairs; plaster extends partly under wall L 29	TT 759, Ceramic female figurine fragment
24	88, 89, 93	MB IIC, LB I	Hard bricky layer with charcoal and limestone flecks sub L 1 in S	
25	94	MB IIC, LB I	Apparent pit continuing through W balk from SW 2-8	
29	111, 113	EB, MB IIC	N-S wall from N balk; sub L 1 and L 17; floor L 23 abuts and goes under upper courses; wall extends 1 m and is a possible rebuild of wall L 30	
30	--		N-S wall, of which wall L 29 may be a rebuild	
32	116, 177	EB, MB IIC-1500	Trial trench in NW corner; compact brown = L 35 = L 40	
33	117, 121, 124, 129, 136-143, 157, 161, 162, 164, 178	EB, MB IIC-1500	Trial trench in SW corner sub L 24; compact brown;= L 47 = L 64	

Appendix B—200

Locus number	Basket number/s	Pottery dates	Locus description	Registered Objects
34	118, 122	EB, MB IIC, -1500	Bluish-black ashy pocket in L 33	
35	119, 123, 125, 264	EB, EB III, MB IIC, 1500	Trial trench in NW corner sub L 23; compact brown = L 32 = L 40	
36	--		Pit cleaned out in SW corner = L1	
37			Wall sub L 35 = L 150b of SW 1-7; E face robbed out by pit L 39; is bonded to N face of wall L 38; has red floor L 49 against W face, which = L 159 of SW 1-7; only 1 course deep from 173.87 to 173.70 under which is wall L 71	
39	126		Sub L 35; soft black pit cutting E face of wall L 37 next to wall L 38	
40	127, 128, 209	MB IIC	Compact brown sub L 23 over wall L 41 and on its S face = L 32 = L 35	
41	--		Wall sub L 40 roughly constructed with small stones at 173.68-173.24	
44	133	MB IIC, LB I, 12th cent	Pit sub loose creamy fill, L 1; soft black with charcoal	TT 566, Jar handle with seal impression
46	135, 144, 145	MB IIC, LB I	Firm brown in stone fall S of pit L 44 sub L 1	
47	--		= L 33 = L 64	
49	153	MB IIC	Red floor sub L 35 tipping up against wall L 37 = L 159 of SW 1-7; 173.84	
50	--		Red floor sub L 32 tipping up against N face of wall L 41 at 173.50 = L 52	
52	179	EB, MB IIC	Red and gray floor at 173.55 = L 50	
53	--		Wall sub L 47; 1 course wide with blocked doorway; 173.87-173.24	
54	--		Wall sub L 47; 2 courses wide, 1 course deep; 173.86-173.63; no floor associated with it	
57	189, 203	EB, MB IIC	Compact red and gray layer sub L 46	

Appendix B—201

Locus number	Basket number/s	Pottery dates	Locus description	Registered Objects
64	--		= L 33 = L 47	
69	187	EB, MB IIC	Red floor S of wall L 53; L 69 = L 73 (sub L 72), which is a red floor sunken into pit L 101, which slopes radically down toward the E, suggesting some kind of basin	
70	174, 211, 234, 274	EB, EB III, MB IIC, LB I	Pit = L 25	
71	185	EB, MB IIC	Wall sub wall L 37; 1 course wide; joined to wall L 38 and going into SW 1-7; 173.70-173.52	
73	--		Equals L 69	
75	188, 190, 191, 194, 195, 199-202, 204, 205, 210, 212, 213, 217, 218, 220, 269	EB, EB III, MB IIB, MB IIC	Compact black-brown fill sub L 69; same as L 164, 165 in SW 1-7	
76	192, 193, 196, 198, 219, 222, 223, 225, 228-233, 270	EB, EB III, MB IIC, LB I	Firm brown with large stones sub L 75	
78	197	MB IIC	Child burial in S balk; sub red floor L 69 at 173.20 and in compact brown fill	TT 900, Ceramic female figurine torso
80	--		Wall sub L 76; 2 courses wide; joined wall L 82; 172.77-172.30	
82	--		Wall sub L 76 joining wall L 80; 173.04-172.50	

Locus number	Basket number/s	Pottery dates	Locus description	Registered Objects
83	--		Wall sub L 76 joining walls L 84 , L 82 and SW 1-7 wall L 201 by means of blocked doorway L 110; associated with floors L 85, L 90, and L 112; cut by child burial 53; 173.36-172.52	
84	--		Wall sub L 76; 173.31-172.58	
85	--		Compact brown floor sub L 76 between L 82 and L 84 at 172.59	
87	--		Wall sub L 76 cut by L 70; in W balk from 173.05 to 172.65	
88	243	EB III, MB IIC	Wall sub L 76; 2 courses deep; from 172.69 to 172.20	
89	--		Wall sub L 76; cut by Sellin on E; made corner with wall L 80; associated with floor L 90; possibly making a doorway between itself and L 106; 172.88-172.30	
90	241, 247, 248, 254	EB III	Floor sub L 76; ashy black; associated with walls L 80, L 82, and L89	
95	236	EB III	Ashy black layer sub L 76; above L 102	
98	240	EB III	Thin red circle sub L 97 = L 76; probably a destroyed tabun	
99	239, 242, 251, 254, 258-260, 263, 266, 267	EB III	Firm brown layer = L 109	
100	268, 271	EB III	Yellow-orange bricky burn layer sub L 99 in N part of square = SW 1-7 L 194	
101	245, 246, 248, 250, 252, 253	EB III, MB IIB-C	Pit cut from floor L 73 with child burial, L 46, in it; cuts wall L 94 and burn L 100; loose black	
102	256	EB III	Compact gray floors sub L 95 and above wall L 104; = L 90	
104	--		Wall sub L 108; 1 course wide; not clearly associated with any other floor or wall; 172.40-172.15	

Locus number	Basket number/s	Pottery dates	Locus description	Registered Objects
105	--		Wall sub L 76 in S balk coming from SW 1-8; probably joined with wall L 88; 172.54-172.20	
106			Wall sub L 99 associated with floors L 107 and L 111; not clearly associated with any other wall; cut by pit L 101; 172.19-171.92 (bedrock)	
107	282, 283	EB III	Floor sub L 99	
108	262	EB III	Compact dark brown sub L 102	
109	--		Firm gray and brown = L 99	
110	--		Blocked doorway of wall L 83 in N balk sub L 76	
111	279	EB II	Floor sub L 110 = L 107 with wall L 106	
112	286, 294	EB III	Compact brown floor sub L 76	
116	280	EB III	Hard brown and small stones sub L 111	
117	281	EB III	Firm red-brown layer sub L 116 to bedrock	
118	284	EB III	Compact gray, clayey floor sub L 107	
119	285, 288	EB III	Compact dark brown layer	
121	290, 291, 293	EB III	Firm orange-brown layer sub L 99	

Appendix B—204

Principal Loci in SW 2-7
(with Registered Objects)
Published Pottery from Rast 1978 in Parentheses

Locus number	Basket number/s	Pottery dates	Locus description	Registered Objects
1	1	I_1, I_2, H, A	1 m strip (15 cm deep) through stratum of dark surface soil	
2	2	I_1, I_2, A	Second 1 m strip (15 cm deep) through dark surface stratum	
3	3	LB, I_1, I_2, A	3 m surface strip (15 cm deep) following pattern of L 1 and L 2	
4	4	I_1, I_2, A	2 m surface strip (15 cm deep); as L 1-3	
5	5, 6	MB, LB, I_1, I_2, 6th cent, P, A	2 m sub-surface strip under L 1 and L 2 to absolute 177.75 (NW), 177.58 (NE)	
6	7, 8	MB, LB, I_1, I_2, H, A	2 x 3 m sub-surface strip under L 3 to absolute 177.19	
7			2 m square W of L 6 to absolute 177.19; = L 6	
8	9-13	LB, I_1, I_2, H, A	3 m square under L 3 and L 4 sub surface to absolute 176.55	
9			2 x 3 m extension of L 8 to the W; = L 8	
10	14	LB, I_1, I_2, H, A	Light sub-surface stratum under L 1, 2, and 5	
11	15, 16	I_1-I_2, H, A	Dark colored first occupation stratum sub L 1, 2, 5, 10	
12	17, 18	I_1, I_2, A	Light tan and fairly hard stratum; = L 46	
13	19, 20	MB, I_2, A	Hard gray and bricky later sub L 12	(TT 36) jar, Rast (1978) fig 30:4
14	21, 22	10th cent, I_2, H, A	Layer of light and soft gray fill with many small stones sub dark first occupation stratum	
15	--		E-W I_2 wall extending from W balk to center of square	
16	--		N-S I_2 wall joined to L 15 enclosing area of I_2 jar	
17	23	I_2, A	1 m trial trench running next to S border of wall L 15	

Locus number	Basket number/s	Pottery dates	Locus description	Registered Objects
18	24, 25	I_2, H, A	2 m strip sub L 11 in light tan soil; exploratory activity in top level of square, E side to depth of 25 cm	(TT 306) juglet, Rast (1978) fig 40:5
19	26	LB, I_2, A	Light tan stratum continued sub L 18	
20	27	I_1, I_2, A	Continuation of light tan stratum sub L 18	
21	28, 29	I_2, A	Continuation of trial trench L 17 S of wall L15	
22	--		N-S I_2 wall along E balk	
23	30, 31, 35, 39	I_1-I_2, P, A	Sub L 20; trial trench between wall L 16 and wall L 22 next to N balk	
24	32, 33, 42, 43	LB, I_1, I_2, 10th-7th cent, A	Trial trench between wall L 16 and W balk	TT 94, ceramic figurine fragment
25	34	I_1-8th cent	Floor between walls L 16 and L 22 at 176.55 with slight debris deposit above	

Locus number	Basket number/s	Pottery dates	Locus description	Registered Objects
26	36, 37, 38, 40, 98	± 900	Area E of wall L 16 and N of wall L 15;= room 2	(TT 62) juglet, (Rast 1978) fig 40:7 (TT 63) juglet, (Rast 1978) fig 40:1 TT 71, iron sword (?) (TT 73) pyxis, (Rast 1978) fig 40:14 TT 78, serpentine pendant TT 79, basalt weight (TT 83) jug, (Rast 1978) fig 39:6 TT 116, basalt quern TT 117, limestone rubbing stone (TT 439) bowl, (Rast 1978) fig 42:2 (TT 440) jug, (Rast 1978) fig 37:2 (TT 441) bowl, (Rast 1978) fig 46:8 (TT 443) bowl, (Rast 1978) fig 48:3 (TT 448) bowl, (Rast 1978) fig 48:2

| 27 | 41, 45, 46, 49, 85, 101 | ± 900 | Area adjoining S balk of L 26, with extensive pottery | (TT 64) censer, (Rast 1978) fig 51:3 (TT 65) cooking pot, (Rast 1978) fig 50:3 TT 86, basalt rubbing stone TT 87, stone weight (TT 88) juglet, (Rast 1978) fig 40:6 (TT 89) lamp, (Rast 1978) fig 51:1 TT 90, iron sword (?) TT 91, iron plowshare TT 100, ceramic figurine mold (TT 103) jug, (Rast 1978) fig 37:1 TT 108, iron scythe TT 322, iron scythe (TT 416) bowl, (Rast 1978) fig 45:3 (TT 442) bowl, (Rast 1978) fig 46:13 (TT 444) bowl, (Rast 1978) fig 48:16 (TT 445) bowl, (Rast 1978) fig 45:2 (TT 446) bowl, (Rast 1978) fig 42:1 (TT 447) bowl, (Rast 1978) fig 48:15 (TT 449) bowl, (Rast 1978) fig 47:1 (TT 450) bowl, (Rast 1978) fig 46:7 (TT 451) bowl, (Rast 1978) fig 43:2 (TT 452) bowl, (Rast 1978) fig 46:14 (TT 453) bowl, (Rast 1978) fig 46:3 (TT 487) bowl, (Rast 1978) fig 44:4 (TT 488) pyxis, (Rast 1978) fig 40:12 |

Locus number	Basket number/s	Pottery dates	Locus description	Registered Objects
28	44, 47, 48, 50, 51, 53-59	11th-8th cent	Trial trench extending along wall L 22 S of L 23 to wall L 15 and sub floor L 25; continues W toward wall L 16 through very loose destruction, abundant large sherds from individual pots, frequent lumps of plaster; may suggest walls L 15, 16, and 30 were plaster-lined	TT 132, iron plow points (TT 464) bowl, (Rast 1978) fig 45:6 (TT 471) bowl, (Rast 1978) fig 43:1 (TT 484) juglet, (Rast 1978) fig 40:11 (TT 485) bowl, (Rast 1978) fig 45:1
30	--		E-W wall enclosing northern room as uncovered in L 28	
31	62	8th cent	Northernmost extension of wall L 16 recognized as later phase	
36	69, 70, 76-78, 86, 87, 99, 105, 106, 142	LB I, LB II, 12th, 8th cent, ±900	A strip along wall L 16 between walls L 30 and 32, later extended to entire room beneath L 28 to presumed clay floor	(TT 486) bowl, (Rast 1978) fig 48:1 TT 1842, ceramic human figurine
38	--		Narrow wall that became visible on E side of room 1	
45	100, 102, 103	I_2, P, A	Chocolate occupation stratum in new 3 m extension of S balk	
46	104, 107-111, 120	I_2, P, H, A	Light tan stratum directly sub L 45	TT 257, scarab
47	112-114, 116, 121, 129, 132	I_1, I_2, P, H, A	Crumbly, dark earth, presumably Sellin fill, up to layer of gray fill	
52	121-125	LB I, LB II, 12th, 10th cent	Fine sandy stratum without stones in S room 1 sub L 46	
54	129, 136	LB I, 12th, 10th cent	Loose brown stratum with black ash sub L 52	
55	130-133	LB I	Gray ash destruction layer sub L 54	TT 356, limestone saddle grinder TT 357, basalt quern

Appendix B—209

Locus number	Basket number/s	Pottery dates	Locus description	Registered Objects
57	142, 147, 151, 154, 156, 157, 210-212, 217, 218, 226-228	± 900	1 m square of black ash destruction along S balk	TT 387, fused iron pieces TT 398, bone spatula TT 409, iron arrowhead (TT 415) bowl, (Rast 1978) fig 45:4 TT 430, limestone מצבה TT 431, limestone מצבה TT 432, basalt מצבה (TT 467) jar, (Rast 1978) fig 36:1 (TT 472) cooking pot, (Rast 1978) fig 50:2 (TT 490) jar, (Rast 1978) fig 36:2
58	--		Bricky clay floor cut through in S by L 57	
59	143, 145, 146, 148-150, 152, 153, 155	± 900	Destruction layer of mixed brown, gray and black ash sub floor L 58	TT 320, quartzolite rubbing stone (TT 327) juglet, (Rast 1978) fig 40:4 (TT 476) jar, (Rast 1978) fig 30:2 (TT 483) jar, (Rast 1978) fig 31:1 (TT 489) krater, (Rast 1978) fig 41:1 (TT 1866) jar, (Rast 1978) fig 35:1
60	159, 160-162	± 900	Hard brown clay with black ash intrusion at former E balk of room 1	TT 355, bone spatula (TT 456) cooking pot, (Rast 1978) fig 50:1 (TT 465) bowl, (Rast 1978) fig 46:1

| 61 | 163-166, 168-170, 172-176, 178-206, 208, 209, 214-216, 219-222, 225, 229 | ± 900; 11th cent | Dark hard clay stratum covering entire southern extension of room 1 | TT 323, miniature juglet
TT 324, limestone rubbing stone
TT 342, iron toggle pin
(TT 350) amphora, (Rast 1978) fig 36:3
(TT 351) stand, (Rast 1978) fig 51:4
(TT 352) bowl, (Rast 1978) fig 47:2
(TT 353) bowl, (Rast 1978) fig 46:5
(TT 354) bowl, (Rast 1978) fig 47:4
TT 358, quartzolite quern
TT 359, limestone base
(TT 372) pyxis, (Rast 1978) fig 40:13
TT 373, socketed stone
TT 388, loom weights
TT 389, limestone base
TT 390, limestone base
TT 391, limestone base
TT 392, basalt rubbing stone
TT 393, basalt rubbing stone
TT 394, basalt grinder
TT 395, basalt quern
(TT 410) bowl, (Rast 1978) fig 46:11
(TT 411) bowl, (Rast 1978) fig 46:2
(TT 412) bowl, (Rast 1978) fig 47:3
(TT 414) jug, (Rast 1978) fig 39:4
(TT 454) jug, (Rast 1978) fig 38:1
(TT 455) bowl, (Rast 1978) fig 46:12
(TT 457) bowl, (Rast 1978) fig 46:6
(TT 458) juglet, (Rast 1978) fig 40:9 |

Locus number	Basket number/s	Pottery dates	Locus description	Registered Objects
62	171, 177, 207, 213, 223, 231, 238, 246	MB IIC, LB, I_1-I_2, P, A	2 m square, 5 m S of "olive press," probing for Sellin cistern	
63	224, 230, 232-237	12th-10th cent, ± 900	15-20 cm of brown fill or wash between L 61 and floor beneath it; new SE corner of room 1	(TT 386) juglet, (Rast 1978) fig 40:3 TT 397, bone spatula (TT 468) jug, (Rast 1978) fig 39:2 (TT 481) jar, (Rast 1978) fig 31:2
64	239-241	± 900	Room 1 S and W of wall L16, beginning 130 cm from W balk and widening to 160 cm from W balk	
65	242, 244, 245, 247-248	LB I, LB II, 12th & 10th cent	Area limited to strip W of wall L 16 from the old S balk to the new S balk of room 1	
66	243	I	Pit in the midst of the extension of room 1 area	TT 408, iron armor scale
67	249	± 900	Area under later phase wall on E side of room 1	TT 419, stone weight
68	250-252	I_1-I_2, ± 900, P, A	New 2 m strip S of room 1 through upper occupation levels	TT 423, ceramic disk
69	253-257a	LB-I_2, 12th cent, ± 900, P	Beginning of I_2 occupation in new 2 m strip S of room 1	
70	258, 262, 263, 266	I_1, I_2, P, A, ± 900	= L 71	
71	261	12th-10th cent	2 m strip W of wall L 16 ; brick with white flecks; = L 70	
72	259, 260	I_2, P, A	Soft area, possibly a pit, in SE corner of new 2 m strip	

Locus number	Basket number/s	Pottery dates	Locus description	Registered Objects
73	264, 265	MB IIC, LB, I_1-I_2, P, A	Area covered with stones W and NW of the Sellin "olive press"	
74	267, 268, 269-271, 286	MB IIC, 12th-7th cent, O, A	Test trench 150 cm square along N balk to determine stratification under wall L 30; dug to floor at 175.46; starting at this level earth was peeled off to another floor 8-10 cm below	TT 560, loom weight TT 563, loom weight
76	275-278a	I_1-I_2, P, O, A	Extension of pit from N balk of 1963 season, beginning 175 cm E of W balk and running 150 cm eastward in full width of L 74	
78	281	12th-10th cent	Narrow strip directly N of wall L 16 dug under the wall to confirm the depth level of wall L 16 and to seek continuation of stratigraphy on the E balk of L 74	TT 600, bronze arrowhead
79	282	10th cent	Area in which wall top two courses of L 16, the later phase, were removed	
80	283	10th cent	Earlier phase of wall L 16 down to the floor of rooms 1 and 2 of the cultic structure	
81	284	10th cent	Wall L 15 of 1963 season removed to floor level of rooms 1 and 2	
82	285, 289, 290, 293	LB I, I_1, I_2, A	100-120 cm strip between wall L 16 and W balk, dug to a floor level in the S and mass of smaller stones in the N	TT 667, basalt rubbing stone
83	287	MB IIC, 10th cent, EH, O	Floor below L 74 at level 175.39; 5 cm sub L 83 there was a distinct burn, partly gray, partly black to a depth of 2 cm; sub this came 5 cm of a brown layer, followed by 5 cm of gray ash; finally a cream-colored clay layer of considerable depth appeared; 8 similar strata were visible in the N balk	
84	288, 291, 369, 370	I_2, O, A	Pit in NW corner of SW 2-7; cf. 1963 W balk section drawing	
86	316	± 1000	Fragment of plaster floor with fragment of bowl lodged in it at level 175.53	

Appendix B—213

Locus number	Basket number/s	Pottery dates	Locus description	Registered Objects
87	294, 295-297, 299, 302, 321, 322	MB IIC, LB I, I_1-I_2 to 1000	First presumed floor sub L 86; under several cm of soft gray surface a brown gritty layer 15 cm thick terminated in a hard gray floor. The floor was followed S and E	TT 632, basalt saddle grinder (TT 635) juglet, (Rast 1978) fig 92:2 TT 639, miniature cup TT 646, ceramic whorl TT 732, basalt saddle grinder TT 754, ceramic female figurine
88	298, 300	MB IIC, LB, 12th-11th cent, I_2	Crumbled bricky debris between wall L 89 and the E balk; dug in an effort to find floor corresponding to floor L 87	TT 633, basalt saddle grinder TT 636, basalt rubbing stone TT 688, bone spindle whorl
89	301	Late 11th cent	N-S wall remaining in only one course, presumably connected with wall floor L 87	
90	303, 306	MB IIC, I_1-I_2	Remnant of Sellin fill; soft gray dusty soil S of L 88 extending along E balk to S balk	
91	304, 314	MB IIC, 12th-10th cent	Small shallow pit 1 m in D in NW corner, adjoining L 84	
92	305	MB IIC, 12th-11th cent	E-W wall appearing in NE corner of square	
94	309, 318	LB I-A	Loose gray fill sub L 88 E of wall L 89 and extending to flagstone pavement L 95	
96	308, 311, 317, 319	LB I,-1000	Fairly hard brown colored layer next to W balk sub L 82, ending in hard brown surface at level of L 87	TT 641, ceramic female figurine
100	320	--	Plaster floor at 175.34	
101	--		Plaster floor at 175.01	

Locus number	Basket number/s	Pottery dates	Locus description	Registered Objects
103	323, 324	LB I	Test trench adjoining S balk W of wall L 89 to determine nature and extent of black burn, first thought to be a pit	
104	325, 326	MB IIC, LB I, 12th cent	20 cm thick burn layer of black, gray and creamy ash (balk of L 103), which, however, quickly disappeared and gave way to L 105	
105	327, 330, 332, 337	MB IIC, LB I, 12th cent	Hard gravel layer with many stones sub 104 dug to floor layer 174.74	
108	333, 334	MB IIC, LB I, 12th cent-1000	Pit 100 x 110 x 60 cm adjoining W side of wall L 89	
111	339, 341	LB I, 12th cent	15 cm brown layer culminating in a clear floor level, partly plaster, which may be identical with L 101 on the E side of wall L 89	
114	346-348	LB I	13 cm layer of gray clay, medium hard, culminating in first floor level sub wall L 89, which may be identical with L 100 on the E side of wall L 89	
115	--		Limestone base at 175.08	
116	--		Limestone base at level 175.15	
117	349-354	LB I	Gray bricky layer of varying thickness sub L 100 and sub L 114	TT 856, basalt rubbing stone
118	355-359	MB IIC, LB I	1 x 2.25 m test trench along W balk dug to depth of 65 cm sub L 111	TT 855, ceramic figurine head
119	--		Oblong slab in SE corner of square, appearing to jut out squarely from middle of basin ("olive press"), which is on other side of balk	
120	360	LB I	Continuation southward of 1 m test trench dug to depth of 65 cm sub L 105	
121	361-363	LB I, 12th cent	Pit that appears to cut through gray bricky stratum visible on W balk of L 120	

Appendix B—215

Locus number	Basket number/s	Pottery dates	Locus description	Registered Objects
124	365-368	MB IIC, LB I, 12th cent, ±1200	Pit with extensive gray and black burn, which appeared on W balk of L 118 = L 168	
127	--		Pit between wall L 92 and floor L 101	
128			Pit S of pit L 127 in E balk	
129	377-379	MB IIC, LB I	Hard-packed brown soil mixed with some flecks, sub floor L 111 = L 105, at which digging stopped in 1966 season, dug first to a layer of black ash at 174.77 that was visible in E balk of pit L 124 and in the N rim of pit L 91, but then faded out. This locus was dug in a 1 m N-S strip from pit L 121 to pit L 76, to a depth that reached a new floor at an average of 25-35 cm sub L 111 and L 105	
130	380	MB IIC, LB I, A	Mixed fill at N end of former N-S balk between SW 3-7 and SW 2-7 dug to the level of L 129 and clearing the rim of pit L 84	
131	381	LB I, A	Corridor between pits L 84 and L 124 dug in part to level of floor L 129	
132	382	mixed	Pit corridor sub L 131 brought completely to L 129 level	
133	383	LB I, 1500-1468	Hard-packed brown layer with flecks, 1 m N-S strip adjoining L 129, dug to same floor level	
134	384, 385	LB I pure, 1500-1468	Hard-packed brown layer with flecks, 1 m N-S strip adjoining L 133, dug to the same floor level	
135	386-388	1500-1468	Hard-packed brown layer with flecks, 1 m N-S strip adjoining L 134, dug to same floor level, adjoining S balk of SW 2-7	
141	396-398	MB IIC, 1500-1468	Hard flecked brown layer sub L 134	
145	--		E-W wall that appeared to rest on floor L 135	

Locus number	Basket number/s	Pottery dates	Locus description	Registered Objects
149	--		Stone pavement that appeared in L 141 NW of wall L 145, but apparently unrelated to it	
151	407	MB IIC, LB I	Mixed earth enclosed by stones atop E balk at northern end of SW 2-7	
153	409, 413, 413a	MB IIC, 1500-1468, LB I	Soft fill in E balk sub L 151	
155	411, 414, 417	MB IIC, 1500-1468	Unidentified occupation immediately sub pit L 108; later found to extend northward. Plaster floor level = 174.19	
157	419	1500-1468	Plaster floor sub L 149 that appears to be northern continuation of L 155	
160	499	± 1500	E-W wall tentatively bounded by plaster floors both to the S of L 155 and N of L 157	
166	426	MB IIC, LB I, 13th cent	Removal of balk between SW 2-7 and SW 1-7, S of pit L 113 to level of L 153, N of L 113	
168	429-431, 536	EB, MB IIC, LB I, 12th cent	= L 124	
169	433, 440	MB IIC, LB I	Robber trench 45 cm wide that appears to be northward continuation of wall L 88 on N balk of SW 2-8	
171	--		Stone complex adjoining W balk that may be new wall	
176	442	MB IIC, LB I	Red-orange burn layer E of wall L 130 sub 111	
177	--		"Plaster pallet" sub L 176 with patches of cinnamon brown and orange embedded on surface	

Appendix B—217

Locus number	Basket number/s	Pottery dates	Locus description	Registered Objects
199	473	--	Balk between SW 2-7 and SW 1-7 sub L 166, adjoining pit L 113 of SW 1-7, exposing eastern extension of wall L 160	TT 1167, ceramic female figurine
205	498	EB, MB IIC	Stone pavement adjoining E balk, N of wall L 160	
215	502, 504, 506	EB, MB IIC	1 m trial trench adjoining E balk in N	
216	508	MB IIC-1500	Pit on E side of trial trench L 215, sub L 205	
230	535, 540-542, 544	EB, MB IIC, LB I	Circular pit, partly stone lined, E and S of L 177, top = 173.76, bottom = 172.60	
233	--		E-W wall sub wall L 160, westernmost stone level = 173.93	
235	551, 545	MB IIC, LB I	E-W wall sub pallet L 177, easternmost stone level=174.18	
241	553, 554	EB, MB IIB, MB IIC	Soft brown layer between wall L 235 and N balk, sub L 177	
242	555, 558	--	Child burial No. 22	
244	--		General floor level N of wall L 233, 173.20	
248	634	EB, MB IIC, LB I	Small pit adjoining N balk and half enclosed by it, sub L 241; level at top = 173.26	
256	578-582	EB, MB IIC	Soft gray S of former pit L 230 sub L 244	
257	583, 585-588	EB, MB IIC	Soft brown S of former pit L 230 sub L 256	
280	647-655	EB, EB III, MB IIC	Small pit on W balk in NW corner	

Principal Loci in SW 2-8
(with Registered Objects)
Published Pottery from Rast 1978 in Parentheses

Locus number	Basket number/s	Pottery dates	Locus description	Registered Objects
1	1-4	MB IIC, LB I, I_1, I_2, P, H, O, A	Loose fill in Sellin trench extending from surface level 176.14 to 175.64	TT 497, bronze armor scale
2	5-8	LB, 10th, 9th cent, I_1, I_2, P, EH, H	Area (presumably W of Sellin trench) characterized by emergence of considerable masses of hard, gray clay, apparently fallen debris	
3	9-16	I_1, I_2, P, EH, LH	Loose surface earth extending 28-50 cm sub surface to what appears to be first hard level of occupation	
5	18-21	I_1, I_2, P	A 40 cm-wide cut out of 1963 season S balk to determine strata in SW corner of square	
6	22, 23	9th-7th cent	Sub L 2 and 3, a hard clay layer of considerable depth, as confirmed by newly cut balk, L 5	TT 515, ceramic female figurine head
7	24-34	MB IIC, LB, 10th-9th cent, I_1, I_2, P, EH, O, A	Brown, loose fill sub L 6, exending to 176.00	TT 527, ceramic female figurine torso
8	35-42, 46-51	EB, MB IIC, LB, 12th, 10th-7th cent, P	Gray, medium to soft sub L 7 extending to hard clay floor next to fallen clay debris at level ca. 175.64	TT 549, perforated ceramic disk

Locus number	Basket number/s	Pottery dates	Locus description	Registered Objects
9	43, 53	MB IIC, LB, I$_1$-7th cent, P, H, A	Test trench in SE corner of square to determine nature of strata sub L 8	
10	44, 45, 105, 118	LB I, 12th cent, I$_2$	Clearly outlined black ash burned stratum exposed in W balk of L 9 and running NW several meters from SE corner of square. Black ash lay under a series of 6 stones. In a thickness of 15-20 cm, the black ash rested on a clearly outlined stone floor. The black ash did not darken the stones as a fine bricky layer separated the burn from the floor. The level of the floor is 175.20, on which a circular cooking pot base was resting. The black ash stratum is also visible in S side of pit exposed in the 1963 season.	
11	--		Wall in S balk; apparently the extension of wall L 6 in SW 1-8	
14	54-56	EB, MB IIC, LB, I$_1$ to 7th cent, P, A	Deepening of L 9, turning to include pit L 72 of SW 2-7	
21	66, 67, 69-85	MB IIC, LB I, 1200-1000, I$_1$, I$_2$, P, O, A	Area marking perimeter of pit L 14 that was squared off southward, westward and northward in order to clarify stratigraphy in these 3 directions	(TT 605) juglet, (Rast 1978) fig 93:6 TT 598, iron chisel head (?) TT 669, ceramic figurine legs

Locus number	Basket number/s	Pottery dates	Locus description	Registered Objects
25	86-88	EB, MB IIC, LB I, 12th to 9th cent, I_1, I_2	Hard gray surface area dug in a 2 m strip along N balk; terminates in hard clay floor, presumed to be the floor of the cultic structure found in the 1963 season	
26	89, 91	1200-1000	Probing through L 25 exposing soft pockets and various unrelated large stones, but not reaching new floor level	

27	90, 92, 97	MB IIC, LB I, 12th cent	19 cm D jug in which large collection of weights was found; see TT 701-729	TT 701, scarab
				TT 702, stamp seal
				TT 703, lead bead
				TT 704, bronze bead
				TT 705, bronze trapezoidal weight
				TT 706, bronze trapezoidal weight
				TT 707, bronze turtle-shaped weight
				TT 708, bronze baboon-shaped weight
				TT 709, bronze frog-shaped weight
				TT 710, bronze dame weight
				TT 711, bronze dome weight
				TT 712, bronze dome weight
				TT 713, bronze loaf-shaped weight
				TT 714, bronze loaf-shaped weight
				TT 715, bronze loaf-shaped weight
				TT 716, rectangular bloodstone bar
				TT 717, serpentine dome weight
				TT 718, stone weight
				TT 719, stone weight
				TT 720, stone weight
				TT 721, stone weight
				TT 722, stone weight
				TT 723, stone weight
				TT 724, serpentine weight
				TT 725, stone weight
				TT 727, incisor corroded to knife handle
				TT 728, shells
				TT 729, burnishing stones
				(TT 753) cooking pot, (Rast 1978) fig 91:1

Locus number	Basket number/s	Pottery dates	Locus description	Registered Objects
28	93, 106	EB, MB IIC, LB I, 12th-10th cent	Partially plastered floor on which jug L 27 rested, possibly the northern extension of L10 interrupted in the W by pit L 66 (SW 2-7)	TT 762, ceramic female figurine legs
29	94, 100, 101, 103	LB I, 1200-1000	Crumbly brown fill 25 cm deep in NW corner of square	
31	99	12th cent	Remnant of crudely built wall apparently associated with adjoining plaster floor L 28 and jug full of objects, L27	TT 755, ceramic animal figurine
33	107-110	EB, MB IIC, LB I	Floor sub L 28 in NE corner of square adjoining Sellin cut	
34	111	MB IIC, LB I	Floor sub L 33 in NE corner adjoining Sellin cut; = L 51	
36	--		Large flagstone slab in NW corner of square at 175.05	
40	115	LB I, 12th cent	Hard gray clay layer adjoining L 36 sub L 29 and L36 W of wall L 31 in NW corner of square	
43	120	LB I, 12th cent	Second floor sub L 10	TT 538, ceramic jar stopper
44	121, 122	LB I, 12th cent	Third (presumed) floor sub L 10	
45	123, 127	LB I, 12th cent	Hard rocky brown layer 15 cm thick sub floor L 44	
46	124-126, 129, 131	LB I, ±1200	Mudbrick cube encasing large, water-storage jar at southern end of wall L 31	(TT 1862) jar, (Rast 1978) fig 88:1

Locus number	Basket number/s	Pottery dates	Locus description	Registered Objects
48	132, 133, 136, 138	LB I, 13th cent, ±1200, I$_2$	Sub L 45; brown, fairly soft layer first observed alongside L 46 and dug to level of floor, which may be the same occupation as floor L 34 E of wall L 31	
50	134, 135, 137, 139, 147	EB, MB IIC, LB I, ±1200	Stone-lined pit that emerged sub L 36 in NW corner of square. One of its stones lay 90-113 cm S of N balk has a surface level of 174.76. Bottom of pit is 173.56	TT 548, ceramic jar stopper (TT 832) krater, (Rast 1978) fig 89:1
51	140, 142-144	LB I, ±1200	Medium-hard brown gravel layer E of wall L 31 sub floor L 34; dug to level of presumed floor; = L 34	TT 830, ceramic female figurine torso TT 831, ceramic female figurine torso TT 839, ceramic female figurine legs
52	141, 145, 148	LB I, ±1200, 10th cent, I$_2$	Soft brown clay sub L 48 only on E side of wall L 31	TT 857, ceramic female figurine
55	--		Pavement between wall L 31 and L 39-53 of which the N stone = 174.70 and the S stone = 174.60	
58	--		N-S wall extending from S balk whose second stone is at 174.86	
60	152, 155, 156	MB IIC, LB I, ±1500	Hard brown bricky layer sub L 51 dug ca. 30 cm to level of new firm surface	
62	157, 158	EB, LB I	Continuation of hard brown bricky layer sub L 60	
63	159	LB I, 12th cent	Later northernmost phase of wall L 31	
64	160		Hard mudbrick foundation sub L 63	
65	161, 164	EB, LB I, 13th cent	Hard bricky layer = L 64 of 1966 season sub wall L 63 and wall L 31 and pavement L 55	

Appendix B—224

Locus number	Basket number/s	Pottery dates	Locus description	Registered Objects
67	163, 166, 190, 191	MB IIC, LB I, late 13th-12th cent, ± 1200	Pit with orange-colored sandy fill SW of pit L21 and partially sub pavement L 55	
68	165, 167, 169	MB IIC, LB I, I$_2$	Hard flecky brown sub L 64 and L 65 dug to depth of 25 cm through N half of square; adjacent to pit L 21	
69	312, 312a-312n, 314, 322, 327	10th cent, pure I$_2$, A	Cistern that Sellin placed 5 m S of "olive press" or basin	
75	174	MB IIC, 15th cent	Hard flecky brown layer N and W of pit L 67 sub L 62	
76	175, 178	EB, 15th cent	Hard flecky brown layer N of pit L 21 sub L 60	
77	179, 182, 185	MB IIC, LB I, 13th cent, ± 1200	Pit connected with pit L 67	(TT 1054) lamp. (Rast 1978) fig 90:2
80	183	LB I	Hard bricky brown layer dug to plaster floor sub L 76	TT 1051, ceramic female figurine
81	184, 188, 279	MB IIC, LB I	Chocolate enclosure/storage bin adjoining plaster floor L 85; bottom = 173.30; top of rim = 173.98	
85	--		Plaster floor at 174.02 adjoining large circular tabun-like enclosure L 81 sub L 76	
88	235	MB IIC, LB I	N-S wall built on plaster floor L 85 and appearing to continue N on basis of robber trench L 169 of SW 2-7; = L 118	
93	204	LB I	Hard flecky brown layer sub L 68	

Appendix B—225

Locus number	Basket number/s	Pottery dates	Locus description	Registered Objects
98	--		Plaster floor fragment W of wall L 88 sub L 93	
101	213	--	Balk between SW 2-7 and SW 2-8, level not determined, cut further to bring SW 2-7 and SW 2-8 into phase	TT 1130, female figurine head
110	318	EB, MB IIC	E-W wall in NW corner that goes with plaster floor L 98 and N-S wall L 88	
118			= L 88	
132	--		3-stone N-S wall between wall L 110 and N balk	
140	--		Ground floor level; 173.10 in S, 172.94 in N	
144	274	EB, MB IIC	Soft brown layer sub L 140 in SE corner	
146	276	EB, MB IIC	Trial trench in SE corner sub L 144; hard chunky brown	
156	285-287, 289, 290, 292-297, 302, 305, 309, 311a, 313, 315, 319-321, 369, 370, 374, 395, 396	EB, EB III, MB IIC, LB I, 10th cent, I$_2$, 7th-6th cent	Outlines of pit (cistern L 69) following same lines as pit L 21	TT 1478, bronze scriber (?) (TT 1830) cultic stand, (Rast 1978) fig 54:1 (TT 1853) chalice, (Rast 1978) fig 53:5
157	298-300	EB III, MB IIC	Soft brown layer adjoining balk in SW corner sub L 146	

Appendix B—226

Locus number	Basket number/s	Pottery dates	Locus description	Registered Objects
163	323-326, 328, 331, 334, 335, 340, 342, 344-346, 376, 377, 379, 380, 381-383	EB, EB III, MB IIC	Small pit adjoining EB and MB IIC storage jars	(TT 1855) bowl, (Rast 1978) fig 52:3
164	329, 330	EB, 10th, 7th cent	Bedrock huwar fallen onto floor of pit L 156	
168	391	EB III	Fairly thick plaster floor first discovered in W balk of pit L 156; also seen in sides of pit L 163	
170	347-350	10th cent	Quarter-moon section cut into eastern sector of pit L 156 into soft, dark turab sub light creamy huwar L 164	TT 1540, ceramic animal figurine spout
171	351-357, 359, 360, 361, 363-368, 371-373, 375, 384, 385, 388-390, 392, 397-402, 404, 408, 410	EB III, MB IIC, 12th cent, 10th cent	Coarse, loose brown top stratum showing in section of L 170, about 25-30 cm thick sub L 164	TT 1625, basalt tripod bowl leg TT 1652, loom weight TT 1655, spindle or rod TT 1716, basalt leg fragment from tripod bowl
173	386, 387, 405	EB III, MB IIC	Pit adjoining balks in SE corner sub L 157	(TT 1854) bowl, (Rast 1978) fig 52:9

Appendix B—227

Locus number	Basket number/s	Pottery dates	Locus description	Registered Objects
175	406	EB III, MB IIC	Pit in SW corner adjoining W balk	

**Appendix C:
Registered Objects Found in
SW 1-7; 2-7; 1-8; 2-8
with some objects from SW 1-9
References to Pottery published in Rast (1978)
in Parentheses and Iron I Sub-period (following Object Registration No.)**

Appendix C:
Registered Objects Found in SW 1-7; 2-7; 1-8; 2-8 (with some objects from 1-9) with references to Pottery Published in Rast (1978) in Parentheses and Iron I Sub-period (following Object Registration No.)

Object Registration No.	Area	Locus.basket	Pottery Dates	Dimensions/weight	Description
STONE & PASTE OBJECTS					
TT 78 (Period IIB)	2-7	26.37	±900	W=4 cm.; L=4.9 cm.; Wt=36 grams	Pierced pendant/weight; serpentine; TA 2440/n[1]
TT 79	2-7	26.37	±900	H=2.2 cm.; D=2.5 cm.; Wt=22 grams	Dome weight; basalt; TA 9268/n
TT 81 (Period IIB)	2-7	26.37	±900	L=2.7 cm.; D=2.8 cm.	Loom weight
TT 86 (Period IIB)	2-7	27.46	±900	H=6.8 cm.; Base=6.3 x 4.6 cm.	Neatly-shaped pyramidal rubbing stone; gas bubbles form very rough surface; *basalt scorie* (scorite or foamy basalt)
TT 87	2-7	27.46	±900	H=1.4 cm.; D top=2.3 cm., base=2.1 cm.; Wt=13 grams	Oval stone weight or stopper, undetermined stone
TT 98 (Period IIB)	2-7	27.45	±900	H=4.1 cm.; Base D=4.5 cm.	Rubbing stone; limestone
TT 116 (Period IIB)	2-7	26.38	±900	W=30 cm.; L=56 cm.; H=11.75 cm.	Quern; coarse texture with ashy spot on base; basalt; cf. *Hazor I*, Pl. 145:3 (also in same locus: TT 71, 78, 79, 83, 117)

---

[1] TA with a number is a number assigned to the object in the Tel Aviv laboratory report.

Object Registration No.	Area	Locus. basket	Pottery Dates	Dimensions/weight	Description
TT 117 (Period IIB)	2-7	26.38	±900	L=8.9 cm.; Oval end 6.2 x 5.5 cm.	Oval rubbing stone; rounded end and about half of vertical sides well-polished; broken at top and across one side; limestone; cf.. TT 116; also in same locus, TT 78
TT 170	2-7	39.74	I$_2$, P, H, A	H=7.5 cm.; Base D=4.4 cm.	Basalt rubbing stone; cf. *Hazor I*, LIX:10
TT 260	2-7	46.110	10th-6th cent., P, H, A	L=6 mm.; D=6 mm.	Black stone bead
TT 320 (Period IIB)	2-7	59.149	±900	W=6.5 cm.; L=10.7 cm.; H=5.2 cm.	Rectangular rubbing stone; light, porous; one surface flat, slightly smoothed; quartzolite
TT 324 (Period IIB)	2-7	61.164	±900	H=3.9 cm.; Base D=ca. 3 cm.	Semi-spherical rubbing stone; lines of smoothing visible; white limestone with some black striations; also in same locus TT 322, TT 358, TT 359
TT 356 (Period IIB)	2-7	55.141	±900	W=13.5 cm.; L=23.5 cm.; H=8 cm.	Saddle grinder; incomplete; basalt
TT 357	2-7	55.141	±900	W=36.5 cm.; L=33.5 cm.	Quern; broken, but complete; porous basalt
TT 358	2-7	61.169	±900	W=33 cm.; L=29 cm.; H=15 cm.	Quern; broken and incomplete; quartzolite
TT 359	2-7	61.169	±900	H=13 cm.; D=ca. 21.5 cm.	Round worked stone base (?); flat on one side, irregular on the other; limestone; cf. TT 389, TT 390, TT 391
TT 373 (Period IIB)	2-7	61.205	±900	H=3 cm.; D=3.8 cm.	Socketed stone; mace head (?); undetermined stone
TT 389 (Period IIB)	2-7	61.203	±900	H=12.5 cm.; D=ca. 22.5 cm.	Round worked stone base (?); flat on one side, irregular on the other; partly coated with white plaster-like substance; limestone; cf. TT 359, TT 390, TT 391

Object Registration No.	Area	Locus. basket	Pottery Dates	Dimensions/weight	Description
TT 390 (Period IIB)	2-7	61.203	±900	H=ca. 11 cm.; D=19-21 cm.	Round worked stone base (?); flat on one side, irregular on the other; limestone; same as TT 389; cf.. TT 359, TT 391
TT 391 (Period IIB)	2-7	61.203	±900	H=ca. 10.5 cm.; D=ca. 21 cm.	Round worked stone base (?); flat on one side, irregular on the other; limestone; same as TT 389; cf. TT 359, TT 390
TT 392 (Period IIB)	2-7	61.203	±900	H=7.1 cm.; base D=6 cm.	Rubbing or pounding stone; no surface shows more wear than any other; basalt; in same locus as TT 324, TT 358, TT 359, TT 393
TT 393 (Period IIB)	2-7	61.203	±900	H=6.7; base D=5.7 cm.	Rubbing stone; base worn smooth; basalt; cf. TT 392
TT 394 (Period IIB)	2-7	61.203	±900	W=15.7 cm.; L=31.5 cm.; H=7 cm.;	Plano-convex saddle grinder; smoother on flat side; coarse-textured basalt
TT 395 (Period IIB)	2-7	61.203	±900	W=ca. 28 cm.; L=49 cm.; H=12 cm.	Quern; basalt; cf. TT 357
TT 413	2-7	46.107	7th-6th cent., H, A	H=4.5 cm.; L=8 cm.	Rubbing stone; basalt; chipped
TT 419	2-7	67.249	±900	H=2.3 cm.; D=2.9 cm.; Wt=50 grams	Drum-shaped weight; surfaces show fine scratches; limestone; TA 7685/n
TT 430 (Period IIB)	2-7	57.228	±900	W=18.5 cm.; H=26 cm.; Th=10-12 cm.	Shaped standing stone (מצבה); limestone, partially coated with plaster; cf. TT 431, TT 432
TT 431 (Period IIB)	2-7	57.228	±900	W=18 cm.; H=26.5 cm.; Th=9-14 cm.	Shaped standing stone (מצבה); limestone, partially coated with plaster; cf. TT 430, TT 432
TT 432 (Period IIB)	2-7	57.228	±900	W=14.5 cm.; H=17.7 cm.; Th=11 cm.	Shaped standing stone (מצבה); basalt; cf. TT 430, TT 431
TT 503	1-7	4.13	10th cent., I_2	H=5.5 cm.; base D=5-5.5 cm.	Rubbing stone; assymetrical; trapezoidal; flat on bottom; basalt

Object Registration No.	Area	Locus. basket	Pottery Dates	Dimensions/weight	Description
TT 508	1-8	2.17	MB IIC, I$_1$-9th cent.	H=1.8 cm.; D=2.9 cm.	Spindle whorl; polished dark granite (?); base deeply scratched
TT 509	2-8	6.22	9th-7th cent.	L=1.1 cm; D=1 cm.	Bead; carnelian
TT 520	1-8	2.15	MB IIC, I$_1$-9th cent.	H=5.8 cm.; L=5.3 cm.; W=5.2 cm.	Rubbing stone; basalt
TT 524	1-7	5.37	I$_{1-2}$, H, O, A	H=7.4 cm.; Base=5 cm. x 5.9 cm.	Rubbing stone; fine-grained basalt
TT 532	1-8	4.30	MB IIC, LB, I$_{1-2}$, P, O, A	H=1.5 cm.; D=1.9 cm.	Finely polished white stone
TT 562	2-7	74.268	10th-7th cent., O, A	H=5.5 cm.; Base D.=5 x 5.5 cm.	Medium-grain basalt
TT 578 (Period IIA)	1-7	35.?	10th cent.	W=30.5 cm.; L=ca. 30.5 cm.; H=ca. 16 cm.; bowl D=20.4-21.4 cm.; bowl depth = 11.5 cm.	Mortar; 4-side shape; rim and top edges polished smooth; shape of bowl depression not symmetrical; limestone
TT 596	2-8	22.68	12th-10th cent., A	L=4.4 cm.; W=2.8 cm.; Th. at haft end=8 mm.; Th. at point=1mm.	Black flint point
TT 597	1-7	5.68	Early 10th cent.	H=4 cm.; Base D=5 x 5.5 cm.	Rubbing stone; fine-grained, light gray basalt
TT 612 (Period IA)	1-8	12.76	MB IIC, LB I, 12th cent.	D=9.8-10.5 cm.; H=ca. 5 cm.; Hole D=2.5-6.8 cm.	Basalt ring; coarse grain; size of digging stick weight or counterweight; crude; lower surface is smoother
TT 615	2-8	21.80	10th cent.-P	H=5.2 cm.; Base=5 x 5.5 cm. oval	Basalt rubbing stone; medium grain

Object Registration No.	Area	Locus. basket	Pottery Dates	Dimensions/weight	Description
TT 616	2-7	84.291	I$_2$, O, A	H=8.6 cm.; Base=4.5 x 5 cm. rectangle	Limestone hammer or rubbing stone; base rounded and smooth
TT 623	1-7	68.114	MBIIC, LBI, 12th cent.	W=6.7 cm.; H=13 cm.; Th=2.3-3.2 cm.	Stylized female figurine; no detail other than depressions for eyes, nose/mouth, breasts, navel and vulva; limestone
TT 632 (Period IIA)	2-7	87.302	12th-10th cent.	W=ca. 14.7 cm.; L=32.5 cm.; H=ca. 11 cm.	Saddle grinder; coarse-grained basalt
TT 633	2-7	88.300	MB II C, LB I, 12th-11th cent.	W=10 cm.; L=41.5 cm.; H=5.3 cm.	Saddle grinder; coarse-grained basalt
TT 636 (Period IIA)	2-7	88.300	11th cent.	W=7.6 cm.; L=8.6 cm.; H=6 cm.	Rubbing stone; basalt
TT 638 (Period IIA)	2-7	88.300	MB IIC, LBI, 12th-late 11th cent.	D=6 mm.; H=4 mm.	Carnelian bead; chipped
TT 640 (Period IIA)	2-7	96.308	12th-10th cent.	D=5 mm.; Th.=1 mm.	Blue paste bead
TT 643 (Period IB)	2-8	25.87	MB IIC, I$_{1-2}$, P	H=4.3 cm.; Base D.=ca. 4.7 cm.	Rubbing stone; medium-grained basalt; pitted
TT 667	2-7	82.285	LB; I$_1$; I$_2$; A	H=4.9 cm.; Base=3 x 4.5 cm.	Rectangular rubbing stone with perforated handle; top chipped; *basalt scorie* (foamy basalt); cf. *AASOR* XXII, ¶ 55 and Pl. 13-5 II, Pt. 1; Pl. XXIII:23
TT 670	1-7	23.127	MB IIC, LBI, 12th-10th cent.	H=1 cm.; D=1.1 cm.	Blue paste bead

Appendix C—234

Object Registration No.	Area	Locus. basket	Pottery Dates	Dimensions/weight	Description
TT 716	2-8	27.90	12th-10th cent.	W=1 cm.; L=2.2 cm.; H=1 cm.; Wt=10.6 grams	Rectangular bar weight (?); bloodstone; cf. *Megiddo II*, Pl. 168.15
TT 717	2-8	27.90	12th-10th cent.	H=20 mm.; D=19 mm.; Wt=13 grams	Dome weight; somewhat irregularly shaped; serpentine
TT 718	2-8	27.90	12th-10th cent.	W=10 mm.; L=20 mm.; H=8 mm.; Wt=14.4 grams	Biconical stone weight with flat base; serpentine (?); TA 9255/n
TT 719	2-8	27.90	12th-10th cent.	W=9 mm.; L=27 mm.; H=10 mm.; Wt=8.2 grams	Cylindrical stone weight with flat base and flattened ends; finely finished, fine-grained black stone
TT 720	2-8	27.90	12th-10th cent.	W=14 mm.; L=32 mm.; H=11 mm.; Wt=11 grams	Biconical stone weight with flat base; black stone; TA 9258/n
TT 721	2-8	27.90	12th-10th cent.	W=20 mm.; L=30 mm.; H=17 mm.; Wt=19 grams	Ovoid stone weight with flat base; black stone; TA 9264/n
TT 722[2]	2-8	27.90	12th-10th cent.	W=31 mm.; L=30 mm.; H=25 mm.	Oval stone weight; undetermined black stone; unweighed because corroded to bronze fragment
TT 723	2-8	27.90	12th-10th cent.	W=18 mm.; L=23 mm.; H=16 mm.; Wt=12 grams	Pear-shaped weight with flat base; black stone; TA 9265/n
TT 724	2-8	27.90	12-10th cent.	H=9 mm.; D=15 mm.; Wt=6 grams	Egg-shaped weight; serpentine; TA 9257/n
TT 725	2-8	27.90	12th-10th cent.	H=9 mm.; D=15 mm.; Wt=5.1 grams	Cylindrical weight; serpentine; TA 9267/n
TT 729 (Period IB)	2-8	27.90	12th-10th cent.	varied	Miscellaneous burnishing stones; some smooth and polished; 3 fused to iron knife handle; total 49

---

[2] TT 722 is part of a conglomeration with TT 727.

Object Registration No.	Area	Locus. basket	Pottery Dates	Dimensions/weight	Description
TT 732 (Period IIA)	2-7	87.321	12th-11th cent.	W=10.5 cm.; L=30 cm.; H=ca. 4.5 cm.	Saddle grinder; medium-grained basalt
TT 735 (Period IIA)	2-7	96.319	LB I-12th cent.	D=7-8 mm.; Th=3 mm.	Blue stone bead; one side worn
TT 742	1-8	20.96	MB IIC, LB I	H=9 mm.; D=10 mm.	Carnelian bead
TT 749	1-8	24.93	MB IIC	H=4.3-4.5 cm.; D=5.5 cm.	Cylindrical rubbing stone; fine-grained basalt; rubbing surface slightly concave
TT 789 (Period IA)	2-7	110.338	LB I	H=5 cm.; Base D=4-4.5 cm.	Rubbing stone; medium-grained basalt; chipped
TT 790	2-7	107.331	MB IIC, LB I	H=6 cm.; Base D=ca. 5.4 cm.	Rubbing stone; medium fine-grained basalt; sooty deposit on surface
TT 803 (Period IIB)	1-7	86.161	12th-century-I_1	H=ca. 9.2 cm.; D at widest point=5.8 cm.	Rubbing stone; fine-grained basalt; top chipped like a hammer stone
TT 805 (Period IA)	2-7	112.342	MB IIC, LB I, 12th cent.	H=6.3 cm.; D=5.6 cm.	Rubbing stone; medium-grained basalt
TT 819 (Period IIB)	1-7	75.160	MB IIC, LB I, I_1	L=35.5 cm.; W=ca. 17 cm.; H=4.8 cm.	Saddle grinder; coarse-grained basalt; concave grinding surface; possible mortar?
TT 837 (Period IIB)	1-7	75.160	MB IIC, LB I, I_1	H=ca. 12 cm.; D=ca. 26-28 cm.; D of bowl; 16-17 cm.; Depth of bowl=5.5 cm.	Limestone mortar; pitted with root holes
TT 838 (Period IA)	2-8	51.140	LB I	L=9.5 cm.; W=2.5 cm.; Th=9 mm.	Flint knife blade or sickle point
TT 847 (Period IA)	2-8	50.134	±1200	H=5.5 cm.; L=11 cm.; W=7.5 cm.	Rubbing stone; coarse-grained basalt; pitted

Object Registration No.	Area	Locus. basket	Pottery Dates	Dimensions/weight	Description
TT 856 (Period IA)	2-7	117.353	LBI, 12th-6th cent.	H=4 cm.; Base=4.5 cm. square	Rubbing stone; dark blue with rust stain; fine-grained basalt
TT 901	2-8	60.152	MB IIC, LB I	H=4.2 cm.; Base D=3.6 cm.	Pestle; fine-grained blue basalt
TT 906	1-7	8.215	12th-10th cent.	H=4-5 cm.; D=15.5 cm.	Grinding bowl; medium-grained basalt; light gray
TT 969	1-7	121.246	LB I	D=5 mm.; Th=3 mm.	White paste bead; associated with TT 968
TT 1007	2-7	153.413	MB IIC	L=8.6 cm.; W=ca. 1.9 cm.	Flint knife blade; slight retouch on both edges
TT 1071	2-7	167.428	Late LB I	H=5 cm.; D (at base)=5 cm.	Conical rubbing stone; fine-grained basalt
TT 1078	2-8	80.183	LB I	H=6 cm.; D (at base)=ca. 6 cm	Conical rubbing stone; medium-grained basalt; not worn much on base
TT 1079	1-8	33.117	MB IIC	H=6.4 cm.; D (at base)=5.3-5.5 cm.	Conical rubbing stone; fine-grained basalt
TT 1090	2-8	89.198	MB IIC, LB I	D=9.5-10 cm.; H=8 cm.	Rubbing stone; limestone; rubbing surface well polished
TT 1107	2-8	91.200	MB IIC, LB I	L=2.5 cm.; D=1.1 cm.	Carnelian bead; highly polished; hole drilled through length
TT 1111	1-8	33.117	MB IIC	L=6.5 cm.; D (at widest point)=6.4 cm.	Mace head; limestone; partly drilled; unfinished; cf. *Lachish IV*, Pl. 26:5
TT 1135	1-8	24.93	MB IIC	L=3 cm.; W=9 mm.; Th=5 mm.	Serpentine pendant; cf. *AASOR-TBM*, XXI-XXII, ¶ 55
TT 1137	1-8	33.124	MB IIC	H=4.5 cm.; D (at base)=3.5-4 cm.	Rubbing stone; fine-grained basalt; blue-gray; not much worn

Object Registration No.	Area	Locus. basket	Pottery Dates	Dimensions/weight	Description
TT 1138 (Period IB)	2-8	67.191	MB IIC, LB I, ±1200	H=ca. 5 cm.; D=ca. 5 cm.	Rubbing stone; fine-grained basalt; dark
TT 1170	2-8	104.220	EB, MB IIC, LB I	L=8 cm.; W=2.2cm.; Th=ca. 8 mm.	Flint knife blade; both edges retouched; one edge shiny
TT 1240	2-8	85.198	LB I	H=9 cm.; D (at base)=7.5 cm.	Rubbing stone; limestone; pitted; bottom worn smooth
TT 1249	2-7	215.506	EB, MB IIC	L=10.7 cm.; W=2.6 cm.; Th=1.6 cm.	Diorite pendant; cf. *AASOR-TBM*, XVII, ¶80, Pl. 2/1
TT 1285	1-8	35.119	MB IIC-1500	L=33 cm.; W=12.7 cm.; Th=5.5 cm.	Basalt saddle grinder; complete; convex surface worn
TT 1296	1-7	190.377	EB, MB IIC	D=9.7-10.1 cm.; H=ca. 5.3 cm.; Th=ca. 3.8 cm.	Ring; inside smoothed; top and bottom slightly worn; medium coarse basalt
TT 1297	2-7	177.531	EB, MB IIC	L=12.8 cm.; W=3.6 cm.; Th=1.2 cm.	Flint blade
TT 1324	2-8	138.268	--	H=4 cm.; D (base)=4 cm.	Conical pestle; fine-grained basalt; dark
TT 1325	1-8	67.183	EB, MB IIC	H=7.2 cm.; D (base)=4.5 cm.	Conical pestle or rubbing stone; limestone; base not worn much
TT 1330	2-7	226.525	MB IIC	H=6.1 cm.; D (base)=4.5 cm.	Conical rubbing stone; medium-grained basalt; gray
TT 1332	2-7	221.510	MB IIC-1500	H=3.8 cm.; D (base)=5 cm.	Dome-shaped rubbing stone; fine-grained basalt; light gray
TT 1335	2-7	208.514	EB, MB IIC	H=5 cm.; D (base)=4.7 cm.	Conical rubbing stone; fine-grained basalt; medium gray
TT 1336	2-7	217.507	EB, MB IIC	H=4 cm.; Base=4.2 x 4.2 cm.	Cube-shaped rubbing stone; basalt; 2 surfaces smoothed

Object Registration No.	Area	Locus. basket	Pottery Dates	Dimensions/weight	Description
TT 1344	2-7	211.495	EB, MB IIC, LBI	H=4.5 cm.; D (base)=5 cm.	Dome-shaped rubbing stone; basalt
TT 1346	1-7	166.363	EB, MB IIC	H=7.4 cm.; D=ca. 10.2 cm.	Diorite potter's tournette; well worn; cf. *Lachish IV*, Pl. 49:13, 14, Text, p. 90 f.
TT 1411	2-7	252.571	EB III	D=3.8 cm.; Th=1.2 cm.; H=2 cm.	Basalt ring weight
TT 1412	1-7	189.379	EB	L=5 cm.; W=2 cm.; Th=4 mm.	Flint blade; both edges shiny with one more so
TT 1433	1-7	205.403	MB IIC	H=7.8 cm.; D (base) 5.5 cm.	Conical pestle; fine-grained basalt; base very smooth; entire surface smoothed
TT 1463 (Period IIB)	2-8	156.296	EB III-LBI	L=6.9 cm.; W=1.8 cm.	Flint blade; both edges retouched
TT 1469	1-7	195.401	EB III, MB IIC	H=7.5 cm.; Triangular base ca. 3.9 cm. each side	Pestle; fine-grained basalt; gray; made from stone bowl leg
TT 1479	2-7	267.608	EB III, MB IIC	L=7.2 cm.; W=2.4 cm.	Flint blade; one edge shiny; both edges retouched
TT 1482 (Period IIB)	2-8	157.299	EB III	L=5.8 cm; W=2 cm.	Flint blade; one edge more shiny
TT 1508	1-8	95.236	EB III	D=6 mm.; Th=4 mm.	Carnelian bead; chipped
TT 1548	2-8	153.323	MB IIC	H=6.5 cm.; D (base)=5.7 cm.	Conical rubbing stone; fine-grained basalt; dark
TT 1625 (Period IIB)	2-8	171.404	EB, 12th-10th cent.	W=3 cm.; L=8 cm.; H=10.5 cm.; base d=ca. 25 cm.	Leg from base of tripod bowl; originally ca. 17 cm. tall; fine-grained basalt; cf.. TT 1716 (but not from the same bowl)
TT 1626	1-7	194.421	EB II-III	a) L=11.5 cm.; W=6 cm.; H=5.5 cm.; b) L=10.5 cm.; W=8 cm.; H=3.6 cm.	Rubbing stones; fine grained *basalt scoria*

Object Registration No.	Area	Locus. basket	Pottery Dates	Dimensions/weight	Description
TT 1627	1-8	93.249	EB III	various sizes	Fireplace stones; 9 stones formed fire platform near tabun; re-used grinding stones; all are charred on flat surface
TT 1652 (Period IIB)	2-8	171.352	10th cent.	H=2 cm.; D=2.5 cm.	Loom weight; hole not round nor centered; black stone
TT 1671 (Period IIB)	2-8	171.410	Late 10th cent.	L=ca. 13 cm.; W=7.5 cm.; H=7 cm.	Basalt work stone/grinder
TT 1690	1-7	215.435	Late EB II-early EB III	L=5.6 cm.; W=1.5 cm.; Th=4 mm.	Flint blade; both sides retouched and shiny
TT 1716 (Period IIB)	2-8	171.404	EB, 12th-10th cent.	W=ca. 4 cm.; L=10 ; H=10.4 cm.	Leg fragment from base of tripod bowl; fine-grained basalt; cf. TT 1625 (but not from same bowl)
TT 1732	2-8	128.253	--	H=ca. 20 cm.; L=ca. 32 cm.; W=ca. 30 cm.; Hole D=20-21 cm; depth of hole=ca. 11 cm.	Limestone mortar; edges chipped; hole pitted though smoothed; hole not round
TT 1746	1-8	75.210	EB, MB IIC	H=6.2 cm.; D (base)=4.2 cm.	Rubbing stone; medium-grained basalt; dark; pitted
TT 1748	2-8	104.220	EB, MB IIC, LB I	H=6 cm.; D (base)=ca. 3.3 cm.	Rubbing stone; re-used basalt bowl leg
TT 1750	2-8	125.258	MB IIC	H=ca. 7.6 cm.; D=ca. 7.8 cm.	Rubbing stone; white stone; all surfaces worn smooth; some chips
TT 1808	2-7	62.207	MB IIC, LB I, II	L=4.3 cm.; W=3.2 cm.; Th=7mm. At spine	Flint sickle blade; triangular section; retouched on underside serrations

CERAMIC OBJECTS
(For items in parentheses, see Rast, *Taanach I* for descriptions)

Object Registration No.	Area	Locus. basket	Pottery Dates	Dimensions/weight	Description
(TT 36)	2-7	13.20	960-918		Jar; fig. 30:4
(TT 62) (Period IIB)	2-7	26.40	960-918		Juglet; fig. 40:7
(TT 63) (Period IIB)	2-7	26.38	960-918		Juglet; fig. 40:1
(TT 64) (Period IIB)	2-7	27.41	960-918		Tripod censer or strainer; 2 legs missing; fig. 51:3; cf. *Lachish III*, pl 76:16; *Beth Shan*, Pl. 108:5
(TT 65) (Period IIB)	2-7	27.41	960-918		Cooking pot; handle and rim missing; fig. 50:3
TT 72	2-7	23.35	Arab	H=2.4 cm.; rect. Rim = 7.2 x 7.2 cm.	Bowl; green glaze; broken; piece missing
(TT 73) (Period IIB)	2-7	26.36	960-918		Pyxis; fig. 40:14
(TT 83) (Period IIB)	2-7	26.36	960-918		Jug; fig. 39:6; neck & rim broken, mostly missing
(TT 88) (Period IIB)	2-7	27.46	960-918		Juglet; fig. 40:6; broken; chipped; mended
(TT 89) (Period IIB)	2-7	27.45	960-918		Lamp; broken; incomplete; fig. 51:1

Object Registration No.	Area	Locus. basket	Pottery Dates	Dimensions/weight	Description
TT 94	2-7	24.42	10th-7th cent., A	W=6.1 cm.; H=7.5 cm.	Fragment of †-shaped female figurine with 1, 3-dimensional leg appliqued to a fragment of a cylindrical stand having a D of ca. 18 cm.; 4 small windows; traces of red slip on figurine
TT 100 (Period IIB)	2-7	27.49	±900	W=7.3 cm.; L=18.6 cm.	Female figurine mold
(TT 103) (Period IIB)	2-7	27.45	960-918		Jug; fig. 37:1
TT 107 (Period IIB)	2-7	27.49	I_2	H=8 cm.; D=8 cm.	Loom weight; cf. Gordion, *AJA* 66, p. 165; *Hazor II*, Pl. 18:2; Pl. 20:4
TT 191	2-7	40.88	7th-6th cent., H	H=14.2 cm.	Juglet
TT 253	2-7	47.114	I_{1-2}, P, H, A	L=6.5 cm.; W= ca. 4.1 cm.	Female figurine fragment
TT 306 (Period IIB)	2-7	57.142	I_1		Juglet; broken; mended; handle missing
TT 313	2-7	51.133	LB1-2	D=2.4 cm.; H=2.6 cm.	Loom weight
TT 323 (Period IIB)	2-7	61.164	±900	H=5 cm.	Miniature juglet; neck and rim missing; handle broken
(TT 327) (Period IIB)	2-7	59.149	960-918		Juglet; fig. 40:4
(TT 351) (Period IIB)	2-7	61.184	960-918		Cult stand; fig. 51:4
(TT 352) (Period IIB)	2-7	61.176	960-918		Bowl; fig. 47:2; broken; mended

Object Registration No.	Area	Locus. basket	Pottery Dates	Dimensions/weight	Description
(TT 353) (Period IIB)	2-7	61.181; 63.224	960-918		Bowl; fig. 46:5; broken; incomplete
(TT 354) (Period IIB)	2-7	61.196	960-918		Bowl; fig. 47:4; broken; mended
(TT 372) (Period IIB)	2-7	61.208	960-918		Pyxis; fig. 40:13
(TT 386) (Period IIB)	2-7	63.234	960-918		Juglet; fig. 46:11; piece of rim missing
TT 388 (Period IIB)	2-7	61.219, 220, 221, 222	±900	Type a: H=6.7; D=9.2 cm. Type b: H=5.3; D=10.1 cm.	Fragments of ca. 48 loom weights: 18 in B. 219; 14 in B. 220; 10 in B. 221; fragments of at least 10 others in B. 222
(TT 410) (Period IIB)	2-7	61.216	960-918		Bowl; fig. 46:11; broken; incomplete
(TT 411) (Period IIB)	2-7	61.214	960-918		Bowl; fig. 46:2; broken; mended; incomplete
(TT 412) (Period IIB)	2-7	61.125	960-918		Bowl; fig. 47:3; broken; mended; incomplete
(TT 414) (Period IIB)	2-7	61.187	960-918		Jug; fig. 39:4; broken; incomplete
(TT 415) (Period IIB)	2-7	57.227	960-918		Bowl; fig. 45:4; broken; incomplete
(TT 416) (Period IIB)	2-7	27.101	960-918		Bowl; broken; mended; almost complete
TT 421	2-7	69.256	LB-I$_2$, P	D=1.9 cm.; Th.=3 mm.	Fastener or whorl
TT 423	2-7	68.251	±900	H=2.5 cm.; D=8.5 cm.	Disk with fabric impression; incomplete; cf. *II*, Pl. 228. 2,3

Object Registration No.	Area	Locus. basket	Pottery Dates	Dimensions/weight	Description
(TT 439) (Period IIB)	2-7	26.36-26.40	960-918		Krater; fig. 45:2
(TT 440) (Period IIB)	2-7	26.36-26.40	960-918		Jug; fig. 37:2
(TT 441) (Period IIB)	2-7	26,36; 27.45	960-918		Bowl; fig. 46:8
(TT 442) (Period IIB)	2-7	27.45, 49	960-918		Bowl; fig. 46:13
(TT 443) (Period IIB)	2-7	26.36-26.40	960-918		Bowl; fig. 48:3
(TT 444) (Period IIB)	2-7	27.45	960-918		Bowl; fig. 48:16; mended
(TT 445) (Period IIB)	2-7	27.41, 44, 45	960-918		Bowl; fig. 45:2
(TT 446) (Period IIB)	2-7	27.45	960-918		Bowl; fig. 42:1
(TT 447) (Period IIB)	2-7	27.45	960-918		Bowl; fig. 48:15; mended
(TT 448) (Period IIB)	2-7	26.40	960-918		Bowl; fig. 48:2; mended; complete
(TT 449) (Period IIB)	2-7	27.45	960-918		Bowl; fig. 47:1; mended; incomplete
(TT 450) (Period IIB)	2-7	27.45	960-918		Bowl; fig. 46:7; mended; incomplete

Object Registration No.	Area	Locus. basket	Pottery Dates	Dimensions/weight	Description
(TT 451) (Period IIB)	2-7	27.45	960-918		Bowl; fig. 43:2; mended; incomplete
(TT 452) (Period IIB)	2-7	27.45, 49	960-918		Bowl; 46:14; mended; incomplete
(TT 453) (Period IIB)	2-7	27.45	960-918		Bowl; fig. 46:3; mended; incomplete
(TT 454) (Period IIB)	2-7	61.175	960-918		Jug; fig. 38:1; mended; a few small fragments missing
(TT 455) (Period IIB)	2-7	61.178	960-918		Bowl; fig. 46:12; mended; incomplete
(TT 456) (Period IIB)	2-7	60.160	960-918		1-handled cooking pot; fig. 50:1; mended; incomplete; held 16 sheep/goat astragali
(TT 457) (Period IIB)	2-7	61.179	960-918		Bowl; fig. 46:6; mended; incomplete
TT 458 (Period IIB)	2-7	61.204	±900	H=10.5 cm.	Juglet; mended; incomplete
(TT 459) (Period IIB)	2-7	61.192	960-918		Round-based storage jar; fig. 34:5; mended; a few small pieces missing
(TT 460) (Period IIB)	2-7	61.185	960-918		Hole-mouth jar; fig. 35:2; mended; incomplete
(TT 461) (Period IIB)	2-7	61.195	960-918		Bowl; fig. 44:3; mended; incomplete
(TT 462) (Period IIB)	2-7	61.179	960-918		Bowl; fig. 46:4; mended; several small fragments missing

Object Registration No.	Area	Locus. basket	Pottery Dates	Dimensions/weight	Description
(TT 463) (Period IIB)	2-7	61.200	960-918		Bowl; fig. 48:17; mended; incomplete
(TT 464) (Period IIB)	2-7	27.45, 49; 61.169	960-918		Bowl; fig. 45:6; mended; incomplete
(TT 465) (Period IIB)	2-7	60.162	960-918		Bowl; fig. 46:1; mended; incomplete
(TT 466) (Period IIB)	2-7	61.205	960-918		Juglet; fig. 40:10; mended; rim missing; body incomplete
(TT 467) (Period IIB)	2-7	57.157	960-918		Side-spouted jug; fig. 36:1; mended; rim and base missing
(TT 468) (Period IIB)	2-7	63.234	12th-10th cent.		Jug; fig. 39:2; mended; incomplete
(TT 469) (Period IIB)	2-7	61.205	960-918		Ovoid storage jar; fig. 31:3; mended; rim missing
(TT 470) (Period IIB)	2-7	61.202	960-918		Jug; fig. 38:2; mended; a few body sherds missing
(TT 471) (Period IIB)	2-7	28.57, 59; 57.157; 59.148, 150	960-918		Bowl; fig. 43:1; mended; incomplete
(TT 472) (Period IIB)	2-7	57.226	960-918		Cooking pot; fig. 50:2; mended; incomplete
(TT 473) (Period IIB)	2-7	61.180	960-918		Lamp; fig. 51:2; mended; incomplete

Object Registration No.	Area	Locus. basket	Pottery Dates	Dimensions/weight	Description
(TT 474) (Period IIB)	2-7	61.193	960-918		Ovoid storage jar; fig. 31:1; mended; almost complete
(TT 475) (Period IIB)	2-7	61.191	960-918		Round-based storage jar; fig.34:4; mended; incomplete
(TT 476) (Period IIB)	2-7	59.150	960-918		Jar; fig. 30:2; mended; almost complete
(TT 477) (Period IIB)	2-7	61.174	960-918		Ovoid storage jar; fig. 30:3; mended; incomplete
(TT 478) (Period IIB)	2-7	61.229; 63.236	960-918		Ovoid storage jar; fig. 30:1; mended; incomplete
(TT 479) (Period IIB)	2-7	61.172, 185, 188, 201	960-918		Bowl; fig. 42:4; mended; incomplete
(TT 480)	2-7	61.182-188	960-918		Bowl; fig. 42:3; mended; incomplete
(TT 481) (Period IIB)	2-7	63.230	960-918		Ovoid storage jar; fig. 31:2; mended; almost half missing
(TT 482) (Period IIB)	2-7	61.172, 173	960-918		Round-based storage jar; fig. 34:1; mended; incomplete
(TT 1866) (Period IIB)	2-7	59.143; 61.197	960-918		Round-based storage jar; fig. 31:1; mended; rim incomplete; handle missing
(TT 484) (Period IIB)	2-7	28.53	960-918		Juglet; fig. 40:11; mended; small side pieces missing
(TT 485) (Period IIB)	2-7	28.47; 35.68	960-918		Bowl; fig. 45:1; incomplete

Object Registration No.	Area	Locus. basket	Pottery Dates	Dimensions/weight	Description
(TT 486) (Period IIB)	2-7	36.105	960-918		Bowl; fig. 48:1; mended; incomplete
(TT 487) (Period IIB)	2-7	27.49	960-918		Bowl; fig. 44:4; mended; almost complete
(TT 488) (Period IIB)	2-7	27.45	960-918		Pyxis; fig. 40:12; broken; incomplete
(TT 489) (Period IIB)	2-7	59.155; 61.189, 205	960-918		8-handled krater; mended; incomplete; fig. 41:1; cf.. *Lachish III*, pl 82:124
(TT 490) (Period IIB)	2-7	57.217	960-918		Side-spouted jug; fig. 36:2; mended; incomplete
TT 515	2-8	6.22	9th-7th cent.	W=3 cm.; L=6.2 cm.	Female figurine head with striated coiffure and rounded knob on the bottom (to fit into a slot?); light red; encrusted; nose broken; signs of recarving on coiffure and knob; red paint stripes on back and front
TT 525	1-7	10.23	I_{1-2}, P, A	L=32 cm.; D=10.5-11.5 cm.	Drain pipe; reddish-tan in color
TT 527	2-8	7.31	I_1,I_2, Persian	W=6.8 cm.; L=5.6 cm.	Female figurine torso; head missing; below hips missing; waist band visible, as is pubic triangle line on the right; spine on back; reddish-tan surface
TT 531	2-8	8.40	MB IIC, 12th cent., 10th-7th cent.	D=4.2 cm.; Th.=8 mm.	Perforated disc; broken; mended
TT 538	2-8	9.43	10th-7th cent.	H=ca. 3 cm.; D=4-5 cm.	Jar stopper; irregularly shaped
TT 548	2-8	8.50	10th-7th cent.	H=ca. 4.4 cm.; D=4-4.5 cm.	Jar stopper; unbaked; chipped

Object Registration No.	Area	Locus. basket	Pottery Dates	Dimensions/weight	Description
TT 549	2-8	8.50	10th-7th cent.	D=3.4-3.6 cm; Th. ca. 7 mm.	Perforated disc; cf. TT 531
TT 560	2-7	74.270	MBIIC, 10th-7th cent.	H=ca. 2.5 cm.; D=ca. 2.1 cm.	Loom weight; crude; handmade; mended; thread marks (?)
TT 563	2-7	74.270	MB IIC, 10th-7th cent.	H=2 cm.; D=3.2 cm.	Loom weight
TT 566	1-8	8.44.	MBIIC, I$_1$-7th cent.	Seal impression D=1.3 cm.	X-shaped seal impression on jar handle
TT 583	1-7	5.81	MB IIC, 12th-7th cent., O, A	D=2.7 cm.; H=2.3 cm.	Loom weight; dark
TT 588	1-7	42.67	10th-7th cent.	H=13.7 cm.; Rim D.=38 cm.	Bowl; mended; incomplete
(TT 605)	2-8	21.73	960-918		Juglet; fig. 93:6; cf. *Megiddo II*, Pl. 146.15-17; 88.18
TT 624 (Period IIA)	2-7	88.298	Late MB IIC	L=8.5 cm.; W=7.5 cm.; H=2 cm.	Miniature lamp
TT 625	2-7	82.285	LB I, LB II, A	W=5.2 cm.; H=3.2 cm.	Box; broken; incomplete; tan clay; reddish paint or pigment on parts of exterior surfaces; cf. TT 639
(TT 635) (Period IIA)	2-7	87.302	960-918		Juglet; fig. 92:2; broken; mended; rim chipped
TT 639 (Period IIA)	2-7	87.302	12th-10th cent.	H=ca. 1.8 cm.; rim D=ca. 3.4 cm.; base D=4.2 cm.	Miniature cup; crudely made; possible thread marks on base; cf. TT 625

Object Registration No.	Area	Locus. basket	Pottery Dates	Dimensions/weight	Description
TT 641 (Period IIA)	2-7	96.308	1200-1000	W=5.2 cm.; H=4 cm.	Female figurine torso; head missing; below waist missing; waist line visible; "ball" necklace; hair in single braid on back
TT 645 (Period IA)	1-8	19.84	MB IIC, LB I, LB IIB, I_1-8th cent.		Juglet; handle missing
TT 646 (Period IIA)	2-7	87.299	12th-10th cent.	H=1.3 cm.; D=2.8	Whorl; scratched black surface
TT 669	2-8	21.70	MBIIC, I_1, I_2, P, O, A	W=2.8 cm.; L=3.2 cm.	Figurine legs; knees to ankles only; sex cannot be determined, but probably female
TT 677	1-8	5.41	MB IIC, I_{1-2}, P	Rim D=21 cm.; H=6.6 cm.	Bowl; dark read; lime encrusted; burnished inside and upper outside
TT 683 (Period IA)	1-8	19.84	MB IIC, LB I-IIB, I_1-8th cent.	H=8.8 cm.	Juglet; mended; no handle or rim
TT 687 (Period IA)	1-8	19.84	MB IIC, LB I-IIB, I_1-8th cent.	Rim D=ca. 13 cm.; H=6-6.7 cm.	Bowl; broken; mended; almost complete; tan ware
(TT 753) (Period IB)	2-8	27.97 = plaster floor 28	1150-1125		Cooking pot in which TT 643 and 701-729 were found; broken; mended; incomplete; fig. 91:1
TT 754 (Period IIA)	2-7	87.322	LB-10th cent.	W=4.9 cm.; L=6.8 cm.	Female figurine torso; head mssing; below thighs missing; bracelets; pubic triangle and cleft emphasized; "ball" necklace; back nearly flat except for single braid to waist ; light orange-red ware

Object Registration No.	Area	Locus. basket	Pottery Dates	Dimensions/weight	Description
TT 755 (Period IB)	2-8	31.99	12th, 10th cent.	W=4.7 cm.; L=9.2 cm.; H=3.6 cm.	Hollow-bodied bovine figurine; bottom half only; tan ware; cf. *Lachish IV*, text fig. 5, Pl. 59: 357
T 758 (Period IA)	1-8	19.107	MB IIC, LB I, 12th-10th cent.	H=5.6 cm.; Rim D=8.5 cm.	Bowl; nearly complete; chips out of rim and base; tan ware
TT 759	1-8	23.106	MBIIC, LBI	W=4.5 cm.; L=4 cm.; Th=ca. 9-11 mm.	†-shaped female figurine fragment; head and below waist missing; left breast missing; right breast appliquéd; line of short vertical marks at neck and waist
TT 760	1-8	20.97	MBIIC, LBI	W=1.2 cm.; L=2.5 cm.; Th=8 mm.	Legs of plaque-type figurine; below knees only; sex features not shown but probably female; perhaps legs of TT 759
TT 761 (Period IB)	2-8	10.105	LB I, 12th cent.	W=1.4 cm.; L=2.7 cm.; Th=8 mm.	Bes (Ptah-Sohar) figurine; green faience; 2 chips off back; face worn
TT 762 (Period IB)	2-8	28.106	MBIIC, LBI, late 12th cent.	W=3.5 cm.; L=7 cm.	Female figurine legs; feet missing; bracelets on ankles; pubic triangle and cleft emphasized; tan ware
TT 763 (Period IB)	2-8	33.104	LB I, 12th cent.	L=2 cm.; D=ca. 2.2 cm.	Unbaked loom weight; tan ware
TT 786 (Period IA)	1-8	19.92, 19.102	LB I, 12th-10th cent.	L=16 cm.; W=ca. 16 cm.; H=5.5 cm.	Lamp; greenish ware; mended; incomplete
TT 787 (Period IA)	2-7	105.337	LB I	L=3.5 cm.; Th=8-10 mm.	Egyptian faience sherd; light blue with black lines outside
TT 791 (Period IA)	2-8	43.120	LB, 12th cent.	D=ca. 3 cm.; H=ca. 2 cm.	Unbaked loom weight; marks of shaping and of threads visible on surface
TT 830 (Period IA)	2-8	51.140	LBI, ± 1200	L=7 cm.; w=5 cm..	Female figurine torso; head and legs below knees missing; nude from waist up; pubic triangle and cleft emphasized; cf. TT 831

Object Registration No.	Area	Locus. basket	Pottery Dates	Dimensions/weight	Description
TT 831 (Period IA)	2-8	51.144	LBI, ±1200	W=6 cm.; L=8.4 cm.	Female figurine torso; head and legs below knees missing; nude from waist up; pubic triangle and cleft emphasized; cf. TT 830
(TT 832) (Period IA)	2-8	50.135	±1200		Bowl; broken; mended; incomplete; fig. 89:1
TT 839 (Period IA)	2-8	51.142	LBI, ±1200	W=3.5 cm.; L=5.1 cm.	Female figurine legs; pubic triangle and cleft visible
TT 854	1-7	68.179	LBI	H=4 mm.; D=4 mm.	Blue faience bead
TT 855	2-7	118.356	LBI	L=5.7 cm.; W=4.7 cm.	Figurine head
TT 857	2-8	52.148	LBI, ±1200	W=4.2 cm.; H=5.3 cm.; Th=1 cm.	†-shaped female figurine; waist to knees only; incised decoration at waist and pubic triangle; pubic cleft and navel greatly exaggerated; back flat; tan ware; cf. TT 759
TT 882	1-7	68.192	LBI	W=5 cm.; L=4.1 cm.	Female figurine torso; head missing; below waist missing; "ball" necklace; single braid on back; tan ware
TT 895	1-7	68.196	LB I-12th cent.	W=2 cm.; H=3 cm.	Female figurine legs; shins to feet only; bracelets on ankles; tan ware
TT 900	1-7	68.207	I₂	W=4.5 cm.; L=4.5 cm.	Female figurine torso; head missing; below waist missing; one arm broken; "ball" necklace; single braid on back
TT 902	1-7	93.205	12th-10th cent.	H=10.5 cm.	Juglet; rim and handle missing
TT 965	1-9	92.168	MBIIC, LBI, 13th-12th cent.	W=ca. 3.3 cm.; L=6.5 cm. (dimensions of ear, not of the total fragment)	Human ear; approximately life-size; from mask (?); fragment is finished off behind ear like a rim; wheel marks running inside length of ear; orange-red; cf. *Hazor I*, Pl. 183; *Hazor II*, Pl. 163

Appendix C—252

Object Registration No.	Area	Locus. basket	Pottery Dates	Dimensions/weight	Description
TT 974	1-7	119.242	MBIIC, LBI	W=7 cm.; H=4.5 cm.; Th=ca. 1.2 cm.	†-shaped female(?) figurine torso; head and below waist missing; no appliqued breasts; incised decoration; orange-red
TT 991	2-7	154.412	1500-1468	W=4 cm.; H=3.9 cm.	Female figurine fragment; right arm only; orange-red
TT 997	1-7	117.259	MB IIC, 15th cent.	W=2.6 cm.; L=2.8 cm.; Th=5 mm.	Faience bead spacer; fluted; turquoise blue; cf. *Megiddo II*, Pl. 210:39; *Lachish IV*, Pl. 27.3
TT 999	1-7	119.260	15th cent.		Figurine torso; braid in back; yellow ware
TT 1027	2-8	78.177	15th cent.	L=4 cm.	Female figurine fragment; shoulders and arms only; single braid in back; reddish-tan ware
TT 1045	1-7	125.288	Late MB IIC	D=ca.6.8 cm.; Th (at hub)=2.1 cm.	Wheel; coarse ware; broken; incomplete
TT 1048	2-8	68.167	LBI	W=ca. 1.3-2.6 cm.; L=ca. 3.5 cm.	†-shaped female figurine fragment; right hip and part of pubic triangle only; incised decoration
TT 1051	2-8	80.183	LBI	W=ca. 4 cm.; L=ca. 3 cm.	†-shaped female figurine fragment; pubic triangle; combed, incised decoration; light red ware
(TT 1054)	2-8	78.177	13th cent.		Lamp; mended; complete; fig. 90:2
TT 1087	2-8	89.198	MB IIC, LB I	L=2.2 cm.; D=ca. 1 cm.	Faience bead; white
TT 1089	2-8	89.198	MB IIC, LB I	D=2.5 cm.; H=1.2 cm.	Whorl; yellow; powdery
TT 1100	1-7	158.297	LBI	W=5.8 cm.; L=8 cm.	Female figurine torso; head and below knees missing; pubic triangle and cleft emphasized; single braid in back; orange-tan

Object Registration No.	Area	Locus.basket	Pottery Dates	Dimensions/weight	Description
TT 1101	1-8	34.118	EB, MB IIC to 1500	L=8.5 cm.	Female figurine torso; head and below knees missing; pubic triangle and cleft emphasized; single braid in back; red-orange ware with fingerprints visible on surface
TT 1108	2-7	175.441	Mb IIC, LB I	H=ca. 6 mm; D=8-9 mm.	Faience bead; light blue; fluted
TT 1112	1-7	153.287	MB IIC	L=3 cm.	Figurine feet
TT 1126	2-8	77.185	LB I, 13th cent.	D=ca. 6 cm.	Wheel; edges broken; coarse ware
TT 1127	2-8	92.203	LB I		Painted sherds; white slip with orange, dark red, and gray-brown paint; 9 pieces
TT 1130	2-8	101.213	No pottery	W=2.8 cm.; L=4.1 cm.	Female figurine head with "Astarte" headdress; single braid in back; orange-red
TT 1143	2-8	102.215	MB IIC, LB I	D=ca. 5.4 cm.; H=2.2-2.5 cm.	Miniature bowl; broken; mended; incomplete; orange-red ware
TT 1144	2-8	90.199; 95.199	LB I	H=17.8 cm.	Jar; bichrome painting; green-black on burnished orange-red ware; one handle; broken; mended
TT 1167	2-7	199.473	No pottery	W=4.5 cm.; L=3 cm.	†-shaped female figurine fragment; pubic triangle only; incised decoration; charred black
TT 1174	1-8	47.137	EB, MB IIC, LB I	L=ca. 14 cm.	Juglet; broken; incomplete
TT 1190	2-8	115.231	MB IIC, Early LB I	L=3-3.5 cm.; D=3.5-3.8 cm.	Possibly part of bird-shaped vessel; dark red-brown; hollow inside
TT 1193	2-8	111.228	MB IIC, 1500	H=10 cm.; D=ca. 6 cm.	Loom weight(?); well-fired

Object Registration No.	Area	Locus. basket	Pottery Dates	Dimensions/weight	Description
TT 1202	1-7	108.328	MBIIC, LBI	W=3 cm.; L=5 cm.	Female figurine legs; knees to feet; bracelets on ankles; tan
TT 1204	1-8	63.156	EB, MB IIC	D=1-2 cm.; H=7 mm.	Faience bead; faded light blue
TT 1231	1-7	175.341	EB, MB IIC	H=9 cm.; D (at widest point)=6 cm.	Loom weight; pink-tan ware; well fired
TT 1232	1-7	175.341	EB, MB IIC	H=9 cm.; D (at widest point)=5.5 cm.	Loom weight; pink-tan ware; well fired
TT 1233	2-7	215.504	EB, MB IIC	H=8.3 cm.; D (at widest point)=5.9 cm.	Loom weight; conical; well fired
TT 1234	2-8	115.231	MB IIC	H=9.2 cm.; D (at widest point)=6 cm.	Loom weight; conical; pink-tan ware; well fired; cf. *Megiddo II*, Pl. 169:7
TT 1235	2-8	121.246	MB IIC	H=7.5 cm.; D (at widest point)=5 cm.	Loom weights; poorly fired; pink-tan ware; 4: 2 in fair condition, 2 broken
TT 1236	2-8	115.243	MB IIC	H=9.1 cm.; D (at widest point)=5.8 cm.	Loom weight; pink-tan ware; well fired
TT 1237	2-8	115.243	MB IIC	H=10.6 cm.; D (at widest point)=7.5 cm.	Loom weight; tan ware; well fired
TT 1254	2-8	124.237	MB IIC, LB I	H=2-5.5 cm.; D=ca. 11.5 cm.	Bowl; broken; incomplete
TT 1301	1-7	118.356	MB IIC	H=6.2 cm.; D (at rim) 16 cm.	Bowl; carinated; broken; mended; incomplete; orange-tan ware
TT 1308	1-8	53.186	EB, MB IIC	D=3 cm.; Th=5 mm.	Button with 2 holes; worn

Object Registration No.	Area	Locus. basket	Pottery Dates	Dimensions/weight	Description
TT 1310	2-7	215.506	EB, MB IIC	H=10 cm.; D (base)=6.9 cm.	Loom weight; not well fired; chipped; coarse ware
TT 1311	2-7	223.522	EB, MB IIC, LB I	H=10.6 cm.; D (base)=ca.6.4 cm.	Loom weight; base damaged; blackened; well fired; pink-tan ware
TT 1312	2-7	222.511	EB, MB IIC, LB I	H=9.3 cm.; D (base)=ca. 6 cm.	Loom weight; complete; well fired; pink-tan ware
TT 1313	1-7	165.359	EB, MB IIC	H=10.8 cm.; D (base)=5.2 cm. chipped;	Loom weight; base chipped; well fired; tan ware
TT 1314	1-7	178.345	EB, MB IIC	H=7.5 cm.; D (base)=6.6 cm.)	Loom weight; wheel marks on bottom; well fired; pink-tan ware
TT 1317	2-8	124.254	MB IIC	H=9.5 cm.; D (base)=6 cm.	Juglet; cracked; fragile; double-strand handle; rim missing; tan ware
TT 1320	2-8	133.265	MB IIC	H=9.4 cm.; D (base) 5.5 cm.	Loom weight; well fired; pink-tan ware
TT 1322	2-8	138.268	--	H=7.9 cm.; D (base)=5.1 cm.	Loom weight; not fired; crumbly; tan ware
TT 1323	2-8	138.268	--	H=7.1 cm.; D (base)=4.9 cm.	Loom weight; chipped; base broken
TT 1326	1-7	165.35	MB IIC	H=90 cm.; D (at widest point)=ca. 43.5 cm.	Jar; broken; mended; almost complete; incised decoration at shoulder
TT 1349	1-7	183.375	MB IIC	H=18.5 cm.	Juglet; broken; mended; incomplete; orange-tan ware
TT 1358	2-8	142.272	MB IIC	H=22 cm.	Juglet; broken; mended; incomplete; pink-tan ware
TT 1365	1-8	79.207	MB IIC	H=16 cm.; D=ca. 9 cm.	Juglet; Fired in reducing atmosphere to a silver-black burnished finish; incomplete; double-strand handle; buton base
TT 1370	2-7	246.559	MB IIC	H=16.6 cm.; D=6.5 cm.	Juglet; handle, neck, and rim missing; tan ware

Object Registration No.	Area	Locus. basket	Pottery Dates	Dimensions/weight	Description
TT 1376	1-7	58.204	LB I, 12th cent.	H=8 cm.; D (base)=ca. 5.6 cm.	Loom weight; base chipped; tan ware
TT 1377	1-8	57.203	MB IIC	H=8.8 cm.; D (base)=5 cm.	Loom weight; base chipped; charred; probably fired
TT 1378	2-8	141.271	MB IIC	H=9.9 cm.; D (base)=6 cm.	Loom weight; chipped lengthwise; not fired; coarse, tan ware
TT 1393	1-7	189.279	EB	L=4 mm.; Th=2 mm.	Faience bead; greenish blue
TT 1442	2-7	259.590 d	EB, MB IIC	H=14.2 cm.	Juglet; whole'; orange-tan ware
TT 1444	2-7	259.590 b	EB, MB IIC	H=10.3 cm.	Juglet; broken; mended; Tel el-Yehudiyeh ware
TT 1445	2-7	259.590	EB, MB IIC	H=12.5 cm.; D (rim)=ca. 30.5 cm.	Bowl; broken; mended
TT 1447	2-8	148.291	EB, MB IIC, LB I	H=ca. 43 cm.; D (at widest point)=ca. 32 cm.	Jar; broken; mended; neck and rim missing; combed bands at shoulder and above; pink-tan ware; thin and fine
TT 1448	1-7	165.340	MB IIC	H=ca. 60 cm.; D (at widest point)=ca. 38 cm.	Jar; mended; rim and handles missing; orange-tan ware; thin
TT 1451	2-7	259.590 c	EB, MB IIC	H=20.5 cm.; D (at widest point)=7.5 cm.	Juglet; mended; tan ware with tan slip
TT 1455	2-7	261.599	EB, MB IIC	H=9 cm.; D (bas)=6.2 cm.	Loom weight; pink-tan ware
TT 1465 (Period IIB)	2-8	156.286	EB, MB IIC, LB I	H=9 cm.; D (at widest point)=6.7 cm.	Juglet; handle and neck missing; tan ware
TT 1484	2-7	259.590 e	EB, MB IIC	H=11 cm; D=7 cm.	Juglet; black; charred; not restorable

Appendix C—257

Object Registration No.	Area	Locus. basket	Pottery Dates	Dimensions/weight	Description
TT 1486 (Period IIB)	2-8	156.292	EB, MBIIC, LBI	L=8 cm.	Female figurine torso to knees; single braid in back; pink-tan
TT 1500 (Period IIB)	2-8	69.312 a-g	10th cent.	Fragments of various sizes	Terra cotta cultic stand
TT 1534	1-8	101.252	MB IIC	H=15.5 cm.; D (at widest point)=9.3 cm.	Juglet; mended; red-tan ware; double-strand handle; button base
TT 1535	1-8	101.22	MB IIC	H=12 cm.; D (at widest point)=8.4 cm.	Juglet; mended; orange-tan ware; double-strand handle; button base
TT 1540 (Period IIB)	2-8	170.347	10th cent.	L=6 cm.; D=5.2 cm.	Horse head figurine spout; some mane marks vivisble; gray ware with botanical, basalt, and micro-fossil inclusions; wadi clay; tan slip; cf. *Lachish III*, Pl. 32:7-9
TT 1559	2-8	165.332	MB IIC	H=19.5 cm.	Juglet; broken; mended; almost complete; double-strand handle; button base; tan ware; very thin
TT 1563	2-8	165.332	MB IIC	H=13 cm.	Juglet; whole; double-strand handle; button base; tan ware
TT 1575	2-7	284.669	MB IIC	H=20.5 cm.	Dipper juglet; whole; orange-tan ware
TT 1576	2-7	284.669	MB IIC	H=27 cm.	Dipper juglet; broken; mended; almost complete; tan ware
TT 1578	2-7	284.669	MB IIC	H=17.8 cm.	Juglet; mended; complete; double-strand handle; button base; red slip; ornage-tan ware
TT 1586	2-7	284.669	MB IIC	H=8.5 cm.; D (rim) 18.5 cm.	Bowl; mended; complete; encrusted; carination; orange-tan ware
TT 1587	2-7	280.654	MB IIC	H=10 cm.; D (base)=7 cm.	Loom weight; pink-tan ware
TT 1619	1-7	196.389, 390, 395	Mb IIC	H=ca. 86 cm.	Jar; mended; top incomplete; orange-tan ware

Object Registration No.	Area	Locus. basket	Pottery Dates	Dimensions/weight	Description
TT 1631	1-8	115.278	EB III, MB IIC	H=2 cm.; D=2.5 cm.	Loom weight
TT 1632	2-8	168.383	EB III, MB IIC	H=7.5 cm.; D (base)=ca. 4.8 cm.	Loom weight; in group with TT 1633 and TT 1634; orange-tan ware; string cut base
TT 1633	2-8	168.383	EB III, MB IIC	H=9.3 cm.; D (base)=4.5 cm.	Loom weight
TT 1634	2-8	168.383	EB III, MB IIC	H=9 cm.; D (base)=6-6.5 cm.	Loom weight; hand made; poorly fired if fired at all
TT 1636	1-8	115-278	EB III, MB IIC	H=8.2 cm.; D (base)=6.5 cm.	Loom weight; poorly fired
TT 1642	1-8	99.259	EB III	L=5.3 cm.; W=1.8 cm.; H=3.5 cm.	Horse figurine; chipped; perforated; red paint on tan ware
TT 1648	2-7	280.655	--	H=9 mm.; D=5.3 cm.	Miniature plate or re-used base of another vessel; tan ware
TT 1673	2-7	389.684	EB III, MB IIC	H=7.5 cm.; D (base)=5.5-6 cm.	Loom weight; handmade; pink-tan ware
TT 1697	1-8	114.287	MB IIC	H=24.5 cm.	Juglet; whole; orange-tan ware
TT 1698	1-8	114.287	MB IIC	H=18 cm.	Juglet; whole; orange-tan ware
TT 1703	1-7	194.430	Late EB II-Early EB III	H=17.5 cm.	Juglet; dark ware; dark slip; vertical burnish; incomplete; part of base missing
TT 1751	2-7	284.669	MB IIC	H=9.2-10.5 cm.; D=36.5 cm.	Bowl; broken; mended; almost complete; orange-tan ware

Object Registration No.	Area	Locus. basket	Pottery Dates	Dimensions/weight	Description
TT 1754	1-7	219.441	EB III	H=9.6 cm.; D=11.8 cm.	Bowl; chip off rim; small crack in body; complete; dark burnish
TT 1770	2-7	284.669	EB III	H=43 cm.; W=30 cm.	Jar; mended; incomplete; 1 handle missing
TT 1771	2-8	165.332	MB IIC	H=48.5 cm.; W=37.5 cm.	Jar; mended; incomplete
TT 1772	2-7	242.558	--	H=54.5 cm.; W=36 cm.	Jar; mended; incomplete
TT 1775	2-7	290.687 a	MB IIC	H=80 cm.; D=21 cm.	Jar; mended; incomplete
TT 1776	2-7	290.687 b	MB IIC	H=80 cm.; W=47 cm.	Jar; mended; incomplete
TT 1777	2-7	290.687 c	MB IIC	H=88 cm.; D=20.5 cm.	Jar; mended; incomplete
TT 1778	2-7	290.687 d	MB IIC	H=86 cm.; D=21 cm.	Jar; mended; incomplete
TT 1779	2-7	255.590 a	EB, MB IIC	H=30 cm.; W=12.2 cm.	Juglet; mended; incomplete
TT 1788	2-7	179.439	MB IIC, LB I	H=5.5 cm.; D=ca. 18 cm.	Plate or bowl; mended; incomplete; rim missing; orange-tan ware
TT 1790 (Period IA)	1-8	19.102	LB I	H=ca. 16.5 cm.; D (at widest point)=15 cm.	Spouted jar; neck and handle missing; orange-tan ware
TT 1823	1-7	165.419	EB III, MB IIC	H=12.5 cm.; D (rim)=ca. 12 cm.; D (shoulder)=ca. 12 cm.	Pitcher; mended; incomplete; tan ware
(TT 1830)	2-8	156.320 (cistern L. 69)	960-918		Cultic stand; fig. 54:1

Object Registration No.	Area	Locus. basket	Pottery Dates	Dimensions/weight	Description
TT 1831 (Period IB)	2-8	10.45	I_2-7th cent.	H=ca. 32 cm.; D (at widest point)=ca. 24.5 cm.	Jar; mended; incomplete; rim missing; tan ware
TT 1836	2-7	235.545	MB IIC-LB I	H=ca. 2 m.; D=6.5 cm.	Base; faience; light blue surface with brown hatching; chipped; incomplete
TT 1838	2-7	276.646	Eb-MB	H=ca. 2.8 cm.; D (at widest point)=4.8 cm.	Miniature krater; broken; mended; incomplete; burnished; well made; well fired
TT 1842 (Period IIB)	2-7	36.70	±900	W at upper break=3.4 cm.; L=5.5 cm.	Human figurine; knees to ankles only; sides and corners squared, back flat; gender cannot be determined, but probably female
TT 1848	2-7	74.270	10^1-7th cent., A	L=ca. 8.5 cm.; W=6.5 cm.; Th=ca. 2.5 cm.	Blank rectangular tablet; not fired; one surface smoothed
TT 1849 (Period IIA)	2-7	87.296	MB IIC, LB I, I_1	L=8-8.5 cm.; W=ca. 5.5 cm.; Th=ca. 2 cm.	Blank rectangular unfired tablet
TT 1850	1-8	114.287	--	H=ca. 14.5 cm.; D (shoulder)=ca. 8.5 cm.	Juglet; broken; mended; dark red slip; burnished; double-strand handle; button base
TT 1851	1-7	186.385	EB III	D=10 cm.; H=2.5 cm.	Saucer; reddish coarse clay; broken; mended; incomplete; edges charred at opposite end; used as lamp (?)
(TT 1853) (Period IIB)	2-8	156.313 (cistern L. 69)	960-918		Chalice; fig. 53:5
(TT 1854)	2-8	175.406 (cistern L. 69)	960-918		Bowl; fig. 52:9
(TT 1855)	2-8	163.226 (cistern L. 69)	960-918		Bowl; fig. 52:3

Object Registration No.	Area	Locus. basket	Pottery Dates	Dimensions/weight	Description
(TT 1862) (Period IB)	2-8	46.124	ca. 1200-1150		Encasing jar; fig. 88:1
(TT 1866) (Period IIB)	2-7	59.146, 152	960-918		Jar, fig. 35:1
TT 1867	2-8	87.196	--		Jar; mended
TT 1884	2-7	84.369	I_2, O	D=ca. 1.5 cm.; H=1 cm.	Blue-white faience bead; broken; mended; nearly complete; TA 2662/n
CALCITE ITEMS					
TT 644 (Period IA)	1-8	19.84	MBIIC, LBI, LBIIB, I_1-8th cent.	H=3.2 cm.; rim D=4.4 cm.; base D=3.5 cm.	Unguentarium stand; base chipped; traces of material in "dish" or grinding surface
TT 1869 (Period IB)	2-8	20.64	--	D=ca. 6 cm.; H=6 cm.; Th=1 cm.	Vessel sherd; published (C Klammer)
SHELLS					
TT 728 (Period IB)	2-8	27.90	12th-10th cent.	Type a: L=5.5-7 cm. Type b: L=6.5 cm. Type c: L=ca. 2 cm.	11 complete shell lips and 1 fragment found in a cache with objects TT 643 and TT 701-TT 729; 8 type a; 2 of type b; one type c
TT 1699	1-7	194.423	EBII-III	W=2.3-4 cm.	Cockle shells; 30 small; 6 larger; 1 completely worn smooth; in group on bedrock; all perforated at hinge

Appendix C—262

Object Registration No.	Area	Locus. basket	Pottery Dates	Dimensions/weight	Description
BONE AND IVORY OBJECTS					
TT 355 (Period IIB)	2-7	60.160	±900	L=12.2 cm.; W=1.5 cm.	Spatula; broken and incomplete; pointed at one end and round at the other; cf. Petrie, *Tools and Weapons*, Pl. LXV:128, 129
TT 397 (Period IIB)	2-7	63.236	10th cent.	L=20.7 cm.; W=2.4 cm.	Spatula; complete but broken into 3 pieces; pointed at one end and round at other end; charred; cf. Petrie, *Tools and Weapons*, Pl. LXV: 128, 129 ("netting needle")
TT 398 (Period IIB)	2-7	57.228	±900	L=14.5 cm.; W=2 cm.	Spatula; broken into 4 pieces; maybe parts of 2 spatulas; 1 piece encrusted with powdery substance; round at one end, pointed at the other
TT 420	2-7	69.256	LB-I$_2$, P	H=8 mm.; D=2-6 cm.	Spindle whorl
TT 591 (Period IIA)	1-7	46.90	12th-10th cent.	L=4 cm.; Th=ca. 2 mm.	Bone inlay fragment; palmetto or lotus design (?)
TT 601	2-7	78.281	12th-10th cent.	D=3.5 cm.; Th.=5 mm.	Button; scratch marks visible from original shaping and polishing
TT 626	2-8	21.84	MB IIC, LB I, 12th-10th cent.	L=2.3 cm.; D=1.2 cm.	Polished bone bead
TT 644	2-8	30.96	LB I	L=7.4 cm; D (at widest point)=ca. 1.6 cm.	Spindle or handle; carved; broken; incomplete
TT 668 (Period IIA)	2-7	88.300	MB IIC, 11th cent.	L=7.5 cm.; D=8 mm.	Spindle; carved; broken and incomplete; cf. *Megiddo II*, Pl. 197: 8, 9

Object Registration No.	Area	Locus. basket	Pottery Dates	Dimensions/weight	Description
TT 727 (Period IB)	2-8	27.90	12th-10th cent.	L=ca. 3 cm.	Canine (?) incisor corroded to TT 726
TT 788 (Period IA)	2-7	108.333	MB IIC, 12th-10th cent.	D=2.9 cm.; H=5 mm.	Bone spindle whorl
TT 968	1-7	121.246	LB I	L=6.2 cm.; W=2.9-3.6 cm.; Th=1 to 4 mm.	Ivory inlay or plaque; broken; mended; incomplete; surface is dark brown; back is unmarked
TT 1016	1-7	132.261	EB, MB IIC, 15th cent, 13th cent.	D=2.1 cm.; Th=7 mm.	Bone button
TT 1031	1-7	146.278	1 bowl, 15th cent.	L=3 cm.; W=2 cm.; Th=ca. 1 cm.	Worked astragalus; sanded; flattened; bone now porous
TT 1109	2-8	91.201	MB IIC, LB I	a) L=3.7 cm.; W=1.9 cm.; Th=ca. 1 mm.; b) L=2.5 cm.; W=9mm.	Bone inlay; 2 pieces; both incomplete; mended; cf. *Megiddo II*, funerary boxes
TT 1114	2-8	94.208	MB IIC, LB I	D=2 cm.; H=8 mm.	Bone spindle whorl
TT 1129 (Period IA)	1-8	44.133	MB IIC, LB I, 12th cent	L=3.8 cm.; W=1.9 cm.; Th=1 mm.	Spatula; broken; incomplete; highly polished
TT 1172	2-8	117.233	MB IIC	L=7.6 cm.; W=1.2-1.5 cm.; Th=ca. 2 mm.	Bone inlay; broken; mended; incomplete; discolored; cf. *Megiddo II*, 192-195
TT 1244	1-7	117.269	--	D (handle)=ca. 2.5 cm.	Bone handle and haft; broken; handle in 4 pieces; haft in 2 pieces
TT 1295	1-7	147.357	EB, MB IIC	L=8 cm.; W=1.4 cm.; Th=2 mm.	Bone tool; broken; incomplete

Object Registration No.	Area	Locus. basket	Pottery Dates	Dimensions/weight	Description
TT 1372	2-8	138.268	--	D=3.2 cm.; H=7 mm.	Bone spindle whorl; one chip
TT 1459	1-8	76.230	EB	L=2.8 cm.; W=ca. 1.2 cm.; H=ca. 1.8 cm.	Astragalus; chipped; weatherworn
TT 1475	1-7	197.415	EB III	L=13.8 cm.	Bone awl; broken; mended; encrusted; complete
TT 1502	1-7	197.415	EB III	L=6 cm.; W=3.5 cm.; Th=2 mm.	Ivory comb; broken; mended; incomplete
TT 1653	2-7	280.654	MB IIC	H=2 cm.; D=4.2 cm.	Bone spindle whorl or button
TT 1655 (Period IIB)	2-8	171.367	10th cent.	L=11 cm.; D=5.5 mm.	Ivory rod, handle, or spindle; incomplete
TT 1689	1-7	219.434	Late EBII-early EB III	L=5.8 cm.; W=1.8 cm.; Th=3 mm.	Bone spatula or tool; mended; incomplete
SCARABS, SCARABOIDS AND SEALS					
TT 257	2-7	46a.110	10th-6th cent.	L=12 mm.; W=8mm.; Th=5 mm.; D of hole=2 mm.	Scaraboid picturing 2 worshipers before a cult object (?); smooth back; bone; hole bored through length
TT 701 (Period IB)	2-8	27.90	12th-10th cent.	W=9 mm.; L=11 mm.; H=8 mm.	Scarab picturing hunting scene with 2 animals and 1 man; detailed beetle markings on back and sides; found inside TT 753; bone; cf. *Lachish III*, Pl. 43:49; *Beth Shan*, fig. 109:8
TT 702 (Period IB)	2-8	27.90	Late 12th cent.	H=18 mm.; D=15mm. (at base)	Dome-shaped bone stamp seal picturing a nursing gazelle and a scorpion; found inside TT 753; lime-encrusted; surface chipped; cf. *Lachish III*, Pl. 44: 91, 92; *Megiddo I*, Pl. 69.22, 40
TT 947	1-7	5.225	MB IIC, LB I	L=2.2 cm.; W-1.5 cm.; H=9 mm.	Black stone scarab; cf. *Jericho II*, Fig. 286:14

Appendix C—265

Object Registration No.	Area	Locus. basket	Pottery Dates	Dimensions/weight	Description
TT 1034	1-7	125.284	LB I	L=1.6 cm.; W=1.4 cm.; H=7 mm.	Faience scarab; blue; glazed on top and sides; bottom worn; cf. *Lachish IV*, Pl. 35:177, 400
TT 1641	2-7	284.669	MB IIC	L=15 mm.; W=10 mm.; H=5 nn.	Soapstone scarab: found on forehead of skeleton in burial 51
METAL OBJECTS					
TT 44	2-7	17.23	I_2, A	L=6.4 cm.; D (head) = 2.33 cm.	Iron nail; corroded
TT 71 (Period IIB)	2-7	26.40	±900	Piece 1) L=15.5 cm.; piece 2) L=14 cm.; piece 3) L=14 cm.	Fragments of non-carburized iron knives or sword; 3 pieces; probably 2 blades; broken; corroded; TA 2520/n
TT 90	2-7	27.45, 49	±900	W=5 cm. (At widest point); L=24.8 cm.	Iron knife; 2 pieces; broken; badly corroded; cf. Petrie, *Tools and Weapons*, Pl. 29: 249 and p. 25; *Lachish III*, Pl. 59; TA 2519/n
TT 91 (Period IIB)	2-7	27.49	±900	W=ca. 5 cm.; L=21 cm.	Non-carburized iron plowshare point; broken into 5 pieces; badly corroded; cf. Petrie, *Tools and Weapons*, Pl. 29:249 and p. 25; TA 2510/n (?)
TT 108 (Period IIB)	2-7	27.49	±900	L=11 cm.	Iron scythe or sickle blade; 2 pieces; nearly complete; corroded; cf. Petrie, *Tools and Weapons*, Pl. LIV:15 and p. 46; TA 2521/n
TT 132 (Period IIB)	2-7	28.47	8th cent.	Piece 1) L=20.8 cm.; piece 2) L=20.6 cm.	Iron plow points or ends of goads; 2 points corroded together; both broken into 2 pieces; tip of one missing; cf. *Lachish III*, Pl. 177:2-5; TA 2516/n
TT 258	2-7	46.110	10th-6th cent., P, H, A	L=41 mm.; W=25 mm.	Bronze fibula

Object Registration No.	Area	Locus. basket	Pottery Dates	Dimensions/weight	Description
TT 259	2-7	46.110	10th-6th cent., P, H, A	L=51 mm.; W=32 mm.	Bronze fibula with iron pin (badly rusted); cf. *Lachish III*, Text, p. 93, Pl. 56:37
TT 322 (Period IIB)	2-7	27.85; 61.164	±900	L (a)=3.8 cm.; (b)=10.8 cm.; W=4.1 cm.	Carburized iron sickle or scythe fragment; consists of a) tip or tang, L=2.3 cm.; middle section 4.1 x 10.8 cm.; end section L=2.3 cm., totally corroded; TA 2504/n
TT 342	2-7	61.185	±900	L=6.5 cm.	Iron toggle pin; rusted; broken into 2 pieces
TT 387 (Period IIB)	2-7	57.228	±900	(a) L=16 cm.; (b) L=11 cm.; (c) L=11	2 carburized iron blades or share scrapers fused to a dagger/spearhead or goad (TT 409); totally corroded; cf. *Megiddo II*, Pl. 181.55, 58, 59
TT 408	2-7	66.243	Iron	W=3.3 cm.; L=8.4 cm.; Th=4 mm.	Iron armor scale with 2 perforations; totally corroded
TT 409 (Period IIB)	2-7	57.218	±900	L=8.1 cm.	Non-carburized iron arrowhead; badly rusted; found with TT 387
TT 497	2-8	1.2	LBI, I_1, I_2, H, A	W=2 cm.; L=6.2 cm.; Th=1.5 cm.	Bronze armor scale; slightly curved; corroded; cf. *Megiddo II*, Pl. 177.6; *Nuzi II*, Pl. 126:B-H
TT 572	1-8	7.42	12th-7th cent., P	Head D.=ca 2.3 cm.; L=10.8 cm.	Iron nail; round head; square shaft; corroded
TT 598	2-8	21.69	I_1, I_2, A	L=8.5 cm.	Iron chisel (?); "head" is solid and globular; 2 pieces; corroded
TT 600	2-7	78.281	12th-10th cent.	L=10.3 cm.; W=1.3 cm.	Bronze arrowhead; broken into 4 pieces
TT 602 (Period IIA)	1-7	60.97	12th-10th cent.	W=3 cm.; L=6.3 cm.; Th=2 mm.	Iron armor scale; totally corroded; blue-black shiny remains
TT 671	1-8	15.71	MB IIC, LB, I_{1-2}	L=6.8 cm.	Bronze pin or needle; broken into 2 pieces; incomplete

Object Registration No.	Area	Locus. basket	Pottery Dates	Dimensions/weight	Description
TT 703 (Period IB)	2-8	27.90	12th-10th cent.	D=2.1 cm.; Th=1 cm.; Wt=15 grams	Bronze bead or whorl; rosette motif with about 18 ridges; lime encrusted; corroded and chipped
TT 704 (Period IB)	2-8	27.90	12th-10th cent.	H=8 mm.; D = ca. 10 mm.	Fluted bronze bead
TT 705 (Period IB)	2-8	27.90	12th-10th cent.	L=16.5 mm.; base=7 x 9 mm.; Wt=4 grams	Bronze trapezoidal weight; cf. TT 706
TT 706 (Period IB)	2-8	27.90	12th-10th cent.	L=11 mm.; base=5 x 9 mm.; Wt=3 grams	Bronze trapezoidal weight; cf. TT 705
TT 707 (Period IB)	2-8	27.90	12th-10th cent.	W=1.3 cm.; L=2.2 cm.; Th=6 mm.; Wt=6.2 grams	Bronze turtle weight; cf TT 709
TT 708 (Period IB)	2-8	27.90	12th-10th cent.	H=3 cm.; Wt=41.6 grams	Bronze baboon figurine weight with paws over mouth; cf. *Gezer I*, p. 76, fig. 22, *Lachish III*, Pl. 35:31; *Megiddo II*, Pl. 206.62
TT 709 (Period IB)	2-8	27.90	12th-10th cent.	W=8 mm.; L=1.5 cm.; Th=ca. 7 mm.; Wt=2.3 grams	Bronze frog weight; cf. TT 707; cf. carnelian frog, *Megiddo II*, Pl. 205.25; *Nuzi II*, Pl. 131
TT 710 (Period IB)	2-8	27.90	12th-10th cent.	H=8 mm.; D=10 mm.; Wt=4.3 grams	Bronze dome weight; cf. TT 711, TT 712
TT 711 (Period IB)	2-8	27.90	12th-10th cent.	H=10 mm.; D=13 mm.; Wt=7 grams	Bronze dome weight; cf. TT 710, 712
TT 712 (Period IB)	2-8	27.90	12th-10th cent.	H=15 mm.; D=15 mm.; Wt=19 grams	Bronze dome weight; cf. TT 710, 711
TT 713 (Period IB)	2-8	27.90	12th-10th cent.	W=10 mm.; L=22 mm.; H=10 mm.; Wt=8.1 grams	Loaf-shaped bronze weight; cf. TT 715
TT 714 (Period IB)	2-8	27.90	12th-10th cent.	W=12 mm.; L=24 mm.; H=9 mm.; Wt=8.6 grams	Loaf-shaped bronze weight; corroded; split; cf. TT 713, TT 715

Object Registration No.	Area	Locus. basket	Pottery Dates	Dimensions/weight	Description
TT 715 (Period IB)	2-8	27.90	12th-10th cent.	W=16 mm.; L=32 mm.; H=14 mm.; Wt=24.8 grams	Loaf-shaped bronze weight; cracked; cf. TT 713; TT 715 = TT 713 x 3 in weight
TT 726 (Period IB)	2-8	27.90	12th-10th cent.	W=.9 cm.; L=7.8 cm.; Th=.8-1.2 cm.	Iron chisel with 3 smooth stones (perhaps weights) corroded to it; tip missing
TT 820 (Period IIB)	1-7	75.160	MBIIC, LBI, I$_1$	L=ca. 24.2 cm.; W (blade)=1.0-4.1 cm.; Th (blade)=1.0-2.0 cm.; W (socket)=4.2 cm.; D (shaft hole)=1.7-3.1 cm.	Carburized iron plow point or goad; broken into 4 pieces and 3 small fragments; incomplete; badly corroded; see *BASOR* 185, fig. 18
TT 1008	1-7	133.262	15th cent.	D=ca.2.2 cm.	Bronze ring; badly corroded; possibly not jewelry but a fastener
TT 1028	2-8	76.178	15th cent.	L=8 cm.; W=1.7 cm.	Bronze arrowhead; corroded
TT 1030	1-7	145.276	±1500	L=8.6 cm.; D=1 mm.	Bronze wire pick or pin; broken off at both ends; not badly corroded
TT 1094	2-8	93.204	LB I, late 15th cent.	L=17 cm.; D=ca. 3 mm.	Bronze nail or toggle pin; partly corroded
TT 1095	1-8	24.93	MB IIC	L=7.3 cm.; W=1.7 cm.	Bronze arrowhead; slightly corroded
TT 1131	2-8	94.209	MB IIC, LB I	L=ca. 9 cm.	Bronze needle; broken; bent; eye incomplete; encrusted
TT 1154	2-7	169.444	EB, MB IIC, LB I	L=7.8 cm.	Bronze pin; 2 pieces plus part of needle with eye
TT 1192	1-7	167.326	EB, MB IIC-1500	L=15 cm.	Bronze pin; 2 pieces; corroded at large end
TT 1195	2-8	104.225	MB IIC, LB I	L=6.5 cm.	Bronze pin; broken; both ends missing; corroded

Object Registration No.	Area	Locus. basket	Pottery Dates	Dimensions/weight	Description
TT 1210	1-7	108.328	MB IIC, LB I	L=8 cm.	Bronze needle or pin; broken; incomplete
TT 1215	1-7	173.334	EB, MB IIC	L=11 cm.	Bronze handle or chisel; corroded; fair condition
TT 1216	2-7	211.495	EB, MB IIC, LB I	L=ca. 4.5 cm.	Bronze crescent; part of a pin or handle (?)
TT 1223	1-8	61.168	EB, MB IIC	L=ca. 4.6 cm.	Bronze wire loop; broken; incomplete
TT 1227	1-8	47.161	EB, MB IIC	L=10.5 cm.	Bronze pin; corroded; incomplete
TT 1243	2-8	119.241; 123.241	MB IIC-1500	L (blade)=ca. 17.5 cm.; (haft)=ca. 9 cm.; D (end of haft)=2.7 cm.; Th (haft)=2 mm.; W (blade at widest point)=4.2 cm.; Th (blade)=ca. 1.1 cm.	Bronze spear point; complete except for chip at point; lime encrusted; slightly corroded
TT 1404	2-8	147.277	EB, MB IIC	L=6.5 cm.	Bronze toggle pin; broken; incomplete; corroded
TT 1415	1-7	195.393	EB, MB IIC	L=7.3 cm.; Th=4 mm.	Bronze weapon haft (?); slightly bent; corroded
TT 1443	2-8	21.285	EB, MB IIC, LB I	L=8 cm.; W (at widest point)=1.8 cm.	Bronze arrowhead; bent; corroded
TT 1478 (Period IIB)	2-8	156.305	EBIII, 7th-6th cent.	L=6 cm.; Th=4-5 mm.	Bronze rod/scriber (?)
TT 1507	2-7	274.637	EB, MB IIC	L=3.7 cm.; Th=3 mm.	Bronze hook; somewhat corroded

Object Registration No.	Area	Locus. basket	Pottery Dates	Dimensions/weight	Description
TT 1651 (Period IIB)	2-8	170.350	12th, 10th cent.	W=1.9 cm.; L=3.8 cm.; Th=1-2 mm.	Bronze handle fragment; found with pin or nail fragment; pierced with .5 cm. round hole
TT 1659	2-7	288.675	EB III	L=6.2 cm.; Th=2.5 mm.	Bronze pin; incomplete; bent
TT 1679	1-8	118.284	EB III	L=3.9 cm.; W=2.9-3.6 cm.; Th=4 mm.	Bronxe axe or adze blade; corroded; incomplete
TT 1685	2-7	290.687	EB III, MB IIC	L=10.2 cm.; Th=2.5 mm.	Bronze needle; bent
TT 1798	2-7	70.260	I$_2$, P, A	L=6.5 cm.; W=2.2 cm.; Th.=1.5 mm.	Bronze armor scales; 1 broken but complete; another corroded to it, incomplete
TT 1799	2-7	70.262	I$_2$, P, A	L=4.8 cm.; W=1.9 cm.; Th.=1.5 mm.	Bronze armor scale fragment; TA 2486/n
TT 1879 (Period IIB)	1-7	86.156	?	L=7.9 cm.; W=1.0-2.9 cm.; Th.=.2-1.7 cm.	Unfinished carburized iron object; potentially an axehead
TT 1880	1-7	93.173	?	W=.3-2.1 cm.; L=2.4 cm.; Th.=1-.7 cm.	Unfinished iron blade
TT 1891	2-8	51.40	?	?	Fragment of iron spear point (?); A. Yahyah dissertation

Appendix D:
**Registered Objects Found in SW 1-7; 2-7; 1-8; 2-8 from Period IIB (960-918 BCE)
with references to Pottery Published in Rast (1978) in Parentheses**

Appendix D:
Registered Objects Found in SW 1-7; 2-7; 1-8; 2-8 from Period IIB (960-918 BCE) with references to Pottery Published in Rast (1978) in Parentheses

Object Registration No.	Area	Locus. basket	Pottery Dates	Dimensions/weight	Description
STONE & PASTE OBJECTS					
TT 78 (Period IIB)	2-7	26.37	±900	W=4 cm.; L=4.9 cm.; Wt=36 grams	Pierced pendant/weight; serpentine; TA 2440/n[1]
TT 81 (Period IIB)	2-7	26.37	±900	L=2.7 cm.; D=2.8 cm.	Loom weight
TT 86 (Period IIB)	2-7	27.46	±900	H=6.8 cm.; Base=6.3 x 4.6 cm.	Neatly-shaped pyramidal rubbing stone; gas bubbles form very rough surface; *basalt scorie* (scorie or foamy basalt)
TT 98 (Period IIB)	2-7	27.45	±900	H=4.1 cm.; Base D=4.5 cm.	Rubbing stone; limestone
TT 116 (Period IIB)	2-7	26.38	±900	W=30 cm; L=56 cm.; H=11.75 cm.	Quern; coarse texture with ashy spot on base; basalt; cf. *Hazor I*, Pl. 145:3 (also in same locus: TT 71, 78, 79, 83, 117)
TT 117 (Period IIB)	2-7	26.38	±900	L=8.9 cm.; Oval end 6.2 x 5.5 cm.	Oval rubbing stone; rounded end and about half of vertical sides well-polished; broken at top and across one side; limestone; cf.. TT 116; also in same locus, TT 78
TT 320 (Period IIB)	2-7	59.149	±900	W=6.5 cm.; L=10.7 cm.; H=5.2 cm.	Rectangular rubbing stone; light, porous; one surface flat, slightly smoothed; quartzolite

---

[1]TA with a number is a number assigned to the object in the Tel Aviv laboratory report.

Object Registration No.	Area	Locus. basket	Pottery Dates	Dimensions/weight	Description
TT 324 (Period IIB)	2-7	61.164	±900	H=3.9 cm.; Base D=ca. 3 cm.	Semi-spherical rubbing stone; lines of smoothing visible; white limestone with some black striations; also in same locus TT 322, TT 358, TT 359
TT 356 (Period IIB)	2-7	55.141	±900	W=13.5 cm.; L=23.5 cm.; H=8 cm.	Saddle grinder; incomplete; basalt
TT 373 (Period IIB)	2-7	61.205	±900	H=3 cm.; D=3.8 cm.	Socketed stone; mace head (?); undetermined stone
TT 389 (Period IIB)	2-7	61.203	±900	H=12.5 cm.; D=ca. 22.5 cm.	Round worked stone base (?); flat on one side, irregular on the other; partly coated with white plaster-like substance; limestone; cf.. TT 359, TT 390, TT 391
TT 390 (Period IIB)	2-7	61.203	±900	H=ca. 11 cm.; D=19-21 cm.	Round worked stone base (?); flat on one side, irregular on the other; limestone; same as TT 389, cf. TT 359, TT 391
TT 391 (Period IIB)	2-7	61.203	±900	H=ca. 10.5 cm.; D=ca. 21 cm.	Round worked stone base (?); flat on one side, irregular on the other; limestone; same as TT 389, cf. TT 359, TT 390
TT 392 (Period IIB)	2-7	61.203	±900	H=7.1 cm.; base D=6 cm.	Rubbing or pounding stone; no surface shows more wear than any other; basalt; in same locus as TT 324, TT 358, TT 359, TT 393
TT 393 (Period IIB)	2-7	61.203	±900	H=6.7; base D=5.7 cm.	Rubbing stone; base worn smooth; basalt; cf. TT 392
TT 394 (Period IIB)	2-7	61.203	±900	W=15.7 cm.; L=31.5 cm.; H=7 cm.;	Plano-convex saddle grinder; smoother on flat side; coarse-textured basalt
TT 395 (Period IIB)	2-7	61.203	±900	W=ca. 28 cm.; L=49 cm.; H=12 cm.	Quern; basalt; cf. TT 357
TT 430 (Period IIB)	2-7	57.228	±900	W=18.5 cm.; H=26 cm.; Th=10-12 cm.	Shaped standing stone (מצבה); limestone, partially coated with plaster; cf. TT 431, TT 432

Object Registration No.	Area	Locus. basket	Pottery Dates	Dimensions/weight	Description
TT 431 (Period IIB)	2-7	57.228	±900	W=18 cm.; H=26.5 cm.; Th=9-14 cm.	Shaped standing stone (מצבה); limestone, partially coated with plaster; cf.. TT 430, TT 432
TT 432 (Period IIB)	2-7	57.228	±900	W=14.5 cm.; H=17.7 cm.; Th=11 cm.	Shaped standing stone (מצבה); basalt; cf.. TT 430, TT 431
TT 803 (Period IIB)	1-7	86.161	12th-century-I$_1$	H=ca. 9.2 cm.; D at widest point=5.8 cm.	Rubbing stone; fine-grained basalt; top chipped like a hammer stone
TT 819 (Period IIB)	1-7	75.160	MB IIC, LB I, I$_1$	L=35.5 cm.; W=ca. 17 cm.; H=4.8 cm.	Saddle grinder; coarse-grained basalt; concave grinding surface; possible mortar?
TT 837 (Period IIB)	1-7	75.160	MB IIC, LB I, I$_1$	H=ca. 12 cm.; D=ca. 26-28 cm.; D of bowl; 16-17 cm.; Depth of bowl=5.5 cm.	Limestone mortar; pitted with root holes
TT 1463 (Period IIB)	2-8	156.296	EB III-LB I	L=6.9 cm.; W=1.8 cm.	Flint blade; both edges retouched
TT 1482 (Period IIB)	2-8	157.299	EB III	L=5.8 cm; W=2 cm.	Flint blade; one edge more shiny
TT 1625 (Period IIB)	2-8	171.404	EB, 12th-10th cent.	W=3 cm.; L=8 cm.; H=10.5 cm.; base d=ca. 25 cm.	Leg from base of tripod bowl; originally ca. 17 cm. tall; fine-grained basalt; cf.. TT 1716 (but not from the same bowl)
TT 1652 (Period IIB)	2-8	171.352	10th cent.	H=2 cm.; D=2.5 cm.	Loom weight; hole not round nor centered; black stone
TT 1671 (Period IIB)	2-8	171.410	Late 10th cent.	L=ca. 13 cm.; W=7.5 cm.; H=7 cm.	Basalt work stone/grinder
TT 1716 (Period IIB)	2-8	171.404	EB, 12th-10th cent.	W=ca. 4 cm.; L=10 ; H=10.4 cm.	Leg fragment from base of tripod bowl; fine-grained basalt; cf. TT 1625 (but not from same bowl)

Object Registration No.	Area	Locus. basket	Pottery Dates	Dimensions/weight	Description
CERAMIC OBJECTS (For items in parentheses, see Rast, *Taanach I* for descriptions)					
(TT 62) (Period IIB)	2-7	26.40	960-918		Juglet; fig. 40:7
(TT 63) (Period IIB)	2-7	26.38	960-918		Juglet; fig. 40:1
(TT 64) (Period IIB)	2-7	27.41	960-918		Tripod censer or strainer; 2 legs missing; fig. 51:3; cf. *Lachish III*, pl 76:16; *Beth Shan*, Pl. 108:5
(TT 65) (Period IIB)	2-7	27.41	960-918		Cooking pot; handle and rim missing; fig. 50:3
(TT 73) (Period IIB)	2-7	26.36	960-918		Pyxis; fig. 40:14
(TT 83) (Period IIB)	2-7	26.36	960-918		Jug; fig. 39:6, neck & rim broken, mostly missing
(TT 88) (Period IIB)	2-7	27.46	960-918		Juglet; fig. 40:6; broken; chipped; mended
(TT 89) (Period IIB)	2-7	27.45	960-918		Lamp; broken; incomplete; fig. 51:1
TT 100 (Period IIB)	2-7	27.49	±900	W=7.3 cm.; L=18.6 cm.	Female figurine mold

Appendix D—276

Object Registration No.	Area	Locus. basket	Pottery Dates	Dimensions/weight	Description
(TT 103) (Period IIB)	2-7	27.45	960-918		Jug; fig. 37:1
TT 107 (Period IIB)	2-7	27.49	I_2	H=8 cm.; D=8 cm.	Loom weight; cf. Gordion, *AJA* 66, p. 165; *Hazor II*, Pl. 18:2; Pl. 20:4
TT 306 (Period IIB)	2-7	57.142	I_1		Juglet; broken; mended; handle missing
TT 323 (Period IIB)	2-7	61.164	±900	H=5 cm.	Miniature juglet; neck and rim missing; handle broken
(TT 327) (Period IIB)	2-7	59.149	960-918		Juglet; fig. 40:4
(TT 350) (Period IIB)	2-7	61.186	960-918		Amphora; fig. 36:3
(TT 351) (Period IIB)	2-7	61.184	960-918		Cult stand; fig. 51:4
(TT 352) (Period IIB)	2-7	61.176	960-918		Bowl; fig. 47:2; broken; mended
(TT 353) (Period IIB)	2-7	61.181; 63.224	960-918		Bowl; fig. 46:5; broken; incomplete
(TT 354) (Period IIB)	2-7	61.196	960-918		Bowl; fig. 47:4; broken; mended
(TT 372) (Period IIB)	2-7	61.208	960-918		Pyxis; fig. 40:13
(TT 386) (Period IIB)	2-7	63.234	960-918		juglet; fig. 46:11; piece of rim missing

Object Registration No.	Area	Locus. basket	Pottery Dates	Dimensions/weight	Description
TT 388 (Period IIB)	2-7	61.219, 220, 221, 222	±900	Type a: H=6.7; D=9.2 cm. Type b: H=5.3; D=10.1 cm.	Fragments of ca. 48 loom weights: 18 in B. 219; 14 in B. 220; 10 in B. 221; fragments of at least 10 others in B. 222; found mostly inside or in association with multi-handled krater TT 489
(TT 410) (Period IIB)	2-7	61.216	960-918		Bowl; fig. 46:11; broken; incomplete
(TT 411) (Period IIB)	2-7	61.214	960-918		Bowl; fig. 46:2; broken; mended; incomplete
(TT 412) (Period IIB)	2-7	61.125	960-918		Bowl; fig. 47:3; broken; mended; incomplete
(TT 414) (Period IIB)	2-7	61.187	960-918		Jug; fig. 39:4; broken; incomplete
(TT 415) (Period IIB)	2-7	57.227	960-918		Bowl; fig. 45:4; broken; incomplete
(TT 416) (Period IIB)	2-7	27.101	960-918		Bowl; broken; mended; almost complete
(TT 439) (Period IIB)	2-7	26.36-26.40	960-918		Krater; fig. 45:2
(TT 440) (Period IIB)	2-7	26.36-26.40	960-918		Jug; fig. 37:2
(TT 441) (Period IIB)	2-7	26,36; 27.45	960-918		Bowl; fig. 46:8
(TT 442) (Period IIB)	2-7	27.45, 49	960-918		Bowl; fig. 46:13

Appendix D—278

Object Registration No.	Area	Locus. basket	Pottery Dates	Dimensions/weight	Description
(TT 443) (Period IIB)	2-7	26.36-26.40	960-918		Bowl; fig. 48:3
(TT 444) (Period IIB)	2-7	27.45	960-918		Bowl; fig. 48:16; mended
(TT 445) (Period IIB)	2-7	27.41, 44, 45	960-918		Bowl; fig. 45:2
(TT 446) (Period IIB)	2-7	27.45	960-918		Bowl; fig. 42:1
(TT 447) (Period IIB)	2-7	27.45	960-918		Bowl; fig. 48:15; mended
(TT 448) (Period IIB)	2-7	26.40	960-918		Bowl; fig. 48:2; mended; complete
(TT 449) (Period IIB)	2-7	27.45	960-918		Bowl; fig. 47:1; mended; incomplete
(TT 450) (Period IIB)	2-7	27.45	960-918		Bowl; fig. 46:7; mended; incomplete
(TT 451) (Period IIB)	2-7	27.45	960-918		Bowl; fig. 43:2; mended; incomplete
(TT 452) (Period IIB)	2-7	27.45, 49	960-918		Bowl; 46:14; mended; incomplete
(TT 453) (Period IIB)	2-7	27.45	960-918		Bowl; fig. 46:3; mended; incomplete
(TT 454) (Period IIB)	2-7	61.175	960-918		Jug; fig. 38:1; mended; a few small fragments missing

Object Registration No.	Area	Locus. basket	Pottery Dates	Dimensions/weight	Description
(TT 455) (Period IIB)	2-7	61.178	960-918		Bowl; fig. 46:12; mended; incomplete
(TT 456) (Period IIB)	2-7	60.160	960-918		1-handled cooking pot; fig. 50:1; mended; incomplete; held 16 sheep/goat astragali
(TT 457) (Period IIB)	2-7	61.179	960-918		Bowl; fig. 46:6; mended; incomplete
TT 458 (Period IIB)	2-7	61.204	±900	H=10.5 cm.	Juglet; mended; incomplete
(TT 459) (Period IIB)	2-7	61.192	960-918		Round-based storage jar; fig. 34:5; mended; a few small pieces missing
(TT 460) (Period IIB)	2-7	61.185	960-918		Hole-mouth jar; fig. 35:2; mended; incomplete
(TT 461) (Period IIB)	2-7	61.195	960-918		Bowl; fig. 44:3; mended; incomplete
(TT 462) (Period IIB)	2-7	61.179	960-918		Bowl; fig. 46:4; mended; several small fragments missing
(TT 463) (Period IIB)	2-7	61.200	960-918		Bowl; fig. 48:17; mended; incomplete
(TT 464) (Period IIB)	2-7	27.45, 49; 61.169	960-918		Bowl; fig. 45:6; mended; incomplete
(TT 465) (Period IIB)	2-7	60.162	960-918		Bowl; fig. 46:1; mended; incomplete
(TT 466) (Period IIB)	2-7	61.205	960-918		Juglet; fig. 40:10; mended; rim missing; body incomplete

Appendix D—280

Object Registration No.	Area	Locus. basket	Pottery Dates	Dimensions/weight	Description
(TT 467) (Period IIB)	2-7	57.157	960-918		Side-spouted jug; fig. 36:1; mended; rim and base missing
(TT 468) (Period IIB)	2-7	63.234	12th-10th cent.		Jug; fig. 39:2; mended; incomplete
(TT 469) (Period IIB)	2-7	61.205	960-918		Ovoid storage jar; fig. 31:3; mended; rim missing
(TT 470) (Period IIB)	2-7	61.202	960-918		Jug; fig. 38:2; mended; a few body sherds missing
(TT 471) (Period IIB)	2-7	28.57, 59; 57.157; 59.148, 150	960-918		Bowl; fig. 43:1; mended; incomplete
(TT 472) (Period IIB)	2-7	57.226	960-918		Cooking pot; fig. 50:2; mended; incomplete
(TT 473) (Period IIB)	2-7	61.180	960-918		Lamp; fig. 51:2; mended; incomplete
(TT 474) (Period IIB)	2-7	61.193	960-918		Ovoid storage jar; fig. 31:1; mended; almost complete
(TT 475) (Period IIB)	2-7	61.191	960-918		Round-based storage jar; fig.34:4; mended; incomplete
(TT 476) (Period IIB)	2-7	59.150	960-918		Jar; fig. 30:2; mended; almost complete
(TT 477) (Period IIB)	2-7	61.174	960-918		Ovoid storage jar; fig. 30:3; mended; incomplete

Object Registration No.	Area	Locus. basket	Pottery Dates	Dimensions/weight	Description
(TT 478) (Period IIB)	2-7	61.229; 63.236	960-918		Ovoid storage jar; fig. 30:1; mended; incomplete
(TT 479) (Period IIB)	2-7	61.172, 185, 188, 201	960-918		Bowl; fig. 42:4; mended; incomplete
(TT 481) (Period IIB)	2-7	63.230	960-918		Ovoid storage jar; fig. 31:2; mended; almost half missing
(TT 482) (Period IIB)	2-7	61.172, 173	960-918		Round-based storage jar; fig. 34:1; mended; incomplete
(TT 1866) (Period IIB)	2-7	59.143; 61.197	960-918		Round-based storage jar; fig. 31:1; mended; rim incomplete; handle missing
(TT 484) (Period IIB)	2-7	28.53	960-918		Juglet; fig. 40:11; mended; small side pieces missing
(TT 485) (Period IIB)	2-7	28.47; 35.68	960-918		Bowl; fig. 45:1; incomplete
(TT 486) (Period IIB)	2-7	36.105	960-918		Bowl; fig. 48:1; mended; incomplete
(TT 487) (Period IIB)	2-7	27.49	960-918		Bowl; fig. 44:4; mended; almost complete
(TT 488) (Period IIB)	2-7	27.45	960-918		Pyxis; fig. 40:12; broken; incomplete
(TT 489) (Period IIB)	2-7	59.155; 61.189, 205	960-918		8-handled krater; mended; incomplete; fig. 41:1; cf.. *Lachish III*, pl 82:124

Object Registration No.	Area	Locus. basket	Pottery Dates	Dimensions/weight	Description
(TT 490) (Period IIB)	2-7	57.217	960-918		Side-spouted jug; fig. 36:2; mended; incomplete
TT 1465 (Period IIB)	2-8	156.286	EB, MB IIC, LB I	H=9 cm.; D (at widest point)=6.7 cm.	Juglet; handle and neck missing; tan ware
TT 1486 (Period IIB)	2-8	156.292	EB, MBIIC, LBI	L=8 cm.	Female figurine torso to knees; single braid in back; pink-tan
TT 1500 (Period IIB)	2-8	69.312 a-g	10th cent.	Fragments of various sizes	Rectangular terra cotta cultic stand; .54 m. high when reconstructed
TT 1540 (Period IIB)	2-8	170.347	10th cent.	L=6 cm.; D=5.2 cm.	Horse head figurine spout; some mane marks vivisble; gray ware with botanical, basalt, and micro-fossil inclusions; wadi clay; tan slip; cf. *Lachish III*, Pl. 32:7-9
(TT 1830) (Period IIB)	2-8	156.320 (cistern L. 69)	960-918		Cultic stand; fig. 54:1
TT 1842 (Period IIB)	2-7	36.70	±900	W at upper break=3.4 cm.; L=5.5 cm.	Human figurine; knees to ankles only; sides and corners squared, back flat; gender cannot be determined, but probably female
(TT 1853) (Period IIB)	2-8	156.313 (cistern L. 69)	960-918		Chalice; fig. 53:5
(TT 1866) (Period IIB)	2-7	59.146, 152	960-918		Jar; fig. 35:1

BONE AND IVORY ITEMS

Object Registration No.	Area	Locus. basket	Pottery Dates	Dimensions/weight	Description
TT 355 (Period IIB)	2-7	60.160	±900	L=12.2 cm.; W=1.5 cm.	Spatula; broken and incomplete; pointed at one end and round at the other; cf. Petrie, *Tools and Weapons*, Pl. LXV:128, 129
TT 397 (Period IIB)	2-7	63.236	10th cent.	L=20.7 cm.; W=2.4 cm.	Spatula; complete but broken into 3 pieces; pointed at one end and round at other end; charred; cf. Petrie, *Tools and Weapons*, Pl. LXV: 128, 129 ("netting needle")
TT 398 (Period IIB)	2-7	57.228	±900	L=14.5 cm.; W=2 cm.	Spatula; broken into 4 pieces; maybe parts of 2 spatulas; 1 piece crusted with powdery substance; round at one end, pointed at the other
TT 1655 (Period IIB)	2-8	171.367	10th cent.	L=11 cm.; D=5.5 mm.	Ivory rod, handle, or spindle; incomplete

METAL OBJECTS

Object Registration No.	Area	Locus. basket	Pottery Dates	Dimensions/weight	Description
TT 71 (Period IIB)	2-7	26.40	±900	Piece 1) L=15.5 cm.; piece 2) L=14 cm.; piece 3) L=14 cm.	Fragments of non-carburized iron knives or sword; 3 pieces; broken; corroded; TA 2520/n
TT 91 (Period IIB)	2-7	27.49	±900	W=ca. 5 cm.; L=21 cm.	Non-carburized iron plowshare point; broken into 5 pieces; badly corroded; cf. Petrie, *Tools and Weapons*, Pl. 29:249 and p. 25; TA 2510/n (?)
TT 108 (Period IIB)	2-7	27.49	±900	L=11 cm.	Iron scythe or sickle blade; 2 pieces; nearly complete; corroded; cf. Petrie, *Tools and Weapons*, Pl. LIV:15 and p. 46; TA 2521/n

Object Registration No.	Area	Locus. basket	Pottery Dates	Dimensions/weight	Description
TT 132 (Period IIB)	2-7	28.47	8th cent.	Piece 1) L=20.8 cm.; piece 2) L=20.6 cm.	Iron plow points or ends of goads; 2 points corroded together; both broken into 2 pieces; tip of b) missing; cf. Lachish III, Pl. 177:2-5; TA 2516/n
TT 322 (Period IIB)	2-7	27.85; 61.164	±900	L (a)=3.8 cm.; (b)=10.8 cm.; W=4.1 cm.	Carburized iron sickle or scythe fragment; consists of a) tip or tang, L=2.3 cm.; middle section 4.1 x 10.8 cm.; end section L=2.3 cm., totally corroded; TA 2504/n
TT 387 (Period IIB)	2-7	57.228	±900	(a) L=16 cm.; (b) L=11 cm.; (c) L=11	2 carburized iron knife blades fused to a dagger/spearhead; totally corroded; cf. *Megiddo II*, Pl. 181.55, 58, 59
TT 409 (Period IIB)	2-7	57.218	±900	L=8.1 cm.	Non-carburized iron arrowhead; badly rusted; found with TT 387
TT 820 (Period IIB)	1-7	75.160	MBIIC, LBI, I$_1$	L=ca. 24.2 cm.; W (blade)=1.0-4.1 cm.; Th (blade)=1.0-2.0 cm.; W (socket)=4.2 cm.; D (shaft hole)=1.7-3.1 cm.	Carburized iron plow point or goad; broken into 4 pieces and 3 small fragments; incomplete; badly corroded; see *BASOR* 185, fig. 18
TT 1478 (Period IIB)	2-8	156.305	EBIII, 7th-6th cent.	L=6 cm.; Th=4-5 mm.	Bronze rod/scriber (?)
TT 1651 (Period IIB)	2-8	170.350	12th, 10th cent.	W=1.9 cm.; L=3.8 cm.; Th=1-2 mm.	Bronze handle fragment; found with pin or nail fragment; pierced with .5 cm. round hole
TT 1879 (Period IIB)	1-7	86.156	?	W=1.0-2.9 cm.; Th=.2-1.7 cm.	Unfinished carburized iron object; potentially an axehead

**Appendix E: Astragali from the Cultic Structure
Area B, SW 1-7; 1-8; 2-7; 2-8**

Appendix E: Astragali from the Cultic Structure
Area B, SW 1-7; 1-8; 2-7; 2-8

No.	Foster No.	Lab/Reg. No.	Pottery Date	Locus	L/R	Sheep/goat[1]	M/F[2]	Descriptive Comments[3]
1	140	4596/N	1500-1468	SW 2-7.140.394	L	S/G	M	Polished on lateral and medial faces
2	112	3272/N.1	I₁	SW 2-7.60.160 16 astragali from pot TT 456 (Rast 1978: fig. 33, 38, 170-171) Period IIB	L	S/G	M	4.0 mm. d. hole drilled halfway through bone on the lower end of plantar face, w/ metal oxide coloring remaining (cf. Lapp 1964: 35, n. 50). 4.0 mm. d. shallow hole in middle of lateral face.
3	114	3272/N.2	I₁	same as above	R	S/G	M	—
4	115	3272/N.3	I₁	same as above	R	S/G	M	Some polishing on medial face; butchering marks on lateral face; signs of burning
5	116	3272/N.4	I₁	same as above	R	S/G	M	Signs of burning on plantar face
6	117	3272/N.5	I₁	same as above	R	S/G	?	Partial (about ½ remaining)
7	118	3272/N.6	I₁	same as above	R	S/G	?	Butchering marks on medial face

---

[1] The identifications in this table are from Foster's work and the laboratory report from Tel Aviv University. Where their identifications disagree, the table shows S/G.

[2] Foster's identification

[3] Terminology for parts of astragalus from Driesch, Angela von den, *A Guide to the Measurement of Animal Bones from Archaeological Sites*. Harvard, 1976, pp. 88-89.

No.	Foster No.	Lab/Reg. No.	Pottery Date	Locus	L/R	Sheep/goat[4]	M/F[5]	Descriptive Comments[6]
8	119	3272/N.7	I₁	same as above	L	S/G	M	Signs of burning on dorsal face; shallow 4.0 mm. d. hole in plantar face
9	?	3272/N.8	I₁	same as above	R	S/G	?	Sign of burning on dorsal end
10	?	3272/N.9	I₁	same as above	R	S/G	?	—
11	120	3272/N.10	I₁	same as above	L	S/G	M	Shows signs of burning on distal end and medial face
12	?	3272/N.11	I₁	same as above	?	S/G	?	Partial; dorsal end missing
13	121	3272/N.12	I₁	same as above	L	S/G	M	Butchering marks on distal end; some signs of burning on dorsal end
14	122	3272/N.13	I₁	same as above	R	S/G	M	Darkened on dorsal end (through handling?)
15	?	3272/N.14(?)	I₁	same as above	?	S/G	?	Fragment; part of dorsal and distal ends missing; some signs of burning
16	123	3272/N.15	I₁	same as above	R	S/G	M	Signs of burning
17	124	3272/N.16	I₁	same as above	R	S/G	M	Signs of burning on distal end
18	65	3271/N.1	± 900	SW 2-7.27.45	R	S/G	M	Signs of burning
19	66	3271/N.2	± 900	same as above	R	S/G	M	Signs of burning on distal end

[4]The identifications in this table are from Foster's work and the laboratory report from Tel Aviv University. Where their identifications disagree, the table shows S/G.

[5]Foster's identification

[6]Terminology for parts of astragalus from Driesch, Angela von den, *A Guide to the Measurement of Animal Bones from Archaeological Sites*. Harvard, 1976, pp. 88-89.

No.	Foster No.	Lab/Reg. No.	Pottery Date	Locus	L/R	Sheep/goat[7]	M/F[8]	Descriptive Comments[9]
20	67	3271/N.3	± 900	same as above	L	S/G	M	—
21	?	3271/N.4	± 900	same as above	?	S/G	?	Fragment (about ½), dorsal end missing
22	?	3271/N.5	± 900	same as above	L	S/G	?	—
23	68	3271/N.6	± 900	same as above	L	S/G	M	Some signs of burning with wear after burning
24	69	3271/N.7	± 900	same as above	R	S/G	M	—
25	70	3271/N.8	± 900	same as above	L	S/G	M	—
26	?	3271/N.9	± 900	same as above	R	S/G	?	—
27	71	3271/N.10	± 900	same as above	R	S/G	M	Signs of burning, esp. on dorsal face
28	72	3271/N.11	± 900	same as above	R	S/G	F	Signs of burning, esp. on dorsal face
29	73	3271/N.12	± 900	same as above	L	S/G	M	—
30	74	3271/N.12(?)	± 900	same as above	L	S/G	M	Part of medial face on distal end missing
31	75	3271/N.13	± 900	same as above	R	S/G	M(?)	—
32	?	3271/N.14	± 900	same as above	L	S/G	?	Some polishing on both medial and lateral faces

---

[7]The identifications in this table are from Foster's work and the laboratory report from Tel Aviv University. Where their identifications disagree, the table shows S/G.

[8]Foster's identification

[9]Terminology for parts of astragalus from Driesch, Angela von den, *A Guide to the Measurement of Animal Bones from Archaeological Sites*. Harvard, 1976, pp. **88-89**.

Appendix E—289

No.	Foster No.	Lab/Reg. No.	Pottery Date	Locus	L/R	Sheep/goat[10]	M/F[11]	Descriptive Comments[12]
33	?	3271/N.15	± 900	same as above	L	S/G	?	Some signs of burning on distal end
34	77	3271/N.16	± 900	same as above	L	S/G	M	Repaired
35	?	3271/N.17	± 900	same as above	L	S/G	?	Signs of burning on distal end
36	78	3271/N.18	± 900	same as above	R	S/G	M	Signs of burning on plantar face
37	79	3271/N.19	± 900	same as above	R	S/G	M	Signs of burning on dorsal face
38	80	3271/N.20	± 900	same as above	R	S/G	M	Some polishing on lateral face
39	81	3271/N.21	± 900	same as above	L	S/G	M	Darkening on dorsal end through handling?)
40	?	3271/N.22	± 900	same as above	R	S/G	?	—
41	83	3271/N.23	± 900	same as above	L	S/G	M	—
42	84	3271/N.24	± 900	same as above	R	S/G	F	—
43	85	3271/N.25	± 900	same as above	L	S/G	M	Shiny brown on medial face from calcification
44	?	3271/N.26	± 900	same as above	L	S/G	?	Signs of burning on dorsal end
45	86	3271/N.27	± 900	same as above	L	S/G	M	Signs of burning on distal end
46	87	3271/N.28	± 900	same as above	R	S/G	M	—

---

[10]The identifications in this table are from Foster's work and the laboratory report from Tel Aviv University. Where their identifications disagree, the table shows S/G.

[11]Foster's identification

[12]Terminology for parts of astragalus from Driesch, Angela von den, *A Guide to the Measurement of Animal Bones from Archaeological Sites*. Harvard, 1976, pp. 88-89.

No.	Foster No.	Lab/Reg. No.	Pottery Date	Locus	L/R	Sheep/goat[13]	M/F[14]	Descriptive Comments[15]
47	?	3271/N.29	± 900	same as above	L	S/G	?	Some polishing on medial face; signs of burning
48	88	3271/N.30	± 900	same as above	L	S/G	M	—
49	89	3271/N.31	± 900	same as above	L	S/G	F	Repaired
50	?	3271/N unnumbered	± 900	same as above	?	S/G	?	Signs of repair, but most of dorsal end missing; discoloration from metal oxide in hole(?)
51	?	3271/N unnumbered	± 900	same as above	?	S/G	?	Fragment of distal end
52	?	3271/N unnumbered	± 900	same as above	R	S/G	?	Fragment of dorsal end
53	128	3285	± 900	SW 2-7.27.45a	L	G	—	Totally blackened from burning and fragmentary
54	129	3286	± 900	same as above	L	S/G	M	Totally blackened from burning
55	130	3288	± 900	same as above	L	S/G	—	Totally blackened from burning; fragment of distal end only
56	131	3290	± 900	same as above	L	G	—	Missing; description from Foster
57	132	3291	± 900	same as above	R	G	M	Partially blackened from burning

---

[13]The identifications in this table are from Foster's work and the laboratory report from Tel Aviv University. Where their identifications disagree, the table shows S/G.

[14]Foster's identification

[15]Terminology for parts of astragalus from Driesch, Angela von den, *A Guide to the Measurement of Animal Bones from Archaeological Sites*. Harvard, 1976, pp. 88-89.

Appendix E—291

No.	Foster No.	Lab/Reg. No.	Pottery Date	Locus	L/R	Sheep/goat[16]	M/F[17]	Descriptive Comments[18]
58	133	3292	± 900	same as above	L	S/G	—	Totally blackened from burning; fragment of distal end only
59	134	3295	± 900	same as above	L	S/G	—	Totally blackened from burning
60	1	3299/N.1	± 900	SW 2-7.27.45	R	G	M	Partially blackened from burning
61	2	3299/N.2	± 900	same as above	R	G	M	Partially blackened from burning
62	?	3299/N.3	± 900	same as above	L	G	?	Totally blackened from burning
63	?	3299/N.6	± 900	same as above	R	G	?	—
64	3	3299/N.7	± 900	same as above	R	G	M	Totally blackened from burning
65	?	3299/N.7 (?)	± 900	same as above	R	G	?	Partially blackened from burning
66	?	3299/N.7 (?)	± 900	same as above	L	G	?	Totally blackened from burning
67	6	3299/N.10	± 900	same as above	L	G	M	Partially blackened from burning
68	17	3299/N.12	± 900	same as above	R	S/G	M	Totally blackened from burning
69	7	3299/N.13	± 900	same as above	R	G	F	4.0 mm. d. shallow hole in distal end of plantar face w/ evidence of metal oxide
70	8	3299/N.14	± 900	same as above	R	G	M	Partially blackened from burning
71	9	3299/N.15	± 900	same as above	R	G	M	Totally blackened from burning

---

[16] The identifications in this table are from Foster's work and the laboratory report from Tel Aviv University. Where their identifications disagree, the table shows S/G.

[17] Foster's identification

[18] Terminology for parts of astragalus from Driesch, Angela von den, *A Guide to the Measurement of Animal Bones from Archaeological Sites*. Harvard, 1976, pp. 88-89.

No.	Foster No.	Lab/Reg. No.	Pottery Date	Locus	L/R	Sheep/goat[19]	M/F[20]	Descriptive Comments[21]
72	10	3299/N.16	± 900	same as above	L	G	M	Partially blackened from burning
73	12	3299/N.19	± 900	same as above	R	S/G	F	Totally blackened from burning
74	13	3299/N.20	± 900	same as above	R	G	M	Totally blackened from burning
75	?	3299/N.21	± 900	same as above	R	G	?	Partially blackened from burning
76	?	3299/N.22	± 900	same as above	L	G	?	Totally blackened from burning
77	14	3299/N.23	± 900	same as above	R	G	F	Totally blackened from burning; partial
78	?	3299/N.23(?)	± 900	same as above	R	G	?	Totally blackened from burning; partial
79	22	3299/N.24	± 900	same as above	R	S/G	M	Partially blackened from burning
80	?	3299/N.25	± 900	same as above	R	G	?	Partially blackened from burning;;; 4.0 mm. d. hole drilled part way through on plantar face at distal end
81	15	3299/N.26	± 900	same as above	R	G	M	Totally blackened from burning
82	?	3299/N.28	± 900	same as above	R	G	?	Totally blackened from burning
83	?	3299/N.29	± 900	same as above	L	G	?	All of plantar face missing
84	16	3299/N.30	± 900	same as above	L	G	?	Part of medial face missing

[19]The identifications in this table are from Foster's work and the laboratory report from Tel Aviv University. Where their identifications disagree, the table shows S/G.

[20]Foster's identification

[21]Terminology for parts of astragalus from Driesch, Angela von den, *A Guide to the Measurement of Animal Bones from Archaeological Sites*. Harvard, 1976, pp. 88-89.

No.	Foster No.	Lab/Reg. No.	Pottery Date	Locus	L/R	Sheep/goat[22]	M/F[23]	Descriptive Comments[24]
85	?	3299/N.31	± 900	same as above	L	G	?	Fragment; totally blackened from burning
86	18	3299/N.33	± 900	same as above	L	G	F	Totally blackened from burning
87	?	3299/N.33	± 900	same as above	L	G	?	Totally blackened from burning; medial face missing
88	?	3299/N.35	± 900	same as above	L	G	?	Totally blackened from burning
89	19	3299/N.36	± 900	same as above	L	S/G	?	Totally blackened from burning
90	?	3299/N.37	± 900	same as above	L	G	?	Totally blackened from burning
91	?	3299/N.39	± 900	same as above	?	G	?	Totally blackened from burning; partial
92	20	3299/N.39	± 900	same as above	L	G	M	Partially blackened from burning
93	?	3299/N.40	± 900	same as above	R	G	?	Partially blackened from burning
94	24	3299/N.43	± 900	same as above	L	G	?	Partially blackened from burning
95	?	3299/N.44	± 900	same as above	L	G	?	Totally blackened from burning
96	?	3299/N.46	± 900	same as above	L	G	?	Partially blackened on plantar face from burning
97	?	3299/N.47	± 900	same as above	L	G	?	Partially blackened from burning

[22]The identifications in this table are from Foster's work and the laboratory report from Tel Aviv University. Where their identifications disagree, the table shows S/G.

[23]Foster's identification

[24]Terminology for parts of astragalus from Driesch, Angela von den, *A Guide to the Measurement of Animal Bones from Archaeological Sites*. Harvard, 1976, pp. 88-89.

No.	Foster No.	Lab/Reg. No.	Pottery Date	Locus	L/R	Sheep/goat[25]	M/F[26]	Descriptive Comments[27]
98	?	3299/N.48	± 900	same as above	L	G	?	Partially blackened from burning
99	?	3299/N.49	± 900	same as above	L	G	?	Totally blackened from burning
100	27	3299/N.50	± 900	same as above	L	S/G	M	Totally blackened from burning
101	?	3299/N.52	± 900	same as above	L	G	?	Totally blackened from burning
102	?	3299/N.53	± 900	same as above	L	G	?	Partially blackened from burning
103	26	3299/N.54	± 900	same as above	L	G	M	Totally blackened from burning
104	?	3299/N.55	± 900	same as above	L	G	?	Partially blackened from burning
105	?	3299/N.56	± 900	same as above	L	G	?	—
106	29	3299/N.57	± 900	same as above	L	G	M	Partially blackened from burning
107	30	3299/N.58	± 900	same as above	L	G	M	Totally blackened from burning; lateral face missing; 4.0 mm. d hole drilled part way through plantar face at distal end
108	?	3299/N.61	± 900	same as above	?	G	?	Fragment; partially burned
109	?	3299/N.62	± 900	same as above	?	G	?	Fragment
110	?	3299/N.63	± 900	same as above	L	G	?	Totally blackened from burning

---

[25]The identifications in this table are from Foster's work and the laboratory report from Tel Aviv University. Where their identifications disagree, the table shows S/G.

[26]Foster's identification

[27]Terminology for parts of astragalus from Driesch, Angela von den, *A Guide to the Measurement of Animal Bones from Archaeological Sites.* Harvard, 1976, pp. **88-89.**

No.	Foster No.	Lab/Reg. No.	Date	Locus	L/R	Sheep/goat	M/F	Descriptive Comments
111	?	3299/N Unnumbered or number illegible	± 900	same as above	R	G	?	Totally blackened from burning
112	?	3299/N Unnumbered or number illegible	± 900	same as above	L	G	?	Totally blackened from burning
113	?	3299/N Unnumbered or number illegible	± 900	same as above	R	G	?	Totally blackened from burning
114	?	3299/N Unnumbered or number illegible	± 900	same as above	R	G	?	—
115	?	3299/N Unnumbered or number illegible	± 900	same as above	R	G	?	Totally blackened from burning
116	?	3299/N Unnumbered or number illegible	± 900	same as above	L	G	?	Totally blackened from burning
117	?	3299/N Unnumbered or number illegible	± 900	same as above	R	G	?	Totally blackened from burning

No.	Foster No.	Lab/Reg. No.	Date	Locus	L/R	Sheep/goat	M/F	Descriptive Comments
118	?	3299/N Unnumbered or number illegible	± 900	same as above	L	G	?	Totally blackened from burning
119	?	3299/N Unnumbered or number illegible	± 900	same as above	L	G	?	Totally blackened from burning
120	?	3299/N Unnumbered or number illegible	± 900	same as above	R	G	?	Totally blackened from burning
121	?	3299/N Unnumbered or number illegible	± 900	same as above	R	G	?	Totally blackened from burning
122	?	3299/N Unnumbered or number illegible	± 900	same as above	?	G	?	Totally blackened from burning
123	?	3299/N Unnumbered or number illegible	± 900	same as above	?	G	?	Fragment; lateral or distal face only; totally blackened from burning
124	?	3299/N Unnumbered or number illegible	± 900	same as above	?	G	?	Fragment; dorsal end only; totally blackened from burning

Appendix E–297

No.	Foster No.	Lab/Reg. No.	Date	Locus	L/R	Sheep/goat	M/F	Descriptive Comments
125	?	3299/N Unnumbered or number illegible	± 900	same as above	?	G	?	Fragment of plantar face, dorsal end with 4.0 mm. d. hole drilled through; totally blackened from burning
126	?	3299/N Unnumbered or number illegible	± 900	same as above	?	G	?	Fragment; totally blakened from burning
127	?	3299/N Unnumbered or number illegible	± 900	same as above	?	G	?	Fragment; totally blakened from burning
128	?	3299/N Unnumbered or number illegible	± 900	same as above	?	G	?	Fragment; totally blackened from burning
129	?	3299/N Unnumbered or number illegible	± 900	same as above	?	G	?	Fragment; totally blackened from burning
130	?	3299/N Unnumbered or number illegible	± 900	same as above	?	G	?	Fragment, totally blackened from burning
131	345 (?)	4582/N (a)	I	SW 1-7.86.161	L	S/G	M	Partially blackened from burning
132	348 (?)	4582/N (b)	I	same as above	R	S/G	M	Partially blackened from burning

Appendix E—298

No.	Foster No.	Lab/Reg. No.	Date	Locus	L/R	Sheep/goat	M/F	Descriptive Comments
133	346 (?)	4582/N (c)	I	same as above	L	S/G	F	Light and porous
134	347 (?)	4582/N (d)	I	same as above	L	S/G	M	Partially blackened from burning
135	344 (?)	4582/N (e)	I	same as above	?	S/G	?	Fragment of distal end
136	349	4595/N	12th-10th cent.	SW 2-7.96.308	R	S/G	F	Butchering marks on lateral face, distal end
137	141	4614/N	MB IIC	SW 2-7.251.569	R	G	M	Medial and lateral faces flattened
138	?	4619/N	EB III, MB IIC	SW 2-7.269.122	R	G	?	Medial face flattened
139	289	4641/N	EB, MB IIC	SW 1-8.32.116	L	S/G	M	—
140	290	4642/N (a)	EB, MB IIC	SW 1-7.165.359	L	G	M	—
141	291	4642/N (b)	EB, MB IIC	same as above	?	S/G	M	—
142	292	4643/N	12th cent.	SW 1-7.57.93	R	S/G	M	Medial face partially flattened
143	293	4644/N	MB IIC	SW 1-7.5.229	L	S/G	M	—
144	294	4645/N	I	SW 1-7.17.138	L	G	M	Lateral and medial faces flattened
145	295	4647/N (a)	EB, MB IIC	SW 1.7.165.363	L	S/G	M	—
146	296	4647/N (b)	EB, MB IIC	same as above	L	S/G	F	—
147	296	4647/N (c)	EB, MB IIC	same as above	R	G	M	—
148	297	4647/N (d)	EB, MB IIC	same as above	R	S/G	?	—
149	299	4647/N (e)	EB, MB IIC	same as above	R	G	M	—

No.	Foster No.	Lab/Reg. No.	Date	Locus	L/R	Sheep/goat	M/F	Descriptive Comments
150	300	4648/N	EB, MB IIC	SW 1-7.165.362	L	G	M	—
151	301	4649/N	EB, MB IIC, 1500	SW 1-7.167.326	R	G	M	Medial face flattened
152	?	4654/N (a)	EB, MB IIC	SW 1-7.178.345	R	*Sus domesticus*	?	—
153	?	4654/N (b)	EB, MB IIC	same as above	L	*Sus domesticus*		4654/N (a) and 4654/N (b) appear to be a matched pair of pig astragali
154	195	4740/N	EB III, MB IIC	SW 2-8.158.301	R	G	?	Flattened on lateral and medial sides; mineralized
155	196	4741/N	MB IIC	SW 2-8.125.249	L	G	M	—
156	197	4742/N	MB IIC	SW 2-8.120.248	L	G	M	Partially mineralized
157	201	4745/N	MB IIC, LB I	SW 2-8.14.54	R	S/G	M	Butchering marks on medial face
158	202	4746/N	EB, I-, P	SW 2-8.14.56	R	S/G	M	—
159	225	4758/N (a)	10th-9th cent., P	SW 2-8.21.76	R	S/G	M	Charred from burning
160	224	4758/N (b)	10th-9th cent., P	same as above	R	G	F	—
161	227	4758/N (c)	10th-9th cent., P	same as above	L	G	F	Charred from burning
162	226	4758/N (d)	10th-9th cent., P	same as above	L	G	M	Charred from burning
163	228	4758/N (e)	10th-9th cent., P	same as above	L	G	?	Charred from buring; lateral face only

---

[28]Identified as domestic pig by Tel Aviv University lab.

No.	Foster No.	Lab/Reg. No.	Date	Locus	L/R	Sheep/goat	M/F	Descriptive Comments
164	368	5506/N (a)	EB-MB IIC	SW 2-7.280.650	R	S/G	M	—
165	369	5506/N (b)	EB-MB IIC	same as above	R	S/G	M	—
166	142	5507/N (a)	EB-MB IIC	SW 2-7.280.651	L	Sus domesticus d = 31.99 mm.	?	—
167	?	5507/N (b)	EB, MB IIC	same as above	R	G	?	—
168	381	5508/N	EB, MB, LB	SW 2-7.216.632	R	G	M	Lateral side flattened
169	370	5509/N	EB II, MB IIC	SW 2-7.274.639	R	S/G	M	—
170	357	5510/N (a)	EB I-10th-7th cent.	SW 2-8.164.329	R	G	F	—
171	358	5510/N (b)	EB I-10th-7th cent.	same as above	R	S/G	M	Totally blackened from burning
172	365	5511/N	EB III, MB IIC	SW 2-7.275.640	R	S/G	M	Partially mineralized
173	390	5512/N	EB III, MB IIC, LB I	SW 2-8.156.319	L	S/G	M	—
174	389	5513/N	EB III	SW 1-8.116.280	L	S/G	M	Partially blackened from burning; butchering marks on medial face, distal end
175	374	5514/N	EB-MB	SW 1-8.115.278	R	?	M	Flattened on medial and lateral faces
176	332 (?)	5515/N (a)	EB III, MB IIC, 10th cent.	SW 2-8	L	S/G	M	—

---

[29] Identified as a domestic pig astragalus by Tel Aviv University lab and by G. Foster.

[30] Found in the cult stand cistern

No.	Foster No.	Lab/Reg. No.	Date	Locus	L/R	Sheep/goat	M/F	Descriptive Comments
177	339 (?)	5515/N (b)	EB III, MB IIC, 10th cent.	same as above	L	S/G	M	—
178	336 (?)	5515/N (c)	EB III, MB IIC, 10th cent.	same as above	L	S/G	M	—
179	333	5515/N (d)	EB III, MB IIC, 10th cent.	same as above	L	S/G	M	Totally blackened from burning
180	338 (?)	5515/N (e)	EB III, MB IIC, 10th cent.	same as above	L	S/G	?	Butchering marks on dorsal and medial faces
181	335 (?)	5515/N (f)	EB III, MB IIC, 10th cent.	same as above	R	S/G	M	Flattened on medial face; partially mineralized
182	334 (?)	5515/N (g)	EB III, MB IIC, 10th cent.	same as above	R	S/G	M	—
183	337 (?)	5515/N (h)	EB III, MB IIC, 10th cent.	same as above	R	S/G	M	Surface eroded, showing porous structure of bone
184	338 (?)	5515/N (i)	EB III, MB IIC, 10th cent.	same as above	R	S/G	?	—
185	340	5516/N(a)	EB III, MB IIC, 10th cent.	SW 2-8.171.375	R	S/G	M	—
186	341	5516/N (b)	EB III, MB IIC, 10th cent.	same as above	R	S/G	M	—
187	367	5517/N	EB	SW 2-8.167.336	L	S/G	M	—
188	388	5518/N	MB IIC, 10th cent.	SW 2-8.163.335	L	?	M	—
189	352	5520/N (a)	10th cent.	SW 2-8.170.349	R	S/G	M	Butchering marks on dorsal face
190	?	5520/N (b)	10th cent.	same as above	L	S/G	?	Butchering marks on distal end
191	386	5521/N	10th cent.	SW 2-8.163.324	L	S/G	M	Partially mineralized; butchering marks on distal end
192	364	5522/N	10th cent.	SW 2-8.69.312	L	S/G	M	Irregular hole in dorsal face with metal oxide coloring

"Worked" Astragali from Loci Outside the Cultic Structure

Foster No.	Lab/Reg. No.	Locus	Left/Right	Sheep/goat	Male/Female	Descriptive Comments
137	697	SW 1-9.41.85 697	L	S	12.63/6.94 M	3, 4.0 mm. d. holes drilled from plantar face through to dorsal face
136	618	SW 6-7.63.36	R	—	—	Smoothed on all faces; smoothed and flattened on dorsal face
—	1230	SW 5-8	R	*Bos Taurus*	M	32 x 52 mm.; 48.1 mm. d.; significantly flattened on all faces

**Appendix E: Astragali from the Cultic Structure
Area B, SW 1-7; 1-8; 2-7; 2-8**

Appendix E: Astragali from the Cultic Structure
Area B, SW 1-7; 1-8; 2-7; 2-8

No.	Foster No.	Lab/Reg. No.	Pottery Date	Locus	L/R	Sheep/goat[1]	M/F[2]	Descriptive Comments[3]
1	140	4596/N	1500-1468	SW 2-7.140.394	L	S/G	M	Polished on lateral and medial faces
2	112	3272/N.1	I_1	SW 2-7.60.160 16 astragali from pot TT 456 (Rast 1978: fig. 33, 38, 170-171) Period IIB	L	S/G	M	4.0 mm. d. hole drilled halfway through bone on the lower end of plantar face, w/ metal oxide coloring remaining (cf. Lapp 1964: 35, n. 50). 4.0 mm. d. shallow hole in middle of lateral face.
3	114	3272/N.2	I_1	same as above	R	S/G	M	—
4	115	3272/N.3	I_1	same as above	R	S/G	M	Some polishing on medial face; butchering marks on lateral face; signs of burning
5	116	3272/N.4	I_1	same as above	R	S/G	M	Signs of burning on plantar face
6	117	3272/N.5	I_1	same as above	R	S/G	?	Partial (about ½ remaining)
7	118	3272/N.6	I_1	same as above	R	S/G	?	Butchering marks on medial face

[1] The identifications in this table are from Foster's work and the laboratory report from Tel Aviv University. Where their identifications disagree, the table shows S/G.

[2] Foster's identification

[3] Terminology for parts of astragalus from Driesch, Angela von den, *A Guide to the Measurement of Animal Bones from Archaeological Sites*. Harvard, 1976, pp. 88-89.

No.	Foster No.	Lab/Reg. No.	Pottery Date	Locus	L/R	Sheep/goat[4]	M/F[5]	Descriptive Comments[6]
8	119	3272/N.7	I₁	same as above	L	S/G	M	Signs of burning on dorsal face; shallow 4.0 mm. d. hole in plantar face
9	?	3272/N.8	I₁	same as above	R	S/G	?	Sign of burning on dorsal end
10	?	3272/N.9	I₁	same as above	R	S/G	?	—
11	120	3272/N.10	I₁	same as above	L	S/G	M	Shows signs of burning on distal end and medial face
12	?	3272/N.11	I₁	same as above	?	S/G	?	Partial; dorsal end missing
13	121	3272/N.12	I₁	same as above	L	S/G	M	Butchering marks on distal end; some signs of burning on dorsal end
14	122	3272/N.13	I₁	same as above	R	S/G	M	Darkened on dorsal end (through handling?)
15	?	3272/N.14(?)	I₁	same as above	?	S/G	?	Fragment; part of dorsal and distal ends missing; some signs of burning
16	123	3272/N.15	I₁	same as above	R	S/G	M	Signs of burning
17	124	3272/N.16	I₁	same as above	R	S/G	M	Signs of burning on distal end
18	65	3271/N.1	± 900	SW 2-7.27.45	R	S/G	M	Signs of burning
19	66	3271/N.2	± 900	same as above	R	S/G	M	Signs of burning on distal end

[4]The identifications in this table are from Foster's work and the laboratory report from Tel Aviv University. Where their identifications disagree, the table shows S/G.

[5]Foster's identification

[6]Terminology for parts of astragalus from Driesch, Angela von den, *A Guide to the Measurement of Animal Bones from Archaeological Sites*. Harvard, 1976, pp. 88-89.

No.	Foster No.	Lab/Reg. No.	Pottery Date	Locus	L/R	Sheep/goat[7]	M/F[8]	Descriptive Comments[9]
20	67	3271/N.3	± 900	same as above	L	S/G	M	—
21	?	3271/N.4	± 900	same as above	?	S/G	?	Fragment (about ½), dorsal end missing
22	?	3271/N.5	± 900	same as above	L	S/G	?	—
23	68	3271/N.6	± 900	same as above	L	S/G	M	Some signs of burning with wear after burning
24	69	3271/N.7	± 900	same as above	R	S/G	M	—
25	70	3271/N.8	± 900	same as above	L	S/G	M	—
26	?	3271/N.9	± 900	same as above	R	S/G	?	—
27	71	3271/N.10	± 900	same as above	R	S/G	M	Signs of burning, esp. on dorsal face
28	72	3271/N.11	± 900	same as above	R	S/G	F	Signs of burning, esp. on dorsal face
29	73	3271/N.12	± 900	same as above	L	S/G	M	—
30	74	3271/N.12(?)	± 900	same as above	L	S/G	M	Part of medial face on distal end missing
31	75	3271/N.13	± 900	same as above	R	S/G	M(?)	—
32	?	3271/N.14	± 900	same as above	L	S/G	?	Some polishing on both medial and lateral faces

---

[7]The identifications in this table are from Foster's work and the laboratory report from Tel Aviv University. Where their identifications disagree, the table shows S/G.

[8]Foster's identification

[9]Terminology for parts of astragalus from Driesch, Angela von den, *A Guide to the Measurement of Animal Bones from Archaeological Sites*. Harvard, 1976, pp. 88-89.

No.	Foster No.	Lab/Reg. No.	Pottery Date	Locus	L/R	Sheep/goat[10]	M/F[11]	Descriptive Comments[12]
33	?	3271/N.15	± 900	same as above	L	S/G	?	Some signs of burning on distal end
34	77	3271/N.16	± 900	same as above	L	S/G	M	Repaired
35	?	3271/N.17	± 900	same as above	L	S/G	?	Signs of burning on distal end
36	78	3271/N.18	± 900	same as above	R	S/G	M	Signs of burning on plantar face
37	79	3271/N.19	± 900	same as above	R	S/G	M	Signs of burning on dorsal face
38	80	3271/N.20	± 900	same as above	R	S/G	M	Some polishing on lateral face
39	81	3271/N.21	± 900	same as above	L	S/G	M	Darkening on dorsal end through handling?)
40	?	3271/N.22	± 900	same as above	R	S/G	?	—
41	83	3271/N.23	± 900	same as above	L	S/G	M	—
42	84	3271/N.24	± 900	same as above	R	S/G	F	—
43	85	3271/N.25	± 900	same as above	L	S/G	M	Shiny brown on medial face from calcification
44	?	3271/N.26	± 900	same as above	L	S/G	?	Signs of burning on dorsal end
45	86	3271/N.27	± 900	same as above	L	S/G	M	Signs of burning on distal end
46	87	3271/N.28	± 900	same as above	R	S/G	M	—

[10]The identifications in this table are from Foster's work and the laboratory report from Tel Aviv University. Where their identifications disagree, the table shows S/G.

[11]Foster's identification

[12]Terminology for parts of astragalus from Driesch, Angela von den, *A Guide to the Measurement of Animal Bones from Archaeological Sites*. Harvard, 1976, pp. 88-89.

No.	Foster No.	Lab/Reg. No.	Pottery Date	Locus	L/R	Sheep/goat[13]	M/F[14]	Descriptive Comments[15]
47	?	3271/N.29	± 900	same as above	L	S/G	?	Some polishing on medial face; signs of burning
48	88	3271/N.30	± 900	same as above	L	S/G	M	—
49	89	3271/N.31	± 900	same as above	L	S/G	F	Repaired
50	?	3271/N unnumbered	± 900	same as above	?	S/G	?	Signs of repair, but most of dorsal end missing; discoloration from metal oxide in hole(?)
51	?	3271/N unnumbered	± 900	same as above	?	S/G	?	Fragment of distal end
52	?	3271/N unnumbered	± 900	same as above	R	S/G	?	Fragment of dorsal end
53	128	3285	± 900	SW 2-7.27.45a	L	G	—	Totally blackened from burning and fragmentary
54	129	3286	± 900	same as above	L	S/G	M	Totally blackened from burning
55	130	3288	± 900	same as above	L	S/G	—	Totally blackened from burning; fragment of distal end only
56	131	3290	± 900	same as above	L	G	—	Missing; description from Foster
57	132	3291	± 900	same as above	R	G	M	Partially blackened from burning

---

[13]The identifications in this table are from Foster's work and the laboratory report from Tel Aviv University. Where their identifications disagree, the table shows S/G.

[14]Foster's identification

[15]Terminology for parts of astragalus from Driesch, Angela von den, *A Guide to the Measurement of Animal Bones from Archaeological Sites*. Harvard, 1976, pp. 88-89.

Appendix E—309

No.	Foster No.	Lab/Reg. No.	Pottery Date	Locus	L/R	Sheep/goat[16]	M/F[17]	Descriptive Comments[18]
58	133	3292	± 900	same as above	L	S/G	—	Totally blackened from burning; fragment of distal end only
59	134	3295	± 900	same as above	L	S/G	—	Totally blackened from burning
60	1	3299/N.1	± 900	SW 2-7.27.45	R	G	M	Partially blackened from burning
61	2	3299/N.2	± 900	same as above	R	G	M	Partially blackened from burning
62	?	3299/N.3	± 900	same as above	L	G	?	Totally blackened from burning
63	?	3299/N.6	± 900	same as above	R	G	?	—
64	3	3299/N.7	± 900	same as above	R	G	M	Totally blackened from burning
65	?	3299/N.7 (?)	± 900	same as above	R	G	?	Partially blackened from burning
66	?	3299/N.7 (?)	± 900	same as above	L	G	?	Totally blackened from burning
67	6	3299/N.10	± 900	same as above	L	G	M	Partially blackened from burning
68	17	3299/N.12	± 900	same as above	R	S/G	M	Totally blackened from burning
69	7	3299/N.13	± 900	same as above	R	G	F	4.0 mm. d. shallow hole in distal end of plantar face w/ evidence of metal oxide
70	8	3299/N.14	± 900	same as above	R	G	M	Partially blackened from burning
71	9	3299/N.15	± 900	same as above	R	G	M	Totally blackened from burning

[16]The identifications in this table are from Foster's work and the laboratory report from Tel Aviv University. Where their identifications disagree, the table shows S/G.

[17]Foster's identification

[18]Terminology for parts of astragalus from Driesch, Angela von den, *A Guide to the Measurement of Animal Bones from Archaeological Sites.* Harvard, 1976, pp. 88-89.

No.	Foster No.	Lab/Reg. No.	Pottery Date	Locus	L/R	Sheep/goat[19]	M/F[20]	Descriptive Comments[21]
72	10	3299/N.16	± 900	same as above	L	G	M	Partially blackened from burning
73	12	3299/N.19	± 900	same as above	R	S/G	F	Totally blackened from burning
74	13	3299/N.20	± 900	same as above	R	G	M	Totally blackened from burning
75	?	3299/N.21	± 900	same as above	R	G	?	Partially blackened from burning
76	?	3299/N.22	± 900	same as above	L	G	?	Totally blackened from burning
77	14	3299/N.23	± 900	same as above	R	G	F	Totally blackened from burning; partial
78	?	3299/N.23(?)	± 900	same as above	R	G	?	Totally blackened from burning; partial
79	22	3299/N.24	± 900	same as above	R	S/G	M	Partially blackened from burning
80	?	3299/N.25	± 900	same as above	R	G	?	Partially blackened from burning;; 4.0 mm. d. hole drilled part way through on plantar face at distal end
81	15	3299/N.26	± 900	same as above	R	G	M	Totally blackened from burning
82	?	3299/N.28	± 900	same as above	R	G	?	Totally blackened from burning
83	?	3299/N.29	± 900	same as above	L	G	?	All of plantar face missing
84	16	3299/N.30	± 900	same as above	L	G	?	Part of medial face missing

---

[19]The identifications in this table are from Foster's work and the laboratory report from Tel Aviv University. Where their identifications disagree, the table shows S/G.

[20]Foster's identification

[21]Terminology for parts of astragalus from Driesch, Angela von den, *A Guide to the Measurement of Animal Bones from Archaeological Sites.* Harvard, 1976, pp. 88-89.

Appendix E—311

No.	Foster No.	Lab/Reg. No.	Pottery Date	Locus	L/R	Sheep/goat[22]	M/F[23]	Descriptive Comments[24]
85	?	3299/N.31	± 900	same as above	L	G	?	Fragment; totally blackened from burning
86	18	3299/N.33	± 900	same as above	L	G	F	Totally blackened from burning
87	?	3299/N.33	± 900	same as above	L	G	?	Totally blackened from burning; medial face missing
88	?	3299/N.35	± 900	same as above	L	G	?	Totally blackened from burning
89	19	3299/N.36	± 900	same as above	L	S/G	?	Totally blackened from burning
90	?	3299/N.37	± 900	same as above	L	G	?	Totally blackened from burning
91	?	3299/N.39	± 900	same as above	?	G	?	Totally blackened from burning; partial
92	20	3299/N.39	± 900	same as above	L	G	M	Partially blackened from burning
93	?	3299/N.40	± 900	same as above	R	G	?	Partially blackened from burning
94	24	3299/N.43	± 900	same as above	L	G	?	Partially blackened from burning
95	?	3299/N.44	± 900	same as above	L	G	?	Totally blackened from burning
96	?	3299/N.46	± 900	same as above	L	G	?	Partially blackened on plantar face from burning
97	?	3299/N.47	± 900	same as above	L	G	?	Partially blackened from burning

[22]The identifications in this table are from Foster's work and the laboratory report from Tel Aviv University. Where their identifications disagree, the table shows S/G.

[23]Foster's identification

[24]Terminology for parts of astragalus from Driesch, Angela von den, *A Guide to the Measurement of Animal Bones from Archaeological Sites*. Harvard, 1976, pp. 88-89.

No.	Foster No.	Lab/Reg. No.	Pottery Date	Locus	L/R	Sheep/goat[25]	M/F[26]	Descriptive Comments[27]
98	?	3299/N.48	± 900	same as above	L	G	?	Partially blackened from burning
99	?	3299/N.49	± 900	same as above	L	G	?	Totally blackened from burning
100	27	3299/N.50	± 900	same as above	L	S/G	M	Totally blackened from burning
101	?	3299/N.52	± 900	same as above	L	G	?	Totally blackened from burning
102	?	3299/N.53	± 900	same as above	L	G	?	Partially blackened from burning
103	26	3299/N.54	± 900	same as above	L	G	M	Totally blackened from burning
104	?	3299/N.55	± 900	same as above	L	G	?	Partially blackened from burning
105	?	3299/N.56	± 900	same as above	L	G	?	—
106	29	3299/N.57	± 900	same as above	L	G	M	Partially blackened from burning
107	30	3299/N.58	± 900	same as above	L	G	M	Totally blackened from burning; lateral face missing; 4.0 mm. d hole drilled part way through plantar face at distal end
108	?	3299/N.61	± 900	same as above	?	G	?	Fragment; partially burned
109	?	3299/N.62	± 900	same as above	?	G	?	Fragment
110	?	3299/N.63	± 900	same as above	L	G	?	Totally blackened from burning

---

[25]The identifications in this table are from Foster's work and the laboratory report from Tel Aviv University. Where their identifications disagree, the table shows S/G.

[26]Foster's identification

[27]Terminology for parts of astragalus from Driesch, Angela von den, *A Guide to the Measurement of Animal Bones from Archaeological Sites*. Harvard, 1976, pp. 88-89.

No.	Foster No.	Lab/Reg. No.	Date	Locus	L/R	Sheep/goat	M/F	Descriptive Comments
111	?	3299/N Unnumbered or number illegible	± 900	same as above	R	G	?	Totally blackened from burning
112	?	3299/N Unnumbered or number illegible	± 900	same as above	L	G	?	Totally blackened from burning
113	?	3299/N Unnumbered or number illegible	± 900	same as above	R	G	?	Totally blackened from burning
114	?	3299/N Unnumbered or number illegible	± 900	same as above	R	G	?	—
115	?	3299/N Unnumbered or number illegible	± 900	same as above	R	G	?	Totally blackened from burning
116	?	3299/N Unnumbered or number illegible	± 900	same as above	L	G	?	Totally blackened from burning
117	?	3299/N Unnumbered or number illegible	± 900	same as above	R	G	?	Totally blackened from burning

Appendix E—314

No.	Foster No.	Lab/Reg. No.	Date	Locus	L/R	Sheep/goat	M/F	Descriptive Comments
118	?	3299/N Unnumbered or number illegible	± 900	same as above	L	G	?	Totally blackened from burning
119	?	3299/N Unnumbered or number illegible	± 900	same as above	L	G	?	Totally blackened from burning
120	?	3299/N Unnumbered or number illegible	± 900	same as above	R	G	?	Totally blackened from burning
121	?	3299/N Unnumbered or number illegible	± 900	same as above	R	G	?	Totally blackened from burning
122	?	3299/N Unnumbered or number illegible	± 900	same as above	?	G	?	Totally blackened from burning
123	?	3299/N Unnumbered or number illegible	± 900	same as above	?	G	?	Fragment; lateral or distal face only; totally blackened from burning
124	?	3299/N Unnumbered or number illegible	± 900	same as above	?	G	?	Fragment; dorsal end only; totally blackened from burning

Appendix E—315

No.	Foster No.	Lab/Reg. No.	Date	Locus	L/R	Sheep/goat	M/F	Descriptive Comments
125	?	3299/N Unnumbered or number illegible	± 900	same as above	?	G	?	Fragment of plantar face, dorsal end with 4.0 mm. d. hole drilled through; totally blackened from burning
126	?	3299/N Unnumbered or number illegible	± 900	same as above	?	G	?	Fragment; totally blackened from burning
127	?	3299/N Unnumbered or number illegible	± 900	same as above	?	G	?	Fragment; totally blakened from burning
128	?	3299/N Unnumbered or number illegible	± 900	same as above	?	G	?	Fragment; totally blackened from burning
129	?	3299/N Unnumbered or number illegible	± 900	same as above	?	G	?	Fragment; totally blackened from burning
130	?	3299/N Unnumbered or number illegible	± 900	same as above	?	G	?	Fragment, totally blackened from burning
131	345 (?)	4582/N (a)	I_1	SW 1-7.86.161	L	S/G	M	Partially blackened from burning
132	348 (?)	4582/N (b)	I_1	same as above	R	S/G	M	Partially blackened from burning

Appendix E—316

No.	Foster No.	Lab/Reg. No.	Date	Locus	L/R	Sheep/goat	M/F	Descriptive Comments
133	346 (?)	4582/N (c)	I₁	same as above	L	S/G	F	Light and porous
134	347 (?)	4582/N (d)	I₁	same as above	L	S/G	M	Partially blackened from burning
135	344 (?)	4582/N (e)	I₁	same as above	?	S/G	?	Fragment of distal end
136	349	4595/N	12th-10th cent.	SW 2-7.96.308	R	S/G	F	Butchering marks on lateral face, distal end
137	141	4614/N	MB IIC	SW 2-7.251.569	R	G	M	Medial and lateral faces flattened
138	?	4619/N	EB III, MB IIC	SW 2-7.269.122	R	G	?	Medial face flattened
139	289	4641/N	EB, MB IIC	SW 1-8.32.116	L	S/G	M	—
140	290	4642/N (a)	EB, MB IIC	SW 1-7.165.359	L	G	M	—
141	291	4642/N (b)	EB, MB IIC	same as above	?	S/G	M	—
142	292	4643/N	12th cent.	SW 1-7.57.93	R	S/G	M	Medial face partially flattened
143	293	4644/N	MB IIC	SW 1-7.5.229	L	S/G	M	—
144	294	4645/N	I₁	SW 1-7.17.138	L	G	M	Lateral and medial faces flattened
145	295	4647/N (a)	EB, MB IIC	SW 1.7.165.363	L	S/G	M	—
146	296	4647/N (b)	EB, MB IIC	same as above	L	S/G	F	—
147	296	4647/N (c)	EB, MB IIC	same as above	R	G	M	—
148	297	4647/N (d)	EB, MB IIC	same as above	R	S/G	?	—
149	299	4647/N (e)	EB, MB IIC	same as above	R	G	M	—

Appendix E—317

No.	Foster No.	Lab/Reg. No.	Date	Locus	L/R	Sheep/goat	M/F	Descriptive Comments
150	300	4648/N	EB, MB IIC	SW 1-7.165.362	L	G	M	—
151	301	4649/N	EB, MB IIC, 1500	SW 1-7.167.326	R	G	M	Medial face flattened
152	?	4654/N (a)	EB, MB IIC	SW 1-7.178.345	R	*Sus domesticus*[28]	?	—
153	?	4654/N (b)	EB, MB IIC	same as above	L	*Sus domesticus*		4654/N (a) and 4654/N (b) appear to be a matched pair of pig astragali
154	195	4740/N	EB III, MB IIC	SW 2-8.158.301	R	G	?	Flattened on lateral and medial sides; mineralized
155	196	4741/N	MB IIC	SW 2-8.125.249	L	G	M	—
156	197	4742/N	MB IIC	SW 2-8.120.248	L	G	M	Partially mineralized
157	201	4745/N	MB IIC, LB I	SW 2-8.14.54	R	S/G	M	Butchering marks on medial face
158	202	4746/N	EB, I₁₋₂, P	SW 2-8.14.56	R	S/G	M	—
159	225	4758/N (a)	10th-9th cent., P	SW 2-8.21.76	R	S/G	M	Charred from burning
160	224	4758/N (b)	10th-9th cent., P	same as above	R	G	F	—
161	227	4758/N (c)	10th-9th cent., P	same as above	L	G	F	Charred from burning
162	226	4758/N (d)	10th-9th cent., P	same as above	L	G	M	Charred from burning
163	228	4758/N (e)	10th-9th cent., P	same as above	L	G	?	Charred from buring; lateral face only

---

[28] Identified as domestic pig by Tel Aviv University lab.

No.	Foster No.	Lab/Reg. No.	Date	Locus	L/R	Sheep/goat	M/F	Descriptive Comments
164	368	5506/N (a)	EB-MB IIC	SW 2-7.280.650	R	S/G	M	—
165	369	5506/N (b)	EB-MB IIC	same as above	R	S/G	M	—
166	142	5507/N (a)	EB-MB IIC	SW 2-7.280.651	L	Sus domesticus d = 31.99 mm.[29]	?	—
167	?	5507/N (b)	EB, MB IIC	same as above	R	G	?	—
168	381	5508/N	EB, MB, LB	SW 2-7.216.632	R	G	M	Lateral side flattened
169	370	5509/N	EB II, MB IIC	SW 2-7.274.639	R	S/G	M	—
170	357	5510/N (a)	EB I-10th-7th cent.	SW 2-8.164.329	R	G	F	—
171	358	5510/N (b)	EB I-10th-7th cent.	same as above	R	S/G	M	Totally blackened from burning
172	365	5511/N	EB III, MB IIC	SW 2-7.275.640	R	S/G	M	Partially mineralized
173	390	5512/N	EB III, MB IIC, LB I	SW 2-8.156.319	L	S/G	M	—
174	389	5513/N	EB III	SW 1-8.116.280	L	S/G	M	Partially blackened from burning; butchering marks on medial face, distal end
175	374	5514/N	EB-MB	SW 1-8.115.278	R	?	M	Flattened on medial and lateral faces
176	332 (?)	5515/N (a)	EB III, MB IIC, 10th cent.	SW 2-8.[30]	L	S/G	M	—

[29]Identified as a domestic pig astragalus by Tel Aviv University lab and by G. Foster.

[30]Found in the cult stand cistern

Appendix E—319

No.	Foster No.	Lab/Reg. No.	Date	Locus	L/R	Sheep/goat	M/F	Descriptive Comments
177	339 (?)	5515/N (b)	EB III, MB IIC, 10th cent.	same as above	L	S/G	M	—
178	336 (?)	5515/N (c)	EB III, MB IIC, 10th cent.	same as above	L	S/G	M	—
179	333	5515/N (d)	EB III, MB IIC, 10th cent.	same as above	L	S/G	M	Totally blackened from burning
180	338 (?)	5515/N (e)	EB III, MB IIC, 10th cent.	same as above	L	S/G	?	Butchering marks on dorsal and medial faces
181	335 (?)	5515/N (f)	EB III, MB IIC, 10th cent.	same as above	R	S/G	M	Flattened on medial face; partially mineralized
182	334 (?)	5515/N (g)	EB III, MB IIC, 10th cent.	same as above	R	S/G	M	—
183	337 (?)	5515/N (h)	EB III, MB IIC, 10th cent.	same as above	R	S/G	M	Surface eroded, showing porous structure of bone
184	338 (?)	5515/N (i)	EB III, MB IIC, 10th cent.	same as above	R	S/G	?	
185	340	5516/N(a)	EB III, MB IIC, 10th cent.	SW 2-8.171.375	R	S/G	M	—
186	341	5516/N (b)	EB III, MB IIC, 10th cent.	same as above	R	S/G	M	—
187	367	5517/N	EB	SW 2-8.167.336	L	S/G	M	—
188	388	5518/N	MB IIC, 10th cent.	SW 2-8.163.335	L	?	M	—
189	352	5520/N (a)	10th cent.	SW 2-8.170.349	R	S/G	M	Butchering marks on dorsal face
190	?	5520/N (b)	10th cent.	same as above	L	S/G	?	Butchering marks on distal end
191	386	5521/N	10th cent.	SW 2-8.163.324	L	S/G	M	Partially mineralized; butchering marks on distal end
192	364	5522/N	10th cent.	SW 2-8.69.312	L	S/G	M	Irregular hole in dorsal face with metal oxide coloring

Appendix E—320

"Worked" Astragali from Loci Outside the Cultic Structure

Foster No.	Lab/Reg. No.	Locus	Left/Right	Sheep/goat	Male/Female	Descriptive Comments
137	697	SW 1-9.41.85 697	L	S	12.63/6.94 M	3, 4.0 mm. d. holes drilled from plantar face through to dorsal face
136	618	SW 6-7.63.36	R	—	—	Smoothed on all faces; smoothed and flattened on dorsal face
—	1230	SW 5-8	R	Bos Taurus	M	32 x 52 mm.; 48.1 mm. d.; significantly flattened on all faces

Appendix F: Overall Taanach Astragali Data

Appendix F: Overall Taanach Astragali Data[1]

Acqui-sition No.	Laboratory Number	Side L/R	Sheep/ Goat Ratio[2]	Male/ Female Ratio[3]	Circumfer-ence in mm.	Longitudinal Diameter in mm.	Burnt/ Unburnt	Cut/Polished Uncut/Unpolished	Remarks
1	3299/N 1	R	14.65/14.14 G	11.85/6.58 M	6.4	24.44	B	U	Intact
2	2	R	14.32/14.12 G	11.65/6.86 M	6.2	24.03	B	U	Intact
3	7	R	15.44/15.88 G	13.28/7.73 M	6.5	24.66	B	U	Intact
4	8	R	—	12.12/5.26 F	5.7	21.92	B	U	Intact
5	9	R	15.12/13.95 G	11.38/5.95 M	6.4	23.99	B	U	Intact
6	10	L	17.12/15.98 G	12.59/7.19 M	6.5	24.78	B	U	Intact
7	12	R	16.23/13.85 S	12.56/8.61 M	6.8	26.60	B	U	Intact
8	13	R	13.95/15.34 G	11.37/5.88 F	6.2	24.94	B	U	Intact
9	14	R	14.23/13.80 G	11.88/6.33 M	6.4	23.92	B	U	Intact
10	15	R	15.31/14.45 G	11.36/7.85 M	6.0	24.04	B	U	Intact
11	16	L	16.20/13.89 G	11.33/7.54 M	6.6	25.47	B	U	Intact
12	17	R	15.24/13.57 S	12.23/8.14 M	6.5	25.49	B	U	Intact
13	19	R	15.40/14.54 G	11.49/5.71 F	6.0	21.90	B	U	Intact
14	20	R	13.74/14.74 G	11.07/6.91 M	6.0	23.25	B	U	Intact
15	23	R	—	10.42/4.28 F	6.1	23.01	B	U	Intact

---

[1] Based on the measurements and analysis of Giraud V. Foster, M. D., Ph.D. and Muhammad Al-Zawahra. Palestinian Institute of Archaeology, Birzeit University.

[2] The numerator is Foster's measurement of the depth lateral of the astragalus; the denominator is his measurement of the depth medial. S = sheep (*Ovis Aries Linné*); G = goat (*Capra Hircus Linné*). If the ratio of the numerator to the denominator is 1.1 or greater, Foster calculates that the bone is from a sheep. If it is 110 or less, he evaluates it as coming from a goat.

[3] An M or an F indicates identification as male or female.

Acquisition No.	Laboratory Number	Side L/R	Sheep/Goat Ratio	Male/Female Ratio	Circumference in mm.	Longitudinal Diameter in mm.	Burnt/Unburnt	Cut/Polished Uncut/Unpolished	Remarks
16	24	R	15.87/14.17 S	11.42/8.04 M	6.1	24.00	B	U	Intact
17	26	R	13.74/12.71 G	113.4/7.65 M	6.0	23.13	B	U	Intact
18	30	L	11.30/12.09 G	—	5.4	21.61	W	U	Intact
19	33	L	15.15/13.70 S	10.85/5.89 F	6.2	23.72	B	U	Intact
20	36	L	—	—	6.0	22.83	B	U	Intact
21	39	L	13.08/12.57 G	10.81/6.24 M	5.9	23.46	B	U	Intact
22	41	L	13.64/12.31 S	10.50/6.12 M	5.8	22.38	B	U	Intact
23	43	L	15.65/15.61 G	—	6.5	25.61	B	U	Intact
24	45	L	15.81/15.18 G	11.67/6.57 M	6.5	25.47	B	U	Intact
25	47	L	—	13.04/7.04 M	6.4	24.80	B	U	Intact
26	50	L	14.71/14.50 G	12.14/7.94 M	6.5	25.23	B	U	Intact
27	51	R	16.09/12.92 S	12.64/5.46 F	6.3	23.52	B	U	Intact
28	54	L	14.36/14.10 G	10.99/6.90 M	6.3	24.00	B	U	Intact
29	57	L	12.95/13.64 G	—	6.2	23.13	W	U	Intact
30	58	L	15.39/14.75 G	11.73/6.59 M	6.6	25.51	B	U	Intact
31	[4]	L	13.30/11.54 S	10.85/7.09 M	5.9	23.08	B	U	Intact
32		L	14.46/13.20 G	10.83/6.65 M	6.0	23.08	B	U	Intact
33		L	13.70/13.47 G	11.05/7.59 M	5.8	22.67	B	U	Intact
34		L	—	—	6.0	22.69	B	U	Intact
35		R	—	—	6.2	23.77	U	U	Intact
36		L	12.28/12.27 G	11.01/7.29 M	5.8	22.77	B	U	Intact
37		L	17.71/17.34 G	13.02/8.75 M	7.1	27.24	B	U	Intact

[4] The following astragali were unnumbered or the registration number could not be read.

Acqui-sition No.	Laboratory Number	Side L/R	Sheep/Goat Ratio	Male/Female Ratio	Circumference in mm.	Longitudinal Diameter in mm.	Burnt/Unburnt	Cut/Polished Uncut/Unpolished	Remarks
38		L	—	11.73/7.29 M	6.6	27.26	B	U	Intact
39		L	—	10.86/5.18 F	6.1	23.40	B	U	Intact
40		L	14.77/13.01 S	11.38/7.78 M	6.1	23.53	B	U	Intact
41		L	14.86/14.43 G	12.24/7.03 M	6.5	25.21	B	U	Intact
42		R	15.72/15.22 G	11.68/5.90 F	6.4	24.56	B	U	Intact
43		R	16.01/15.11 G	11.63/7.53 M	6.7	25.64	B	U	Intact
44		L	15.30/14.72 G	11.69/5.34 F	6.5	25.14	B	U	Intact
45		L	14.73/13.38 S	11.60/7.57 M	6.0	23.21	B	U	Intact
46		R	13.89/13.38 G	11.37/6.54 M	5.8	23.00	B	U	Intact
47		R	—	10.72/6.86 M	5.8	22.64	B	U	Intact
48		R	—	11.18/6.57 M	6.3	24.20	B	U	Intact
49		L	14.12/13.32 G	11.42/7.38 M	6.1	23.39	B	U	Intact
50		R	17.12/14.09 S	12.57/7.71 M	6.4	25.23	B	U	Intact
51		R	16.85/14.06 S	11.92/6.22 F	6.5	24.56	B	U	Intact
52		R	15.71/14.07 S	10.85/7.32 M	6.0	22.99	B	U	Intact
53		R	G	8.93/5.11 M	5.6	21.91	B	U	Intact
54		L	13.70/13.63 G	9.96/6.21 M	5.8	23.11	B	U	Intact
55		L	—	11.89/7.52 M	~6.4	25.48	B	U	Fragment
56		R	15.24/14.19 G	—	~6.1	23.48	B	U	Fragment
57		R	—	—	~6.3	24.28	B	U	Fragment
58		L	—	—	~6.5	25.86	B	U	Fragment
59		L	—	—	~5.8	22.72	B	U	Fragment
60		L	—	—	—	—	B	U	Fragment
61		L	—	—	~5.7	~22.14	W	U	Fragment

Acqui-sition-No.	Laboratory Number	Side L/R	Sheep/Goat Ratio	Male/Female Ratio	Circumference in mm.	Longitudinal Diameter in mm.	Burnt/Unburnt	Cut/Polished Uncut/Unpolished	Remarks
62		L	—	—	~5.8	~22.89	U	U	Fragment
63		R	—	—	—	—	B	U	Fragment
64		L	—	—	6.6	26.10	B	U	Fragment
65	"Light colored" 3271/N 1	R	G	10.06/6.57 M	6.1	23.58	U	U	Intact
66	2	R	12.65/12.96 G	9.87/6.19 M	5.4	21.01	U	U	Intact
67	3	L	13.12/12.12 G	11.17/6.23 M	5.8	22.80	U	U	Intact
68	6	L	G	9.97/6.20 M	5.8	22.79	U	U	Intact
69	7	R	G	11.12/7.26	6.1	22.54	U	U	Intact
70	8	L	14.01/14.42 G	11.94/8.55 M	6.3	24.21	U	U	Post mortem mark on anterior surface
71	10	R	G	10.57/7.10 M	6.5	24.42	U	U	Post mortem mark on anterior surface
72	11	R	14.23/14.20 G	13.59/6.44 F	6.7	25.57	B	U	Post mortem mark on anterior surface
73	12	L	—	11.45/7.65 M	6.0	25.001	U	U	Post mortem mark on anterior surface
74	12[5]	L	—	10.49/6.45 M	5.9	23.42	U	U	Mended double ?
75	13	R	G	11.18/5.81 M	6.1	23.81	U	U	Mended double ?
76	13	R	15.17/14.43 G	13.29/7.46 M	5.8	22.47	U	U	Mended double ?
77	16	L	13.14/13.11 G	12.60/7.26 M	6.4	25.07	U	U	Mended double ?
78	18	R	15.30/14.93 G	12.00/7.33 M	7.0	25.97	U	U	Mended double ?

[5] Here, and in several instances below, the same number was assigned to more than one astragali by the excavators.

Appendix F—326

Acqui-sition No.	Laboratory Number	Side L/R	Sheep/Goat Ratio	Male/Female Ratio	Circumference in mm.	Longitudinal Diameter in mm.	Burnt/Unburnt	Cut/Polished Uncut/Unpolished	Remarks
79	19	R	15.29/13/36 S	11.92/6.58 M	6.2	24.10	U	U	Mended double ?
80	20	R	14.72/14.23 G	11.27/6.04 M	6.2	23.79	U	?	Side part polished
81	21	L	G	12.46/8.36 M	6.7	25.70	U	U	Side part polished
82	21	L	14.14/13.26 G	11.33/7.32 M Acquistion	6.2	24.64	U	U	
83	23	R	14.80/13.79G	10.36/7.17 M	6.5	25.15	U	U	Intact
84	24	R	G	12.26/6.22 F	6.6	25.26	U	U	Intact
85	25	L	G	11.60/8.49 M	6.8	26.44	U	U	Intact
86	27	L	G	12.58/8.55 M	7.0	26.89	U	U	Intact
87	28	R	G	11.46/6.78 M	6.7	25.56	U	U	Intact
88	30	L	16.09/15.91 G	12.70/6.88 M	7.0	27.08	U	U	Intact
89	31	L	13.83/13.58 G	10.45/5.07 F	6.2	22.62	U	U	Intact
90	32	L	G	11.36/6.19	6.3	24.51	U	U	Intact
91	6	L	17.87/15.88 S	12.85/7.77 M	7.0	26.17	U	U	Intact
92		R	16.02/14.61 G	12.70/6.25 F	6.4	24.93	U	U	Intact
93		R	13.22/12.73 G	11.18/6.66 M	6.1	24.10	U	U	Intact
94		R	G	—	5.7	22.66	U	U	Intact
95		R	G	12.31/7.69 M	6.2	24.00	U	U	Intact
96		R	11.16/15.30 G	12.70/5.87 F	6.7	25.47	U	U	Intact
97		L	—	—	~6.6	25.06	U	U	Fragment
98		R	G	—	~6.9	25.93	U	U	Fragment
99		L	—	—	~6.9	26.03	U	U	Fragment

[6]The following astragali are unumbered or the number could not be read.

Acqui-sition No.	Laboratory Number	Side L/R	Sheep/Goat Ratio	Male/Female Ratio	Circumference in mm.	Longitudinal Diameter in mm.	Burnt/Unburnt	Cut/Polished Uncut/Unpolished	Remarks
100		L	—	—	—	—	U	U	Fragment
101		R	—	—	~6.6	~25.22	U	U	Fragment
102		R	—	—	~6.2	~23.95	U	U	Fragment
103		L	—	—	—	—	U	U	Fragment
104		R	—	—	—	—	U	U	Fragment
105		R	—	—	—	—	U	U	Fragment
106		R	—	—	—	—	U	U	Fragment
107		L	—	—	—	—	U	U	Fragment
108		L	—	—	—	—	U	U	Fragment
109		L	—	—	—	—	U	U	Fragment
110		L	—	—	—	—	B	U	Fragment
111	?	L	—	—	—	—	U	U	Fragment[7]
112	3272/N (Pot 456) 1	L	16.45/15.94 G	14.83/9.95 M	7.1	27.78	B	U	Drilled w/ metal
113	?	R	13.78/12.13 S	11.37/5.73 F	6.0	23.25	U	U	Intact
114	2	R	15.61/16.50 G	12.95/7.13 M	7.1	27.41	U	U	Intact
115	3	R	14.37/2.93 G	11.97/7.94 M	6.8	26.44	B	U	Intact
116	4	R	G	11.45/8.05 M	6.8	26.93	U	U	Intact
117	5	R	—	—	—	—	U	U	Intact
118	6	R	—	—	6.0	23.06	U	U	Intact
119	7	L	G	11.25/7.04 M	6.2	23.73	U	U	Intact
120	10	R	13.94/12.97 G	10.91/6.31 M	6.0	24.04	B	U	Intact

---

[7] In addition, there were 8 fragments that were unidentifiable, of which 3 were burnt.

Acqui-sition No.	Laboratory Number	Side L/R	Sheep/Goat Ratio	Male/Female Ratio	Circumference in mm.	Longitudinal Diameter in mm.	Burnt/Unburnt	Cut/Polished Uncut/Unpolished	Remarks
121	12	L	14.88/14.60 G	10.50/6.36 M	5.7	21.98	B	U	Intact
122	13	R	15.72/12.45 S	9.31/7.35 M	6.4	24.76	U	U	Intact
123	15	R	G	11.10/6.90 M	6.1	23.43	U	U	Intact
124	16	R	G	9.70/6.28 M	5.4	20.47	U	U	Intact
125	8	R	G	11.11/6.46 M	6.3	21.18	B	U	Intact
126		R	G	M	5.8	~20.29	U	U	Intact
127		R	14.21/13.47 G	11.55/7.48 M	6.0	23.67	U	U	Intact
128	SW 2-7.27.45A 3285	L	—	—	~6.6	~25.70	B	U	Intact
129	SW 2-7.27.45A 3286	L	G	11.11/6.37 M	6.5	23.95	B	U	Intact
130	SW 2-7.27.45A 3288	L	—	—	—	—	B	U	In 3 pieces
131	SW 2-7.27.45A 3290	L	14.70/15.49 G	—	~6.6	~25.53	B	U	2 pieces, 1 with hole in inf. surface
132	SW 2-7.27.45A 3291	R	G	12.38/8.45 M-	6.3-	24.66	B/W	U	2 pieces, 1 with hole in inf. surface
133	SW 2-7.27.45A 3292	L	—	—	—	—	B	U	2 pieces, 1 with hole in inf. surface
134	SW 2-7.27.45A 3295	L	G	—	6.0	23.41	B	U	2 pieces, 1 with hole in inf. surface
135	4654/N	L	16.00/15.20 G	11.91/7.89 M	6.4	24.32	U	U	2 pieces, 1 with hole in inf. surface
136	SW 6-7.63.36 618	R	—	—	6.9	27.05	U	—	Flattened on all 6 sides
137	SW 1-9.41.85 697	L	16.92/15.17 S	12.63/6.94 M	6.7	25.19	U	—	3 holes, sup./inf.

[8]The following astragali were unnumbered or had numbers that could not be read.

Acqui-sition No.	Laboratory Number	Side L/R	Sheep/Goat Ratio	Male/Female Ratio	Circumference in mm.	Longitudinal Diameter in mm.	Burnt/Unburnt	Cut/Polished Uncut/Unpolished	Remarks
138	SW 1-7.B278. L. 146 1031	L	—	—	~6.6	25.56	U	—	Flattened on 4 sides; sup./inf.; ant./post.; bone porous
139	SW 1-8.230.76 1459	L	G	11.47/7.51 M	6.3	24.35	U	—	1 central hole; chipped; weather worn
140	SW 2-7.140.394 4596/N	L	G	10.57/7.52 M	5.9	23.17	U	—	2 sides flattened: lat. & medial
141	4614/N[9/10]	R	G	10.33/8.47	6.5	24.96	U	—	2 sidesd flattened: med. & lat.
142	SW 2-7. 569.257 SW 2-7. 269. b. 122 5500[11/12]	R	13.59/13.49 G	10.42/7.09 M	5.8	22.22	U	U	—
143	SW 2-7.264. b. 122 6135	R	13.55/11.96 S	13.02/6.90 F	5.7	22.11	U	U	—
144	4604	L	13.57/11.96 S	11.96/6.83 M	6.0	23.60	U	U	Beginning of box w/ "non-cultic" bones
145	4650	R	13.17/11.32 S	10.17/6.06 M	5.4	20.43	U	U	?
146	4657	L	—	12.24/6.24 F	6.6	25.54	B	?	?
147	4652	L	—	—	6.0	22.53	U	—	2 sides flattened: med. & lat.
148	4653	L	16.82/15.20 S	11.73/6.63 M	6.6	25.16	U	U	—
149	4653	L	G	12.51/5.56 M	6.8	25.30	U	U	2 sides flattened: med. & lat.

---

[9]Sus astragalus; TT 4755, d. = 40.86

[10]Sus astragali (2 specimens); TT 4854, d. = 3309; TT 4656, d. = 33.11

[11]Sus astragali; TT 4686; SW 1-9.83.44, d. = 31.03.

[12]Sus astragali; TT 5507; SW 2-7.651.280, d. = 31.19.

Acqui-sition No.	Laboratory Number	Side L/R	Sheep/Goat Ratio	Male/Female Ratio	Circumference in mm.	Longitudinal Diameter in mm.	Burnt/Unburnt	Cut/Polished Uncut/Unpolished	Remarks
150	4653	R	14.44/13.23 G	11.12/6.57 M	6.1	23.26	U	U	—
151	4654	L	—	11.20/5.74 F	5.7	22.27	U	U	1 side flattened: med.
152	4655	R	14.32/14.43 G	11.72/6.80 M	6.0	23.49	U	—	2 sides flattened: med. & lat.
153	4655	L	16.45/15.43 G	11.97/6.37 M	6.1	23.41	U	—	2 sides partially flattened: med. & lat.
154	4655	L	15.88/13.31 S	11.67/5.69 F	5.9	23.22	U	U	—
155	4656	R	16.38/14.49 S	12.34/7.29	6.8	25.37	U	U	—
156	4657	L	G	M	6.1	23.68	U	—	2 sides partially flattened: sup. & lat.
157	4657	L	G	M	6.2	23.51	U	—	2 sides partially flattened: sup. & lat.
158	4657	L	14.96/14.31 G	10.66/5.69 M	5.9	22.95	U	U	—
159	4657	L	—	12.95/6.32 F	7.1	27.33	U	U	—
160	4657	R	16.16/13.33 S	12.50/5.65 F	6.2	23.74	U	U	—
161	4658	R	12.62/12.36 G	9.42/5.86 M	5.4	21.05	U	U	—
162	4659	L	14.97/12.74 S	10.43/5.83 M	5.9	21.66	U	U	—
163	4660	L	15.18/12.90 S	11.49/5.58 F	5.8	22.4	U	U	—
164	4661	L	16.24/14.56 S	12.15/6.95 M	6.4	24.96	U	U	—
165	4662	L	17.19/13.91 S	11.87/7.09 M	6.6	25.18	U	U	—
166	4662	R	13.39/12.13 G	10.45/6.90 M	5.9	22.56	U	U	—
167	4671	L	13.15/13.12 G	10.89/6.52 M	5.7	22.81	U	U	—
168	4671	L	15.43/15.35 G	13.69/8.50 M	6.3	24.09	U	U	One side partially flattened: lat.
169	4671	L	12.51/12.29 G	10.81/6.03 M	5.4	20.87	U	U	—
170	4671	R	G	10.71/6.31 M	6.1	23.29	U	U	—
171	4672	L	14.01/12.25 S	11.29/6.59 M	6.0	24.34	U	U	—
172	4673	L	G	10.31/6.0 M	5.9	23.09	U	U	—
173	4673	L	14.46/13.35 S	12.47/8.25 M	6.3	25.62	U	U	—

Acquisition No.	Laboratory Number	Side L/R	Sheep/ Goat Ratio	Male/ Female Ratio	Circumference in mm.	Longitudinal Diameter in mm.	Burnt/ Unburnt	Cut/Polished Uncut/Unpolished	Remarks
174	4674	R	15.75/12.53 S	10.57/5.45 F	6.7	23.55	U	U	—
175	4674	R	16.95/14.45 S	12.36/6.39 F	6.5	24.45	U	U	—
176	4675	L	G	11.38/7.06 M	6.5	24.84	U	U	—
177	4677	L	16.97/15.45 G	12.29/7.52 M	6.5	24.71	U	U	—
178	4678	R	—	—	6.2	24.54	U	—	Sup. surface flattened
179	4679	R	14.54/12.19 S	10.77/6.73 M	6.2	23.61	U	U	—
180	4679	R	G	11.45/5.90 F	6.3	23.72	U	U	—
181	4679	R	—	11.77/6.55 M	5.8	22.40	U	U	—
182	4680	L	G	11.68/7.01 M	6.5	24.56	B	U	—
183	4681	R	G	11.35/7.10 M	6.4	25.10	U	U	—
184	4682	L	G	M	6.0	23.15	U	U	Flattened lat. & med.
185	4683	R	15.50/15.30 G	13.37/6.38 F	6.0	23.33	B	U	—
186	4685	L	17.76/16.80 G	12.89/8.71 M	7.2	24.25	U	U	—
187	4687	R	16.46/15.47 G	12.13/8.35 M	6.7	24.96	U	U	—
188	4688	L	16.43/14.35 S	11.37/6.40 M	6.3	24.41	B	U	—
189	4688	L	16.88/15.07 S	11.90/6.92 M	6.3	24.41	U	U	—
190	4689	L	15.40/13.27 S	10.92/6.97 M	5.7	21.72	U	U	—
191	4690	R	17.45/14.49 S	12.13/7.13 M	6.5	24.84	U	U	—
192	4691	R	—	12.02/6.60 M	~6.6	~25.18	U	U	—
193	4692	L	13.73/14.49 S	10.79/6.45 M	5.7	22.60	B	U	—
194	4693	L	16.40/14.76 S	13.58/8.72 M	6.6	25.82	U	U	—
195	4740	R	—	—	5.9	22.94	U	U	Flattened on lat. side
196	4741	L	14.35/13.08 G	10.57/6.47 M	5.5	21.86	U	U	—
197	4742	L	15.49/14.51 G	108.2/6.44	5.9	22.66	U	U	—

Appendix F—332

Acqui-sition No.	Laboratory Number	Side L/R	Sheep/ Goat Ratio	Male/ Female Ratio	Circumfer- ence in mm.	Longitudinal Diameter in mm.	Burnt/ Unburnt	Cut/Polished Uncut/Unpolished	Remarks
198	4743	L	14.28/14.26 G	108.7/6.87 M	6.2	23.70	B	U	—
199	4744	R	—	12.59/7.83 M	6.7	24.63	U	U	—
200	4744	L	22.75/22.81 G	16.15/10.48 M	8.9	34.37	U	U	—
201	4745	R	16.21/14.72 S	12.75/7.88 M	6.4	25.13	B on ant./med. surfaces	U	
202	4746	R	14.81/12.86 S	10.77/6.44 M	6.1	24.73	U	U	—
203	4748	L	—	12.21/7.78 M	6.3	24.49	U	U	—
204	4748	R	145.8/136.8 G	10.28/5.15 F	5.8	22.65	U	U	—
205	4754	L	16.84/14.88 S	10.99/6.53 M	6.3	24.37	U	U	—
206	4756	L	—	13.06/8.80 M	6.7	25.68	U	U	—
207	4759	R	—	—	—	—	U	U	—
208	4767	R	G	10.38/6.07 M	6.3	24.67	U	U	—
209	4767	R	22.05/22.01 G	17.35/9.68 M	9.0	34.99	U	U	—
210	4767	L	17.57/15.34 S	11.59/6.75 M	6.7	25.72	U	U	—
211	4767	R	16.03/13.75 S	—	6.2	24.63	U	U	—
212	4774	L	—	11.90/8.03	~6.4	~25.30	B	U	—
213	4768	R	G	M	6.5	25.38	U	U	—
214	4768	L	15.14/13.09 S	11.13/6.08 M	6.0	23.04	U	U	—
215	4769	L	G	12.68/6.15 F	6.5	24.56	B	U	—
216	SW 1-26.2.32 4770	R	—	11.32/6.31 M	6.8	25.90	U	U	—
217	SW 3-6.166 4775	R	14.99/13.33 S	11.02/6.10 M	6.2	24.76	U	U	—
218	SW 1-26.162 4771	R	G	—	6.3	24.17	U	U	—

Appendix F—333

Acqui-sition No.	Laboratory Number	Side L/R	Sheep/Goat Ratio	Male/Female Ratio	Circumfer-ence in mm.	Longitudinal Diameter in mm.	Burnt/Unburnt	Cut/Polished Uncut/Unpolished	Remarks
219	SW 3-6.144 4777	R	17.12/14.15 S	13.18/6.46 F	6.5	25.33	U	U	—
220	SW 3-0.214 4779	L	16.79/15.59 G	12.61/7.78 M	6.7	25.32	U	U	—
221	SW 1-26.164 4780	L	16.17/14.17 S	12.01/5.74 M	6.1	23.57	U	U	—
222	4789	R	—	11.39/8.70 M	6.5	25.37	U	U	Med. & Lat. flattened
223	4789	L	15.52/13.66 S	11.65/6.53 M	6.3	24.33	U	U	—
224	SW 2-8.21.76 4758/N	R	G	13.57/7.03 F	6.5	25.49	U	U	—
225	4758/N	R	16.27/13.75 S	12.80/8.08 M	6.4	24.69	B	U	—
226	4758/N	L	14.11/13.81 G	11.27/6.86 M	6.0	23.05	B	U	—
227	4758/N	L	15.38/14.76 G	11.04/5.65 F	6.0	22.87	B	U	—
228	4758/N	L	—	—	—	—	B	U	—
229	4620	L	14.21/12.43 S	10.42/7.15 M	5.7	22.44	U	U	—
230	4620	R	15.85/13.53 S	10.23/7.18 M	5.8	22.34	U	U	—
231	4621	R	16.69/13.24 S	11.97/6.30 F	6.7	25.78	U	U	—
232	4622	L	17.38/15.61 S	13.95/7.82 M	7.0	27.05	U	U	—
233	4622	R	16.56/16.71 G	12.21/7.05 M	6.7	26.19	U	U	—
234	4623	L	17.39/16.43 G	12.56/6.83 M	6.6	25.42	U	U	—
235	4624	L	G	11.58/7.44 M	6.3	24.60	U	U	—
236	4626	L	15.66/13.60 S	11.73/6.78 M	6.3	24.45	U	U	—
237	4627	R	14.58/13.60 G	10.02/5.46 M	6.0	22.31	U	U	—
238	4628	R	17.19/14.84 S	11.14/6.10 M	6.6	24.40	U	U	—
239	4628	L	15.11/14.56 G	11.2/7.89 M	6.2	25.25	U	U	—
240	4629	L	14.2/14.71 G	10.54/7.30 M	6.3	24.36	U	U	—

Acqui-sition No.	Laboratory Number	Side L/R	Sheep/ Goat Ratio	Male/ Female Ratio	Circumfer-ence in mm.	Longitudinal Diameter in mm.	Burnt/ Unburnt	Cut/Polished Uncut/Unpolished	Remarks
241	4631	R	13.6/12.18 G	9.5/6.00 M	5.7	21.40	U	U	—
242	4631	R	13.61/12.06 G	10.37/7.21 M	6.1	22.14	U	U	—
243	4623	R	G	11.45/7.03 M	6.0	22.58	U	U	—
244	4633	R	16.11/14.01 S	12.24/6.29 F	6.2	23.42	U	U	—
245	4634	L	G	1135/7.34 M	6.9	26.05	U	U	—
246	4634	L	G	11.22/6.96 M	5.9	23.23	U	U	—
247	4643	L	G	11.10/8.05 M	7.1	26.53	U	U	—
248	4643	R	15.68/14.63 G	11.99/6.02 F	6.3	23.85	U	U	—
249	4634	L	—	12.98/8.31 M	7.1	27.11	U	U	—
250	4634	L	—	11.37/7.53 M	6.2	22.74	U	U	—
251	4634	L	—	—	6.2	24.05	U	U	Sup. & inf. surfaces flattened
252	4634	R	—	—	6.3	23.70	U	U	—
253	4634	L	—	13.56/7.95 M	7.3	28.14	U	U	—
254	4634	R	S	12.15/6.28 F	6.6	25.26	U	U	—
255	4634	R	—	11.41/6.87 M	5.7	21.54	U	U	—
256	4634	R	13.36/11.62 S	10.71/7.62 M	5.7	25.60	U	U	—
257	4634	L	—	10.55/5.76 M	5.9	23.02	U	U	—
258	4634	L	16.65/14.94 S	—	7.0	26.84	U	U	—
259	4634	L	G	11.09/6.04 M	6.2	22.97	U	U	—
260	4634	L	—	—	6.5	25.05	U	U	—
261	4634	R	—	—	—	—	U	U	—
262	4634	R	—	—	6.7	26.19	U	U	—
263	4634	R	—	9.68/7.73 M	6.2	23.70	U	U	—
264	4636	R	15.23/14.63 G	11.25/6.36 M	6.3	24.06	U	U	—

Acquisition No.	Laboratory Number	Side L/R	Sheep/Goat Ratio	Male/Female Ratio	Circumference in mm.	Longitudinal Diameter in mm.	Burnt/Unburnt	Cut/Polished Uncut/Unpolished	Remarks
265	4637	R	11.82/10.25 S	8.99/5.50 M	5.2	19.86	U	U	—
266	4638	L	—	10.71/7.22 M	5.8	23.08	U	U	—
267	4639	R	15.50/13.76 S	11.36/8.52 M	6.2	24.04	U	U	—
268	Unnumbered	R	13.52/12.83 G	10.52/6.02 M	5.7	22.17	B	U	—
269	Unnumbered	R	12.85/12.65 G	10.48/6.86 M	5.6	21.90	B	U	—
270	SW 1-7.165.354 Unnumbered	L	14.16/13.64 G	9.89/6.83 M	6.1	23.11	U	U	—
271	SW 1-7.165.354 Unnumbered	R	13.77/13.99 G	11.59/6.98 M	6.1	23.91	U	U	—
272	SW 1-7.165.354 Unnumbered	L	—	10.63/7.08 M	6.2	23.89	U	U	Med. & lat. sides flattened
273	SW 1-7.165.354 Unnumbered	R	12.70/11.70 G	10.82/6.36 M	5.7	22.09	U	U	—
274	SW 1-7.165.354 Unnumbered	R	—	—	6.5	25.12	U	U	—
275	SW 1-7.165.354 Unnumbered	L	G	M	6.4	24.80	U	U	Med. & lat. sides flattened
276	SW 1-7.165.354 Unnumbered	R	—	11.91/7.19 M	6.3	24.09	U	U	—
277	SW 1-7.165.354 Unnumbered	L	16.35/14.91 G	12.86/8.18 M	6.7	25.58	U	U	—
278	SW 1-7.165.354 Unnumbered	R	13.88/13.47 G	—	5.6	22.00	U	U	—
279	SW 1-7.165.354 Unnumbered	L	—	—	5.7	21.72	U	U	—
280	SW 1-7.165.354 Unnumbered	L	14.59/13.54 G	10.79/6.87 M	5.9	22.93	U	U	—
281	SW 1-7.165.354 Unnumbered	L	G	11.88/8.72 M	6.7	25.72	U	U	—

Acquisition No.	Laboratory Number	Side L/R	Sheep/ Goat Ratio	Male/ Female Ratio	Circumference in mm.	Longitudinal Diameter in mm.	Burnt/ Unburnt	Cut/Polished Uncut/Unpolished	Remarks
282	SW 1-7.165.354 Unnumbered	L	14.38/13.94 G	11.10/7.50 M	6.1	23.85	U	U	Lat. side flattened
283	SW 1-7.165.354 Unnumbered	L	14.76/14.19 G	10.81/6.35 M	5.8	22.46	U	U	—
284	SW 1-7.165.354 Unnumbered	R	—	10.49/5.39 F	5.6	22.53	U	U	—
285	SW 1-7.165.354 Unnumbered	L	14.51/13.89 G	11.03/7.50 M	5.9	22.81	U	U	—
286	SW 1-7.165.354 Unnumbered	R	17.26/14.70 S	11.52/7.48 M	6.4	24.46	U	U	—
287	SW 1-7.165.354 Unnumbered	L	15.54/12.15 S	10.71/7.10 M	6.1	23.16	U	U	—
288	4640	L	14.24/13.52 G	—	6.2	23.60	U	U	—
289	4641	L	16.49/14.50 S	11.40/7.52 M	6.0	22.62	U	U	—
290	4642	R	—	11.64/7.57 M	—	—	U	U	—
291	4642	L	15.15/13.57 S	10.49/6.04 M	6.0	23.15	U	U	—
292	4643	R	16.74/14.17 S	11.93/6.59 M	6.4	24.55	U	U	—
293	4644	L	16.48/13.97 S	10.72/5.83 M	6.1	23.38	U	U	—
294	4645	L	16.39/15.71 G	11.63/6.98 M	6.6	25.26	U	U	Lat. & med. sides flattened
295	4647	L	16.82/15.19 S	11.78/7.58 M	6.4	23.68	U	U	—
296	4647	R	15.12/15.15 G	11.87/6.18 M	6.3	24.31	U	U	—
297	4647	R	11.55/8.42 S	—	6.1	23.15	U	U	—
298	4647	L	16.74/14.54 S	11.20/5.36 F	6.3	24.71	U	U	—
299	4647	R	G	10.08/6.20 M	5.5	20.58	U	U	—
300	4648	L	13.51/13.06 G	11.01/6.70 M	5.9	2.32	U	U	—
301	4649	R	—	11.52/7.64 M	6.4	24.15	U	U	—
302	4612	R	—	—	6.0	23.00	U	U	—

Appendix F—337

Acquisition No.	Laboratory Number	Side L/R	Sheep/Goat Ratio	Male/Female Ratio	Circumference in mm.	Longitudinal Diameter in mm.	Burnt/Unburnt	Cut/Polished Uncut/Unpolished	Remarks
303	4613	R	15.0/13.04 S	10.54/6.64 M	6.0	22.75	U	U	—
304	4613	R	16.60/14.80 S	12.88/6.70 F	6.6	25.44	U	U	—
305	4631	L	—	—	8.8	34.29	U	U	—
306	4615	L	13.22/13.19 G	10.78/6.37 M	5.5	21.71	U	U	—
307	4618	L	15.98/14.85 G	11.57/6.89 M	6.8	25.63	U	U	—
308	4600	L	16.02/15.25 G	11.06/7.20 M	6.4	24.15	U	U	—
309	4602	R	16.2/14.77 S	11.93/6.38 M	6.6	25.35	U	U	—
310	4603	R	G	11.75/5.90 F	6.5	24.90	B	U	—
311	4604	R	15.38/15.36 G	13.03/6.55 F	6.5	24.33	U	U	—
312	4604	L	15.98/15.08 G	12.58/6.75 M	6.3	24.39	U	U	—
313	4605	R	—	12.25/7.96 M	6.7	25.34	U	U	—
314	4606	R	15.75/13.81 S	12.08/6.46 F	6.6	25.35	U	U	—
315	4607	R	15.92/14.73 G	12.18/5.17 F	6.4	23.94	U	U	—
316	4608	R	15.63/16.74 G	11.70/7.16 M	6.5	25.72	U	U	—
317	4609	R	16.45/15.36 G	11.67/6.85 M	6.5	25.05	U	U	—
318	4601	L	—	11.17/7.12 M	6.4	24.85	U	U	—
319	Unnumbered	L	—	12.46/7.46 M	6.4	24.80	B	U	—
320	4751/N SW 2-8 l. 21 b. 72 4751	R	15.56/14.26 G	11.53/7.25 M	6.2	23.64	B	U	—
321	4751/N SW 2-8 l. 21 b. 72 4751	R	—	—	—	—	B	U	—

Appendix F—338

Acqui-sition No.	Laboratory Number	Side L/R	Sheep/Goat Ratio	Male/Female Ratio	Circumference in mm.	Longitudinal Diameter in mm.	Burnt/Unburnt	Cut/Polished Uncut/Unpolished	Remarks
322	4751/N SW 2-8 l. 21 b. 72 4751	R	—	—	6.0	22.94	B	U	—
323	4751/N SW 2-8 l. 21 b. 72 4751	L	15.16/12.43 S	11.12/5.77 F	6.1	23.57	B	U	—
324	4656	R	—	12.41/7.37 M	6.6	25.04	U	U	—
325	4558	R	16.08/15.76 G	12.09/9.25 M	6.2	24.38	U	U	—
326	4654	L	15.50/14.08 S	11.30/6.43 M	6.1	23.72	U	U	—
327	4574	L	—	—	—	—	U	U	—
328	4577	L	15.98/14.77 G	12.82/8.38 M	6.5	21.23	U	U	—
329	4588	R	13.23/12.61 G	11.05/6.91 M	5.8	22.21	U	U	—
330	4594	R	S	10.61/5.33 F	6.0	23.58	U	U	—
331	SW 2-8.171 5515	R	14.19/12.07 S	10.61/6.98 M	5.8	22.37	U	C	sup. & lat.
332	SW 2-8.171 5515	L	15.04/14.99 G	11.69/7.44 M	6.1	25.10	U	U	*
333	SW 2-8.171 5515	L	G	11.95/6.53 M	5.6	22.39	B	U	—
334	SW 2-8.171 5515	R	15.65/15.29 G	11.91/6.94 M	6.2	24.36	U	U	—
335	SW 2-8.171 5515	R	16.09/16.09 G	12.54/8.38 M	6.7	26.62	U	U	—
336	SW 2-8.171 5515	L	14.48/13.69 G	11.08/7.13 M	6.1	24.02	U	U	—
337	SW 2-8.171 5515	R	—	12.21/7.66 M	6.0	21.95	U	U	—

Acquisition No.	Laboratory Number	Side L/R	Sheep/ Goat Ratio	Male/ Female Ratio	Circumference in mm.	Longitudinal Diameter in mm.	Burnt/ Unburnt	Cut/Polished Uncut/Unpolished	Remarks
338	SW 2-8.171 5515	L	—	9.16/4.66 F	5.3	20.35	U	U	—
339	SW 2-8.171 5515	L	13.99/13.99 G	10.8/7.79 M	5.9	2327	U	U	—
340	SW 2-8.171.375 5516/N	R	18.85/15.75 G	13.01/8.49 M	6.9	24.52	U	U	—
341	SW 2-8.171.375 5516/N	R	18.21/15.97 S	13.11/9.03 M	6.7	27.16	U	U	—
342	SW 6-2 5528/N	L	17.70/16.49 G	13.08/8.06 M	6.8	2643	U	C	Sup., med., & lat.
343	SW 6-2 5532/N	L	17.41/16.42 G	12.60/7.47 M	6.8	2579	U	U	—
344	SW 1-7.86.161 4582/N	L	—	—	—	U	U	U	—
345	SW 1-7.86.161 4582/N	—	15.47/13.86 S	10.95/6.27 M	6.1	23.19	U	U	—
346	SW 1-7.86.161 4582/N	—	—	13.72/7.08 F	6.3	24.30	U	U	—
347	SW 1-7.86.161 4582/N	—	—	12.31/6.90 M	6.5	25.71	U	U	—
348	SW 1-7.86.161 4582/N	—	15.74/14.94 G	10.13/5.97 M	6.0	23.43	U	U	—
349	SW 2-7.96.308 4595/N	—	18.35/16.47 S	14.85/7.92 F	6.8	26.17	U	U	—
350	SW 6-2 5527	—	15.29/15.11 G	13.07/8.26 M	6.9	26.86	U	U	—
351	SW 3-6 3481/N	—	16.48/13.22 S	12.41/7.21 M	6.5	24.85	U	U	—
352	SW 2-8.170.349 5520/N	R	15.67/13.92 S	10.96/6.02 M	6.2	23.02	U	U	—
353	3763/N	L	15.82/14.17 S	12.12/5.58 F	6.3	23.69	U	C	Sup. & post.

Appendix F—340

Acquisition No.	Laboratory Number	Side L/R	Sheep/ Goat Ratio	Male/ Female Ratio	Circumference in mm.	Longitudinal Diameter in mm.	Burnt/ Unburnt	Cut/Polished Uncut/Unpolished	Remarks
354	3769/R	R	15.03/13.83 G	10.30/7.83 M	6.1	22.44	U	U	—
355	3769/N	L	15.07/12.80 S	11.21/6.70 M	6.4	25.20	U	U	—
356	3769/N	L	14.66/14.00 G	10.74/8.44 M	6.0	23.25	U	U	—
357	SW 2-8 5510	R	14.84/14.84 G	11.55/5.40 F	6.3	24.47	U	U	—
358	SW 2-8 5510	R	15.70/13.17 S	11.49/6.46 M	6.1	23.67	B	U	—
359	SW 3-7 5539/N	R	15.72/13.71 S	11.21/7.31 M	5.9	23.04	U	U	—
360	SW 1-9 5541/N	L	15.73/13.32 S	12.24/8.60 M	6.1	23.80	U	U	—
361	SW 3-30 5538/N	R	15.84/13.84 S	12.22/9.30 M	6.6	25.70	U	U	—
362	SW 3-7 5523/N	R	15.82/13.75 S	11.20/6.71 M	5.9	23.08	U	U	—
363	SW 3-7 5523/N	R	14.28/12.17 S	9.86/5.02 F	5.5	21.36	U	U	—
364	SW 2-8 5522/N	L	16.60/16.02 G	12.40/7.00 M	6.5	25.03	U	U	—
365	SW 2-7 5511/N	R	13.92/13.08 G	10.98/6.52 M	5.6	21.57	U	U	—
366	SW 2-8 5529/N	R	17.35/14.85 S	11.07/7.53 M	6.4	25.40	U	U	—
367	SW 2-8.167.336 5517/N	L	14.34/14.34 G	12.09/6.86 M	5.9	22.87	U	U	—
368	SW 2-7 5506/N	R	16.37/15.27 G	11.66/6.54 M	6.4	24.31	U	U	—
369	Unnumbered	R	12.48/12.44 G	10.69/6.31 M	5.8	22.33	U	U	—

Acqui-sition No.	Laboratory Number	Side L/R	Sheep/ Goat Ratio	Male/ Female Ratio	Circumfer-ence in mm.	Longitudinal Diameter in mm.	Burnt/ Unburnt	Cut/Polished Uncut/Unpolished	Remarks
370	SW 2-7.274.639 5509/N	R	13.99/13.33 G	10.74/6.42 M	5.9	23.36	U	U	—
371	SW 6-2 5540/N	L	15.04/14.98 G	11.00/7.97 M	5.6	21.64	U	U	—
372	SW 1-9 5531/N	R	14.49/12.24 S	11.92/7.07 M	6.4	23.93	U	U	—
373	SW 1-9 5530/N	L	14.60/14.42 G	10.42/7.40 M	6.0	23.43	U	U	—
374	SW 1-8 5514/N	R	13.67/13.39 G	10.42/7.40 M	6.0	22.50	U	C	Med. & lat. sides flattened
375	SW 1-9 5545/N	R	—	—	~5.6	21.32	U	C	Med. & lat. sides flattened
376	SW 3-7 Unnumbered	R	15.01/12.62 S	—	6.4	~23.42	U	U	—
377	SW 3-7 5536/N	L	—	—	6.2	24.40	U	U	—
378	SW 3-7 5544/N	L	15.64/12.97 S	10.78/6.76 M	5.8	22.48	U	U	—
379	SW 6-7 5533/N	R	15.94/14.31 S	11.19/5.93 F	6.1	23.28	U	U	—
380	SW 6-28 5502/N	R	13.65/12.30 S	10.00/7.14 M	5.9	23.14	U	U	—
381	SW 2-7.216.632 5508/N	R	—	M	5.7	22.17	U	C	Right side flattened
382	SW 3-7 5519/N	L	15.67/14.46 G	11.19/5.80 F	6.0	23.52	U	U	—
383	SW 5-4 5535/N	R	16.33/14.35 S	12.74/8.65 M	6.7	26.21	U	U	—
384	SW 7-7 5542/N	L	14.29/14.02 G	10.84/7.32 M	6.1	23.92	U	U	—

Appendix F—342

Acqui-sition No.	Laboratory Number	Side L/R	Sheep/Goat Ratio	Male/Female Ratio	Circumference in mm.	Longitudinal Diameter in mm.	Burnt/Unburnt	Cut/Polished Uncut/Unpolished	Remarks
385	SW 5-2 5543/N	L	G	11.27/6.77 M	5.9	23.37	U	U	—
386	SW 2-8 5521/N	L	G	10.62/7.02 M	5.9	22.46	U	C	3 sides: sup., lat. & post.
387	SW 6-2 5534/N	L	15.10/13.93 G	11.65/7.80 M	6.3	25.18	U	C	3 sides: sup., lat., & post.
388	SW 2-8.163.335 5518/N	L	G	9.79/5.60 M	5.6	22.78	U	U	—
389	SW 1-8.116.280 5513/N	L	16.27/13.21 S	11.42/7.13 M	6.2	24.50	B	U	—
390	SW 2-8.156.319 5512/N	L	14.38/14.35 G	11.13/7.07 M	6.0	23.67	U	U	—

Appendix F—343

SOURCES CONSULTED

Ackerman, S.
1989 "And the Women Knead Dough": The Worship of the Queen of Heaven in Sixth-Century Judah." In P. L. Day (editor), *Gender and Difference in Ancient Israel*. Minneapolis: Fortress Press: 109-124.

Ahlström, G. W.
1982 *Royal Administration and National Religion in Ancient Palestine*. Leiden: E. J. Brill.

Al-Zawahra, Muhammad M.
1997 Private Communication.

Amiran, R.
1967 "A Note on Figurines with 'Disks.'" *Eretz-Israel*. 8: 99-100 (Hebrew).

Barry, Lewis R.
1988 "Old World Dice in the Protohistoric Southern United States." *Current Anthropology*, vol. 29, no. 5, December, 1988: 759-768.

Bass, George F.
1967 *Cape Gelidonya: A Bronze Age Shipwreck*. Transactions of the American Philosophical Society, N.S., vol. 57, part 8. Philadelphia: The American Philosophical Society.

Beck, Pirhiya.
1994 "The Cult-Stands from Taanach: Aspects of Iconographic Tradition of Early Iron Age Cult Objects in Palestine." In Israel Finkelstein and Nadav Na'aman (editors), *From Nomadism to Monarchy: Archaeological and Historical Aspects of Early Israel*. Jerusalem: Yad Itzhak Ben-Zvi for the Israel Exploration Society: 325-381

Ben-Tor, Amnon, ed.
1989 *Hazor III-IV. Text*. Jerusalem: Ben-Zvi.

Binford, L. R.
1981 *Ancient Men and Modern Myths*. New York: Academic Press.

Biran, Avraham.
1994 *Biblical Dan*. Jerusalem: Israel Exploration Society/Hebrew Union College-Jewish Institute of Religion.

Boessneck, J., H. H-Müller, and M. Teichert.
1964 "Oesteologische Unterscheidungsmerkmale zwischen Schaf (*Ovis Aries* Linné) und Ziege (*Capra hircus* Linné)." *Kühn-Archiv* 78: 1-129.

Brody, Aaron J.
1996 "Maritime Religion of the Canaanites and Phoenicians: Aspects of the Specialized Sacral Beliefs and Practices of Levantine Seafarers." Unpublished Ph. D. Dissertation, Harvard University.
1997 Personal Communication.

Buren, E. D. van.
1930 *Clay Figurines of Babylonia and Assyria.* Yale Oriental Series, 16. New Haven: Yale University Press.

Chambon, Alain.
1984 *Tell el-Fâr'ah I: L'Âge du Fer.* Recherche sur les Civilisations, Mémoires no. 31. Paris: A.D.P.F.

Coogan, Michael.
1987 "Of Cults and Cultures: Reflections on the Interpretation of Archaeological Evidence." *Palestine Exploration Quarterly* 119: 1-8.

Daviau, P. M. Michéle.
1994 "Traces of Cultic Behaviour in the Bronze Age Orthostat Temple at Hazor." In Jean-Claude Petit et al. (editors), *"Ou demeueres-tu?" (Jh 1, 28) La maison depuis le monde biblique. En homage au professeur Guy Coutuner a l'occasion de ses soixante-cinq ans.* Quebec: Fides: 72-90.
1993 *Houses and their Furnishings in Bronze Age Palestine.* JSOT/ASOR Monograph Series, no. 8. Sheffield: Sheffield Academic Press.

De Vaux, R.
1951 "La Troisième Campagne de Fouilles à Tell el-Far'ah, près Naplouse." *Revue Biblique* 58: 393-430.

Dever, William G.
1970 *Gezer I: Preliminary Report of the 1964-66 Seasons.* Jerusalem: Hebrew University Press.
1983 "Material Remains and the Cult in Ancient Israel: An Essay in Archaeological Systematics." In C. L. Meyers and M. O'Connor (editors), *The World of the Lord Shall Go Forth. Essays in Honor of David Noel Freedman in Celebration of His Sixtieth Birthday.* Winona Lake: ASOR/Eisenbrauns: 571-587.
1984 "Asherah, Consort of Yahweh? New Evidence from Kuntillet 'Ajrûd." *Bulletin of the American Schools of Oriental Research* 255: 21-37.
1987 "The Contribution of Archaeology to the Study of Canaanite and Early Israelite Religion." In P. D. Miller, et al. (editors), *Ancient Israelite Religion: Essays in Honor of Frank Moore Cross.* Philadelphia: Fortress Press: 209-147.
1990 *Recent Archaeological Discoveries and Biblical Research.* Seattle and London: University of Washington Press.

1994 "The Silence of the Text: An Archaeological Commentary on 2 Kings 23." In M. D. Coogan et al. (editors), *Scripture and Other Artifacts: Essays on the Bible and Archaeology in Honor of Philip J. King.* Louisville, KY: Westminster/John Knox: 143-168.
1995 "'Will the Real Israel Please Stand Up?' Part II: Archaeology and the Religions of Ancient Israel." *Bulletin of the American Schools of Oriental Research*, 298: 37-58.

Finkelstein, Israel.
1988 *The Archaeology of the Israelite Settlement.* Jerusalem: Israel Exploration Society.

Foster, Giraud V.
1984a *Personal communication to Albert E. Glock, March 15.*
1984b "The Bones from the Altar West of the Painted Stoa." *Hesperia* 53/1: 73-82.
1985 *Personal communication to Albert E. Glock, September 18.*
1986 "Ovicaprid Astragali." In P. E. McGovern, *The Late Bronze Age and Early Iron Ages of Central Transjordan. The Baq'ah Valley Project, 1977-1981.* Philadelphia: The University Museum: 317-319.

Fowler, M. D.
1984 "Concerning the 'Cultic' Structure at Taanach." *Zeitschrift des Deutschen Palästina-Vereins* 100: 30-34.

Frick, F. S.
1971 "The Rechabites Reconsidered." *Journal of Biblical Literature* 90: 279-287.
1992 "Rechab." In D. N. Freedman et al. (editors), *The Anchor Bible Dictionary.* New York: Doubleday. 5: 630-632.

Gesell, G. C.
1985 *Town, Palace and House Cult in Minoan Crete.* Swedish Inistitute of Mediterranean Archaeology, LXVII. Göteborg: Paul Åströms Förlag.

Gilmour, Garth.
1995 "The Archaeology of Cult in the Southern Levant in the Early Iron Age: An Analytical and Comparative Approach." Unpublished Ph. D. dissertation, St. Cross College, Oxford.
1997 "The Nature and Function of Astragalus Bones from Archaeological Contexts in the Levant and Eastern Mediterranean." *Oxford Journal of Archaeology*, 16/2: 167-175.

Gitin, Seymour.
1989 "Tel Miqne-Ekron: A Type-Site for the Inner Coastal Plain in the Iron Age II Period." In S. Gitin and W. G. Dever (editors), *Recent Excavations in Israel.* AASOR 49. Winona Lake, IN: Eisenbrauns: 23-58.
1990 "Ekron of the Philistines Part II: Olive-Oil Suppliers to the World." *Biblical Archaeology Review* Vol. XVI, No. 2 (March/April): 32-42.

1993 "Seventh Century Cultic Elements at Ekron." In A. Biran and J. Aviram (editors), *Biblical Archaeology Today, 1990.* Proceedings of the Second International Congress on Biblical Archaeology, Jerusalem, June-July 1990. Jerusalem: Israel Exploration Society, 258-258.

Glock, A. E.
1975 "Taanach." *Encyclopedia of Archaeological Excavations in the Holy Land*, Volume IV. Englewood Cliffs, N.J.: Prentice-Hall: 1428-1433.

Glock, Lois.
N.D. Unpublished notes on "Astragali from SW 2-7, Locus 27 and Locus 60."

Goodenough, E. R.
1956 *Jewish Symbols in the Greco-Roman Period. Volume Five: Fish, Bread, and Wine.* Bollingen Series, XXXVII. NY: Pantheon Books.

Graesser, Carl F.
1972 "Standing Stones in Ancient Palestine." *Biblical Archaeologist* 35: 34-63.

Guy, P. L. O. and G. M. Engberg.
1938 *Megiddo Tombs.* Chicago: University of Chicago Press.

Haran, Menahem.
1993 "'Incense Altars'—Are They." In A. Biran and J. Aviram (editors), *Biblical Archaeology Today, 1990.* Proceedings of the Second International Congress on Biblical Archaeology, Jerusalem, June-July 1990. Jerusalem: Israel Exploration Society: 237-247.

Harrison, Jane E.
1912 *Themis.* Cambridge: Cambridge University Press.

Hesse, B.
1988 "Patterns of Palestinian Pork Production." Unpublished paper presented at the ASOR/SBL Annual Meeting, Chicago, November 1988.
1990 "Pig Lovers and Pig Haters: Patterns of Palestinian Pork Production." *Journal of Ethnobiology* 1 / 2: 195-225.
1995 "Husbandry, Dietary Taboos and the Bones of the Ancient Near East: Zooarchaeology in the Post-Processual World." In D. B. Small (editor), *Methods in the Mediterranean.* Leiden: E. J. Brill: 197-223.

Hesse, B, and P. Wapnish.
1985 *Animal Bone Archaeology. From Objectives to Analysis.* Washington: Taraxacum.

Hestrin, Ruth.
1987 "The Cult Stand from Ta'anach and its Religious Background." *Studia Phoenicia* V: 61-78.

1991 "Understanding Asherah: Exploring Semitic Iconography." *Biblical Archaeology Review* Vol. XVII, No. 5 (September/October 1991): 50-59.

Hillers, D. R.
1962 *Tell Ta'annek and a Gleaning of Tell Ta'annek.* Unpublished translation of Sellin (1904).
1970 "The Goddess with the Tambourine: Reflections on an Object from Taanach." *Concordia Theological Monthly* 41: 606-619.

Holland, T. A.
1977 "A Study of Palestinian Iron Age Baked Clay Figurines, with Special Reference to Jerusalem: Cave 1." *Levant* 9: 121-155.

James, Frances.
1966 *The Iron Age at Beth Shan: A Study of Levels VI-IV.* Philadelphia: The University Museum.

Kantor, H. J.
1962 "A Bronze Plaque with Relief Decoration from Tell Tainat," *Journal of Near Eastern Studies* 21: 93-117.

Kempinski, Aharon.
1989 *Megiddo: A City-State and Royal Centre in North Israel.* München: C. H. Beck.

Lamon, Robert S. and Geoffrey Shipton.
1939 *Megiddo I: Seasons of 1925-34, Strata I-V.* Oriental Institute Publications, 42. Chicago: University of Chicago.

Lapp, Paul W.
1964 "The 1963 Excavation at Ta'annek." *Bulletin of the American Schools of Oriental Research* 173: 4-44.
1967a "The 1966 Excavations at Tell Ta'annek." *Bulletin of the American Schools of Oriental Research* 185: 2-39.
1967b "Taanach by the Waters of Megiddo." *Biblical Archaeologist* 30/1: 2-27.
1969 "The 1968 Excavations at Tell Ta'annek." *Bulletin of the American Schools of Oriental Research* 195: 2-49.
1969b "A Ritual Incense Stand from Taanak," *Qadmoniot* 2: 16-17 (Hebrew).

Levine, Louis D.
1993 "Response." In A. Biran and J. Aviram (editors), *Biblical Archaeology Today, 1990.* Proceedings of the Second International Congress on Biblical Archaeology, Jerusalem, June-July 1990, A. Biran and J. Aviram, eds. Jerusalem: Israel Exploration Society: 267.

Loud, Gordon.
1948 *Megiddo II: Seasons of 1935-39. Text and Plates.* The University of Chicago Oriental

Institute Publications, vol. 62. Chicago: University of Chicago Press.

McCown, C. C.
1950 "Hebrew High Places and Cult Remains." *Journal of Biblical Literature* 69: 205-219.

May, H. G.
1935 *Material Remains of the Megiddo Cult.* University of Chicago Oriental Institute Publications, vol. XXVI. Chicago: University of Chicago Press.

Meehl, Mark W.
1995 "A Stratigraphic Analysis of the Unpublished Early Iron Age Materials from Tell Ta'annek in Light of Recent Jezreel Valley Excavations." Unpublished Ph.D. dissertation, Johns Hopkins University.

Meshel, Zeev.
1978 *Kuntillet 'Ajrûd: A Religious Centre from the Time of the Judean Monarchy on the Border of the Sinai.* Jerusalem: The Israel Museum..

Mettinger, T. N. D.
1995 *No Graven Images? Israelite Aniconism in Its Ancient Near Eastern Context.* Conlectanea Biblica, Old Testament Series 42. Stockholm: Almqvist & Wiksell International.

Meyers, Carol L.
1976 *The Tabernacle Menorah: A Synthetic Study of a Symbol from the Biblical Cult.* ASOR Dissertation Series 2. Missoula: Scholars Press.
1987 "A Terracotta in the Harvard Semitic Museum and Disc-Holding Female Figures Reconsidered." *Israel Exploration Journal* 37.2-3: 116-122.
1995 "An Ethnoarchaeological Analysis of Hannah's Sacrifice." In D. W. Wright et al. (editors), *Pomegrantes and Golden Bells: Studies in Biblical, Jewish, and Near Eastern Ritual, Law, and Literature in Honor of Jacob Milgrom.* Winona Lake, IN: Eisenbrauns: 77-91.

Pedley, J. G.
1993 *The Sanctuary of Santa Venera at Paestum, I,* ed. M. Torelli, with contributions by T. V. Buttrey et al. (Archaeologica 104, Arhaeologia Perusina II). Rome: Giorgio Bretschneider.

Potts, T. F.
1985 "The Late Bronze-Early Iron Ages." In T. F. Potts et al. "Preliminary Report on the Sixth Season of Excavation by the University of Sydney at Pella in Jordan." *Annual of the Department of Antiquities of Jordan* 29: 181-210.
1992 "The Cultic Stands." In R. H. Smith and T. F. Potts (editors), "The Iron Age." In A. W. McNicoll et al. *Pella in Jordan 2.* Mediterranean Archaeology Supplement 2: Sydney: Meditarch: 83-101.

Powell, Marvin A.
1992 "Weights and Measures." *The Anchor Bible Dictionary*, ed. David N. Freedman. Vol. 6: 897-908. New York: Doubleday.
1997 "Weights and Measures." *The Oxford Encyclopedia of Archaeology in the Near East*, ed. Eric M. Meyers. Vol. 5: 339-342. New York: Oxford University Press.

Pritchard, James B.
1943 *Palestinian Figurines in Relation to Certain Goddesses Known through Literature*. American Oriental Series, 24. New Haven: Yale University Press.
1954 *The Ancient Near East in Pictures Relating to the Old Testament*. Princeton: Princeton University Press.
1959 "Inscribed Weight." In *Hebrew Inscriptions and Stamps from Gibeon*. Philadelphia: The University Museum: 29-30.
1975 *Sarepta: A Preliminary Report on the Iron Age. Excavations of the University of Museum of the University of Pennsylvania, 1970-72*. Philadelphia: The University Museum.

Prummel, Wietske and Hans-Jörg Frisch
1986 "A Guide for the Distinction of Species, Sex and Body Side in Bones of Sheep and Goat." *Journal of Archaeological Science* 13: 567-577.

Rappaport, Roy A.
1970 "Sanctity and Adaptation." *Io* 7: 46-71.
1971a "The Sacred in Human Evolution." *Annual Review of Ecology and Systematics*. 2: 23-44.
1971b "Ritual, Sanctity and Cybernetics." *American Anthropologist* 73: 59-76.
1984 *Pigs for the Ancestors: Ritual in the Ecology of a New Guinea People*. New, enlarged edition. New Haven: Yale University Press.

Rast, Walter E.
1977 "Cakes for the Queen of Heaven." In A. L. Merrill and T. W. Overholt (editors), *Scripture in Hisory and Theology: Studies in Honor of J. Coert Rylaarsdam*. Pittsburgh: Pickwick Press: 168-180.
1978 *Taanach I: Studies in Iron Age Pottery*. Cambridge, MA: American Schools of Oriental Research.
1994 "Priestly Families and the Cultic Structure at Taanach." In M. D. Coogan, J. C. Exum, and L. E. Stager (editors), *Scripture and Other Artifacts: Essays on the Bible and Archaeology in Honor of Philip J. King*. Louisville, KY: Westminster/John Knox: 355-365.

Reese, D. S.
1989 "On Cassid Lips and Helmet Shells." *Bulletin of the American Schools of Oriental Research*, 275: 33-39.

Renfrew, Colin.
1985 *The Archaeology of Cult. The Sanctuary at Phylakopi*. British School of Archaeology at

Athens. London: Thames and Hudson.

Renfrew, Colin and Paul Bahn.
1991 *Archaeology: Theories, Methods and Practice.* NY: Thames and Hudson, Ltd.

Roberts, John M., Malcom J. Arth, and Robert R. Bush
1959 "Games in Culture." *American Anthropologist* 61: 597-605.

Sellin, Ernst.
1904 *Tell Ta'annek.* Denkschriften der Kaiserlichen Akademie der Wissenschaften in Wien, Philosophisch-historische Klasse 50, IV Abhandlung. Wien: Carl Gerhold's Sohn.

Sheffer, Avigail.
1981 "The Use of Perforated Clay Balls on the Warp-Weighted Loom." *Tel Aviv* 8: 81-83.

Shiloh, Yigal.
1979 "Iron Age Sanctuaries and Cult Elements in Palestine." In F. M. Cross (editor), *Symposia Celebrating the Seventy-fifth Anniversary of the Founding of the American Schools of Oriental Research.* Cambridge, MA: American Schools of Oriental Research: 147-157.

Stager, Lawrence E. and Samuel R. Wolff
1981 "Production and Commerce in Temple Courtyards: An Olive Press in the Sacred Precinct at Tel Dan." *Bulletin of the American Schools of Oriental Research* 243: 95-102.

Stech-Wheeler, T. J., J. D. Muhly, K. R. Maxwell-Hyslop, and R. Maddin.
1981 "Iron at Taanach and Early Iron Metallurgy in the Eastern Mediterranean." *American Journal of Archaeology* 85: 245-268.

Taylor, J. G.
1993 *Yahweh and the Sun: Biblical and Archaeological Evidence for Sun Worship in Ancient Israel.* Sheffield: JSOT Press.

Tuffnell, O., C. H. Inge, and L. Harding.
1940 *Lachish II. The Fosse Temple.* London: Oxford University Press.
1953 *Lachish III: The Iron Age.* London: Oxford University Press.

Wapnish, Paula.
1993 "Archaeozoology: The Integration of Faunal Data with Biblical Archaeology." In A. Biran and J. Aviram (editors), *Biblical Archaeology Today, 1990.* Jerusalem: Israel Exploration Society: 426-442.

Yadin, Yigael et al.

1958-
1961   *Hazor: An Account of the Excavations, 1955-1958.* 4 vols. In 3. Jerusalem: Goldberg's Press, Ltd.

1985   "New Gleanings on Resheph from Ugarit." In A. Kort and S. Morschauer (editors), *Biblical and Related Studies Presented to Samuel Iwry.* Winona Lake, IN: Eisenbrauns: 259-274.

Yeivin, S.
1973   "Temples That Were Not." *Eretz-Israel* 11:163-175 (Hebrew with English summary, 28*).

Zertal, Adam.
1994   "'To the Land of the Perizzites and the Giants': On the Israelite Settlement in the Hill Country of Manasseh." In Finkelstein, Israel and Nadav Na'aman, *From Nomadism to Monarchy: Archaeological and Historical Aspects of Early Israel.* Jerusalem: Israel Exploration Society: 47-69